MURDER MOST FOUL

Murder is shocking, no matter what the circumstances. But the perversity of some murders stun even hardened investigators. Mutilated corpses, sick rituals and obscene souvenirs are some of the ingredients that make certain murders truly bizarre.

Now, from the authentic files of *True Detective Magazine,* read the horrifying true crime accounts of the vicious killers who committed Bizarre Murders, including: John Perry, who chopped up his wife and fed her organs to Katie, the family cat; John Calvaresi, a teenager whose fondness for Stephen King movies led him to reenact a gruesome murder; or Daniel Kimball, who killed his girlfriend and had sex with her corpse!

BIZARRE MURDERERS

FROM THE FILES OF *TRUE DETECTIVE* MAGAZINE

BIZARRE MURDERERS II

Edited by
**ROSE G.
MANDELSBERG**

PINNACLE BOOKS
WINDSOR PUBLISHING CORP.

The editor wishes to express her sincerest thanks and appreciation to Stan Munro whose painstaking efforts made this book possible.
A special mention to all the talented and dedicated writers in this book.

For more true crime reading, pick up TRUE DETECTIVE, OFFICIAL DETECTIVE, MASTER DETECTIVE, FRONT PAGE DETECTIVE, and INSIDE DETECTIVE magazines on sale at newsstands every month.

TABLE OF CONTENTS

"HE HAD SEX WITH ROSEMARY'S ROSARY-BEADED CORPSE!"

by Krist Boardman

As the chief and formerly the only detective of a 12-man police department, William F. Grow thought he'd seen it all.

True, there weren't many homicides in the city of Shamokin, Pennsylvania, a pleasant city of 10,000 nestled in a valley of the anthracite coal region in Northumberland County. It had actually been 11 years since the city's last homicide in 1977, and that was a humdinger—an arson fire set by a couple of firemen that resulted in nine deaths.

But now, on July 24, 1988, this one homicide was worse.

Detective Grow was in his camper trailer several miles out of town when he received a call on his cellular phone to report to the 500 block of one of Shamokin's main thoroughfares, named, appropriately enough, Shamokin Street. By this time it was one o'clock in the morning on Saturday. When Grow arrived, he found waiting for him Chief of Police James Hodge, Corporal Marlin Marose, and Northumberland County Assistant District Attorney Tony Rosini.

Detective Grow soon learned that a short time earlier, Corporal Marose had received a phone call from a relative of Rosemary Kleinsmith to check up on her.

The relative had told Marose that it was several days since she had heard from or spoken with Rosemary, and it was highly unusual not to be in touch with her every day. She feared something was wrong. Consequently, Corporal Marose entered the Kleinsmith apartment and saw that the relative's fears were confirmed. He secured the scene and then promptly called the chief and also Detective Grow.

Having abandoned his plans to be an electrician for a career in law enforcement 19 years earlier, Detective Grow had seen plenty, both in and out of uniform, as a police officer. But he wasn't quite ready for the shock he now encountered.

"When I entered the bedroom I observed a nude body. It was terrifying, horrifying," Grow would later recount. "I never as a police officer had seen anything like this at that time. The body was nude. Rosary beads draped from her mouth to her vagina. Also, there was a set of rosary beads draped between her breasts. There were ashes sprinkled over her body." It was a grotesque sight.

Blood coming from the victim's nose indicated that she had also suffered some kind of trauma to the face and neck.

The room was hot. Summer temperatures outside were soaring, and the apartment temperature was approximately 90 degrees. The odor from apparently three days of decomposition was mitigated somewhat by a box fan that was left running and was still on. The windows to the first-floor apartment were still open when the police arrived.

The sparsely furnished apartment was not in the best of shape. Rosemary Kleinsmith kept a lot of her things in plastic bags on the floor. The mattress where her body lay was also directly on the floor.

One of the first things police noticed when they arrived at the apartment, even before Detective Grow got there, was that the cord to the telephone was missing. It was impossible to use the phone to make any calls for assistance at the scene.

Detectives learned from the victim's family that Rosemary Kleinsmith had been living on the edge for some time. Slightly retarded, she had slipped into the bar scene to the point where she had an acknowledged drinking problem. In addition, her relatives said, she was a person who tried to please others to a fault — particularly men. As Detective Grow soon learned, there were plenty of men to look at as suspects in Rosemary's murder.

After the crime scene photographer finished his work, the body was removed by emergency paramedics to the Sunbury Community Hospital some 17 miles away, where Deputy Coroner Quay Olley declared the victim dead. Not much later, the body was moved again to a hospital in Allentown, Pennsylvania, for autopsy by Dr. Isidore Mihalakis, a forensic pathologist who frequently assisted in homicide investigations throughout eastern Pennsylvania.

Sleuths also learned that the victim had a cat. That was clear because there were numerous cat hairs throughout the apartment, yet the cat was nowhere to be found. By checking with people living throughout the neighborhood, the cat was eventually located nearby. This event would play a critical role in the developing investigation.

Meanwhile, the state police in Montoursville, Pennsylvania, were called in to dust the apartment for fingerprints. After a meticulous dusting, the team was unable to find a single unusual print.

To both Detective Grow and his counterpart from the state police, Corporal David Shinski, who assisted him, the absence of usable fingerprints in the victim's apartment was immediately suspicious. They knew the victim was in and out of the apartment many times with various friends, and they expected the prints to reflect that kind of activity as well as to point to possible suspects. The absence of fingerprints on obvious objects such as the top of the TV, doorknobs, glasses,

9

and ashtrays, suggested that the surfaces had be
wiped clean.

"I knew for a fact that a number of people would
going in and out of her apartment," Detective Gr
would later say. "It sort of seemed funny that
couldn't come up with any fingerprints in the apa
ment, not even one of her own."

The lack of such direct evidence meant that Gr
and the force of investigators gathering around hi
from both Shamokin and the state police would ha
to work harder on other leads. During the next f
days, they focused on locating every possible pers
who had anything to do with Rosemary Kleinsmith

One witness who lived on the third floor of the sar
apartment building as Rosemary told investigato
that he was sleeping in the middle bedroom of I
apartment on the night of the murder.

"I was sleeping and I was awakened by Rosema
screaming, 'Help me.' Either, 'He is choking me,'
'They're choking me.' So I got up, looked at the cloc
walked to the front room, looked out the window.
didn't see nothing. I didn't hear anything else. So
more or less went back to bed and went to sleep."

He added that he thought it was about 1:45 a.m.
Thursday, July 21, 1988.

Meanwhile, at the Lehigh Valley Medical Cent
Dr. Mihalakis was completing his autopsy. He fou
four areas of bruising on the victim's head, face a
neck, injuries that were received before death. He al
found the victim's blood alcohol level at .28, indic
ting "marked alcoholic intoxication. She was outrig
drunk . . . and had her last drink within one ho
prior to death."

As for her head and face injuries, Dr. Mihalak
thought they were not fatal. What did appear fat
were fractures in the hyoid bone around the voice b
in the throat, usually indicative of strangulatio
However, there were no marks on the victim's throa
meaning that strangulation was most likely manu

10

and not with a ligature, he determined.

As Detective Grow got deeper into the case, he realized that the biggest of his problems was eliminating suspects. They seemed to come out of the woodwork.

The first suspect was an unknown assailant who just earlier in the week, before Rosemary was murdered, was accused of raping her. Rosemary had reported the incident to the police. A man she'd never met before gave her a ride in his pickup truck and took her out into the country where he raped her, then brought her to a truck stop and dropped her off. Because of this incident, Rosemary went to the local hospital, where she was examined and later interviewed by a county social worker who was advised of what happened in the incident.

The only problem was that the medical exam was inconclusive as to whether Rosemary had been raped. And without an identification of the alleged rapist or any other confirmation of this incident, medical authorities, the social worker and the police were puzzled over whether the incident had occurred at all.

Rosemary had also said that during the rape, her ribs were broken. Hospital X-rays taken of her at the time she was examined for the rape indicated that Rosemary's ribs were indeed broken, but they appeared to be on the mend for some time, perhaps two months, indicating that they weren't hurt at the time of the rape.

Still, if the rape had occurred, it loomed as a motive for her murder. Was someone trying to silence her? detectives wondered.

One of Rosemary's boyfriends, Manfred Gillo, also surfaced as an active suspect when police received information that she'd been in a fight with him in a bar earlier in the evening on July 20th. Shamokin police were very familiar with Gillo because he was a known drug abuser and petty drug dealer with a string of convictions on his record.

When Gillo was brought in for questioning, he ad-

11

mitted being with Rosemary but claimed it was only for a short time after he was leaving one bar and heading for another. He met Rosemary on the street, Gillo said, and they did have an argument. He claimed Rosemary was being obnoxious because of her drinking, and he was getting irritated with her and didn't want to have anything to do with her.

Detective Grow tended to believe Gillo, that Rosemary had a tendency to get on people's nerves when she was drinking. That didn't rule out Gillo as a suspect, but it still didn't mean that Grow had any information that Gillo had murdered her.

News of the crime apparently unleashed a flood of guilt from one unlikely quarter. Shamokin police found a note stuffed in the mailbox overnight from a man named Billy Radowski who confessed to the crime. Billy went on profusely, describing his misdeeds for the police. He was known as another retarded person who was also one of Rosemary's boyfriends. The only problem with his confession was that it didn't match up with the details from the crime scene.

"He had no inkling about the rosary beads," said Detective Grow after evaluating and effectively dismissing Radowski's confession.

Sleuths also brought in for questioning another boyfriend of Rosemary's. He lived in the nearby town of Kulpmont and occasionally was known to be with Rosemary. But he told police he was with another girlfriend, and no one in Shamokin could put him in the town any time near when Rosemary was last seen alive.

When detectives canvassed local bars in Shamokin, they found two bar employees who recalled seeing Rosemary on the evening of July 20th. One, a bartender in a tavern across the street from Rosemary's apartment, said he recalled seeing the victim sitting at a bar stool with a man. The man gave Rosemary a necklace, he said.

"She was excitable and she constantly spoke about two subjects—her boyfriends and her cat," the bartender recalled.

When Detective Grow asked the witness to be more specific about whom Rosemary was with at that time, the bartender replied, "I remember him handing her this necklace and speaking of marriage. And of course, that was a frequent statement of Rosemary when she would come in with someone. They were always going to get married. So I didn't pay much attention to that part of it."

The bartender also said he thought the couple had left about 1:00 a.m. and proceeded to walk across the street.

The second bar employee worked at a tavern further down the street. She said she saw Rosemary walking—or staggering because she was so drunk—along with a man she did not recognize. What seemed a little unusual about this man was that he was a lot more clean-cut and more muscular than the men Rosemary usually consorted with, the witness said.

"I looked back and saw them again," she recounted. "I took notice because . . . he wasn't the type of gentleman she was usually with."

The bartender where Rosemary and her male friend had been drinking asserted investigators further when he helped them locate a bar patron who was also there that evening. This patron, a woman who lived in the neighborhood and who knew Rosemary casually, told detectives that she was in the bar for several hours that evening and happened to be sitting only a few bar stools away from Rosemary. She said Rosemary had come in by herself a little earlier, then left. About 15 minutes later, Rosemary came in with the man whom Rosemary called "Dan." While Rosemary and her companion were there, Rosemary mentioned that she hadn't seen him for some time and asked him if he'd missed her.

"He said that he had just come back from out West,

13

and that was the reason she hadn't seen him for a while," the bar patron recalled. "He said he brought her a gift . . . a necklace, and it was in a little box, and he gave it to her. And apparently it had one of those little round things on for a catch because she couldn't open it. . . . He took it and opened the catch for her and put it on her neck."

The patron said she couldn't hear everything that the couple said. She wasn't deliberately eavesdropping, but at the same time, she was close to them and did hear some things. She said Rosemary asked Dan if he missed her and Dan said he did. "Why don't we get married?" Rosemary had asked him.

"He talked like he seriously intended to," the woman continued. "He said, 'Well, we can't get married here. We'll have to go away.' "

Rosemary also asked Dan if he had a key to her apartment. She'd given out copies to a number of men and couldn't remember if she'd given one to Dan, the bar patron explained. But Dan told her he didn't have one. Soon thereafter, the couple left the bar.

Because of the seriousness of the crime, the lack of clues and large variety of possible suspects, Corporal Thomas Brennan of the Pennsylvania State Police was brought in to conduct a criminal profile of the murderer, based on evidence available at the crime scene.

Trained by the FBI in the newly developed discipline of criminal profiling, Brennan predicted that the killer was a drifter who had been married before, who had some religious background, and who also had some prior involvement with retarded people. He was a white male between 20 and 30 years old, and he may have been in some previous trouble with the law.

Detective Grow and Corporal Shinski perked up when they heard the accounts of both the bartender and the bar patron, particularly with reference to the gold necklace. There was no gold necklace found on the victim. The fact that the victim was manually strangled indicated that whoever had killed Rosemary

14

had taken off her necklace, perhaps to avoid detection through a trace on it. Who but the very person who had put on the necklace would have thought to take it off? lawmen wondered. For the first time in the probe, the sleuths felt they had gotten a solid lead.

By asking around, they learned that the "Dan" who had just blown into town about a week or so earlier was named Daniel Kimball. Probers learned he was staying in a friend's apartment only a few blocks away.

Detective George Allen of the Northumberland County District Attorney's Office and Trooper Walter Mazeikas, a criminal investigator of the state police substation at Stonington, located Kimball and brought him into the Shamokin Police Department for questioning.

Kimball appeared very calm and self-assured. He seemed to have an answer for every question that Detective Grow asked him, even before he could finish asking it.

The suspect admitted that he was with Rosemary Kleinsmith during the evening in question but he maintained that they separated immediately after leaving the bar, with her going one way toward her apartment and with him going in the direction of his friend's apartment.

Kimball also admitted that he'd given Rosemary the gold necklace but denied taking it back. He seemed unruffled by Detective Grow's questions.

"He sat back, very cool, said he'd been in the area a couple days, that he was working in Philadelphia in a restaurant," said Detective Grow. "But he was too calm. I just had a feeling about him. As a police officer you have a feeling. He was very quick with the answers, even before you had the question asked."

A further interview with the female bar employee indicated that she'd seen the man with Rosemary in the evening. They were walking down the alley toward the rear of Rosemary's apartment. This was directly at odds with what Daniel Kimball had told the police

15

about parting ways with Rosemary after they left the tavern. It had the effect of making him the number-one suspect in the murder.

Investigators did a background check on Daniel Kimball. They discovered that there was an outstanding arrest warrant on him in Chester County in suburban Philadelphia for failure to appear in court for sentencing on a drunken-driving conviction. Consequently, Chester County authorities found him and jailed him on that charge.

When detectives showed up at the friend's apartment where Kimball had been staying, they were looking for something specific in addition to Kimball—some of his clothing. In this effort they were successful, as Kimball's friend gave the probers several garments. Investigators were looking for cat hairs on the clothing and had the hairs compared to those recovered from Rosemary's cat.

The result was that they were similar—not conclusive given the inconclusive nature of such evidence, but at least it still pointed in the direction of Kimball.

The investigation also hit an unexpected vein of criminal wrongdoing. Kimball's friend in Shamokin was interviewed to get more information about Kimball. Investigators were interested in learning more about Kimball's activities during the night in question to see if Kimball had really come back to the apartment at the time he said he and Rosemary parted. Kimball also told the detectives that there was a young boy who was naked in the apartment with his friend at the time he returned, and that the boy and the friend were drinking beer. But Kimball couldn't offer any explanation as to why the boy was there and what he was doing.

While the friend didn't shed much light on the situation with Kimball, except to say that he did come home sometimes in the early hours of the morning, the presence of the minor did arouse suspicion of a different kind. Further investigation revealed that

16

Kimball's friend was regularly enticing youngsters to his apartment, where he'd ply them with beer, then fondle them in bed. Subsequently, the friend was arrested and charged with three counts of corruption of minors, for which he was sentenced to five years in prison.

However, this unexpected side trip down another alley of wrongdoing didn't keep lawmen away from their main task, as they tried to zero in on Daniel Kimball as a primary suspect in Rosemary Kleinsmith's murder.

A visit to the Chester County Prison, where Kimball was now being held, helped a little. Kimball told detectives that he'd been with another woman, whose name he supplied, earlier that evening before meeting up with Rosemary, whom he met outside as she was sitting on some railroad ties on a side street off Shamokin Street.

When asked to explain the discrepancy between the story of the eyewitness who saw him and Rosemary walking down the alley toward the rear of her apartment and his own account of parting company with the victim immediately after leaving the bar, Kimball admitted that he'd fibbed about that because he didn't want sleuths to think he'd killed Rosemary. He now said he *did* go into the victim's apartment with her. He said he later went out to get some beer, returned with it, and then left the apartment again soon after. Kimball said they'd just visited the apartment a short time and then he left.

Investigators told Kimball that they didn't believe him, that they believed he'd done more than that.

Kimball snapped, "If you think I did it, you prove it! I don't want to talk to you any more. I want to go eat."

Kimball did have a couple of valid points, detectives reasoned. Legally he didn't have to talk to the police anymore if he didn't want to. He'd already admitted to going inside Rosemary's apartment, then leaving to

17

get some beer at another nearby tavern which he named, and then leaving Rosemary's apartment a second time. That still left open the possibility that someone else might have come in after he left. After all, probers knew that a number of other men had keys to the victim's apartment and were known to crash there at any time. So it was entirely plausible that this could have happened and that Kimball was innocently trying to keep himself out of the middle of the crime scene.

It was plausible, but the investigators didn't believe Kimball was innocent. As Detective Grow felt, they all just had a gut feeling that the restaurant worker from Chester County, Pennsylvania, knew more about the murder than he was telling.

Then, in October 1988, Northumberland authorities received help from an unexpected quarter. A letter from the Chester County District Attorney's Office revealed that a person in the Chester County Prison had some information he wanted to pass along about a possible homicide that occurred in Shamokin.

The inmate, a former co-worker at the restaurant in Chester County where Kimball worked, said he shared a room with Kimball while both of them were on the outside. No angel himself, the inmate had been involved in a series of petty thefts and forgery charges. He said Kimball spoke with him at length when they were together about Rosemary Kleinsmith's murder.

Investigators knew that the inmate had solid information when he described how Kimball had given Rosemary Kleinsmith the gold necklace in the bar. The inmate also told probers that Kimball later purchased a six-pack of beer and, while in the apartment, Kimball and Rosemary started arguing over whether there would be some sex.

Kimball had also told the inmate that he was extremely concerned over the possibility that DNA matchups of semen taken from the victim's mouth and vagina could be made with his own body fluids. This was the first that detectives had heard of a sexual as-

18

sault; semen samples were not recovered because they would have decomposed during the three days since the body's discovery and Rosemary's death.

The inmate said Kimball told him that after choking Rosemary with his hands, he wrapped a phone cord around her neck to make sure she was dead. Then he removed from her neck the gold chain that he'd given her earlier in the night. It was then that Kimball had sex with Rosemary's dead body.

With this information, Kimball was brought from the Chester County Prison to Northumberland County on November 2, 1988, to be charged with first-degree murder. While he was in Northumberland County, he was transferred to Shamokin, where Rosemary Kleinsmith was murdered, to talk further with police officers about the case. Pennsylvania State Police Trooper Francis Bowers and Corporal Shinski were with Detective Grow from the Shamokin Police Department, to assist in the interview.

As the preliminaries progressed, Trooper Bowers established a friendly rapport with Kimball, while Corporal Shinski was very hostile to him. As this developed, eventually Kimball asked if Shinski could leave the room. When the corporal did as he was asked, Kimball admitted that he'd killed the victim.

After drawing some pictures of the scene and giving some other descriptions, Kimball was asked if he'd had sex with Rosemary's body after she was already dead. Kimball didn't answer the question.

"Officer Grow, from the first day you interviewed me, I knew you wouldn't give up till you got me," Kimball told him.

As Daniel Craig Kimball's trial approached, the defense focused on his sanity and competency. As it turned out, Kimball's unusual background became the focus of a lengthy pretrial hearing over his sanity.

A defense psychiatrist on whom much of the insanity motion of the defense rested told the court that he thought Kimball's "long term prognosis clinically is

19

poor. He has not only a bipolar disorder, but he has an antisocial personality."

The uncertainty as to the time when Kimball may have had sex with Rosemary Kleinsmith—either before or after her death—worked in the defendant's favor. None of the injuries normally associated with rape were found on the victim, which tended to support the theory that the sexual assault occurred after she was dead. While this didn't shed any favorable light on Kimball, it did rule out the filing of rape charges, since one cannot, legally speaking, rape a body that is already dead. One can, however, be charged with the lesser crimes of abuse of a corpse and perverted sexual practices.

But in court testimony, Kimball steadfastly denied having sex with Rosemary's body after she died.

In addition, Kimball's defense centered on the theory that the victim's death was accidental and not premeditated. They contended that she died from a fight that got out of hand when Kimball gave Rosemary a couple of karate chops. This argument not only had the potential to reduce the charges to second or third-degree murder but would highlight the testimony of the pathologist testifying both for the commonwealth and the defense.

Dr. Isidore Mihalakis, the commonwealth pathologist, testified that the hyoid bone fractures in the victim's throat indicated that she died from strangulation, not from karate chops.

"The karate chop to the neck kills primarily by two mechanisms. One is swelling of the neck and occlusion of the artery, because of a lot of swelling there. The windpipe is narrowed and the person can't breathe. I found no such swelling at the time of the autopsy," he said.

"Secondly, a karate chop to the neck can also compress or injure vital nerves which control heart activity and potentially put the heart into a standstill. But a normal, healthy heart cannot be so affected."

In addition, Dr. Mihalakis said that "the [hyoid] V-shaped bone . . . is in such a well-protected area, to cause a fracture with anything other than strangulation is extremely difficult, if not impossible."

As for whether there was ligature strangulation, the witness said he saw no evidence of it, even though Kimball said he wrapped the phone cord around Rosemary's neck and later disposed of the cord in some bushes.

For the defense, a doctor testified that he could not state for sure if manual strangulation was the cause of death. He said the hyoid bone and thyroid cartilage could have been injured from two blows to the left and right sides of the victim's neck. Those blows "could have produced those injuries," he concluded.

Another witness, a relative of Kimball's, was flown in from Idaho Falls, Idaho. She told the court that she talked to Dan on the phone and had gotten his letters, when he indicated he was a suspect in Rosemary's murder.

"He said he didn't do it . . . I think he just said that they went and had a couple of beers," she testified. Dan said the police were "trying to frame him . . . on trumped-up charges."

But then, later, as he talked with her more about it, "he did say he did kill her accidentally. . . . He said that he karate-chopped her and she fell backwards and hit her head either on a chair or table or something. . . .

"He said they got a six pack of beer and went to her apartment. She wanted to have sex with him and he didn't want to because she had V.D."

One prosecution witness said that the defendant had experienced behavioral problems throughout his childhood. He was rejected by both regular and special schools. Eventually his problems caused him to be adjudicated as a juvenile delinquent, and he was eventually sent to a mental hospital after a nervous collapse while serving in the U.S. Navy. During his stay in

21

the hospital, he declared, "Nobody here knows I'm Jesus Christ."

During the defense phase of the case, Assistant Public Defenders Elizabeth Beroes and Jeffrey Mensch put a few minor witnesses on the stand. Their big surprise, however, was in allowing Daniel Kimball to testify. Perhaps they could not have prevented him from testifying, because as it turned out, Kimball appeared to love the attention he was getting in court as a witness in his own trial.

With Defense Attorney Beroes directing the questioning, Kimball described what happened in Rosemary Kleinsmith's apartment:

"I got the phone cord. She was already dead for I don't know how many minutes. She was turning blue. I don't remember. I wrapped the phone cord around her neck, and I braided it. I weaved it around her neck. . . . I didn't want them looking for anybody who knew martial arts. . . . My mind is going a million miles an hour. And my heartbeat is thumping a million miles an hour. . . . I can't believe this. I didn't know what was going on. And I couldn't believe that she was dead, and I was still talking to her."

After putting the beads on her, Kimball continued, "I said a few more prayers—it was, I don't know if I said the last rites or the Lord's Prayer and something else, I'm not sure. I sort of had a nervous breakdown. I didn't know what to do. I panicked. So I put the rosary beads on her body, and I took the phone cord off her neck. . . . I would like to point out to each and every one of you that Rosemary was a friend of mine. She was a good friend of mine. She was a good woman. She didn't have any bad in her. She was a happy-go-lucky woman who would help anybody."

"Did you plan and intend to kill this woman?" asked Defense Attorney Beroes.

"No, I did not," replied Kimball. "It was an accident. I didn't intentionally, deliberately, purposely kill anybody and never have, and I don't think I even will, or ever would. It was an accident. She was a friend of mine. I feel terrible about her death. . . . I apologize to everyone for putting them through this."

Under cross-examination, District Attorney Robert B. Sacavage tried to paint a less remorseful portrait of the defendant.

"Now, let's find out how Rosemary Kleinsmith had her clothes taken off," began Mr. Sacavage. "What is your story there? Explain to the jury what you didn't explain on direct examination."

"Why is that so necessary?" asked Kimball.

"Just answer the question, please, Mr. Kimball," directed Samuel C. Ranck, President Judge of Northumberland County's Circuit Court.

"I took her clothes off," said Kimball.

"You just took her clothes off, for the heck of it?" pressed Sacavage.

"I just took them off."

"When did you take them off?"

"After she was dead," responded Kimball. He added that he had sex with her body twice, once in the mouth and once in the vagina, after her body was naked.

Prosecutor Sacavage read into the court record several previous statements made by Kimball:

"All I did was accidentally kill some girl, crushed her neck with two karate chops. So what? . . . Accidents do happen. I should have taken out an insurance policy on her for double indemnity for accidental death."

Sacavage wanted to know whether Kimball in fact made these statements.

"I was being facetious," the defendant replied. "Maybe I was upset about being in jail. Maybe I was having a hard time dealing with the fact that I killed somebody."

"And this is what you were writing about your good friend Rosemary, right?" asked Sacavage.

The prosecutor asked Kimball about a letter to one

23

of his relatives, saying that there was a possibility of acquittal. There are "no prints, no evidence, no eye-witnesses, nobody to testify against me," Kimball wrote. "My confession is as phony as a three-dollar bill. And phony signature, Mr. D.C. Kimball. My legal signature is Daniel Kimball."

Later, Kimball denied under cross-examination that he'd had sex twice with Rosemary's corpse.

"So you just made it up that you had two orgasms, just for the heck of it, just to throw it in? Is that your testimony?"

"So I made it up," answered Kimball. "So what?"

"If it was such an accidental death," asked Prosecutor Sacavage, "and you were only there to be friends with her, why was she undressed? Why were her clothes off? Explain that to the jury?"

"I don't know," responded Kimball. "What do you usually do after you kill somebody?"

"I'm asking the questions. Mr. Kimball, I never killed anybody. Tell the jury, explain to the jury why she was undressed."

"I did accidentally kill her and I have no explanation for anything I did after that," the defendant replied.

"Did she accidentally become undressed?"

"I don't — no, I took her clothes off. I remember taking her clothes off."

In July 1991, Daniel Craig Kimball was convicted of first-degree murder. But the commonwealth failed in its effort to obtain a death penalty as a sentence.

During the sentencing phase of the trial, the court ruled that the aggravating factor of the crime was that "the offense was committed by means of torture."

The mitigating factors were that the defendant "had no significant history of prior criminal convictions," and "was under the influence of an extreme mental or emotional disturbance, had suffered from substance abuse, and was an abused or neglected child."

On July 29, 1991, Daniel Kimball received a life senence for his murder conviction. Even as he remains under custody of Pennsylvania correctional officials, various aspects of his case are being debated in higher courts within the appeals process.

EDITOR'S NOTE:
Manfred Gillo and Billy Radowski are not the real names of the persons so named in the foregoing story. Fictitious names have been used because there is no reason for public interest in the identities of these persons.

"LITTLE ANGEL WAS RAVAGED BY DEMENTED DEVIL!"

by Dan Buttaro

Summer Days in Vero Beach, Florida, are usually balmy mixture of sunshine and wind. Afternoons a often punctuated by a brief shower or two. The down pour cleanses the beaches and streets. Twenty minut later one can't even tell it rained.

The children of this quaint and quiet community of Florida's southeastern coastline take advantage of nature's generosity by spending most of their time out doors. But on August 20, 1979, the peaceful ambience of the seaside town was shattered when a family discovered one of its children missing.

It seemed as if the ocean breeze had kicked up an mysteriously blown the 4-year-old child away.

Angel Halstead spent most of that Monday after noon playing outside with friends. Around s o'clock, Angel's brother was sent to find her and te her it was time to come home. The boy trekked dow the residential lane to the end of 25th Avenue, whe he found Angel playing in a neighbor's driveway wit a friend and a kitten. She said she didn't want to com home yet, so the boy returned home alone.

Fifteen minutes later, the boy was sent back with or ders to fetch his sister. When the boy returned som time later, he said Angel was nowhere to be found.

26

The girl's family, upset by her sudden disappearance, began a street-by-street search. An hour passed and they were still unable to locate the missing girl. Neighbors and friends joined in the frantic quest. Fear for Angel's safety grew as the sun sank lower in the sky. Around 9:00 p.m., Angel's parents decided to notify the Vero Beach Police Department to get some help.

Vero Beach Police Chief Sam McCall, along with Lieutenant John D'Agosto, quickly arrived at the Halstead residence and took charge of the search. The neighborhood, known for its tranquility, was lined with modest homes and surrounded by woodlands. Crime and missing children weren't part of the neighborhood's lifestyle. In contrast, this was the second time in a day that police were dispatched to a 25th Avenue address. Chief McCall expected that Angel would probably be found playing at a friend's house.

During the preliminary questioning of Angel's parents, friends and neighbors, Chief McCall reconstructed the events leading up to the phone call to police. The missing girl had been playing outside with other youngsters earlier that day. The veteran officer learned of the brother's two trips to fetch his sister home. However, the young boy's timing of events didn't fully coincide with other information.

"When I went down the street, she was down there playing with a friend," he remembered. "When I went back home to eat, Mommy told me to go and get Angel. The police were down the street breaking up a fight, and Angel was down there. When I went back down the street, the police were gone and so was Angel." When Chief McCall checked the police dispatch log, he discovered that the altercation the boy recollected didn't occur until 8:00 p.m., almost two hours after the boy's second venture to find Angel.

Another witness added more information. Apparently, Angel Halstead had left her friend in the driveway, shortly after her brother departed, to look for a

27

kitten the couple had been playing with. The black kitten with white paws had run off into the nearby woods, and Angel feared it would be lost forever if she didn't locate it before dark.

The stories led the chief to conclude that the last confirmable sighting of Angel Halstead was around 6:30 p.m. The officer made a notation of the wooded area. He also marked the exact locations where the family and neighbors had searched during the two and a half hours before the police were notified.

One-by-one, teams of family members, friends, neighbors and police officers reported back to Chief McCall. Angel was still missing.

Around 2:00 a.m., the next morning, the chief ordered Lieutenant D'Agosto to phone Detective-Sergeant David Carter, an ace sleuth, and instruct him to meet the chief at the 25th Street location. Within an hour, under a blanket of stars, Sergeant Carter took charge of the case, setting up a command post in front of the Halstead house. Chief McCall personally updated the detectives with what little information he had obtained.

After the meeting, Carter's natural optimism began to give way to the gravity of the worsening situation. He knew it was destined to be a fretful — and lonely — night for everyone.

The search resumed early Tuesday morning. Sergeant Carter released a description of the missing girl. Angel was 3 feet 6 inches tall and weighed about 42 pounds. She had short brown hair and was last seen wearing a pink halter top, pink shorts, and no shoes.

Off-duty Vero Beach officers and deputies from the Indian River County Sheriff's Department bolstered the on-duty force of the organized search parties. Local firms, agencies, and volunteers offered time and equipment to locate the missing girl.

Several airplanes from Piper Aircraft Corporation in Vero Beach, took to the skies. Residents watched the planes circle a Palm Beach County Sheriff's helicopter, which was dispatched to lend air support in the hunt. On the ground, police dogs belonging to Corporal Chester Blair of the Vero Beach Police Department and other canines from the county correctional facility and a local kennel joined the woodland teams.

The dogs, following the scent of the missing child, tracked Angel's movements from the driveway, down 25th Street, to a trail leading into a wooded area. The hounds pulled searchers along the trail to a spot where it appeared a vehicle had turned around. The dogs lost the girl's scent at that point.

In three nearby lakes, Vero Beach Fire Department divers worked a grid pattern but found no clues. More searchers encircled the area as the morning sun climbed into the sky.

When asked about the progress of the undertaking, Sergeant Carter remarked, "I'm very happy with the effort these people made. We're satisfied that the girl is not in the lakes. We'll keep looking as long as is necessary."

Firemen, correctional guards, and members of the sheriff's department explorers post assisted the teams of city police officers and county deputies. A local CB club set up a communications link to assist the field and car units of volunteers. In all, more than 150 searchers combed the area.

Local radio and television stations added to the communications network by broadcasting announcements about the missing child. During the hot, humid Tuesday afternoon, several citizens stopped at the 25th Street command post saying they had spotted a girl fitting Angel's description. Police quickly checked out each lead, none of which ultimately panned out.

The sun was setting and Angel Halstead had now been missing for more than 24 hours. Outside the command post a relative spoke about the missing girl to reporters.

"She always likes to play," he said. "She'll play with all the children in the neighborhood. They all seem to congregate in this yard. Angel also likes to play with her dolls and other toys. She is really good at coloring."

But the fearful adult was at a loss to explain the child's disappearance. "I just don't know what to think about this situation," he added.

Inside Sergeant Carter's patrol car—turned into a command post—Carter knew what to think. Every police officer realizes the mounting seriousness as each hour passes after the disappearance of a child.

The headline in Wednesday morning's Vero Beach *Press-Journal* said it all. The front-page banner read "Foul Play Suspected in Girl's Disappearance."

As the search parties departed to their assigned locations the following morning, Carter reviewed all the information collected with other investigators. Some of the facts garnered took the sleuths on a wild goose chase.

For example, Sergeant Carter's reason for putting the command post in front of Angel's house was based on his knowledge of a possible domestic problem. The detective's probing disclosed that the girl's natural parents were divorced. The split had involved a bitter custody battle over the missing girl and her sister.

Although Angel's mother had won the battle, the detective worked on the theory that the war between the estranged couple might still be going on.

But Angel's natural father quickly disproved the theory. The father arrived immediately at the scene after being notified of Angel's disappearance and remained active in the search effort. His sincere demonstration of concern left Sergeant Carter facing the worse case scenario—foul play.

Carter based this speculation on the fact that police dogs lost Angel's scent at a specific spot. The sudden interruption of her trail seemed to imply that Angel had been abducted by a person who used a vehicle. Being the most logical assumption, the sleuth directed

30

most of the search parties to that particular area. To be on the safe side, however, some of the team continued to explore other possible explanations for Angel's disappearance.

A fellow officer approached Carter with a suspicion. One of the neighborhood youths, he said, had been asking questions. Even though most people are curious about police work, this boy was just a little too inquisitive. His constant badgering for information drew initial suspicion, but one particular question the youth asked struck the officer as peculiar.

Carter asked what the boy wanted to know.

"Can they take fingerprints off a body?" the officer quoted the boy.

The question hit Sergeant Carter between the eyes.

The detective directed the officer to monitor the boy's movements. Maybe he was genuinely curious, but maybe he knew more about Angel's disappearance than police did, Carter stressed.

By 9:00 a.m., the sun began baking the search teams when, suddenly, a searcher discovered a few pieces of clothing dangling from some scrub brush. He quickly alerted others. As the team of volunteer firemen approached the bush they realized it was a small halter, a pair of shorts and a pair of panties. The halter and shorts were pink. Fear struck the group as a member sprinted off to inform the police.

Within minutes Sergeant Carter arrived and began moving some palmetto fronds that someone had apparently carefully lain on the ground. Slowly he uncovered the body of a child, its face buried in the sand. Bruises covered the body's back. The detective gently turned over the corpse. It was a girl whose face had been beaten beyond recognition. But no one doubted that the search for Angel Halstead was suddenly over and had ended tragically.

Within minutes, news of the grim discovery rumbled through the area. Neighbors stood in silence as police officers and firemen, back from the crime scene openly wept. To police officers, homicide is a fact of life. But the killing of this innocent 4-year-old girl was just too much to accept.

The stark reality of the discovery came into focus when those standing near the command post heard the loud, hollow shrill of a woman's voice from inside Angel's house.

The officer who told Carter about the boy with the inquisitive questions grabbed the detective. The patrolman reported that he observed the boy following the team that found Angel's body during the morning. He also watched as the boy placed his arms around one of the dead girl's relatives, offering his condolence. It didn't make sense. But the veteran sleuth knew most homicides never make sense.

Sergeant Carter ordered Detectives Ronald B. Blanton and James Attkisson to find the boy and bring him in for questioning. The pair of sleuths located the 14-year-old sitting on the hood of a car, along with a few friends, in front of his home. He readily agreed to accompany the pair of probers to the police station. Before taking the lad down to the Vero Beach Police Department, the sleuths drove the boy to his mother's place of employment.

The officers explained to the woman that Angel Halstead's body had been found and that they were interested in knowing what information her son could shed on the discovery. She agreed to escort the officers to the station.

An hour and a half after Carter issued the order to pick up the boy, Brooks Bellay, the teen and his mother walked into the Vero Beach Police Station. Carter looked at the lad, who was big for his age. Bellay stood 6 foot 1 and weighed about 185 pounds. The teen's size only strengthened the detective's gut hunch as his two partners prepared to interrogate the teenager.

Bellay offered to talk with the sleuths, but not in the presence of his mother. She was asked to wait in an adjoining room. They began the questioning by reading Bellay his rights. At first the teenager denied everything, but the officers kept urging Bellay to tell them what he knew.

"It's something you can never live with," Attkisson warned. "You have to talk about it. You just don't know what it's going to be like to try and sleep with this. You want to talk now? You want to tell? You can't take something like this to your grave."

Slowly, the boy recounted the story of Angel Halstead's horrible death. Bellay acknowledged that he followed the girl into the woods as she searched for her black kitten with white paws. But then he told the detectives that the 4-year-old willingly took off her clothes and approached him in a seductive manner, grabbing his genitals. He admitted hitting her in the face with his fist, but he said he couldn't remember how many times he hit her. The boy, looking for a way to confess and yet save face, seemed to be twisting his story.

Incredibly, he said it was Angel who asked him to have sex with her. So he did it, he said, and then struck her when he was finished. Then he dragged her body about 20 yards, covered it, and tossed away her clothes. Detective Blanton and his partner thought it odd that Bellay got the crime off his chest by passing the blame onto Angel Halstead, a 4-year-old little girl. Finally, the detectives asked Bellay to prepare and sign a statement. Bellay ended the interrogation with his signature. The sleuth walked out of the interrogation room thinking about how the suspect had calmly spent the first evening of the search for Angel at her house watching television.

When the probers spotted Sergeant Carter, the interrogators received one more shock. Another search party had found " more pairs of panties draped across another palmetto bush near the crime scene. The undergarments were placed on the bush in a similar manner as the slain girl's clothing.

Sergeant Carter instructed an officer to alert the state attorney's office about the cache of undergarments discovered by the other team. Right now he had his hands full with a teenage suspect who just signed a confession to murder. And information coming into police headquarters indicated that the suspect had been a problem in the neighborhood just a few weeks before Angel's death.

As a result, Brooks Bellay was scheduled to appear in juvenile court the following Monday to face charges for burglary and improper exhibition of a weapon. The charges stemmed from an incident at another home on 25th Avenue on June 23rd. According to a witness, the incident began across the street at a neighbor's home, where a 13-year-old girl was babysitting two younger sisters.

"I was in the bedroom with the lights out, watching what was happening," the woman recalled. "He was harassing the girls and they were screaming. Then Brooks kicked in the front door with a knife in his hand. One of the girls hid in a bedroom while the other came over here to tell us what had happened.

"All three girls were able to escape the house safely, and as soon as police arrived, Brooks was coming out of the house."

"Two days later the girls' father and I went to the Florida Division of Youth Services (DYS) where affidavits were signed against Brooks," the witness added. "I told the DYS people that he should be helped. They were told about his sexual drives, which he has had for the past year. I said that if something wasn't done soon, a terrible thing would happen. Now, six weeks later, it did. They just didn't listen to us."

According to the police report, Brooks Bellay had dumped a pitcher of Koolaid on the carpet and thrown popcorn on the floor while he was in the house. Authorities, under the law, could only question and release the youth. Neighbors spotted him back in the area a few hours later.

State Attorney Robert Stone attempted to explain to an angry community how the system works.

"The DYS has the responsibility to the people of the state as well as the offender," the state attorney commented. "An act of violence is not normal for a child. The police can have probable cause when making an arrest, but our office has to have proof beyond a reasonable doubt."

In any event, it was a foregone conclusion that the first-degree murder charge would postpone the teenager's day in the juvenile court system.

At the suspect's hearing, which was hastily scheduled around 8:00 p.m. Wednesday evening before Judge Philip Nourse, Detective Blanton indicated that Angel Halstead had been beaten before she died.

The detective described how the girl had several marks on her chest and head. Her clothing, he added, was found hanging on several fronds above her nude body. Blanton, who had attended the victim's autopsy, told the judge that the medical examiner had discovered marks on Angel's genital area which made the forensic pathologist believe the victim had been sexually assaulted.

The state attorney then made an unusual plea. Stone requested that Bellay be committed to the Indian River County Jail instead of the juvenile detention center. The prosecutor's reason for the motion was "for the best interest of the person charged and the community as a whole."

Stone argued that the boy should be placed in solitary confinement with his cell next to the jailer's office rather than in a room with other youths at the detention center. While this attempted move bothered Public Defender Paul Kanarek, the suspect's attorney, it was Prosecutor Stone's future intentions that worried him. The prosecutor was apparently attempting to shift the gears of the legal system.

The state attorney indicated that a grand jury would be empaneled, as early as the next week, to determine

35

whether Brooks Bellay should be tried as a juvenile or an adult. If Bellay were to be tried as an adult, the teenage suspect would face the possibility of capital punishment if convicted of first-degree murder.

The judge decreed that he had no choice, under Florida statutes, but to send the teenager to the youth detention center. While the defense had won the first round, Defense Attorney Kanarek still carried reservations. He knew Prosecutor Stone was only sparring and hadn't started any serious punching yet.

A few days later, Stone revealed to the press that the victim had died from massive internal bleeding caused by severe multiple injuries. The senior prosecutor added that based on his analysis of the pathologist's report, there was evidence that Angel Halstead had been sexually assaulted.

Although Stone wouldn't elaborate on the detail of the autopsy, he said, "The public needs to know that this girl didn't fall down and die. It was severe."

He cut the news conference short when a reporter asked if Angel had died immediately.

"No, it wasn't instantaneous," Stone snapped back. "That's all I have to say."

Angel Halstead was laid to rest on August 25th in a ceremony attended by about 30 relatives and friends. A framed photograph of the little girl sat on top of the small white casket surrounded by flower arrangements.

"Angel attended our church," the pastor said during the funeral service. "She rode the bus. She came and was told about Jesus Christ. She knows where she's going."

Two days later Brooks Bellay made news again. The youth had been involved in a card-game fight while in custody, and now the supervisor of the detention center was fearful of the suspect's safety in the institution. This time the public defender agreed to transfer Bellay from the youth facility to the Indian River County Jail. The judge approved the move.

36

Outside, after the hearing, the supervisor told newsmen there were other reasons, in addition to the fight, which led him to believe that Bellay's life would be in danger if he stayed at the detention center. From his conversation two things were evident: Inmates didn't like the accusations leveled against Bellay, and the youth's behavior had been less than sterling.

A few days after the victim's funeral, and before the small town had a chance to rebound from the effects of the slaying, a news story shook Vero Beach again. According to the article, Angel Halstead's body had been exhumed from the cemetery.

The state attorney declined to comment on the reason, telling reporters he had been instructed by the judge not to discuss the case. To veteran newspersons it was obvious there was some sort of problem with the autopsy report. The journalists pushed the prosecutor for another comment.

State Attorney Stone emphasized that he was hesitant to comment in detail on the autopsy report, not only because of the judge's order, but because of the anguish it could potentially cause the victim's family. That statement ended the news conference. When reporters returned to their newsrooms, the rest of the story was waiting for them.

The state attorney's office subpoenaed the local news media demanding that photographs, negatives, and film relating to the death of Angel Halstead be immediately turned over to his office.

A few days later, on August 30th, an Indian River County grand jury took a few minutes over five hours to return a first-degree murder indictment against the teenage suspect. Brooks Bellay was going to trial as an adult. Following the hearing, Prosecutor Stone said he hadn't decided whether or not he would seek the death penalty in the case.

"You have a fourteen-year-old boy involved, but you also have to consider the heinous nature of the crime," Stone remarked, while not ruling out the possibility of a plea bargain. The state attorney then returned to the courtroom.

Stone revealed that Angel's body had been exhumed from the cemetery plot in order to make a positive identification through dental records. The examination, conducted by Dr. Richard Souviron, took place at the Dade County Medical Examiner's Office. Dr. Souviron, who had received much media attention for his bite pattern testimony in the Ted Bundy case, confirmed the body was that of Angel Halstead.

The state attorney left the courthouse that afternoon with one more victory.

Judge Nourse ordered a local newspaper to comply with the state attorney's request for photographs. His request for one particular picture, a photo of a tree covered with panties near the crime scene, was granted. The newspaper turned over the photograph and Stone's office vacated the remaining subpoenas.

The media now realized the rationale behind the prosecutor's request. Stone was gathering evidence to paint the suspect as being sexually perverted. While the prosecution was loading its guns, the defense made an attempt to have the suspect released.

Bellay's lawyer went into court the following day and requested that his client be released on bond. During the hearing, Detective-Sergeant Carter testified that Vero Beach Police Department sleuths had questioned the suspect and obtained a signed confession. The judge ruled that Bellay should remain confined, without bond, in the county jail.

During the following weeks, Prosecutor Stone won a motion to have hair and blood samples taken from the suspect. The defense introduced another motion to dismiss the charges, but it was denied. The motion was based on the fact that the medical examiner didn't testify before the grand jury. The defense then asked for a change of venue, which was also denied. Bellay's attorney began one motion after another, including briefs to an appeals court. After months of legal

38

wrangling the defense finally won a change of venue. Bellay's impending trial was moved to Martin County, 40 miles south of Vero Beach.

"I am pleased that the trial was moved to Martin County," Defense Attorney Kanarek commented after finally winning one round.

Bellay's day in court was scheduled to begin Monday, July 7, 1980.

Early Monday morning, 150 prospective jurors waited in an adjoining room as State Attorney Robert Stone and Assistant State Attorney Bruce Colton approached the bench in another courtroom. Public Defender Paul Kanarek stood next to the prosecutors. Courtroom spectators watched as the attorneys whispered to each other and Circuit Judge Royce R. Lewis.

Moments later the pool of prospective jurors were told that they wouldn't be needed that day. The state of Florida and Brooks Bellay had apparently struck a deal. The young man, now 15 and legally an adult as ruled by the grand jury, decided to plead guilty to second-degree murder.

Judge Lewis, sitting high above the youth, questioned Bellay at length. By law the judge was required to make sure that Bellay comprehended the significance of the plea bargain. His attorney, with his hand on the teenager's shoulder, stood behind him.

"When you're entering a guilty plea, you are admitting the charge against you is the truth," Judge Lewis said. "Do you understand that?"

"Yes, sir," Bellay responded.

"You admit to the court at this time and under oath that you did kill Angel Halstead?"

"Yes, sir," the lad repeated.

The judge then asked Bellay if anyone told him or promised him that the sentence would be less than life in prison. He responded negatively.

"Have you thought that you might have to spend the rest of your natural life in prison?" Lewis questioned.

"Yes sir," Bellay replied in a quiet monotone voice.

At the end of the questioning the judge accepted the defendant's plea, ordered a presentence investigation, and remanded Bellay to the Indian River County Jail, adding that he would sentence the confessed killer in two weeks. Sheriff's deputies handcuffed Bellay who was dressed in a blue golf shirt with blue double-knit trousers, and led him from the courtroom.

Part of the plea agreement stipulated that Bellay waive his rights to the Youthful Offender Statute sentencing procedure. Under that canon, Brooks Bellay would have been limited to a maximum of four years in prison. In addition to the youthful offender waiver, he also waived all rights to any future appeal.

The plea bargain saved Bellay from facing a capital charge, but it didn't help his chances for an early release. The minimum sentence he faced was 25 years in prison.

Stone, Colton, Kanarek and Public Defender Elton Schwarz left the courtroom to face the contingent of reporters waiting outside. They demanded a reason for what had happened just moments before inside the Martin County courtroom.

Schwarz told reporters that had Bellay been convicted of first-degree murder, the prosecutors would not have sought the death penalty.

"We had been working on a plea bargain for several months," Schwarz admitted. "We reached a tentative agreement on Sunday, but it wasn't final until seven-thirty Monday." The public defender added that the plea bargain was in his client's best interest, considering the circumstances.

"By pleading guilty to the second-degree charge, Bellay will be eligible for parole in about six to ten years," he added. "I would consider the plea bargain a victory. With the evidence they had there was no question of his guilt, just to the degree."

Assistant State Attorney Colton elaborated on the public defender's remarks. He explained that the state had agreed to the plea bargain because of possible problems in obtaining a first-degree murder conviction. Originally the medical examiner filed a report saying the victim had been sexually assaulted before she was killed. This gave the prosecution the ammunition it needed for the first-degree charge.

However, after the body was exhumed and examined by another forensic pathologist, who said he found no evidence of any sexual assault, the medical examiner changed his report, Colton added. The medical examiner said there had been a typographical error on the original report, the assistant state attorney said, and it should have read that there was no evidence of any sexual assault.

Colton said they needed the medical testimony to corroborate the taped statement of Bellay. Without it, Colton emphasized, the state would have been hard pressed to prove premeditation.

"We probably could have gotten the statement admitted at the trial, but there was a question about any other independent evidence of rape," Colton concluded.

While it was obvious that Prosecutors Stone and Colton accepted the plea with regrets, it was equally apparent that Schwarz and Kanarek were delighted. But even in their moment of delight the public defender had to admit the fear of inevitable defeat.

"I told Brooks to expect life, and if he gets anything less he can be pleasantly surprised," Schwarz confided. "I never try to second-guess a judge."

Schwarz, a veteran defender, knew what he was talking about.

On July 17th, Judge Lewis, before passing sentence, told Brooks Bellay that this was the most awesome sentence he had ever had to impose because the lad had "his whole life to look forward to." But the judge also said that Bellay "snatched the life away from a little girl who never got to experience a life of her own."

Judge Lewis then sentenced Brooks Bellay to prison

for the remainder of his natural life, remanding him to the Florida Department of Corrections.

"Son, may God have mercy on your soul," Lewis concluded.

While the judge pleaded for mercy from above, the Vero Beach newspaper ran an editorial blitz on the sentence. Part of the paper's opinion read:

"It is shameful. A merciless teenage killer takes the life of an innocent young girl and, yet, it is possible he could be back on the streets in ten years.

"Does ten years in prison make up for the pain and agony little Angel suffered on that tragic afternoon?

"Does ten years in prison compensate for the heartache, anger and sleepless nights experienced by her family?

"Is this justice?

"Bellay's mother and his attorneys asked for mercy at the youth's sentencing. Yet, where was the mercy on the afternoon of August 20, 1979?"

The newspaper — in not so subtle way — attempted to warn its readers what the future held for Angel Halstead's killer.

The average person often thinks a life sentence is just that — a banishment to the penal system until death. But convicts know better. Life means nothing more than being placed on hold until one can qualify for parole. They know it's a judicial waiting game.

Brooks Bellay's turn at the parole bat came up 11 years after his plea bargain sentence, in April 1991.

Usually the State Attorney's Office receives advance notification prior to a convict's hearing before the Florida State Probation and Parole Commission. However, in Bellay's case, the commission failed to apprise the prosecutor. Bruce Colton, now the state attorney in Vero Beach, learned of the hearing through a chance phone call on Thursday, April 25th.

A parole officer from Palm Beach County called Colton asking for the present address of the victim's parents. The officer told the prosecutor that Bellay's parole hearing was scheduled for May 1st — a mere six days away. Should his request be approved, Bellay would be released on June 20th.

As soon as the parole officer hung up, Colton made a few phone calls of his own.

The following morning, the Vero Beach *Press-Journal* published a story about the convicted killer's scheduled hearing and possible release. Colton and the slain girl's family hoped the article would spark enough community reaction to keep Bellay behind bars at the correctional institute in Polk County.

By the afternoon it was evident to some residents of Vero Beach that one of Angel's family members wasn't taking any chances. The relative canvassed residences, city streets, and shopping centers asking everyone he met to sign a petition to keep Bellay behind bars.

All weekend long, the victim's relative solicited signatures. His plea revived the community's memory of the girl who had died trying to find a lost kitten. Many remembered the horror of Angel Halstead's death and were furious to learn her killer might be set loose. One by one — as the day of Bellay's hearing neared — pages of the petition accumulated more endorsements.

On Wednesday, May 1st, the convict's hearing began. Bellay's attorney, Stephen Johnson, said his client would agree never to return to Vero Beach as a condition of the parole. If released, Bellay planned to move in with a relative in Tampa on Florida's west coast.

But the opposition wasn't about to let matters rest there.

Two relatives of little Angel Halstead made a tearful plea to keep the convicted killer behind bars. They amplified their request with a petition, signed by 3,095 local and seasonal residents, opposing the parole request. Commission members, noticeably astounded by the petition, focused their eyes on the next witness, State Attorney Bruce Colton.

Colton revealed that problems with the medical examiner's 1979 report, along with questions about Bellay's confession, had forced prosecutors at that time to accept Bellay's second-degree murder plea in exchange for a life sentence. It was a sentence too short for such a heinous crime, Colton argued.

"This was, in fact, a first-degree murder and sexual battery," the prosecutor said.

State Attorney Colton went on to say that the convict's plans to move in with his relative would not last very long since that relative was terminally ill. Furthermore, although Bellay had had a job interview, he had no commitment of employment.

Then the state attorney, who served as an assistant during Bellay's plea bargain, went for the jugular. Colton pointed out to the parole board that Bellay now denied he ever admitted having sex with the slain 4-year-old girl. Colton concluded by recommending that the convict undergo psychological counseling prior to any consideration of parole in the future.

Parole Commission Chairman A.M. Fontana then told other panel members that his office had received more than 100 telephone calls disapproving of the convict's request for supervised freedom. In the end, the commission voted to extend Bellay's parole date to at least June 20, 2001.

The prosecutor and relatives of Angel Halstead returned to Vero Beach satisfied that justice had been done. Bellay was taken back to the Polk Correctional Institute. Justice had tossed him three quick pitches and struck him out. Now he would have to wait another 10 years before coming to bat again.

About two weeks later, Prosecutor Colton, who usually shies away from publicity, wrote a letter to the editor of the Vero Beach newspaper.

"Based upon a review of the facts of the case," the letter said, "Bellay's lack of remorse and failure to seek or receive treatment while in prison for sexually oriented mental disorders, and the outpouring of community sentiment, the Parole Commission unanimously voted to postpone a projected parole date for Bellay until June 2001.

"I wish to express my appreciation to all of those members of our community who wrote letters, made telephone calls and signed petitions in the successful effort to keep Bellay in prison where he belongs."

Because of a prosecutor, a family and a community who didn't forget the little girl who became a victim of a senseless killing, a convict lost his request to be released into a society that didn't want him back.

"I feel certain that he would do something like this again," Colton emphasized as he closed another chapter on the Angel Halstead homicide.

"MASKED CORPSE IN THE BLACK BRA!"

by Tom Basinski

Maria Cruz looked out the window of her run-down shack on the outskirts of Tijuana, Mexico, on the early morning of September 12, 1990. Near the side of the road about 50 feet from where she lived, Maria spotted what looked like a colorful blanket and two pillows.

Most people probably wouldn't give a discarded blanket more than a passing thought. But Maria was poor, and she thought she could use another blanket, especially with the cold, damp autumn nights starting to arrive.

Maria Cruz walked toward the object. She had already decided which of her four daughters would get the blanket. It would be the baby because the blanket was so pink and colorful. As she approached the object, she saw that it was decorated with the cartoon character Strawberry Shortcake. Although Maria's family was poor, the children knew which cartoon characters were popular.

Maria fluffed the pillows and decided they would do just fine. When Maria went to pick up the "blanket," she discovered that it was really a sleeping bag, and it was heavy, as though something was inside it.

46

Maria unzipped the bag at the top and saw a head of black hair. It was a body, and the face was covered with a kind of "mask" made from strapping tape. Maria was not accustomed to violence. She was shocked beyond belief.

Maria ran to her neighbor's house about a quarter of a mile away. Maria's neighbor had a jeep. After Maria told him about her grisly find, she ran back home to tend to her children. Her neighbor drove to a small restaurant near Tijuana's famous Bullring by the Sea and the State Judicial Police notified.

In less than half an hour about 25 police officers, some on motorcycles, some in patrol cars, and some in old detective sedans, were on the scene. Most were milling about, smoking cigarettes, and talking with one another.

Finally, a short man wearing a sport shirt on the outside of his trousers arrived. He was the detective in charge. He produced a 35mm camera and shot a roll of pictures of the sleeping bag. He motioned to two men standing off to the side. The men walked up to the sleeping bag, picked it up, along with the pillows, and put everything in the back of a van.

Within two minutes, everyone was gone. Maria Cruz knelt in her living room with her children surrounding her. She lit a candle and said a prayer to Our Lady of Guadalupe, both for the dead soul of whoever was in the bag, and for the safety of her own family.

At the Tijuana morgue, the body was removed from the sleeping bag and prepared for autopsy. The deceased was an Asian female, about 5-foot-4 and weighing 120-pounds. She was wearing an ornate black bra — and nothing else. Her hands were taped together in front.

The mask of clear packaging tape was carefully removed from the victim's face. Underneath, the Mexican pathologist found a rag over the victim's mouth. It was all very curious indeed. Decomposition had

47

barely begun so the officials did not believe the victim had been dead very long.

The makeshift mask and the rag over the mouth were saved along with the sleeping bag. The cause of death was found to be asphyxiation. The officials were able to lift at least one fingerprint from the taped mask. The detectives hoped the print did not belong to someone other than the victim or the killer.

The Mexican detectives looked through a pile of missing persons reports on a clipboard. The authorities in Mexico do not have a nationwide crime database on computer. No person described on the clipboard seemed close in description to whoever was dead in the embalming room. The lead detective lit a cigarette, sat down, and hoped something would happen.

Meanwhile, the next night in San Diego, Lydia Ortega and her husband sat in front of the television. Lydia's husband was reading a story in the Mexican newspaper *El Sol* about the woman found in the sleeping bag. That story had not made it into the American papers.

When he told Lydia the description of the body, Lydia's face clouded over in a frown. A woman who worked for Lydia had not been to work in two days. The woman was very dependable and never missed work unless she was sick in bed.

Lydia said, "I'm afraid it's Diane. I've got to call somebody." The next morning Lydia called personnel and obtained the name and phone number of the next-of-kin of Diane Casora, 33, who worked for Lydia at a branch office of a large utility company.

Lydia called relatives of Diane Casora and relayed her fears to them. The relatives had also been trying to get in touch with Diane, but they, too, had been unsuccessful. The relatives had not yet seen the Spanish-language newspaper.

Lydia and her husband went to Tijuana the next morning to find the morgue, while Diane Casora's rel-

48

atives went to the police department in Chula Vista, where Diane lived.

Diane's relatives relayed the story to a Community Service Officer at the front desk of the police station. After the relatives left, the officer personally carried the report to Sergeant Richard Strickland, the man in charge of missing persons and homicide.

Strickland decided to wait for Lydia Ortega to return from Tijuana before making a move. He did not have to wait long. Just after noon, Diane's relative called to say that her worst fears had been confirmed: the masked body in the black bra was Diane Casora.

The Tijuana officials allowed Lydia to look at a photo of the face of the deceased. Without a doubt it was Diane.

Sergeant Strickland's first step was to call Detective Harry Comer, who was at home on his day off, and tell him to get to work. Then, he assembled the rest of the homicide team: Detectives Wayne Maxey, John Heggestuen, Laura Coulson, and Bob Rutledge. Rutledge spoke Spanish, but Strickland decided that the services of Rey Franco would also be needed. Franco whose first language was Spanish, normally worked burglary.

The team had worked international cases before and it was decided that more than one liaison officer would be needed. Supervising lab technician Bill Johnson was alerted, and his camera equipment and crime-detecting kit were placed in the evidence van. Then Strickland, Rutledge, Franco, and Johnson headed south to Tijuana.

Once there, they discovered the autopsy had already been completed. The Mexican detectives believed the case was theirs since the body had been found in their territory. The American crime fighters tried to explain that the case was probably an abduction, which meant it was Chula Vista's case. A compromise was reached, and the Mexicans allowed the Americans to "borrow" the evidence for analysis.

Meanwhile, back in Chula Vista, Detectives Laura Coulson and Jon Heggestuen had been to Diane Casora's apartment, which was located about one block from the police station. A search warrant had been obtained and evidence collection got under way.

There was no forced entry to the dwelling, the sleuths noticed. Diane's relative said the sleeping bag and the pillows that Diane was found in belonged to Diane. In the trash can, the detectives found an empty dispenser for packaging tape of the kind used to bind Diane and make the mask. They also found a plastic wrapped cardboard used to hold a new pair of scissors and an empty film box.

After the search of the house was completed, Detective Laura Coulson obtained information on Diane's 1989 Volkswagen Jetta, which was missing. Coulson filled out a stolen-car report and had it entered into the nationwide computer with the request to notify Chula Vista police if the vehicle was recovered. The detectives also planned to check with U.S. Customs to see if the vehicle had crossed the border into the United States recently.

The scissors and tape containers found in the wastebasket suggested that Diane Casora had been abducted from her home. She had apparently been wrapped in that tape before she was taken. It was not, as the Tijuana police had theorized, that Diane had left a bar with someone and been killed in Tijuana.

This new information was relayed to Sergeant Strickland and his team. They told the Tijuana detectives, who agreed with their American colleagues that it was now a Chula Vista case. Strickland thanked the detectives for their help and said he wanted to take the body back to the United States for further processing of evidence.

The Mexican detectives bowed politely and said they would cooperate. The body of Diane Casora was en route back to the United States within two days.

The Chula Vista homicide sleuths now had their

work cut out for them. Their first task was to speak with friends, co-workers, and relatives of Diane Casora to find out who might have wanted to see Diane dead. The detectives also tried to get to know the victim through what her friends told them.

The sleuths looked for information on the victim's habits. Did she gamble, go to bars and leave with strangers, abuse drug and alcohol? the sleuths asked Diane's friends. They also checked on insurance policies to see who Diane's beneficiaries were.

It was a long and tedious process, but it had to be done. The detectives hoped that Diane's friends would be truthful. They were well aware that friends often cover up information because it might prove embarrassing to the memory of the deceased.

Generally, the officers learned that Diane Casora was a well-liked person. She was a good worker. She was divorced and her ex-husband was in the military, several hundred miles away, but still in California. There was one child who was with the ex-husband.

Two names cropped up for females who worked with Diane and who did not get along with her. The detectives checked this information out thoroughly, but they were correct in assuming that it did not amount to a serious problem. It turned out that one of the women was going to get married. Apparently, Diane had taken her aside and told her she was too young and that she should wait. The woman resented this and had not spoken to Diane since. That was hardly a reason to kill her, although probers knew people had been killed for pettier reasons.

It was now September 15th, three days after Diane's body had been found and one day after she had been identified. Sergeant Strickland was holding his daily meeting to bring everyone up to date on the case and to assign the various duties for the day.

Detective Laura Coulson received information from U.S. Customs that Diane's vehicle had crossed from Mexico into the United States on September 12th at

51

3:44 a.m. Each time a vehicle crosses, the Customs officer at the booth punches the license number into the computer. This information stays in the computer for 60 days. The computer retains the date and time the vehicle crossed, through which lane it entered, and which officer was on duty at the lane.

Don Hunter, a detective from the sex crimes unit, came into the meeting and asked to be heard when they could fit him in. Hunter explained that he'd worked a rape case on July 15th. Diane Casora was the victim.

Hunter said, "I don't know much about your case, but here's what happened in mine. Diane falls asleep. She wakes up and some guy is in her bedroom. She thinks it's her boyfriend, but she can't see because it's dark.

"The guy comes over, puts some kind of rag over her mouth and nose and she goes out cold. She wakes up the next morning and finds out somebody raped her while she was under.

"We checked the rag and somebody chloroformed her. At first, she said she thought it was her boyfriend because he liked to do some weird stuff to her. So I scheduled another interview with her to get into the nitty gritty of what happened.

"Just before the interview, she calls up, tells me it wasn't her boyfriend, and just to forget the whole thing. By now I figure it must be her boyfriend and she's covering up for the S.O.B."

When Detective Hunter mentioned chloroform, the entire room fell silent. Wayne Maxey told Hunter that they suspected chloroform had been used in this case. Hunter said, "If I was you, I'd talk with the boyfriend. His name is Mark Cadiz. He's a bouncer at a sleazy bar in National City."

Detective Bob Rutledge spoke with a friend of Diane about Mark Cadiz. The friend said that Mark had seen Diane earlier in the week. Mark had returned a cassette tape to Diane. None of Diane's friends liked

Mark. They all said he was "slimy."

Detectives Harry Comer and Wayne Maxey went to the bar and asked to speak with the manager. Even though it was only 10 o'clock in the morning, the place was half-filled with sailors who had pulled the night watch from the nearby 32nd Street Naval Station.

Also in attendance were night-shift workers from a steel and shipbuilding company and several women.

The manager was not eager to help. She was visited regularly by the National City Police Department for a variety of violations. Comer thought this fact might make her more cooperative, but the opposite proved to be true. Fights at the bar were legendary, and it was said that you were not truly a National City cop until you had to break up a knock-down free-for-all that had started inside this bar and spilled out onto National City Boulevard.

The manager said she did not have the timesheets so she could not say when Mark Cadiz worked last. Neither did she have his home address and phone number. She could not say when Mark would be in to work again.

Detective Wayne Maxey was too cool to let this person get his goat. He said, "Okay, we'll be back. Thanks for all your help." The sleuths moved on.

When Detectives Maxey and Comer arrived back at Chula Vista headquarters, they spoke with Laura Coulson who had been present at the American autopsy on Diane Casora conducted by Dr. Christopher Swalwell. The pathologist complimented the Mexican authorities on their handling of the body and concurred with their findings.

The rag was of primary importance to the detectives. Everyone believed the substance on it was chloroform. The lab would make an official determination, but it would take some time.

Later that same night, Detectives Maxey and Comer returned to the bar and spoke with Mark Cadiz, who was on duty. They did not tell him that Diane was dead. They told him they were working her as a missing person. Cadiz thought a minute and told the two detectives that he had not seen her in about three weeks.

As they left, Mazey said, "Bingo! We've got him in his first of probably many lies. The friend said he saw Diane earlier when he returned the cassette tape."

Detective Laura Coulson, in the meantime, had found out that Mark Cadiz had a previous arrest record and his fingerprints were on file with the San Diego Sheriff's Department. She went there and obtained a copy of those prints.

Detective Coulson delivered the original prints along with the taped mask to Mary Kay Arsenault, an expert fingerprint examiner with the Chula Vista Police Department. The lifted print that Arsenault had to work with was of low quality. But it was what the Chula Vista officers could salvage from the Tijuana officers. After a lot of painstaking work, Arsenault said there were enough identifiable points to prove that the prints belonged to Mark Cadiz.

Another meeting was called and the sleuths were very upbeat. Chula Vista had experienced a string of unsolved homicides and this lack of success was wearing on the sleuths. In at least two of the cases, they knew who did the killing but could not prove it. Now, in this case, they at least had some proof.

Their job would not be done by merely arresting Cadiz, however. There were several possible defenses Cadiz would likely employ, and it was the job of the detectives to anticipate these defenses and overcome them.

The first order of business was to find out where Mark Cadiz lived. The probers wanted to get a search warrant, but they could not merely say they wanted a warrant for "wherever Mark Cadiz lives." They had to have the warrant for a specific place. Also, they needed to find out about his vehicles so they could check the Customs computer to see if the vehicle had returned from Mexico.

Once these things were done, they would arrest Cadiz. From interviews with friends and relatives of Diane Casora, sleuths were able to enumerate two addresses where Mark Cadiz lived at least part-time. One was with his current girlfriend and another was with a relative.

The detectives reasoned there was not likely to be evidence at the girlfriend's address, but they obtained a warrant for there nonetheless. They also swore out a search warrant for Cadiz's relative's house.

The sleuths learned Cadiz owned a motorcycle. His license number was run through the computer at Customs, but it was learned the cycle had not crossed into the United States.

Surveillance and arrest teams were formed. Detectives Mitch Hayes and Dan Linney were assigned to check out the girlfriend's house. If ever there was a "Mutt and Jeff" team, Hayes and Linney were it. If Hayes stood on a stool, he would be lucky to reach 5 feet 8 inches. If the 6-foot-2 Linney removed one of his massive legs, he might weigh only 250 pounds.

These two sleuths were never famous for being inconspicuous. Yet, they did excellent work. In one case, several Chula Vista patrol units and some undercover officers were helping state prison officials look for an escapee who had decided that he'd picked enough weeds as part of a road gang on the freeway. The search went on for several hours, foiling even the police dogs and helicopter units that were called in. Nobody had any luck.

Just before nightfall, Detective Hayes was standing outside his car near a freeway on-ramp, drinking a cup of coffee, when a large bearded man covered with tattoos strolled up and said, "Hey brother, think you can give me a lift?" Hayes eyed the man and asked, "Yeah, you in trouble?" The man answered, "Yeah, some guys are after me."

Hayes coolly pointed his semi-automatic handgun

at the suspect and said, "Don't move. I'll just use the radio and get your ride here in a second."

Detectives Linney and Hayes were given an old booking photo of Mark Cadiz and they set off for the stakeout at about nine o'clock in the morning on September 21st. It was a typical surveillance. About 50 men who resembled Cadiz walked down the street while the detectives waited, but for the longest time, there was no sign of Mark Cadiz himself.

Finally, at about 3:40 p.m., a dark-skinned male with a thin build emerged from the upstairs apartment and began walking down the sidewalk.

The two detectives converged on him. Mark Cadiz froze when Linney said, "Police officers, Mark. Stay right where you are."

Cadiz eyed the bulk of Linney and gave a brief thought of hoofing it out of there. But he could see that both officers had walkie-talkies and guns. He decided to do what they told him.

Sergeant Strickland assigned Detectives Wayne Maxey and Harry Comer to conduct the interview while Detectives Jon Heggestuen and Laura Coulson served the search warrant at Cadiz's relatives house. Rutledge and Franco served the warrant at the girlfriend's house. Strickland buzzed back and forth between those places and managed to put together a press release in the meantime.

Before Detectives Maxey and Comer went into the interview room to take on Mark Cadiz, they reviewed what they had and formulated a game plan for the interview. The case looked pretty good. No matter what Mark Cadiz could come up with by way of explanation, he would be hard-pressed to make a convincing argument that he was not involved in Diane Casora's death.

The start of the interview was very low-key. In fact, for the first two hours the three men made small talk while the detectives obtained the usual booking information about next-of-kin, marks, scars, tattoos, and medical history.

When the interview turned to the nuts and bolts of the case, Mark Cadiz denied having anything to do with Diane's death. He could not, however, account for his whereabouts on the night of the killing. The detectives had learned that he had missed work on the night they believed Diane was killed.

The detectives confronted Cadiz about his original statement — that he had not seen Diane in three weeks. They reminded him that he had returned a tape earlier in the week. His memory suddenly improved. He still denied doing any harm to Diane, though.

The talk eventually got around to evidence. Cadiz asked the sleuths what evidence they had. Wayne Maxey replied, "Well Mark, what we have is a fingerprint." That piqued Cadiz's interest. "What fingerprint? Where? I've been in her place a thousand times. My prints are all over her apartment. Naw, you guys are going to have to do better than that."

Once again Wayne Maxey carried the ball. "Mark, don't be more stupid than you've already been. Do you really think we would haul you in here just because we found your prints in her place? Come on! Mark, when you made the mask for Diane, you left a fingerprint on the tape. It's a great surface. The print is beautiful."

Mark Cadiz slumped in his chair and let out a deep breath of air. Detective Maxey said, "Tell us about it, Mark. We've been in this business long enough to know that nothing is cut and dried. Something happened before Diane died. Tell us what it was."

Cadiz sat there for what seemed like several minutes. He said, "I'm trying. I want to tell you. I can see myself outside her house. I'm looking through the window. But, there's a wall there. I can't get through the wall. If I could get in I could tell you. I'm trying. I really am."

Detectives Maxey and Comer looked at each other. Finally, Maxey said, "Mark. It isn't a wall. It's her

57

door. Open the door and go in."

Cadiz's face brightened and his cloud seemed to lift. He went on to yell about his four-year relationship with Diane Casora. Toward the end, it was on-again, off-again, though it was mostly off. In spite of everything they had a good sexual relationship, Cadiz said.

On the night of the "incident," as Mark Cadiz put it, he went to Diane's apartment. She wanted to have sex so they went to the nearby motel and rented a room.

Detective Comer stopped Cadiz with a wave of his hand. "Wait a minute, Mark. Diane's child was with the father. Diane lived alone. Why did you need to rent a room?" he asked.

Mark Cadiz managed a smile. "Diane was a screamer. At least with me she was. She liked to let go—know what I mean? She was afraid of letting go in her place because of the neighbors and whatnot. So we rented a room. We had rented a room at the [motel] several times before."

Detective Comer asked, "Did Diane go with you when you paid for the room?"

Cadiz replied, "No. She hid in the car. It costs extra for another person. I paid for a single to save a couple of bucks. Anyway, we get down there, and she liked to get tied up, you see. We do the thing where I tie her up. I used tape this time. The next thing I know she's dead."

Detective Maxey said, "Whoa, you jumped ahead a little. Where did the mask come in?"

As if he just remembered, Cadiz answered, "Oh yeah. The mask. That was her idea. She liked to have all her senses numbed, you know, like she couldn't see or smell or even hear. The only thing she liked to be aware of was me being with her. Know what I mean?"

Maxey said, "Well, I'm trying. What about the chloroform?"

Cadiz said, "I don't know anything about any chloroform. She died on me while we were going at it. It

58

was an accident. I felt awful about it."

Detective Comer asked, "What did you do after Diane died?"

Cadiz responded, "Like I said, I felt awful. I stayed that night with her in the room. I paid for an extra day and told them not to clean the room. Then, that night I put her in the trunk of her car. I had to go to work. After work I went down to Tijuana and found a place where I could put her.

"I drove her car back across. The next night I went back to see if she was still there. She was gone. I left her car down there and walked back across the border. That's about it. It was an accident. I swear."

The interview was concluded and Mark Cadiz was booked into the county jail. Of course the interviewing sleuths believed only a fraction of what Cadiz had told them. His statement was very self-serving.

By the time the interview was over, the search warrant teams had returned. Nothing of value was found at the suspect's girlfriend's house. However, the sleuths had possibly struck paydirt at his relative's house. There, they found a briefcase containing a camera with film in it, lubricating jelly, and tape.

The film in the camera was now in the process of being developed at the photo service that the police department contracted with.

In the meantime, the detectives left to get a sandwich. When they returned, the photos were ready. The snapshots made even those experienced officers wince.

There were shots of Diane taped up and wearing various skimpy costumes. In all of the shots she did not appear to be conscious. In some of the shots she appeared to be dead. Shockingly enough, there were pictures of yet another woman who also appeared to be unconscious.

The photos were graphic and bizarre in nature. The women were taped up spread-eagled on the bed. Detectives now knew this was definitely a strange man they were dealing with.

The detectives knew Cadiz's statements to them would be admissible in court. The facts would show he had lied to them.

First, Diane Casora did not go willingly to the motel. Sleuths knew this for two reasons. If Diane had gone willingly, why did she bring her daughter's Strawberry Shortcake sleeping bag and pillows? No, she had been chloroformed at ther place, wrapped in the sleeping bag, stuffed in the car and taken to the motel.

Secondly, the detectives verified with the motel management that Mark Cadiz had been a semi-regular customer at he motel. He was usually accompanied by an Asian female, presumably Diane.

Cadiz's line about Diane hiding so they would not have to pay for two people smelled like baloney to the sleuths. The motel management verified that the price for a room was the same whether one or two people rented it. Therefore, the sleuths knew Diane was not hiding the night she was killed. They knew she was out cold, probably in the trunk.

The case was assembled and presented to Deputy District Attorney Bill Collins. At Cadiz's arraignment, Collins asked Municipal Court Judge Gale E. Kaneshiro to set bail at $750,000. Instead, Judge Kaneshiro set it at a cool $1 million.

Before trial, the detectives met with D.A. Collins and went over the scenario for him. They believed Cadiz was angry with Diane for some reason, so he went to her house with his tape, scissors, and chloroform. When she answered the door, he put the cloth over her mouth and nose and put her out.

Cadiz then wrapped Diane's body in the sleeping bag and carted her off to the motel. He liked to have sex with her while she was unconscious, so he kept applying the chloroform to her in doses just enough to keep her under. When she would stir, he would give her a little more. Things got out of hand. He applied too much of the dangerous knockout drug, and she died. He dumped the body after spending the night with her. End of story.

D.A. Collins believed he had a good case. He apparently was correct as Mark Cadiz pleaded guilty to second-degree murder on November 19, 1990. On March 25, 1991, he was sentenced to 15 years to life in prison. Cadiz is now in the California prison system.

Meanwhile, detectives are still searching for the unidentified woman who was photographed unconscious and in sexually explicit poses on Mark Cadiz's film.

EDITOR'S NOTE:
Maria Cruz and Lydia Ortega are not the real names of the persons so named in the foregoing story. Fictitious names have been used because there is no reason for public interest in the identities of these persons.

"HE BIT OFF THE BLONDE BEAUTY'S BREASTS!"

by Don Lasseter

With her golden air shimmering in the sun and her blue eyes reflecting the clear April sky, Lynea Kokes was gorgeous. Even in the white terry cloth shorts and matching blouse she had donned for the move in preparation for her new job, Lynea was beautiful.

Managing apartments was Lynea's specialty, and the building she and her husband were taking over in Panorama City, California, 18 miles north of Los Angeles, was a real challenge. Tenants had complained of drug deals and shady characters on the premises. The new owner, for whom Lynea Kokes worked, made a practice of purchasing troubled apartment complexes, cleaning them up, and turning them into profitable businesses. His main troubleshooter was Lynea Kokes, who would take over the managing duties as soon as she had moved in.

Even though she was only 28, the attractive woman was one of the owner's best managers. Lynea had a way with people, a perfect ability to deal with all tenants, no matter how cranky or stubborn they were. She happily accepted the challenge of converting the apartment complex, despite becoming a new mother just 10 months earlier.

The comely manager caught the eye of several

62

apartment residents. "Could we give you a hand with those heavy boxes?" one of them asked.

Lynea gratefully accepted the man's kind offer for assistance. Another tenant joined in, and soon, the two men were struggling up the stairs with assorted boxes and furniture. When they had completed the task, Lynea thanked them with a smile. They left her in the apartment, apparently, all by herself.

The complex had darkened by 8:20 p.m., April 18, 1988, when Lynea Kokes' husband returned from an errand that had taken most of the day. He walked into apartment 238, with his child at his side, expecting to hear the laughter of his beautiful wife. Instead, he saw a chilling sight that would tear at his heart for the rest of his life.

Lynea Kokes lay crumpled on the dark brown carpet, naked except for ankle-length white stockings and terry cloth shorts clinging to one of her feet. Her sightless eyes stared vacantly at the ceiling. The delicate features of her pretty face were battered black and blue. Her eyes were swollen and discolored with blood. A trail of crimson ran from her broken nose, down her cheek, around her ear, and onto her neck. Blood pooled under her matted hair.

The victim's slim, curvaceous body was twisted, as if she had died in terrible pain. Gaping wounds marred her bare chest. The nipples of both breasts had been torn or chewed off.

Later, the horrified husband could not recall the excruciating shriek that tore from his throat. He could not even remember who called 911 to report the tragedy in apartment 238.

Officer Tim Bergstrom of the Los Angeles Police Department was on night watch patrol with his partner in Panorama City, a suburb of Los Angeles, when he got a radio call at 8:30 p.m. Bergstrom was told to proceed to an apartment complex on Van Nuys Boulevard, where there was a possible code 187, the California penal code for murder.

When the officers arrived, paramedics had just entered the apartment. Within moments, they declared Lynea Kokes dead and covered her brutalized body with a baby blanket taken from the pile of furniture that would never be used by the new occupant.

Officer Bergstrom secured the crime scene with yellow tape, made certain that nothing else was disturbed, and waited for the arrival of the detectives from the homicide unit.

Detective Mel Arnold and his partner, Detective Dan Riehl arrived soon after the uniformed officers. Mel Arnold, a 17-year veteran of the LAPD, six years with the homicide unit, stood two inches over six feet tall. His distinguished gray hair and white mustache gave him an authoritative look, which was balanced by a soft-spoken good humor that immediately set people around him at ease.

Dan Riehl, solidly built and disarmingly amiable, had been paired with Arnold for one year of his four-year tenure with the LAPD. That experience was complemented by a degree in criminology he had earned at California State University in Long Beach, just 30 miles south of his Van Nuys office.

The team had investigated dozens of murders and had been instrumental in solving a notorious local case wherein a man had been sexually mutilated. Arnold and Riehl discovered that the man who committed the murder had been hired by a female friend who wanted to collect insurance on the victim. The investigation helped the district attorney convict the perpetrators, and send the woman, Maureen McDermott, to join only one other woman on California's death row.

Now Detectives Mel Arnold and Dan Riehl faced the grueling task of finding another killer who had cruelly mutilated the victim.

Riehl saw Lynea's body first. The detective was appalled at the obvious brutality. In addition to the bruises on the victim's face, Riehl noticed a large laceration over Lynea's left eye and the contusions to her badly swollen lips. His eyes traveled down to her neck and came to a sudden halt at the gruesome sight.

A black cloth belt circled the dead woman's neck. It had evidently been used as a ligature to strangle her. Just above the belt, a slash wound in the front of her neck gaped open. Below the belt, another gash in her throat had bled freely, leaving a pool of blood on the carpet.

The detective counted seven deep stab wounds to the woman's chest. One particularly vicious puncture had been delivered with such force that the wound gaped open almost one inch.

Detective Riehl watched as criminalist Lloyd Mahaney used a sexual assault kit to collect evidence to determine whether Lynea Kokes had been raped. Blood around her vagina and anus seemed to indicate a brutal rape. The technician used swabs to take samples of fluids from the various body cavities, and carefully applied the fluids to glass slides. These slides would later prove that spermatozoa had been deposited in the victim's vagina, anus, and mouth.

The technician also found a black hair on the body of the light-complected, blonde woman. He carefully dropped the hair into a glassine bag for use as possible evidence.

The meticulous search for evidence continued well into the night as the team of medical and forensic personnel scoured every inch of the apartment. Flashes from cameras illuminated dark corners of the four rooms as police photographers recorded everything at the crime scene that might lead to the killer. One technician found a bloody palmprint on a table used for changing the baby's diapers. The print was carefully photographed and preserved.

A purse, presumably belonging to the victim, had been emptied on the floor, but until the investigators could interview Lynea's husband, they had no way of knowing what, if anything, was missing.

Lynea Kokes' body was carefully lifted onto a gurney and transported to the Los Angeles County Coroner's laboratory for an autopsy. Deputy Medical Examiner Joan Shipley would conduct the postmortem examination of the violated body. She would eventually report that the cause of death was "hemopneumothorax which was the result of perforations of the heart and lungs due to even penetrating stab wounds of the chest, and also due to near strangulation."

"What is near strangulation?" she would be asked.

"That means that there was not complete obstruction of the air vents into the respiratory passages." The ligature had damaged Lynea's ability to breath but had not caused her death.

The medical examiner also found that the victim's nipples had been "avulsed," meaning torn off. There were marks apparently made by teeth around the wounds. Abrasions and bleeding around the victim's genitalia indicated that she had been raped.

All of the injuries, except the stab wounds to the heart, were antemortem; they had occurred before Lynea's death.

The investigation at the apartment continued under the supervision of Detective Mel Arnold. "Sometimes, you need to get lucky on such investigations," Arnold would say. "But luck, as I define it, is when preparation meets opportunity."

The detectives, well prepared with their combined experience and education, were doing everything they could to create the opportunity to solve the heinous murder.

As Detective Dan Riehl would later put it, "There are many suspects until each person is cleared or confirmed as a possible perpetrator." The investigators first wanted to clear up or confirm the obvious possibilities, people who knew the victim or might have a reason to want her dead.

Lynea Kokes' husband was questioned extensively.

Even though he was visibly distraught, it was essential to discover whether he was a possible suspect in the crime. The investigators knew that many such murders were committed by relatives or acquaintances. But Mr. Kokes was quickly cleared of any suspicion whatsoever.

During the questioning, however, he was able to tell the sleuths that his wife's driver's license, several credit cards, and a change purse were all missing from her bag.

The apartment complex in which the victim lived had been the location of some activities involving drugs, the detectives knew. They would have to question all the tenants to see if the killing was somehow related to drugs. Maybe a drug deal had gone bad or the new manager had seen something she shouldn't have seen.

A good place to begin, the investigators figured, was to question the manager Lynea Kokes was replacing. Could he be angry or jealous because Mrs. Kokes was going to supersede his authority?

The interview of the manager revealed that he had been in and out of the office for most of the day and hadn't seen anything unusual. Mrs. Kokes, he said, had been moving her stuff in, and a couple of guys helped her. He couldn't think of anyone who might have killed the victim, since she had been at this location such a short time, not even long enough to make any enemies. His answers to the investigators' questions were forthright and clear. Both detectives had gut feelings that he was not the man they were looking for.

Residents of the complex stood around in small groups, whispering and wondering, as the investigating team performed their tasks. The tenants were curious about what was going on. Some of them speculated about the crime, but few of them really had any inkling of what had happened. They were questioned, individually, by the detectives.

Once again talking to the manager, the detectives wanted to know if there had been any unusual occurrences around the apartment during the day.

"I can't think of anything, other than one of the tenants was caught snooping around the office earlier today," he said.

"Tell us about that," the sleuths urged their helpful witness.

"Well, the guy who lives up in apartment 252 was in the office by himself, and the maid came in. She caught him behind the counter, snooping around where he shouldn't have been. She told me about it, so I told the guy that he had to move. He was behind on his rent anyway, so I told him to move out."

Detectives Riehl and Arnold wanted to talk to the occupant of apartment 252. Their knock on the door was answered by a slim young man in his 20s who was noticeably nervous. Donald Williamson had been drinking but was not in a drunken state. Both detectives were adept with interview techniques, and they had no difficulty getting Don Williamson to agree to talk to them. But first he wanted to go outside. He didn't want to bother his roommate.

Don Williamson shared his apartment with another young man, with whom he had been drinking and playing cards most of the afternoon. Williamson worked at Universal Studios as a chef in the employees' commissary. His roommate worked just across the street from the apartment at a convalescent home.

"Where were you during the afternoon?" the detective asked.

"I have Mondays and Tuesdays off from my job," he answered. "I was just taking it easy around the house today and doing some laundry. My roommate Mark and I got up about nine this morning and went out to get a tape recorder. We got back before noon. He went across the street to where he works and told them that he needed the day off 'cause of a death in the family.

That wasn't really true. He just wanted to hang out with me today. Then we had a few drinks and played some cards. We just got back a little while ago from McDonald's where we had something to eat."

"How long have you guys lived here?"

"A little over a month."

"We heard you are being evicted because you were snooping around in the manager's office," the detectives said.

"It wasn't me. It was my roommate. He came upstairs a few hours ago and told me that he had been down in the office and heard a buzzer go off, an alarm or something. The door was ajar, so he walked in, assuming the manager was there. But nobody was there, then the maid came in and accused him of breaking in the office. So now we're getting kicked out because we're four days behind on the rent."

Don Williamson described how the two men had packed their things and were preparing to drive to central California where his roommate, Mark Bradford, wanted to go.

"What were you guys drinking this afternoon?"

"Black Velvet whiskey and some beer. I had a bottle, one liter, that was about three-quarters full, and we finished that off. Then I gave Mark twenty bucks and he went to the store to get some more. But that was over a period of several hours that we drank it."

"Do you know anything about what happened in apartment two-thirty-eight?"

Don Williamson hesitated several moments, as if in deep thought. When he finally answered, he said, "Well, a little while ago we were standing around with some of the other guys, watching the cops. Nobody seemed to know anything, but Mark, my roommate, said that he had heard what happened. He told me about it. He was in and out of our room all afternoon, talking to people."

"What did he tell you?"

"That some girl down the hallway got beat up and

raped, and her throat was slashed."

Detectives Arnold and Riehl were puzzled about how Don Williamson's roommate had known that much. Of course, rumors had been flying around the complex all evening, so maybe the speculation had been accidentally accurate. Or just maybe Don Williamson knew more than he was revealing.

Williamson's agitation and nervousness prompted the detectives to suspect that the young man had more to tell them. They encouraged him to keep talking. Despite the coolness of the evening, beads of perspiration popped out on the man's forehead. Williamson sputtered and stammered for a bit, and then, as if a valve in his vocal cords had been opened, he couldn't seem to stop talking.

"I called a relative of mine in Nebraska who's been a sheriff for thirty-five years to ask his advice. He told me that I should tell you guys everything I know," Williamson confided.

The two detectives gave Williamson their full attention.

"This afternoon, when that pretty lady was moving in, Mark wanted to make a bet with me that he could get her in bed before her husband came home. Then he went downstairs and helped her move some boxes to her apartment. A Puerto Rican guy helped, too. Mark came back in, and told me about the incident in the office and that we had to move. Then he said he was going to go over and talk to the new manager, that lady, and see if she would maybe let us stay."

"What time was that?"

"Oh, around five-thirty or six. He was gone a little while and I was taking a nap. When he came back in, he went straight to the shower. He got sick, and threw up all over the bathroom. I went in there while he was cleaning up the vomit with some towels."

Williamson stopped again, looked into the eyes of both detectives, took a deep breath, and continued. "I have some knives I use at the commissary that I keep in a knife case here. One of them had a broken tip, so I'd left it on the counter in the kitchen. I saw it on the bathroom floor. But it was just the handle. The blade was broken off, with only about one inch of the blade left attached to the handle."

A broken knife on the bathroom floor didn't mean much, but the detectives wanted to hear more.

"Mark took the towels down to the laundry room. When he came back, he was real antsy and nervous. I noticed that his hands were bloody and bruised like he had hit something. I asked him about it, and he said he was mad 'cause we were getting kicked out and had hit a wall. Then, we went to McDonald's, just a quarter of a mile down Van Nuys Boulevard, to get something to eat."

Bloody hands, plus a broken knife, might add up to a real suspect, the two cops thought.

Williamson continued. "When we got back, I went into the laundry room to get the towels. I heard something metallic clanking inside the dryer. When I pulled the towels out, I saw what was making the noise. It was the broken blade of my knife. I recognized it 'cause the tip was missing. It's still in there. That's when I called my relative in Nebraska, and then decided I'd better tell you guys about it. I don't know if it all means anything, but I thought you guys had better know about it."

Detectives Arnold and Riehl thought that Williamson's information meant a lot. Dan Riehl checked the dryer, found the broken blade, and asked one of the uniformed officers to stand guard over it until a criminalist could remove it and preserve the chain of evidence. Then the two detectives called for backup to make the arrest of Mark Bradford, Don Williamson's roommate.

Officer Tim Bergstrom, who had been the first uniformed officer on the scene when the victim's body was discovered, arrived again a little after 11:00 p.m. Detective Mel Arnold, with his partner Dan Riehl and

Bergstrom backing him up, stepped into apartment 252, leveled his handgun at Mark Alan Bradford, handcuffed him, and informed him that he was under arrest.

Before taking Bradford to the squad car for transportation to the jail, Officer Bergstrom searched the suspect. In the back pocket of his jeans, Bergstrom found the knife handle with the broken blade.

The investigators later removed a duffel bag and a brown suitcase from the apartment. Among the contents of the duffel bag were a pair of blue jeans and a blue shirt, both bloodstained. The suitcase contained credit cards and a driver's license inscribed with the name Lynea Kokes.

Early the following morning, Mark Bradford was taken to the jail processing room where he was fingerprinted and booked. Station Officers Synthia Gordon and Monique Denby were on duty in the processing room, and were just completing the "courtesy" fingerprinting of a detective for administrative reasons.

The detective looked up at Mark Alan Bradford and saw a clean-cut young man, 25 years old, 6 feet tall, hazel eyes, well-groomed dark brown hair, and nice looking. Smiling, the detective, who didn't know the charges against Bradford, asked, "You in for a traffic ticket, or a warrant?"

"Murder," Bradford candidly responded.

The officers, taken aback, looked at him inquisitively but said nothing. The detective had pressing duties and left. Bradford just kept talking. "I helped the lady move in. I was drinking some whiskey, and when I was in her apartment, I started watching her, and I don't know what came over me, but all of a sudden I wanted to kill her."

Wide-eyed, the two processing officers listened in shocked silence. Finally, Monique Denby asked, "Did you dislike her?"

"No. She seemed real nice," Bradford responded in

a dull monotone. "I crushed her throat with my hands, then I put my hand over her mouth so she couldn't scream, then I raped her and left her there. About an hour later, I went back because I realized she wasn't dead. When I got there, she was gasping for air."

"You went back?" asked Denby, in shocked disbelief.

"Yes," Bradford continued, as if describing some simple routine job or other trivial incident. "I knew her husband and child weren't there. So after I went in, I slit her throat and then I stabbed her in the chest."

Horrified, the two officers continued to question Bradford. Synthia Morgan asked, "After you slit her throat, why'd you stab her in the chest?"

With a weak smile, Bradford replied, "Because I wanted to make sure she was dead when I left. When I got home, I started cleaning myself up when the police broke in with their guns and said, 'You're under arrest.' There's one thing I still don't know — how they knew it was me. And another thing, the officer said I cut her nipple off. Now *that* I don't remember doing."

The emotionless young man continued his remarkable tale, telling the officers how he had asked that his parents not be notified because he didn't want them to know what he had done. He concluded his story by saying, "I don't have any bad feelings about what I have done, but I do feel sorry for the little kid because he has no mother and her husband will be mad. What can I say? I've killed her so I might as well smile and be happy. This is the first time I've ever done anything like this. I was in jail before, but it was for robbery or some charges."

Officers Morgan and Denby completed the booking and fingerprinting job, sent Bradford back to his cell, and immediately called a member of Detective Mel Arnold's investigating team to report the entire conversation.

Mark Alan Bradford had made a complete confession of murdering Lynea Kokes. But it was completely useless. The two booking officers were not investigators and had not recited the well known Miranda warning of the suspect's rights. The confession could not be used by prosecutors in a trial, except for cross examination.

The confession was corroborated by some hard evidence. Forensic Print Specialist Anthony Clark Stewart had compared the bloody palmprint taken from the table in the victim's apartment to examples of Mark Bradford's prints. They matched perfectly.

Detective Mel Arnold was frustrated by the useless confession, but he was encouraged that the prints implicated Bradford as the killer. He also had the bloody clothes found in the duffel bag that the suspect wore in the crime, and the credit cards Bradford had stolen from the victim. But the killer's fate would be sealed, Arnold thought, if he could get a confession that could be used in court. If Bradford would talk so frankly to the booking officers, surely he would talk to Arnold, the sleuth reasoned.

On April 20, 1988, Detective Arnold sat across from Mark Bradford in an interview room, with a tape recorder rolling. The detective thought that this young man was the antithesis of the notion that you could tell a man was a killer just by looking at him. Bradford was clean-cut, good looking, exceptionally polite, and agreeable. The suspect had telephoned from the jail and told another detective that he wanted to talk to Arnold.

After carefully reciting the Miranda rights several times, Mel Arnold handed the young man paper and pen. Bradford wrote, "I was advised of my rights," and, "I agree to give up my rights to remain silent and to have an attorney present." Only then, did Mel Arnold begin the questioning.

"Why did you want to talk to us?"

"I had some questions and I'll probably talk, I don't

74

know," Mark Bradford replied. "I already know I'm going to the penitentiary, and I want to know, do I get some help down there?"

Detective Arnold asked what kind of help he meant. Bradford said he thought he needed some help for "things going on inside his head." Arnold told him that mental health therapy was available in the prison system.

That seemed to satisfy Mark Bradford, so he agreed to answer any of Detective Arnold's questions.

Starting with Bradford's background, Mel Arnold learned that Mark had experienced a stormy relationship with his adoptive parents. He had graduated high school and had served a stint in the United States Army. He had been trained as a chef, but when he moved to California from Colorado with his friend, Don Williamson, he had been unable to find employment as a cook, as Williamson had, so he took a few short-term jobs and wound up working in the convalescent home near the apartments.

Mark Bradford had a criminal record that included breaking and entering and several arrests for drunkenness. He admitted to having a problem with alcohol and to experimenting with drugs a few times, but not with anything "heavy."

Answering Detective Arnold's questions, Mark Bradford's account of the events leading to the death of Lynea Kokes agreed, for the most part, with the description given by Donald Williamson. Bradford had helped the victim move, he said, for about 45 minutes, then had left. He returned to her apartment later, he said, to "see what she could do about us working out a monthly rent, since she was taking over the next day." Mrs. Kokes had agreed to try to help.

"What did you do after that?"

"I grabbed her throat."

"No warning?"

"No, sir."

"What were you wearing?"

75

"Some faded blue jeans, bleach-washed, and a blue shirt."

That description matched the bloody garments that had been retrieved from Bradford's duffel bag.

Bradford described how he had choked the victim until she fell down, then how he had removed her clothing. He told Arnold, in specific detail, how he had raped the victim while she desperately gasped for air. "That's when I hit her with my fist. I just knocked her out." Then, he said, he left her lying on the floor gasping for breath.

Back in his room, Bradford stated, he took a shower to cleanse himself of the blood all over him.

The detective asked, "You said that after you got back to your room, you started thinking about her. What were you thinking?"

"If she was gonna live, you know, and ratting me off."

Bradford described how he decided to return to the victim, and finish her off so she couldn't tell on him. On his way, he grabbed Williamson's knife from the kitchen.

"When you got back in her apartment, where was she?"

"Still on the floor, still gasping for breath."

"What happened then?"

"I rolled her over and slit her throat. I put her on her stomach and grabbed the back of her head and tipped her head up and sliced her throat twice. Then I rolled her over on her back and stabbed her a bunch of times, I don't know how many."

"Now, something happened while you were stabbing her in the chest?"

"The knife broke, I believe."

Bradford couldn't remember whether he had tried to strangle the victim with the black cloth belt before or after he had stabbed her. The placement of the slash wounds on the throat indicated that he had applied the ligature first.

After stealing the victim's credit cards and identification, Bradford said, he left her apartment, being careful to lock it, and returned to his own room. "I talked to Don about leaving. I told him I wanted to go to Selma, California. I told him I could hitchhike. He offered to drive me if we got all of our stuff moved to another buddy's place. Then Don came up and told me that the police were all over the place. I told him I was ready to leave. We went to McDonald's to eat, then came back."

The incredible story chilled the experienced detective, who thought he had heard it all. Detective Arnold had developed that protective shell most experienced homicide cops develop to maintain sanity, but it still startled him to hear how someone who had just murdered and mutilated a victim in a bloody massacre could calmly go to a fast-food restaurant and eat afterward.

Arnold reflected on the ease with which Bradford had simply grabbed the woman, raped her, and killed her. Something had just snapped in Bradford's mind, something unexplainable, and he had succumbed to the urge to rape and kill. Detective Mel Arnold wondered if he would ever really understand the working of the sociopathic minds of such killers.

On May 15, 1990, a jury found Mark Alan Bradford guilty of first-degree murder with the special circumstances of rape and robbery. They recommended that he be sentenced to death.

Superior Court Judge Michael Farrell accepted the recommendation, and on July 6, 1990, sent Mark Bradford to join more than 300 other men waiting for a date in California's gas chamber.

In a confession that Bradford made prior to the full story he had related to Detective Mel Arnold, the killer had been asked, "What do you think ought to happen to you?"

Bradford had readily replied, "I should be killed. I mean, I believe in the death penalty. If you got a problem, you ought to seek help. If they can't help you, they ought to kill you. That's the way I look at it."

It remains to be seen whether Mark Alan Bradford will stick to that philosophy when he faces his own execution.

EDITOR'S NOTE:
Donald Williamson is not the real name of the person so named in the foregoing story. A fictitious name has been used because there is no reason for public interest in the identity of this person.

"HELLO DOLLY,
GOODBYE DAVID!"

by Bill G. Cox

The moon rode high and bright over Amarillo,
Texas, on the Monday night of August 15, 1988. It was
a perfect night for riding around and listening to music. The usual kinds of music filled the airways in this
city of 156,000, from country and western to heavy
metal to rock 'n' roll to golden oldies to easy listening.
On a moonlit night made for love and romantic music,
the tunes sent forth by a small radio station on the
city's northeast side were the choice of some Amarillo
listeners. Easy-listening instrumentals and vocals —
nice to kiss by, if you were so inclined.

As it turned out, though, songs such as "Your
Cheating Heart" and maybe even the real oldie,
"Frankie and Johnny," would have been more fitting
for the shocking events that started with a bang at that
easy-listening radio station.

Love and hate — such a thin line between them.
Sometimes emotions and circumstances combine to
blow love all to hell and shove it over to the hate side
of that narrow line.

What started in that easy-listening radio station
came to public attention with a crashing crescendo on
this Monday night when the city streets were bathed in
moonlight.

A young woman was parked in front of a residence waiting for a friend to come out when she heard a loud clanking and clattering noise. Glancing behind her, she saw a speeding pickup pulling a wrapped object behind. The cumbersome bundle seemed to be lashed to a conveyance with wheels that jogged and bounced along the street like a large beach ball on rough waters. As the pickup flashed by, the startled woman got the vivid impression that the bouncing bundle was a human body!

Even as she wondered if she were imagining things, the woman's friend appeared at her car, exclaiming, "Did you see what I just saw?"

As the pair drove away from the curb, they saw the same pickup coming back toward them on the street. They only caught a glimpse of a dark figure in the pickup cab, but they noticed that the bundle was now gone from the trailing rig that had carried it.

A block further down the street, the two witnesses saw the blob lying in the middle of the road. They steered gingerly around it and pulled up to a house where lights were on to notify the police department. They had seen enough to confirm in their minds that the wrapped and tied bundle contained a human body.

The police radio room received the call reporting a body in the street at 10:11 p.m.

A police unit driven by Patrolman Jim Burgess was dispatched to investigate the report. However, the patrol car was given the address from where the reporting call had come, and when Burgess arrived there, he saw nothing that looked like a body in the street.

At the same time, Patrolman Efrin Contreras, only a short distance away, was preparing to drive a prisoner to the city jail. The officer had arrested a woman on a charge of prostitution in an area frequented by hustlers. Strung along East Amarillo Boulevard are cheap motels, strip joints, bars and similar establishments. The area that surrounds the boulevard, which some cops refer to as "The Strip of Sin," really jumps

80

on Saturday nights. On Mondays, the activity is slower, but police still happen on a paid-love transaction in progress even on the quiet nights.

Contreras had grilled and released the potential john, a motorist who the high-heeled lady had solicited on the street. The nervous man, relieved not to be in the clutches of the law, drove away. But a minute or so later, Contreras was surprised to see the man back again.

"It looks like someone has been hit by a car—there's a body in the middle of the street down there," he yelled, pointing in the direction from which he had come.

With the lady of the night still in tow, the uniformed officer drove to the spot two blocks away. When he got out of the car and looked closer at the trussed bundle, Contreras picked up his radio mike and notified the radio clerk of the discovery.

Patrolman Burgess heard the radio traffic and sped to the nearby location given by his fellow officer. The patrolmen observed what appeared to be a portion of a human arm visible from what looked like white sheets tied with different sizes of rope.

A strong and sickening smell of decomposed flesh was immediately apparent as the patrolmen made a cursory examination. The brief look was enough for Burgess to return to his police car and place a call to the Special Crimes Unit.

The Special Crimes Unit is a crack homicide squad peopled with specially assigned investigators from the Amarillo Police Department and the sheriff's departments of Potter and Randall Counties. Amarillo lies in both counties. The Special Crimes Unit was created to probe murders in Amarillo and the two-county area. Its record of solved crimes and its investigative techniques have inspired other police forces in the Southwest to set up similar homicide units.

The Special Crimes roster has an assortment of personalities. Lieutenant Sandy Morris, the unit's assistant coordinator, directs the field investigations. A veteran homicide detective with more than 25 years' experience, he's a crusty individual who has seen the "old school" police procedures of hitting the sidewalks and tapping informants change with new laws and court decisions into the highly skilled forensic police techniques of today. The unit includes younger men and women who have come up through the ranks to their present jobs of investigators and ID and crime technicians.

It's a crew that gets a homicide probe off the ground with the efficiency of a scientific space launch. They felt lucky that the call to duty on this Monday night didn't come in the wee hours of the day, which happens to them all too often.

Accompanied by a detail of regular duty police officers at the crime scene, the Special Crimes Unit force included Lieutenant Jimmy Stevens, the crime scene coordinator who was administrator and overall unit supervisor at the time; Lieutenant Morris and Investigator David Thurman; and Investigator Greg Soltis, an ID and crime scene officer. Aided by one of the uniformed officers, Investigator Soltis took measurements and drew crime scene diagrams in addition to photographing the body and immediate vicinity.

Potter County Justice of the Peace Haven Dysart, acting as coroner, came to the scene to conduct a preliminary inquest.

As the lawmen examined the trussed heap in the street, they saw that the body appeared to be wrapped in curtains or drapes instead of a sheet as first believed. Underneath, they found that a brown plastic garbage sack covered the victim's head, and the feet were inside a black plastic bag. The stench hanging in the air was the result of the advanced decomposition of the body, which appeared to be male. Because of the body's condition the investigators were uncertain of the dead man's race or how he had been killed. The body had been trussed with two different-sized ropes,

82

the sleuths noted.

Questioning the man and woman who had phoned police after witnessing the hop-and-skip ride of the body behind the pickup, the detectives came up with little information.

The witnesses told officers they thought the pickup had been blue and white in color. They also thought that the driver had been wearing a cap similar to a baseball cap, but they had gotten only a glimpse of the driver.

Officers were assigned to go house to house in the residential area. The neighborhood canvass produced little more than what already had been learned.

Some witnesses who had been on their front porches and were drawn to the speeding pickup and its trailing load by the racket they made also mentioned the blue and white colors. Others who had seen the strange and noisy ensemble thought the pickup might have been another color.

Adding to the confusion, one or two witnesses thought the blue-and-white pickup was not the one that had carried the bizarre bundle, but one that had slowed so its driver could see what was left in the middle of the street after the load had been dislodged from another pickup. One witness contacted by the investigators thought he had seen two persons in the pickup pulling the bundle on wheels.

All of those who had viewed the unusual scene agreed that the pickup had been speeding along Northeast 10th Avenue, going at least 50 mph in a residential area limited to 30 mph. The mysterious driver had obviously been hellbent for somewhere when the towed body was suddenly dislodged by its bumpy, tumultuous ride over the pavement.

The investigators' search for clues along the trail of the fast-moving pickup revealed drag marks and debris at various points that confirmed the last ride of the unidentified body had been a rough one. The corpse had been separated from the pulling vehicle at the intersection of Northeast 10th Avenue and North Arthur Street. This was a short distance from the address to which Officer Burgess had been dispatched before the body's actual location was established.

As he looked over the crime scene and heard the stories of witnesses, Lieutenant Morris formulated a theory on which he speculated to his colleagues. The veteran homicide sleuth wondered why the body had been dragged behind the pickup after being wrapped and trussed so compactly. He felt that this indicated the killer was a person of small stature and limited strength — perhaps even a woman — who had been unable to lift the bound package into the back of the pickup.

Whatever had been the case, the investigators, who had worked about every kind of homicide in the books, agreed on one thing: This had to be the most bungled — and weirdest — job of body disposal they had ever come across.

Presumably, after becoming aware that the body in back was no longer aboard, the killer had not bothered to retrace the route to retrieve it for fear of being seen with the misplaced corpse.

Lieutenant Morris was of the opinion that the body might have been loaded somewhere in the immediate vicinity. Deciding to look for the start of the drag trail, which was visible sporadically along the street, the lieutenant got into his car, accompanied by Investigator Thurman, and drove slowly along the route, scanning the streets that intersected Northeast 10th.

Meanwhile, after the body had been released from the scene by the acting coroner, it was taken to a county building for thorough examination and photographing. Soltis was assigned as the ID man who would record on film the distasteful sorting out of the victim's remains as they were removed from the wrappings.

As the outside covering and plastic bags were peeled away, the investigators saw that the victim had been nude when encased in the crude shroud. The body was that of a well-built man with short reddish hair and mustache. On the right shoulder was a tattoo that could help in making the identification. The red, yellow, and black tattoo depicted a rearing unicorn.

A wound that appeared to be a bullet hole was evident in the victim's forehead, though it could have been the result of the body being dragged on the pavement, the officers thought. As the last covering was pulled away, a shell casing dropped to the floor.

The examination also revealed abrasions on the buttocks and the inside of the thighs, undoubtedly the result of friction during the body's extended drag over the rough pavement.

There was no clothing or anything else that might contribute to the dead man's identification. It looked as though he had been slain while naked or had been undressed after the killing to prevent identification, the investigators theorized.

Although the body's decomposition was far advanced—indicating that the corpse may have been kept someplace for a period of time before the killer decided to get rid of it—Investigator Soltis noted that it probably would be possible to obtain some fingerprints in spite of the badly deteriorated flesh.

Later, this was done successfully so that prints could be sent to the usual sources—namely, the fingerprint records of the FBI and the Texas Department of Public Safety—for linking the murder victim with a name.

It was hard to tell for sure, but it appeared the victim had been in his 20s or 30s.

It was hoped an autopsy scheduled within the next few hours would throw more light on how the unidentified man had been killed and how long he had been dead before the body ended up in the street.

In the vicinity where the bound body had been found, Lieutenant Morris and Investigator Thurman drove slowly along the trail left by the dragging body.

They came upon some tracks that turned onto the road from an alley.

Thurman got out of the car to check the newest find. For months after the murder probe, the investigator would be kidded by his fellow officers about literally being a bloodhound on the case. But the truth was that when Thurman stooped to look closely at the drag marks from the alley, he knew they were on the right trail. The fluids from the decaying body left an evilly repugnant smell. He grimaced as he bent over the tracks and the rank odor assailed his senses.

"That's where it came from," he said as he returned to Lieutenant Morris in the car. Looking at his investigator's face, Morris hoped he didn't become sick.

Continuing down the alley, the investigators saw that the nauseating trail left the alley and digressed into the driveway of a garage attached to a small apartment. The beams of the sleuths' flashlights fell upon what looked like plastic curtain hooks in the drive. More signs of the body having been dragged from that location were also evident.

As the two men got out of their car, the stench in the air was overpowering.

Almost gagging on his words, Morris said, "This has got to be it." He indicated the small structure adjacent to the garage. The officers saw that there was a carport or breezeway next to the garage, and on the other side of that was a larger building that faced the intersecting street.

Finding the door of the small apartment locked, Morris and Thurman turned their attention to the other building. Turning the corner, they saw that it was a radio station. There were lights on inside.

A man who identified himself as a disc jockey answered the door. After the detectives told him that they suspected the smaller building at the rear might have been where a body found several blocks away had come from, the radio station employee tried to find the key to the apartment. He said the apartment was

86

vacant and no one lived there. It was owned by the radio station and had been used only for storage in recent weeks.

Unable to find the key, he said he would phone the program director. Meanwhile, he gave the officers a verbal consent to enter the apartment.

"I don't know what became of the key to the place," he explained. The record that was playing was about to end. Turning away in a hurry, he said he'd be back with the detectives after calling the program director.

Lieutenant Morris got on his radio and notified the officers at the scene of the body discovery that he believed the murder site — or at least the place where the body might have been stored — had been found. Within minutes, the contingent of investigators gathered at the radio station.

Corporal Wayne Randolph, who had been summoned to process the apartment and determine whether it was the place where the red-haired man had been killed, removed a pane of glass from the front door to gain entry. Meanwhile, the program director advised he was on his way to the station.

As the apartment's door was opened, the terrible smell hit the investigators full force. A light was switched on, and they saw that they had indeed found the crime scene. Blood smears and other blood traces were found. It looked as if the killer had tried to clean up the signs of violent death.

The apartment was bare except for some items that had been stored by the radio station. Checking through the rooms, the investigators found a discharged bullet in one side of a stainless steel sink. Looking closely at the slug, the detectives noted it was a jacketed-type bullet with the nose hollowed out.

Examining a shower stall, the crime scene technicians found traces of blood in the bottom of the stall, even though the stall looked as if it had been scrubbed.

Close scrutiny of the shower stall also disclosed a dent or small round impression that could have been left by a bullet. The scar on the wall was to the left of the shower stall on the level of an individual's head if he were taking a shower, the officers observed. There was a smear of blood on a baseboard that probably was left when the body was dragged from the shower.

As the crime scene technicians diagrammed and photographed the apartment interior, Morris and other members of the investigative unit quizzed the program director and the station manager, who had also come to the scene.

The radio station officials confirmed that the apartment had been unoccupied for several weeks and was being used only for storage. Among items that had been stored there were white drapes from the radio station. The detectives surmised that these had been used to wrap the body after the victim had been shot to death.

According to the officials, the only key to the unused apartment had been kept in the radio station, but the key was missing. They had no idea who had taken it or where it might be.

It seemed logical that, since only radio station employees had access to the key, the missing key was probably taken by a station employee. If someone else had taken the key to enter the apartment, it had gone undetected by the staff on duty.

The station employees were baffled as to who might have entered the apartment to kill a man there. They were also at a loss to identify the victim or explain what he was doing in the apartment.

Pursuing their theory that the killer was probably a small woman or a frail person who had not been able to lift the trussed body into the pickup and had ended up dragging it behind on some kind of makeshift trailer, Morris and Thurman quizzed the station manager about the female employees.

The disc jockey recalled that he had arrived shortly before 11:00 p.m. to relieve his counterpart in the broadcasting studio. The DJ on duty then had been a woman. He also told the detectives that he noticed her pickup, a light blue Ford, was parked in its usual spot outside. When he showed up, the disc jockey had presumably left in her pickup. He said she had acted normally.

Answering questions about the woman, the radio station personnel said they knew that she was having domestic problems and was in fact involved in a divorce proceeding with her husband. But they added that her spouse didn't match the description of the murder victim as given by the investigators. The description didn't fit any man they knew, the witnesses told the detectives.

The lawmen realized that the lady disc jockey's pickup might be similar in appearance to the blue-and-white pickup involved in the wild and macabre drive down Northeast 10th with the bouncing body behind. Quizzing the station employees further, the detectives learned that it would not have been impossible for the woman DJ to have left the broadcast booth temporarily.

The radio officials explained that since the station had an "easy-listening" format, music frequently was played automatically in time blocks up to 15 minutes without interruption.

Later, a detective ran a time test by driving the route of the pickup, from the station to the spot where the body came loose in the street and then back to the station. It was found that the round trip could have been made in under four minutes.

Was it possible that the woman DJ had attempted to dispose of the body during her allotted time on the air to try and establish a perfect alibi, the detectives wondered? Stranger things had happened, and such a deception in fact was a timeworn fictional plot.

Obtaining the DJ's home address, Lieutenant Morris and Investigator Thurman drove to the location across town to talk with the employee. But as they pulled up in their car, they saw that the residence was dark. The pickup described by the woman's fellow employees was nowhere in sight, nor was there any answer to the detectives' knocking.

As Morris and Thurman pondered their next move, discussing whether to issue a pickup bulletin for the woman and her truck and have a surveillance team on her house, the radio in their unit came to life. It was a brisk message from an investigator still at the radio station. He requested that the detectives return to the station immediately because of a new development.

Since the body in the street had been reported, nearly eight hours had elapsed, and the murder investigation dragged into the wee hours of the morning. It was shortly after 5:00 a.m. when Morris and Thurman reached the radio station.

As Morris stepped from the car, he was met by Sergeant Janice Whisenhunt of the Special Crimes team. The information she passed along to her supervisor was startling and bizarre, to say the least.

At about 4:55 a.m., the radio station manager had emerged suddenly from the station, excitedly telling Whisenhunt, "I've solved your case!"

It sounded like a piece of dialogue from an old radio murder mystery of the pretelevision days.

According to the manager, he had phoned another station official to tell him about the murder and the weird developments involving the radio station, now the focal point of the homicide investigation.

The call was answered by a woman the manager recognized as the girlfriend of the official. He said the woman was a secretary employed by the station.

When the station executive told the secretary the shocking news and mentioned that the police were looking for one of the female disc jockeys to see what she knew about the murder — if anything — the secretary had responded out of the blue:

"She didn't do it. I did!"

Flashes of the old *Perry Mason* TV show must have played across the radioman's mind as he heard the words. It was like one of those dramatic radio or TV courtroom scenes when the truth blares forth at the peak of plot tensions.

The station manager told Sergeant Whisenhunt that the secretary had said she would come to the station to surrender and then quietly hung up.

It was about 5:30 a.m. when a car pulled up at the station. It was driven by a man who turned out to be the station official with whom the secretary was living. A striking but distraught-looking young blonde wearing blue jeans and a long-tailed shirt stepped from the passenger side of the vehicle.

She introduced herself to the waiting officers as Deborah Sue Garre. Thurman escorted the 27-year-old woman to the police car in which he and Morris were riding and advised her fully of all legal rights.

The blonde woman suddenly volunteered that the gun she used was at the house where she and her radio station boyfriend were living. She said she would lead the officers to the weapon.

Driving to the designated address, Morris and Thurman followed Deborah Garre inside to a bedroom. The blonde pointed to a handgun still holstered and lying on the floor beside the bed. Before touching anything, Lieutenant Morris summoned an ID technician to photograph the house interior and the gun.

The sleuths recognized the weapon as a semiautomatic .380-caliber Walther pistol. Later, the suspect also identified a red pickup parked at the house as the vehicle she used when trying to dispose of the body. She told the detectives that she had borrowed the pickup from an unsuspecting relative. Checking the vehicle's interior, crime scene technicians and the detectives found pieces of rope behind the seat that matched those with which the draped body had been tied.

The suspect readily identified the dead man as 36-year-old David Lee Cain, formerly of Florida. Cain was the third side of a love triangle that Garre had

91

opted to remove, as she subsequently related in a statement given that morning to Lieutenant Morris at the Special Crimes Unit offices. In the close quarters of the small office where Deborah Garre was interrogated, the stench was like an odious poison gas. The blue jeans the woman was wearing were the same ones she had on when she wrapped the body and dragged it to the pickup. The jeans were saturated with the body fluids from the decomposing corpse, and the stench was terrible.

The suspect didn't seem to notice or care as she related the details of the romantic affair that ended in the calculated and cold-blooded murder of one of her lovers, according to the story she told Lieutenant Morris.

Garre related that after her husband had died in 1985, she became romantically involved with the radio station employee, an older man with whom she lived for several months.

But after some time, she decided to break off the relationship and move to Florida. It was in Tampa in 1987 that she met David Cain, a 36-year-old guitar player and member of a band. She met him in the singles' bar where the band played.

In the statement given to investigators, Deborah Garre related that she and Cain became lovers. However, she still kept in touch with the radio station employee back in Amarillo with phone calls and letters. She explained that she was indecisive as to which of the two boyfriends she really loved. Whenever she talked to Cain about ending their affair, he threatened to kill himself, Garre said.

"After a certain period of time, I began to believe that he meant it," the blonde said. "I didn't want to be responsible for something like that." The irony of the suspect's remark wasn't missed by the detectives.

Meanwhile, the Amarillo radio official came to Tampa, and Deborah decided to go back with him and resume their relationship. But the old indecision haunted her again. She recalled that she kept in touch with Cain in Florida, calling him and exchanging love letters.

Finally, Garre told Cain it was over between them. She loved the man in Amarillo, she said, and was going to remain with him. According to the story she told the officers, Cain made some threats and told Deborah that he was coming to Amarillo.

Cain kept his word, and when he arrived, the woman was once again involved in two romances and plagued with a bad case of not knowing which man she preferred. While she tried to make up her mind, she obtained the key to the small apartment behind the radio station and told Cain that he could stay there at night.

Cain kept away from the place during the day when radio station employees were on duty in force. But at night, when most of the staff was gone and only a single disc jockey manned a broadcast studio, he would slip back into the apartment.

Deborah, who was working as a secretary at the station, came back for nighttime rendezvous with Cain. They were careful to keep the lights off, since they weren't needed anyway.

The catch-as-catch-can romance in the apartment, when night settled over the radio station, continued for two weeks. But David Cain wasn't happy that he had to share his intimacies with the blonde. Deborah told the investigators that David threatened to tell her older boyfriend of the situation.

It was a fateful decision for the guitar player. It would be his last.

Deborah Garre said she picked up Cain on Saturday evening, August 14th, and drove him to the apartment. Inside they talked at length — Deborah saying it was all over, David threatening to blow the whistle on the love triangle to the older lover.

At one point, David told Deborah he was going to take a shower. (Detectives said later it wasn't clear

whether the couple had made love or intended to.)
While David headed for the shower, Deborah said, she
stepped outside to her car to get a pistol, the Walther
semiautomatic that she had borrowed.

She related that she came back inside and stealthily
approached the shower stall, where she could hear the
water running. Like a scene from Alfred Hitchcock's
movie *Psycho,* Garre approached the shower. David
was naked under the shower stream, facing toward the
shower head.

According to Deborah's statement, she raised the
pistol and shot him in the back of the head.

As it would be reconstructed later from results of
the autopsy and the evidence found in the shower
stall, the slug had exited from Cain's forehead between
his eyes and struck the shower wall. It left a nick in the
wall and fell to the shower floor, as did Cain.

Faced with the problem of not knowing what to do
with the body, the woman pulled the nude man from
the shower. She wrapped the body in the shower curtain and the white drapes she found in the apartment,
placing a brown plastic bag over the victim's head and
another similar bag around the feet. She then lashed
the clumsy bundle of death together with pieces of
rope and sashes from the drapes.

The body was heavy—too heavy for Garre to lift,
she said. For a few minutes, panic swept over her.
Deborah decided to leave the body in the apartment,
since no one had any reason to enter it.

She tried to tidy up the death scene, running water
in the shower, wiping the floor to remove blood and
tissue. Blood was smeared on a baseboard as the body
was dragged to another spot. As the investigators later
learned, the gun-wielding blonde had picked up the
slug from the shower stall and tossed it into the stainless steel sink, apparently thinking it went down the
drain.

She dropped the discharged shell in with the body.
She left the apartment unnoticed. No one had heard

94

the shot. There had been no witnesses to the arrival of the couple at the apartment or to the suspect's departure.

For the rest of the weekend, Deborah tried to act her normal self, but fear followed her like a black shadow. She was afraid that at any moment, the dead man in the apartment might be found, if someone from the station just happened to need something that was stored in the residence behind the station.

Deborah hoped no one would notice that the apartment key was missing and launch a search for it. She feared someone would ask questions that could lead somehow to discovery of the corpse in storage.

In the August weather, the daytime temperatures were blazing hot. Inside the apartment, the wrapped body was reacting naturally to the heat and time—it was decomposing fast.

Radio station employees, when they came to and from the station, sniffed the air and commented on the nasty stench that was present. Luckily for Deborah, they blamed it on the wind coming from the direction of the cattle feedlot. When the wind was right—or wrong, if you wish—the feedlot "B.O." descended on the area like a thick cloud of fog.

By Monday, the feedlot complaints were getting louder and more frequent. Deborah knew she had to do something before someone following the trail of stench too closely made a gruesome discovery.

When Monday night came, Deborah made preparations to get rid of the victim. She wasn't sure where she would take it, but she knew she had to get Cain's body out of that apartment.

She went to a television station and borrowed a dolly, saying she needed it to move some belongings. She put it in the back of her red pickup and headed for the death apartment. A few minutes later, Deborah was startled to learn that she had lost the dolly out of the truck somewhere along the way.

Deborah did an amazing thing at this point—a

piece of action that made the detectives wonder about the icy cool calmness of this young blonde who had shot down one of her lovers. She went to the Amarillo Police Department, which is only a few blocks away from the radio station, and asked to talk to someone in the "lost and found" department. When directed to the officer handling such requests, Deborah Garre reported that she had lost a dolly from her pickup. The officer took down the information and she left.

Then, strangely enough, as she was driving back to the radio station, Deborah spotted her lost dolly in the street. She retrieved it and drove on to the radio station.

Back in the apartment, she struggled and managed to drag and push the now thoroughly odious wrapped body onto the dolly.

Even under the night's darkness, Deborah was terrified that any second she might be seen with her dolly-load of horror. She wheeled the heavy load to the rear of her pickup, which she had pulled up close to the apartment door. In the next few minutes, she struggled and strained to lift the body from the dolly into the pickup bed.

If Deborah Garre knew she was getting drenched with body fluids on her clothing, she seemingly ignored it in her state of near panic. Finally, she did what she thought was the next best thing. She found a piece of garden hose, tied it to the back gate supports of the pickup, then looped the hose around the upper part of the dolly and made it as secure as she could. She lashed the wrapped body to the dolly with rope and curtain sashes.

The late David Cain was ready for love's last ride — a wild and bizarre trip, as it turned out.

Getting into the pickup, Deborah burned rubber as she sped away from the station, first down an alley, then onto Northeast 10th Avenue. She roared down the residential street at a speed later estimated at more than 50 mph, with the dolly bouncing and clanking behind. This was the unbelievable scene witnessed by several residents attracted by the noise and the weird, bouncing "trailer" behind.

Unaware until several minutes later that she had lost the body from the dolly at some point in the journey, Deborah reacted with sheer panic when she finally did notice it. But she decided that wherever it was, it could stay for someone to find. At least it would be a few blocks from the radio station.

Deborah later returned the borrowed dolly and drove home to be with her older boyfriend.

Deborah told the detectives that she had Cain's wallet and the apartment key at her house. She later turned them over to investigators. She also told of throwing Cain's clothing, along with a packet of love letters she had penned to him, in a dumpster near the radio station, where the investigators recovered them.

Why had she killed him? the officers wanted to know.

"He wouldn't listen to reason," the blonde was quoted as telling the investigators on the night of her statement detailing the murder plot that went awry like some madcap comedy.

At 8:15 a.m. on Tuesday, August 16th, Deborah Garre, still clad in the smelly blue jeans and shirt, was booked into the city jail on a charge of murder. Long before that, Lieutenant Morris had tried to air out his office.

Lieutenant Jimmy Stevens, the Special Crimes Unit coordinator, held a press conference announcing the finding of the corpse in the street and the surrender of the suspect, who had made a statement admitting the killing. The highly unusual homicide case got another heavy ride on local TV, radio, the newspapers, and the wire services.

Stevens disclosed that investigators had quizzed the suspect's surviving boyfriend. They were convinced that he had no knowledge of the killing or even that Cain had arrived in Amarillo two weeks earlier and that Deborah Sue had been seeing him in the apartment behind the radio station.

The accused slayer was arraigned before Judge Don Emerson of 320th State District Court at midmorning. She was ordered held in lieu of $10,000 bond.

That morning, a police lieutenant, after hearing about the grisly murder, recalled a report received on Saturday night from a woman reporting she had lost a two-wheel dolly from her pickup truck. The revelation that the murder suspect had brazenly notified police of the lost dolly left the Special Crimes Unit investigators shaking their heads, amazed at the suspect's unmitigated gall.

On September 2, 1988, a Potter County grand jury returned an indictment charging Deborah Sue Garre with murder in the shooting death of David Cain, originally of Lutz, Florida.

A jury was selected to hear the case on November 6, 1989, in 320th State District Court. The sensational trial in the county's courts building drew a steady crowd of spectators as the bizarre testimony unfolded over the next week.

After Special Crimes Unit investigators detailed the finding of the body and the ensuing investigation that culminated with the volunteered admission to the killing by Deborah Sue Garre on the telephone, a forensic pathologist testified about the autopsy results.

The pathologist told the jury that David Cain did not die immediately from the gunshot wound in the head. The shooting victim probably was unconscious, however, and breathed heavily and painfully before he died, said the medical witness. If Cain had received medical attention shortly after being wounded, he would have survived because the shot fired at close range resulted in little brain damage, added the doctor.

With the state's case completed, the defense called its star witness to the stand—the defendant herself, Deborah Garre presented an entirely different appearance to the jury than she did to detectives on that fateful night when the bedraggled blonde, still wearing clothing stained with the body fluids of her victim, turned herself in to the investigators.

Now, Garre's neatly coiffured hair appeared darker; she was smartly dressed and carried a purse slung from her shoulder. To and from the courtroom, she wore dark glasses as the TV camera lights flooded the corridor and newspaper photographers' cameras flashed. She managed a smile for photographers.

In her two days on the witness stand, Garre told a far different story about what happened on the night she fatally shot her lover in the shower stall.

First, she related the details of the mixed-up love relationship with two boyfriends and her pursuit of simultaneous romances. Two days before the shooting, Deborah testified, she went to the apartment where she had stashed Cain and told him news he had heard before—that everything was over between them. She said tearfully that Cain's response was to throw her on the floor and rape her.

"The control had finally been taken away from me," she said.

Garre added that she didn't report the rape to police or tell anyone because she didn't want other persons to get hurt. Cain was threatening not only to kill her other boyfriend—who was unaware of the ongoing romance of Deborah and her "former" lover—but also a relative, the witness testified.

"I wasn't going to take the risk of anyone else getting hurt," Garre explained.

On Saturday night, August 13, 1988, Deborah received a call from Cain saying he had something important to show her. Deborah said she replied she didn't want anything further to do with him, but Cain insisted. She relented because she thought he was going to tell her that he was leaving, she told the jury.

But she was being too optimistic, Deborah said. Instead of the news she was so anxious to hear, Cain told her that they were going to get an apartment together and that he would kill her older boyfriend if there was any trouble.

Then, she testified, he raped her again, after which he boasted, "Now I've put a baby in you. Now you can't leave me!"

Cain instructed Deborah to wait in the living room while he took a shower, she testified. But she went to her vehicle and got the pistol.

She explained, "I thought if I went back in with that to back me up, that he would have to take me seriously." But she related that Cain grabbed her when she got close to the shower and then she blacked out. She said she did not know how she shot Cain because she didn't remember pulling the trigger.

Deborah said that when she saw Cain lying bleeding on the floor, she first thought that he had fallen. "My mind couldn't conceive what happened," she said.

The attractive witness testified that thoughts of suicide entered her mind, but they were replaced with the urgent need to keep the radio station and her other boyfriend out of it. Deborah said she didn't know what to do, but decided after two days that she had to remove the body from the apartment. She detailed how she wrapped the body and tied it to the dolly, then tied the dolly to her pickup after her efforts to lift the body were futile. She said she never went back to look for the body after discovering it was gone.

Deborah Garre testified that she wanted to spend one more night with her surviving boyfriend before killing herself. But the phone call from the station manager, saying police had traced the dead man to the radio station and apparently suspected another woman employee, stopped her suicide plans. Instead, she turned herself in.

Deborah told the jury that she had an abortion after learning she was pregnant from the sexual assaults by Cain. She said she did so against the advice of her attorney, who mentioned that the jury might give her a lighter sentence if she kept the baby.

"I didn't want that kind of child—it was from violence," she said.

Next, the defense called a psychologist to try to explain the defendant's conduct. "She tried to handle it in her own way, and she totally screwed it up," he said.

When pressures she couldn't deal with built up, sudden passions took over. Since Deborah didn't see herself as a person who could kill, she blacked out the shooting. Furthermore, said the medical expert, he believed her story.

He added that Garre had a history of not facing up to problems, ignoring them with the hope they would disappear, trying to live up to a "good little girl" image instilled during childhood. When pressure became too intense, she became irrational. And that's what happened after she shot David Cain, said the witness.

Not reporting the two rapes by Cain was consistent with her "good little girl" syndrome, he added. She didn't mention the sexual assaults to police when she confessed to the slaying because she didn't make the mental connection between the rapes and the shooting until later, the psychologist said.

The defense also called to the stand a woman who testified that, while she was married to Cain, he had threatened to kill himself when she told him she was leaving. One of those times, he pointed a gun at a police officer after barricading himself in a house. Once he tried to kill her and bragged about it later to a friend, the witness related.

During final arguments to the jury, the defense said that Deborah's actions had proved she was guilty only of voluntary manslaughter and not murder. She didn't show good judgment and made hundreds of mistakes, said the attorney. "She finally shot him because the pressure got too great at some point."

The prosecuting attorney said he thought the purported rapes and the defendant's memory lapse were nothing more than stories made up to sway the jury.

"She killed him because she didn't know how to resolve the conflict," he told the jury. Referring to Deborah's having lived with Cain for nearly three weeks in a romantic relationship after his return to Amarillo, the state's attorney asked, "Does that look like someone who's going through an emotional trauma?"

After their deliberations, the jury returned a verdict finding Deborah Sue Garre guilty of voluntary manslaughter. They set her punishment at 20 years in prison, the maximum for that offense.

"BIZARRE CARVINGS ON THE VICTIM'S FACE"

by Robert Carlsen

SEATTLE, WA.
FEBRUARY 25, 1988

Perhaps the best way to describe 63-year-old Norman Clement Gould of Seattle, Washington, was old and tough. One of the younger kids in the neighborhood, awed by his prowess, once called him "nuclear" because of his remarkable physical abilities. Gould knew how to handle himself, and could manhandle some men many years younger. But despite his strength, in July of 1987, he was no match for a ruthless pair of thugs out to get his savings and jade jewelry.

It was 11:40 a.m. on July 24, 1987 when a young man called on Gould. He found Gould's door standing open, and thought that was unusual because Norman was a cautious fellow. He had to be, considering the neighborhood he lived in, and also considering the rumors that he possessed some valuable items. You would never know this, judging by the outside of his modest home.

As a young man entered, calling out Norman's name as he went in, he saw that the rooms in the house were in disarray. When he got to a back bedroom, he found out why. The sight made his blood run cold and the hair on his head bristle.

Norman Gould was on his bed. Gould's legs hung over the side, and he was sprawled out on the bed. A blanket covered his torso, but his head was showing. The man saw that Gould's head was covered with blood and there was a gaping wound on Gould's throat.

The young man staggered backwards out of the room, searched for the telephone and found it in the living room. He picked up the receiver, and without listening for a dial tone, dialed 911. Nothing happened. It took a moment for him to realize the phone was dead. Then he fled to a neighbor's house to call for help.

Uniformed officers were on the scene within minutes, and thus began a case that would take detectives more than two months to solve; a case that would take them across the state requiring the efforts of lawmen in other jurisdictions.

The first person detectives questioned was the man who discovered the body. He explained how he'd been working with Gould, a maintenance worker, on a variety of jobs and came by the house to pick Gould up. He noticed Gould's van was gone, so he drove around the area in search of Gould prior to returning to the home, discovering the door open and subsequently finding Gould's body.

"You said the van is missing?" confirmed Detective Jerry Trettevik, the chief investigator assigned to the case.

"That's right. It was a '67 Volkswagen. Pale blue."

"You know the license number?"

"Sure."

The fellow paused while Trettevik anxiously awaited the number. Finally, the detective prodded, "You care to tell it to me?"

"Let's see. I think it had an O, and a Z, and the number seven in it."

"I'll get it through records. Thanks anyway." The detective next asked the man to tell everything he touched while in the house.

"I've been in there lots of times before, so my prints will probably be all over the place," the man said. "But today, the only thing I touched was the door going into his bedroom and the telephone. Other than that, nothing."

The man's clothes had no bloodstains on them, the detective noticed, and judging from the condition of the victim and the amount of blood at the crime scene, the killer surely would have gotten bloody. Of course it was always possible that the guy making the discovery went home after committing the murder and changed, but Detective Trettevik believed the young man's story, although the man couldn't be entirely eliminated as a suspect.

The county's medical examiner estimated the time of Gould's death was between 11 p.m. the prior evening and 8 a.m. that morning.

"It looks like the guy was bludgeoned as well as stabbed," the medical examiner said. "The throat wound certainly would be fatal. The beating could have been fatal without medical treatment, but might have been survivable. I'll know more once we conduct the autopsy."

The body was hauled off, and detectives began their laborious crime scene search. Because of the condition of the home, the task would be long and tiring. Other officers started moving through the neighborhood, contacting the neighbors.

What the officers discovered, much to their surprise, was that a number of the people in the neighborhood were aware of the fact that Norman Gould had either been burglarized or assaulted by a young man named Frank Larson. What became even more interesting was the fact that Larson was a relative of the man who had reported the discovery of Gould's body. Furthermore, Frank Larson was a former boyfriend of a woman who was shacking up with a new boyfriend who was living just a few houses down the street from the homicide scene.

Detectives questioned Larson's former girlfriend about the alleged burglary/assault committed by Frank Larson while he and the woman were still romantically involved.

"You got it all wrong," the woman told detectives. "It was Gould who came after Franky, accusin' him of robbin' him."

"By robbing, do you mean burglarizing?" a detective asked.

"Of course. What's the difference?"

There was a difference, but the detective figured it wasn't worth being confrontational with her, so he let the woman go on. Her information was more important than her terminology.

"And it was Gould who beat up on Franky," she told detectives, "for burglarizing the place."

"So a burglary did occur? Franky did rip Gould off."

"Well, maybe, but not for anything important. And that was a long time ago, and it don't mean nothin' much now. And besides, I don't think Franky ever threatened to kill the old man. I think the fossil was just makin' that up. Maybe he wanted my sympathy or something."

"Franky threatened to kill Gould?" Detective Trettevik asked.

"I never said that. I said the old man said that. After he pounded on Franky for robbin' him, Gould told me, 'Then the little punk threatened to kill me.' That's what Gould said. I never heard nothin'."

Sleuths contacted Frank Larson who denied, as they expected, committing the homicide. Larson was of small stature, and the probers could understand how Gould, if he really was as tough as his reputation, could have taken him on even though he was 40 years Larson's senior.

While that leg of the investigation was taking place, the crime scene was being processed, and detectives learned some interesting things there.

The telephone cord had been cut, and the cutting instrument was a wire snipper kept in the toolbox normally stored in a cabinet.

Burglars and robbers who invade homes often cut telephone wires as part of their routine. This prevents the victim from calling for help. But the culprit normally does it using a snipper which he has brought for that purpose.

But in this instance, the killer used a snipper kept secluded in a toolbox in a cabinet. How did the killer know where to find the snipper, and why was he allowed to do so? Surely Gould would have heard him getting into the cabinet and toolbox; unless Gould already was dead. But then there would have been no reason to cut the phone cord.

It was almost as if the killer knew where the wire snipper was kept, and also had ample time to get it. This suggested but one thing. Perhaps the killer knew Gould, and asked Gould if he could use the wire cutter, and Gould said sure. But Gould certainly would have been alarmed once the phone was not working, probers reasoned. How did the killer get the better of the old man?

Detectives got their answer when they found a bloody softball bat leaning against a wall in a corner of the home. That was the instrument used to bludgeon Gould into submission. And the killer would have needed that instrument, detectives realized, when they found evidence supporting Gould's reputation of being a tough, athletic old man. In Gould's household possessions, sleuths found a two-year-old snapshot of him doing a handstand on a kitchen chair, an impressive stunt for a young man, let alone somebody Gould's age.

A large, muscular man would have been able to handle Gould. But somebody like Frank Larson would have needed a baseball bat, the detectives knew. So Larson was put under a microscope. But despite the effort they put into investigating the suspect, detectives couldn't find any evidence to prove he was at the murder scene during the hours it was believed the crime occurred.

And another thing happened that muddied the waters in the case. Through records, Detective Trettevik learned that the victim's stolen van's license plate number was OZT 167.

Seattle Police Department officers patrolling south-central Seattle spotted the van and tried to pull it over. A short pursuit ensued. When the van stopped, three figures piled out different doors and each ran in a different direction. None were caught. The van was towed into the impound garage and dusted for prints. Nothing of any value toward the probe was found.

Detectives had lifted a welter of prints from Gould's house, and had a total of 67 print cards, of which 27 were of good quality prints. It would take some time to eliminate those of the victim and others who could not be considered suspects. To their dismay, none of the prints lifted from the home belonged to Frank Larson. But some did belong to his relative, the man who had reported discovering the dead body. Detectives wondered if the murder might have been a two-man operation, and Franky, being the most experienced hood, was more careful and didn't leave any prints.

Taking an inventory of the items in the house was a lengthy process, but with the help of others, detectives determined that stolen from the home had been a jade elephant, a small, circular jade piece, some jewelry, possibly an unknown amount of cash, and some suits. None of those items had been in the possession of suspect Frank Larson or the man who reported finding the corpse, and detectives checked into that closely. So it seemed that Larson, their most likely suspect, was clean.

It had been clear to the detectives that the condition of the home indicated the thieves were searching for something of particular value. Many valuable tools and other items had been overlooked by the killer or killers. Perhaps it had just been the jewelry and jade pieces they wanted. But then why would Gould's suits be missing? It didn't make much sense. On one hand, things of value were stolen, and on the other, materials that could be obtained at a Goodwill store were also taken. Again it seemed like an experienced eye had been at work, and somebody just out of the chute for the first time was also on the prowl, thus suggesting two people were involved.

The results of the autopsy also supported the theory that the thieves wanted something in particular. "There was no quick death here," the medical examiner told detectives. "Gould died a slow and agonizing death. The beating would have been hard enough to take. He was hit all over his body, on his shins, upper legs, torso, head. The head taps were just enough to hurt, but not enough to put him out. The killer wanted him alive for the next phase of torture — the knifings. There were many knife wounds on his body. But they were all about one-eighth-inch deep, enough to cause intense pain, but none fatal.

"The killer carved the letter S on one cheek and the letter X on the other; again, intense pain but hardly lethal. Out of all this, there was one lethal wound — the slashed throat."

It was a gruesome description, one that even made the detectives nervous to think that somebody so ruthless was out wandering the streets. Somebody capable of doing such a thing once surely was capable of repeating the act.

Sleuths continued their investigation and didn't give up on their prime suspect Frank Larson. Detectives still could learn nothing to indicate Larson was the killer. And if Larson did do it, he certainly wasn't letting the police pressure bother him. He was cool as a cucumber and made no effort to alter his routine behavior, a good portion of which was comprised of being a little thief.

Larson was nailed on a burglary rap and put in jail but that still did nothing to further the cause of the homicide case. But at least detectives knew where to find him, at least for a while until the revolving door of justice would spring him.

Detectives were impressed by the loyalty Larson's former girlfriend showed for him. They thought just to spite him, she might nail him to the cross for the murder, but no such thing occurred.

"Just our luck," one of the detectives muttered one day while reviewing the case. "We get as our prime suspect a guy that was good to his woman and never did her wrong, so there's no hard feelings to exploit."

Detectives made no progress in the case until August 28th, when Seattle homicide Sergeant Donald Cameron received a telephone call from Spokane, Washington. Washington State Patrol Detective Powell Shoemaker was on the line to relate an interesting story.

"I got a call from a woman who says she has information about a homicide in your jurisdiction," Shoemaker told Sergeant Cameron. "I'm not sure how reliable it is, but I'll give it to you and you can determine if it means anything."

"Sure," Sergeant Cameron said. Both he and Shoemaker knew that many times so-called hot tips turn out to be washouts. But the sergeant felt that if Shoemaker's instincts had prompted him to call the Seattle police, there might be something to this one.

"She said that two black males, one by the name of Wadelin Drummer, and the second named Malcolm Hardwicke, had beaten a man to death with a baseball bat and then used a buck knife to slash his throat. This occurred somewhere in Seattle's south end. This mean anything to you?"

It was one of those instances when Sergeant

110

Cameron was grateful he'd taken good care of his teeth throughout his life, because if he'd had false ones, he surely would have swallowed them.

"She also told me that this all came about when a prostitute saw the victim with some money, and so she told the two guys about it, and they went there and killed him. She also told me that Hardwicke and the hooker had taken the guy's van, and after the murder had nearly been captured while riding in it."

Sergeant Cameron knew Detective Shoemaker's snitch could bust the case wide open, because Shoemaker was revealing information that hadn't been made public. It was information only the killer(s) and lawmen close to the case could have known.

"She also indicated to me that Drummer had thrown one of his bloody sweatshirts into Lake Washington over there," Detective Shoemaker continued, while Sergeant Cameron remained silent and scribbled notes. "One of Drummer's friends, a guy named Carlos Rashan, is supposed to know all the details. He lives in the victim's neighborhood, I was told. Any of this sound familiar?"

"Familiar? Hell, you just wrote out our affidavit for probable cause," Cameron replied. "You sure your source isn't the killer?"

"I don't think her blood runs that cold. But I can't speak for the guy she's bedding down. I think that may be your man, if this information is legitimate, as you say it is."

"I'll need this woman's name," Sergeant Cameron said.

"Well, that's the problem. I don't know why she picked me to give the information to, but she insisted on remaining anonymous. She was pretty darn scared, and if she calls back, I'll tell her to call you guys. I think she'll agree to talk. I don't think the idea of sleeping with a murderer suits her."

"I hope so," Cameron said. "We're nowhere on this case until now."

111

As soon as he finished that telephone conversation, Sergeant Cameron contacted Seattle P.D. fingerprint expert Marsha Jackson, who has played a critical role in many homicide investigations.

When she got the word, she pulled out the print cards from the homicide case. Having 27 of the cards with valuable prints and Drummer's and Hardwicke's prints on file, she began comparing. She determined that one of Drummer's fingerprints was found on a doorknob between a bathroom and bedroom at the murder scene. She matched Hardwicke's print to a screwdriver that had been found on a kitchen chair.

Armed with the new information, Detective Trettevik renewed his efforts, this time with new suspects upon whom he could focus his attention.

He learned on the day before Gould's murder, Gould was having trouble with his Volkswagen van. Drummer and Hardwicke got chummy with Gould and even helped him with mechanical repairs to the van. They lived in the same area and knew each other.

This also explained how the suspects used Gould's wire snipper to cut the telephone line. They knew the snipper was in the toolbox, and the box was kept in the cabinet in the house.

On September 3rd, Detective Trettevik located Carlos Rashan, who had convictions for theft and forgery in King County. Rashan indicated that Wadelin Drummer had admitted to him that the "old man was dead."

"That's how he put it. 'The old man is dead,' and he told my woman how he had stabbed him. He told my woman this about four or five days after the murder."

Detective Trettevik interviewed Rashan's live-in girlfriend. She said, "Wadelin told me, 'He's dead, you know. What else can I tell you? He's dead.' Then it was a couple of days later that Wadelin's girlfriend from Spokane came over and took him back across the state with her. I don't think she knew he killed the guy. She comes over here every now and then, and this time Wadelin went back with her when she asked him to come back."

It was through Carlos Rashan and his girlfriend that Detective Trettevik was able to find the anonymous caller who'd originally contacted Detective Shoemaker in Spokane. It was somebody the detective had come in contact with years earlier but had long forgotten. But she hadn't forgotten Detective Shoemaker, for he'd been kind to her, and that's why she chose him as her confidant.

The anonymous phone call was traced to her and on September 17, 1987, she provided Trettevik with a statement implicating Wadelin Drummer in the homicide of Norman Gould.

She told Detective Trettevik: "When I got Wadelin over to Spokane, I could tell something was bugging him, but he didn't want to talk about it. But finally he told me that he and Malcolm Hardwicke had tried to rob this guy and that he didn't want to give up the money and they killed him. Wadelin's the one who stabbed him with the knife."

The woman said she didn't come to police directly with the information because she was terrified of Drummer, especially after he told her about the brutal murder. Then he started dropping hints that she should keep her mouth shut, otherwise he might shut it for her. Drummer told her how he had once taken a woman to the top of a remote mountain, and had buried her alive, vertically in the ground with only her head sticking out of the ground, and left her there for the night creatures to do their work.

That horrifying tale got her to thinking about what might happen to her if Drummer ever grew weary of their relationship, which had been going on for eight years. She didn't want to die as the other woman had. So she decided to snitch anonymously to Detective Shoemaker.

"Somehow, I knew you'd figure out who called, though," she said to Detective Trettevik. "You guys are smart that way."

The woman told police that Wadelin Drummer was in hiding in the basement of her house on the South Hill in Spokane. The city's police SWAT team was assigned the task of retrieving Drummer for Seattle authorities. The capture went off without any shots being fired. Drummer was tough when he beat on a 63-year-old man with a baseball bat and slashed his throat with a knife. When Drummer was in command, mercy was not something to be considered. But when the shoe was on the other foot, merciful treatment was something he expected, and got.

As Drummer was led away, he glanced at his former lover while passing her. He didn't have to say anything. The look he gave her spoke louder than any words. The look said, "See you on the mountain."

It was shortly thereafter that the woman recanted her original statement. But at a December 14, 1987 court hearing, she testified that her original statement was true, but she had recanted it because of fear of Drummer.

On the day Wadelin Drummer was captured, police searched the basement in which he was living. In one of his pants pockets, they found a buck knife. A trace of human blood was discovered in the shaft of the knife and was determined to be type O, the same type blood as the murder victim's.

Malcolm Hardwicke was located in Seattle and arrested without incident there.

In the latter part of February 1988, Wadelin LeRoy Drummer, 40, and Malcolm Hardwicke, 39, went on trial.

A jury found Hardwicke guilty only of second-degree robbery for his part in the incident, primarily because it could only be proven that he stole a jade elephant and jade oval piece. But it couldn't be proven he actually bludgeoned or stabbed the victim. Hardwicke was sentenced to nine months in jail and is now out.

The same jury found Wadelin Drummer guilty of

first-degree murder. Drummer was sentenced by King County Superior Court Judge Frank Eberharter to 55 years in prison.

The sentence is believed to be the longest on record in a non-aggravated homicide case in King County since new statewide sentencing guidelines went into effect in 1984.

Wadelin Drummer is currently serving his sentence.

EDITOR'S NOTE:
Frank Larson, Malcolm Hardwicke and Carlos Rashan are not the real names of the persons so named in the foregoing story. Fictitious names have been used because there is no reason for public interest in the identities of these persons.

"FREAKY FISH CUTTER FILETED FEMALES!"

by Barry Bowe

The minister's voice soared to an evangelical crescendo as he addressed a crowd of 50 marchers keeping an angry vigil over the memory of eight savagely slashed women. "Has it meant nothing that bone of our bone, flesh of our flesh, has perished before us, brutally murdered in our midst?"

It was late October 1990. A cold, gloomy dusk was settling upon the Frankford section of Philadelphia. The marchers stood in the shadows of the Market-Frankford El, the same train trestle Sylvester Stallone had used to set the mood for Rocky Balboa's silverscreen rise from working-class obscurity to worldwide fame.

"We stand here today to proclaim that it does matter," the reverend railed, hitting his pontifical stride. "They are children of God, and their death is a judgment upon us all, of how we have failed one another. They will not be forgotten."

At that point, the marchers bunched together to shield themselves from the blasts of wind whipping around the four-story brick apartment house on the corner. They huddled together not just because they were cold, but because they were lighting candles from one wick to the next, symbolically spreading the flames of sorrow, hope, and defiance.

The murders had begun five years earlier, when Southeast Pennsylvania Transportation Authority (SEPTA) workers arrived for work at a maintenance yard near the corner of Bridge Street and Frankford Avenue around 8:30 a.m. on Wednesday, August 28, 1985. What they found opened their eyes faster than a slap on the face.

A woman's body was lying on the ground, face up, between stacks of railroad ties. She was naked from the waist down, her legs spread wide, blouse pulled up, breasts exposed. A coroner would later count 19 stab wounds, the worst of which was an incision that extended from the top of her vagina to above her navel. The coroner determined that some of the wounds had been inflicted after death occurred, but he found no signs of sexual abuse.

The victim, 52-year-old Helen Patent, was a regular customer at the bars lining Frankford Avenue.

Four months later, shortly after midnight on January 2, 1986, residents of an apartment building on the 1400 block of Ritner Street in south Philadelphia heard footsteps tiptoeing down the stairs. Because of the lateness of the hour, they didn't open their door to look.

The next afternoon, the residents noticed that the upstairs neighbor's door had been left ajar. They entered her apartment to investigate. In the bedroom next to the bed, they found 68-year-old Anna Carroll lying on her back on the floor. One of Anna's kitchen knives lay atop her carved body.

Naked from the waist down, legs apart, blouse pulled up to expose her breasts, Anna had been stabbed six times. She had also been slit open from the top of her vagina to her breast bone. In addition, her internal organs had been pulled out—"evisceration" was the term the city coroner would use. The coroner would also determine that some of the wounds had been administered postmortem, but he found no signs

117

of sexual activity in the hours preceding the victim's death.

In the City of Brotherly Love, where nearly 500 murders were par for the year, no one linked the Patent and Carroll killings. Four months had passed since Helen Patent's murder. The killings had occurred at opposite ends of the city and different teams of investigators had been assigned to each case. Anna Carroll's habit of frequenting the tap rooms along Frankford Avenue, near where Helen Patent's body was found, did not as yet have any bearing on the case. Homicide detectives had leads in both murders, but nearly a year passed with no arrests being made in either case.

It was around 8:30 on Christmas night and neighbors were returning to their apartment in the 4700 block of Richmond Street. The neighbors noticed that Susan Olszef's door was ajar, and they looked inside. Some people thought the 74-year-old Olszef looked like a bag lady because she was a common sight on Frankford Avenue, poking down the sidewalk in a walker, always carrying bags. The truth was that she was a frequent shopper in the stores along the strip.

Inside the apartment, Susan Olszef was dead. She'd been stabbed six times, all of the wounds to her back. At the time, no one linked Susan Olszef's killing to the murders of Helen Patent or Anna Carroll.

"The first three slayings happened in three different parts of the city," Lieutenant Joseph Washlick would say later. Washlick would become head of the Philadelphia Police Department's Special Investigations Unit (SIU) in 1989. "We could almost give you a different suspect for each job."

Two weeks after Susan Olszef's murder, another stabbing was discovered. On January 8, 1987, at 7:30 a.m., employees of a sidewalk fruit stand in the 5100 block of Frankford Avenue arrived for work only to discover Jeanne Durkin's slashed body underneath the stand. The 28-year-old victim was a street person who

118

slept in doorways and alleys on Frankford Avenue. Hers was a meager life brought to a violet end.

A blood-starved killer had stabbed Jeanne Durkin 74 times before leaving her beneath the fruit stand, face down on the concrete, naked below the waist, legs spread. Three superficial wounds, which the medical examiner later determined had been administered after death, scored her buttocks. Once again, the M.E. found no signs of rape.

The site of this slaying, footsteps away from the SEPTA maintenance lot where Helen Patent's ravaged body had been found nearly a year and a half earlier, caused a change in thinking at the Philadelphia Police Department. The brutality exhibited in both Helen Patent's murder and in Jeanne Durkin's murder was the common thread that initially linked the killings and channeled the investigators' efforts toward finding a serial killer whom the newspapers would dub the "Frankford Slasher."

A task force was hastily assembled. At first appearance, the only thing the four murders had in common was the savageness of the M.O. The detectives struggled to find an identifiable pattern, but they were stumped. Because investigators were needed on other cases, the task force was soon dismantled. Nearly two years passed without a related homicide — 22 months and four days.

Then on the morning of November 10, 1988, Margaret Vaughn, 66, was evicted from her apartment in the 4900 block of Penn Avenue for failing to pay her rent. That afternoon, she drowned her sorrows in the bars along Frankford Avenue. As late as 6:00 p.m., a barmaid remembered seeing the woman, better known along the strip as "Marge with the Bette Davis eyes," sitting at the bar, drinking with a man.

Homicide detectives would later theorize that Margaret Vaughn returned to her apartment building, hoping to gain access to her old apartment. Her building key unlocked the outside door, but the landlord had changed the lock to her unit. She was locked out. With nowhere else to sleep, Margaret must have decided to spend the night in the vestibule, which is exactly where her neighbors found her the next morning.

Margaret Vaughn was fully clothed, sitting on the floor. She had been stabbed 29 times in the head, chest, and back. Her apartment building was less than three blocks from the fruit stand where Jeanne Durkin had been found stabbed to death and not more than a half-mile from the maintenance yard where Helen Patent's stabbed body had been found three and a half years earlier.

Soon after the Vaughn slaying, Lieutenant Washlick became involved in what Philly PD was calling the Frankford Murder Investigation. Washlick noticed the similarities between the murder of Helen Patent and Jeanne Durkin. He reviewed other murder cases that had occurred in the city and the area. Trying to discern a pattern in the killings, he looked at various angles. Did the homicide occur on the same day of the week? On certain days of the month? Under a full moon? Only during the winter?

"It was difficult to show any relation because of the time frame," Lieutenant Washlick recalled. Also, the age variance of the victims was 46 years. Some of the victims were street people, others were not. Some were found lying in the street, others were found inside their own homes.

Working with the barmaid who had seen Margaret Vaughn on the night of her killing, a police artist compiled a composite of the suspect. Describing the man she'd seen drinking with the victim in the hours preceding the murder, the barmaid sent the investigation forward. Although later witnesses would provide slightly different descriptions, SIU was now looking for a heavyset white male between 55 and 60 years of age, 5-foot-7 to 5-foot-8, with short gray hair, a clean-shaven face, a potbelly, and a slight limp.

The only problem, Lieutenant Washlick would later

admit, was that hundreds of men living in apartments above the Frankford Avenue storefronts fit that description.

Nine weeks later, blood-red lightning struck again. Around 6:00 p.m. on January 19, 1989, 30-year-old Theresa Sciortino was pacing back and forth outside a Frankford Avenue tavern. Shortly thereafter, she was seen walking with a middle-aged white man.

Around 6:45, two women living in the 1500 block of Arrott Street heard a "thumping" coming from the unit above them, a unit that had been burglarized only a few days earlier. Out of fear, the women kept their door closed. Moments later, they heard footsteps coming down the stairway.

When the neighbors saw the building manager around nine o'clock, they reported the suspicious noises that they'd heard. At the time, the manager thought nothing of it and went out to have a few drinks in one of the local bars. When the manager was coming home shortly after midnight, he noticed a light shining from a third-floor window. It was unusual for the tenant to be awake so late, so he decided to check it out.

Inside, on the kitchen floor, lay Theresa Sciortino, naked but for a pair of white socks. She had been stabbed 25 times and split up the middle. A piece of wooden-door molding was lying on the floor next to the body. It had apparently been ripped off when the burglar had broken into the apartment a few days earlier.

Criminalists would later determine that the three-and-a-half-foot piece of molding had been inserted into the victim's vagina. The M.E. would later find acid phosphatase in the victim's vagina, indicating that she'd engaged in sexual intercourse sometime during the 24-hour period preceding her death.

The scene of this crime was within blocks of where Helen Patent, Jeanne Durkin, and Margaret Vaughn had been murdered. Another task force was activated, consisting of 12 detectives and two supervisors, Lieutenants Washlick and Richie Harris.

Investigators combed the Frankford Avenue taverns, interviewing bartenders, barmaids, and customers. Soon, they'd gathered enough information for a police artist to sketch two more renderings of men witnesses claimed to have been seen with several of the victims in the hours prior to their murders.

The lawmen theorized that the murderer was a regular customer of the area bars. They believed he followed some of the victims out of the bars and met others on the street as they left a bar or were about to enter. In either scenario, the women felt comfortable with the killer because they knew him from the bars. On some pretense or another, he would induce them to be alone with him. Then he abducted them and fileted them in the darkness of a back alley or in the quiet confines of their own home.

Sergeant Dennis Murray often patrolled Frankford Avenue at night in an unmarked Plymouth, looking for the slasher.

"These were pretty violent struggles," Murray would say later, "and you would think that the person who's doing this, he would have to be covered with blood. But in all the cases, he had never been seen. Somebody should have taken notice to somebody like that.

"There's victim number seven and victim number eight," Sergeant Murray said during one early-morning patrol, spotting two women walking along the street by themselves. "Or you see a couple and you say, 'Well, if we find her in the morning, at least we'll know who she was with.' "

A local bartender described the prevailing lack of concern among most of his customers. "People don't seem to have much fear because it's happened to somebody else. They say, 'So what?' "

In November 1989, Sergeant Murray received a tip from a concerned community leader. "I was talking to a person who believed that there may be witchcraft involved. At this park up here, he came across some sort of cult ceremony. I thought it was bizarre, but I occasionally drive past the park to see if any ceremonies are going on."

Detective Bill Schol was assigned to the probe the previous January. Since then, he'd received a variety of tips from a wide range of sources, some routine, other anonymous, and one of them exotic in nature. The 13-year police veteran said a psychic called him regularly.

"She and a friend in California pray together and came up with their vision of who this person was, who we might want to look for," Detective Schol recalled. "I listened. Rule number one is you listen. Even at five o'clock in the morning, you listen."

Psychics weren't the only ones calling the SIU with tips. Hundreds of calls poured in. Dozens of elderly women warned the detectives about suspicious bus drivers. "SEPTA drivers get a bad rap," Lieutenant Washlick admitted. But he said that the leads were investigated, one by one, and eliminated.

Another woman called to report a man she'd met through a personals ad. After having dinner with her blind date, the woman decided that the man resembled the police composite which had started appearing in the store windows along Frankford Avenue. The officers checked him out and crossed off his name.

Store owners reported nervous customers. Area residents informed on disagreeable neighbors. Women even turned in their boyfriends as possible slashers.

"In a lot of cases, it's probably somebody that's mad at their neighbor or something," Detective Murray said, adding that the results of all the inquiries had turned out negative. "We spend a lot of time checking those people out." In all, the detectives checked out more than 50 leads to men fitting the description of the composites. None of the tips appeared to lead anywhere, but one did look more promising than others.

A bloody sneaker print was left behind on Theresa

Sciortino's kitchen floor. Although he didn't fit the description of the man police were seeking, the investigators hauled in the victim's boyfriend for questioning. Aside from his relationship with Theresa, tipsters had seen him with her prior to the murder, and they told police he usually wore sneakers.

"He was a good suspect at the time," Detective Murray said, but the boyfriend, too, was soon scratched from the suspect list. "His prints were similar but not identical."

That was how the investigation stood as the spring of 1990 rolled around. Investigators worked 12-hour shifts trying to locate the slasher before he struck again.

"It's like looking for buried treasure," said Lieutenant Washlick, a 21-year vet who'd been trailing the slasher for more than a year at that point. "We've dug holes all over the neighborhood, but we keep coming up with empty holes."

Detective Schol missed lots of family meals, but he believed it would be worth the inconvenience if they could nail the killer.

But before the police moved one step closer to a viable suspect, the blood-thirsty night stalker had struck again.

Uniformed Officer Dan Johnson, of the 15th Precinct, was patrolling Frankford Avenue during the graveyard shift on April 28, 1990. At 1:37 a.m., he braked his police car to a stop in the alley behind a seafood market. A robber had hit the Frankford Avenue fish market two weeks earlier and patrolmen had been keeping close tabs on it ever since.

As he was walking toward the back door, Officer Johnson found a woman's body lying in the alley, face up, legs apart. The victim's pants were draped across the body. Her purse was found about 30 feet down the alley. A small amount of money remained inside, but the purse's contents had been spilled on the ground and rummaged through. Without knowing how much money had originally been in the purse, robbery was never ruled out as a motive for the slaying. Despite all outward appearances that a sexual crime might have been committed, no semen was found in the victim's vagina or anus.

Officer Johnson radioed police headquarters, the Roundhouse at 8th and Race Streets. Minutes later, detectives rushed urgently to the scene. Faced with a 2:00 a.m. mandatory closing time for liquor establishments, the officers quickly rounded up customers from the bars around the corner, grabbed sidewalk bystanders, and transported them to the Roundhouse for questioning. Meanwhile, forensic technicians started processing the crime scene.

Looking for the murder weapon, the evidence personnel climbed into sewers, dug into garbage cans and trash dumpsters, and ripped apart discarded furniture that they found strewn in back alleys. But they found nothing.

In the victim's apartment building, investigators located a neighbor who'd seen the victim earlier in the evening. The woman said she'd known the victim by her nickname, Joy, and said she'd seen Joy walking down Frankford Avenue with an older white man. The neighbor's description of the man fit the composite, which led SIU to believe that Carol "Joy" Dowd was the seventh victim of a serial killer who'd started slashing his victims in 1985.

Dawn turned to morning. Policemen were still scouring the alley behind the fish market for clues when Leonard Christopher arrived for work. The 38-year-old black man showed little surprise at the sight of the officers.

"I just thought they broke in again," Christopher told a *Philadelphia Inquirer* reporter who was covering the story. Christopher had worked in the fish market for nine months and lived in an apartment across the street, above a pizzeria. He was familiar with comings and going on Frankford Avenue and in the back alleys.

"It's a hooker's paradise," he said. "They pull their tricks back there." Then he added that drug users and pushers also used the dark alleys to negotiate drug deals.

When Chou Mae Nguyen and her husband, the owners of the fish market, arrived for work around 9:00 a.m., she asked Christopher what was going on. Had they been robbed again?

No, Christopher told his boss, "a white girl was killed. She was about forty-five." Christopher also told his boss that he thought he'd seen the killer. "I saw a white man around one a.m., near Rite Aid."

Systematically, the detectives dragged Frankford Avenue all day, in and out of the bars, talking to workers and customers, stopping people on the street. At night, they did more of the same, talking to the night workers, night customers, and night walkers, prostitutes who worked that strip. But they got nowhere. Nobody saw anything, nobody heard anything—just like the other unsolved cases. When the detectives ran out of people to interview, they started all over again.

The first bit of useful information came from Leonard Christopher. Despite his being black and not matching the composites in any way, the officers scrutinized him as they interviewed him. With no arrests and no meaningful suspect, the officers refused to ignore any possibility.

Christopher appeared calm. The detectives observed no cuts or marks on his person. he had no police record. Still, they asked about his whereabouts on the previous night.

He told them that his girlfriend had been with him in his apartment. Around 1:00 a.m., he'd been standing at the window with her when he spotted a white man, in his 40s and well-dressed, standing on the sidewalk near Rite Aid. What had caught his eye was that the man appeared to be wiping his hands on something, a tissue or a napkin.

126

To verify the fish cutter's alibi, the lawmen spoke with his girllfriend. There, they encountered an unexpected twist. The girlfriend said *no way* had she been with Christopher on the night of the murder. When the investigators confronted Leonard Christopher with his girlfriend's statement, he changed his story completely.

Sensing a crack in the case, the detectives called in the streetwalkers for a third time. This time, Millie Raye sang a different tune. She now said she'd been withholding information "because Chris was my friend." Millie, an admitted prostitute, said she'd seen Carol Dowd walking down Kinsey Street with Chris around 1:00 a.m. They disappeared into the alley behind the fish market. Soon, a woman screamed, but Millie couldn't hang around. A customer had just pulled up in a car. She hopped in the car and drove away. When Millie returned to Frankford Avenue 45 minutes later, all she saw were police cars, flashing lights, and cops.

From Millie Raye, the detectives obtained the name of a second hooker, someone who'd remained on the street when Millie had left with her john. The second prostitute, Martha Jefferson, added to Millie's story.

Martha Jefferson said she'd seen Chris coming out of the alley behind the fish market shortly after 1:00 a.m. According to Martha, Chris was "sweating profusely, had his shirt over his arm, and a 'Rambo knife' was tucked into his belt."

As badly as the detectives wanted an arrest, they knew they needed better corroboration than the testimony of two prostitutes. Without tangible evidence, any circumstantial case was difficult to "make." With no evidence and two hookers as the star witnesses, a defense attorney would blow the state's case right out of court. So the sleuths kept digging.

The next day, they found a 33-year-old mailman who was a regular on the local bar scene. According to the mailman, Carol Dowd was sitting in a bar in the

4500 block, drinking, when Leonard Christopher came in — sometime between 9:45 and 10:00 p.m. The mailman knew Christopher from the bars. He'd seen him quite often in one bar or another along the strip. That night, Chris sat next to Carol Dowd. They drank and talked together for over an hour.

Between 11:20 and 11:45, the mailman said, Chris got up and left the bar. Two minutes later, Carol Dowd left. Less than two hours later, Officer Johnson would find Carol Dowd's body in the alley behind the fish market.

The mailman also said he knew Chris "cut fish and took out the trash" at the fish market. On several occasions in the past, the mailman had seen Chris "with different types of knives — switchblades, sometimes he'd have a folding knife. At work, I'd seen him with all sorts of real sharp knives." Sometimes he'd seen Chris wearing a large knife sheathed from his belt.

Later that day, the detectives interviewed Chou Mae Nguyen.

"When I got to work, [Chris] told me that a white woman had been killed, stabbed multiple times, and mutilated," Nugyen said. "He said that she was forty-five years old, the woman was slashed bad — cut on the face, neck, and chest. She was gutted, and he was motioning."

What made this statement extremely incriminating was that when Chou Mae Nguyen had arrived for work at 9:00 a.m. on the morning of the murder, none of the information pertinent to the case had been released. Except for the investigating officers, no one knew that the 46-year-old victim had been stabbed 36 times and nearly sliced in two, split from her navel to her vagina, had her left nipple hacked off, and been eviscerated — no one, that is, except for the killer.

Christopher's boss told police that by May 3rd, five days after the murder, Chris had started behaving oddly. He told his boss he couldn't sleep. "I said, 'What are you nervous for?' He said, 'I think a white man is trying to kill me because I was a witness.' "

Nguyen said Christopher's behavior bordered on paranoia. According to her, Chris said he "looked in his apartment to see if the white man was hiding in the closet. 'Maybe *I* killed her,' he said to me later. Then he turned around a second later and said, 'No, I didn't.' I said, 'Why would you say that?' I thought he was kidding."

The next day, executing a search warrant, Lieutenant Harris arrested Leonard Christopher at his apartment. In the apartment, detectives found a pair of pants with a tiny bloodstain on one leg. In time, the stain would prove to be too small to be typed. At the time of the arrest, SIU officers weren't at all sure that they'd collared the Frankford Slasher.

"You don't want to put blinders on," Lieutenant Washlick would say later, "to focus so hard on one suspect and be led down a primrose path. Then, if that suspect didn't do the job, you're left with nothing. You just go with the facts. But, at that time, we were *hoping* we had him."

With Leonard Christopher behind bars, crossing the days off the calendar, his December trial date drew nearer. Detectives and evidence technicians, despite their hard work, failed to secure any physical evidence. The circumstantial case for the prosecution would be a house of cards. Then, on September 8th, the plot thickened.

Neighbors in an apartment building in the 1300 block of Arrott Street noticed a "bad smell." Around 1:00 p.m., the building manager unlocked the door to 30-year-old Michelle Martin's apartment. Inside, he found a body that was starting to decompose, lying face up on the floor, legs apart, nude from the waist down, blouse pulled up to expose the victim's breasts. There were 23 stab wounds to Michelle Martin's head, face, and chest, plus some red marks around her breasts. The coroner estimated that she'd been dead about two days.

The SIU detectives learned that Michelle had last been seen outside one of the Frankford Avenue bars around 8:00 p.m. on Thursday, two nights earlier. According to tipsters, she'd been talking to an older white male.

Was the Frankford Slasher still on the loose? Was Michelle Martin's murder a copycat killing? Was Leonard Christopher innocent of murdering Carol Dowd?

In any case, Lieutenant Washlick pressed the investigation onward. He contacted the FBI Behavioral Science Unit in Quantico, Virginia, for assistance in compiling a psychological profile of the killer. In addition, the SIU detectives dug through the files of the unsolved cases, interviewed family members of all the victims, and submitted a VICAP (Violent Criminal Apprehension Program) form to Quantico for processing by the FBI experts.

In December, Leonard Christopher's trial began with Judge George J. Ivins presiding. For six days, a jury of eight men and four women listened to testimony. In all, the state produced five key witnesses — two prostitutes, the mailman, the fish market owner, and the defendant's girlfriend. But there was no physical evidence — no murder weapon, no fingerprints, no blood, hair, or fiber samples — to link the defendant to the crime. Still, Assistant District Attorney Judith Rubino sought not only a first-degree murder conviction, but also the death penalty.

"No one is going to come in here and tell you they saw the crime," Ms. Rubino said in her opening remarks, "but you're going to hear from prostitutes and other people — they were the people out there at one a.m. on April twenty-eighth — who saw things immediately before and after the killing."

In his turn, Defense Attorney Jack McMahon agreed that the victims had suffered a brutal death. "But don't let the blood and guts take away your focus on this case: did the defendant do it?

130

"Two witnesses are little more than prostitutes and junkies. They have been arrested thirty-five times between them and they have nine aliases. Mrs. Rubino is going to say, 'Believe them beyond a reasonable doubt?'

"Leonard Christopher is thirty-nine years old. He's never been in trouble in his life. He's worked all his life. He was a decent man — not like the people who came here to testify against him. He enlisted in the Navy. He's not some dregs of society.

"It just doesn't make sense. This case stinks. It's garbage."

But the assistant D.A. disagreed with her adversary.

"These are the defendant's friends," Ms. Rubino said. "What's their motivation to lie?"

On December 12th, Leonard Christopher awaited the verdict. After eight hours of deliberation, the jury had reached a decision.

Dressed in a gray suit, wearing horn-rimmed glasses, the defendant looked more like a lawyer or a schoolteacher than a killer. With two female jury members wiping tears from their eyes, the verdict was read: guilty.

"The night stalker is still out there," Christopher proclaimed. "I've been railroaded."

More than a year and a half has passed since someone slashed Michelle Martin to death and one thing is certain: Leonard Christopher was in jail when that murder was committed and could not have committed that crime. But there have been no similar slashings in Frankford or the Philadelphia area since then.

Maybe Leonard Christopher *is* the Frankford Slasher who fileted three, four, or seven of the victims. Maybe Michelle Martin's murder was a copycat killing. Maybe the Frankford Slasher was really two, or three, different killers. The answers remain to be seen.

"Surprisingly, we still get phone calls," Lieutenant Washlick said recently, saying that the Frankford Murder Investigation is ongoing to this day. "Leonard

131

Christopher is a suspect in some of the other killings. We have other suspects, as well. Last year we had four hundred and eighty-one homicides in Philadelphia and we solved eighty-two percent of them."

In the meantime, Leonard Christopher is serving a life sentence within the Pennsylvania penal system. After two hours of deliberation, the jury voted against the death penalty and spared his life.

EDITOR'S NOTE:
Chou Mae Nguyen, Millie Raye, and Martha Jefferson are not the real names of the persons so named in the foregoing story. Fictitious names have been used because there is no reason for public interest in the identities of these persons.

"SKELETON IN THE GARTER BELT AND NYLONS"

by Donald L. Dupay

I had been a cop for a long time: six years on the street, most of it working the crime-ridden ghetto, followed by eight years as a detective. I had seen a *lot*. You know what I mean: A lot of gruesome things. Not much fazed me.

Still, August 29, 1975, was one day I'll never forget. I was a detective working the four-to-midnight shift out of the Homicide Detail in Portland, Oregon. I didn't know it yet, but a routine call asking police to check on an unseen occupant of a house was going to turn into the most bizarre case I ever investigated, a textbook case on the perfect crime.

Bessie Mae Staley had been a respected member of her neighborhood. She was a restaurant owner and a staunch Catholic. Bessie owned and operated Staley's, a small restaurant located in the Sanctuary of Our Sorrowful Mother. Known as The Grotto, the beautiful Catholic sanctuary in the northeast section of Portland is a popular attraction. Bessie's little restaurant did well.

Bessie had lived with her husband in the Southeast Portland house they owned until his death. Built in the '20s, it was an old wood-frame, two-bedroom house that had a large kitchen, a bath, a separate dining room, and a large front room with a fireplace. Always the business woman, when her husband died, Bessie converted the second floor of her home into an apartment. She installed an outside stairway and rented it out to two elderly gentlemen.

People in the neighborhood would stop and chat with Bessie Staley when they met her on the street, but she was a busy lady. She had no children and was managing nicely by herself.

Eventually, the neighbors began to see Bessie with a new man whose name was Charles Lewis. Charles was a bookkeeper by trade and took care of the bookkeeping duties at Bessie's restaurant. When they first met, Charles was in his early 50s, and although Bessie was 14 years older than Charles, they fell in love.

In spite of Bessie being a good Catholic, she and Charles never married. For the next 15 years they lived together in her old house, ran the little restaurant, and collected the rent on the upstairs apartment.

As Bessie got older, her health started to deteriorate rapidly, and she became senile. Bessie made out a will leaving everything to Charles, and Charles reciprocated. But other than personal possessions, Charles didn't have anything to leave Bessie. Gradually, Bessie's senility took her mind. She and Charles had to close the restaurant and retire to their home.

As Bessie got into her late 70s, the disease that took her mind altered her personality. According to a distant relative, Bessie had gone completely crazy and was impossible to be around. She had become caustic and nasty in her advanced years.

But Charles was the bookkeeper, so he collected the monthly rent money. And when their Social Security checks would arrive in the mail, Charles would walk the four blocks to the bank and cash them both. After all, even though Charles never had power of attorney, the people in the bank knew that Bessie couldn't take care of herself and were happy to cash the checks and give the money to Charles. Charles would always hurry home because he couldn't leave Bessie alone. He would say hello to the neighbors who spoke to him on the street. "Yes," he'd say, "Bessie's home, but not in good health, thank you." Charles didn't linger in conversation.

One neighbor commented that in the past three years, he had seen Charles only about six times. Charles would get the groceries delivered. They were always left at the back door. He didn't go out much. He just stayed at home and took care of Bessie. Such a nice man; he must love her dearly, the neighbors thought.

One day when the rent was due, the upstairs tenants knocked on Charles and Bessie's back door with the rent money. Through the back door window, they could see Charles lying on the floor. Since he was down on the floor and didn't move when they knocked, they decided to call the police.

When the uniformed cops got there, they couldn't rouse Charles either and broke into the apartment to see what was wrong. They found Charles Lewis face down on the floor. His eyes were open and he was breathing, but he couldn't speak, and he couldn't move. It was obvious that Charles had suffered a serious medical problem and had been lying on the floor for hours or perhaps days. There was no way to tell.

The cops ordered that an ambulance be dispatched. Charles was taken to Oregon's best medical facility, the University Hospital in Southwest Portland. When he was admitted, his identification showed him to be 68 years old.

When the ambulance left the house, the officers secured the door and were ready to leave.

"You leaving?" asked the upstairs tenant.

"Yes," replied the officer. "He's been sent to the hospital. There's nothing more we can do here except lock up."

"But what about Bessie?" the tenant asked. "What shall I do with the rent money?"

135

"There was no one else in the house," answered the cop. "Who's Bessie?"

The tenant went on to explain that Bessie Staley had owned the house and lived there with Charles Lewis. Although no one had seen her for several years, everyone supposed she was by now an invalid. Charles always said he was taking care of her.

The cops didn't think so. Charles had apparently collapsed on the floor in the dining room, and they thought he was alone in the house. Maybe Bessie had gone visiting, but the cops would double-check to make sure. They searched the house again, including the basement and Charles' bedroom, and found no one.

Another door, covered with dust, hadn't been opened yet. An old dusty bath towel was stuffed into the crack between the bottom of the door and the wooden floor. When the officer opened the dusty door, he looked inside the room. Quickly he closed it again, and put in a call for detectives.

When I arrived, I opened the squeaky old wooden door of Bessie Staley's bedroom. I had apparently opened the door of her tomb! A layer of dust blanketed everything. The blinds were pulled tightly shut, and the window curtains had yellowed and frayed. Very little daylight was coming in. Bath towels, like the one under the door, were stuffed in the window cracks too. Dead flies lay on the sill. There were two heat vents in the bedroom. Both were blocked by rags stuffed in them.

In the corner, on a metal stand, was an empty bird cage. At least it looked empty from the doorway. As I walked up to it, I could see a small yellow canary laying dead on the bottom, its water and seed containers empty. My footsteps into the room had left tracks on the dusty floor.

Personal items, like a hairbrush and comb, lay untouched on the dresser top in the thick dust. Dusty photos of people I didn't know were on a nightstand.

Near them was an old wind-up alarm clock that had stopped ticking long ago.

On the old metal-frame bed was a skeleton lying face up. Dead maggots were visible in the empty eye sockets and open jawbone of the victim. Shoulder-length gray hair covered the skull and part of the neck bones. Cloth fragments of what had once been the victim's robe were on the bed under the skeleton. From a sleeve fragment, an arm bone protruded. Both arms were laying at her side. Among the bones and on the bed where her stomach had been was a large pile of dead maggots — several hundred at least.

Looped around the corpse's pelvic bone was a garter belt. The fasteners were still connected to the shredded remains of two nylon stockings. The stockings still contained the leg bones. Feet and toe bones poked through holes in the nylon. The bedding on which the skeleton lay was stiff and hard from the dried blood and ooze that had seeped into it while the body had decomposed.

I looked around the room slowly, taking it all in: the thick dust, the maggots, the skeleton on the bed with long gray hair, the rags stuffed into the window cracks and the dead canary in the cage. It looked exactly like a set from a horror movie. But it wasn't a set, it was real — very, very real. We had obviously found Bessie Staley.

Records showed that Bessie was 82. The coroner would say that she had probably died when she was 79. Charles Lewis had taken good care of Bessie, very good care indeed!

I was anxious to talk to the medical examiner about this case. What could we learn from the autopsy? What was the cause of death? And Charles. Now that we knew where he had been keeping Bessie, I had a few questions for him.

When I entered Charles' hospital room, I saw that the medics had him hooked up to drip tubes and monitors. The old man lay on his side, eyes open, breathing slowly. I told him I was a detective and that I wanted to ask him some questions about Bessie Staley. His steady gaze at nothing didn't change. His eyes didn't flicker or recognize me; he didn't move or respond. The doctor told me Charles was dying. Tests showed that he had terminal cancer, pneumonia, diabetes, and fatal heart disease.

Charles didn't answer any questions posed by me or the doctor. In fact, he never spoke again. I tried to find some of the answers by looking into his eyes, but poor Charles just wasn't there. Seventy-two hours after the ambulance had removed him from the house, Charles Lewis died.

The medical examiner was no help, either. The skeletal remains of Bessie Staley lay on the stainless steel autopsy table, but there were no buckets on the floor to put the organs in, no plastic bags and no cutting tools. With nothing left but a skeleton, there was no body to cut open, no organs to cut out and examine, no brain to remove. The maggots and a lot of time had done all that work.

"I can tell you how she *didn't* die," said the M.E. "She didn't die of a beating. There is not one broken bone, no broken jaw, no cracked skull, no crushed bones in the throat indicating she may have been strangled, and no bullet holes anywhere. She probably dies of natural causes, perhaps a heart attack."

"But remember, she went crazy years before she died," I reminded him. "Maybe Charles couldn't stand her any more. Could he have put a pillow over her face and smothered her while she was laying down?"

"Yes, she could have died that way," the M.E. replied.

"Could he have poisoned a crazy, burdensome old lady?"

"Yes, she could have died that way too," the M.E. answered.

"Could he have starved her to death?" I asked.

"Yes, she could have died that way too. Why are

you asking all these questions?" the M.E. asked.

"Because she didn't just die in her sleep," I replied. "Ladies don't sleep with their garter belt and nylons on."

"But she could have been taking a nap," the M.E. suggested.

"Yes, or she could have been smothered in another room and carried into the bedroom," I said.

"Why do you think he killed her?"

"Because Charles knew he didn't need her anymore. Remember, once he cashed her first Social Security check, he realized he was home free. Charles was fourteen years younger than Bessie, and I think he decided to kill her rather than take care of her sometime after he cashed the first check. He embezzled eighteen thousand dollars. He kept cashing those checks for three years *after* she died.

"Remember the canary?" I asked. "I think the canary's the key to this mystery. I think Charles had a ruthless streak in him. *Why didn't he feed and water the bird?*

"No," I continued, "I think he said goodbye to Bessie and the bird at the same time; he killed them both. He killed them both by shutting the bedroom door and 'burying' them with a towel in the crack under the door."

"We'll never know now," said the medical examiner.

Charles Lewis had apparently committed the perfect crime, embezzlement for sure and probably murder. Nevertheless, the old embezzling bookkeeper had died with his lips sealed. He'd gotten away with it. But what must have gone through the man's mind? Did Charles realize when he shut the bedroom door and "buried" both Bessie and the canary that he had created his own prison too?

With Bessie's body in the bedroom, Charles could never again let anyone in the house. He could only go out to cash the Social Security checks and come right back home. No wonder he didn't stop and chat with the neighbors. Charles had a secret.

What kind of man could live with a dead body in the next room for three years? Although Bessie Staley never got on the homicide status board and was never listed as a homicide, I know what happened to her. A little bird told me!

"120 FATAL THRUSTS WITH A TINY, WEIRD WEAPON"

by Don Lasseter

When Hal Ibison started his daily work routine on Wednesday, December 17, 1987, he had no way of knowing it would turn out to be a day that would stick in his memory forever.

Ibison's pickup truck bounced heavily as he turned from smooth, wet pavement onto the muddy, pothole-riddled ruts that served as a roadway through a large oil-well field. The 15 acres of open, rough terrain were surrounded by the urban sprawl of Huntington Beach, California.

Cold gusts of wind blew from the pounding surf just across Pacific Coast Highway. Drizzling rain kept the truck's windshield wipers working full time. Ibison wrestled the pickup across a deep culvert, past a row of tall evergreen shrubs, and braked to a halt. As he and his partner emerged from the truck to begin inspecting the oil wells, Ibison glanced back toward the shrubs. A sudden sense of dread chilled him. At first, he thought he had seen a large doll lying in a shallow dugout between two of the plants. But as he drew closer, horror wrenched the pit of his stomach.

The nearly nude body of a petite woman was lying on her back in the dugout. The damage to her body made it obvious that her death had not been pretty.

As his partner stood guard over the body, Ibison raced to the nearest telephone to report what they had discovered. It was 1:50 p.m.

Officer William Morris of the Huntington Beach Police Department received the radio call. Within minutes he was at the site of the discovery. Verifying that the report was neither a hoax nor an error, Morris immediately called for the homicide roll-out team.

Consisting of six officers and a supervisor, the team arrived promptly, followed by the crime scene investigation unit. The officers cordoned off the area with the yellow tape universally used by law enforcement personnel.

Homicide Investigator Richard C. "Hoop" Hooper, of the Huntington Beach Detective Bureau's Homicide Unit, headed up the investigation. Hooper's youthful, unlined face, crowned by thick dark hair trimmed in a classic flattop, belied his 18 years of law enforcement experience, six of those on the homicide team.

Kneeling near the woman's body, Hooper began a cursory examination. The victim was lying on her back, legs fully extended. Her right hand reposed on her stomach while her left hand, arm bent at the elbow, extended above her head. A red sweater, still encasing her shoulders, stretched behind her neck.

Except for the sweater and a bra, which was pulled down below her breasts and slightly twisted, she was nude. She was quite slim, a little over five feet tall and weighing about 100 pounds. Detective Hooper felt anger begin to well up inside him as the sheer brutality of the victim's death became apparent.

Severe bruises marred what had once been an attractive face. The flesh around the victim's left eye was swollen and caked with dried blood. Contusions, abrasions, and bruises marked her mouth, buttocks, left thigh, and knees. Her left breast bore a three-inch curved wound. Other bruises indicated that she had been raped.

142

But what Hooper found most appalling was the multiplicity of small, open puncture wounds. Closer examination would subsequently reveal that the victim had been stabbed 120 times! Most of the punctures had bled profusely, but some of them had not bled at all. The wounds were all on the left side of her body, extending from her temple to her abdomen.

"Why?" Hooper asked himself softly. "Why would any human being inflict such cruelty on another person?" The literal overkill didn't make sense.

The investigation team meticulously sifted the surrounding area for any evidence. They found a pair of bloodstained black jeans lying in the mud 10 feet away. The jeans apparently belonged to the victim, as did the knee-high black boots with three-inch heels found near her feet. Wadded beneath the victim's back was a yellow, hooded sweat shirt imprinted with the word "Catalina."

But the incessant rain continued to fall, hindering the probers' efforts and decreasing the chance of finding anything that might help solve this increasingly bizarre puzzle.

The investigators continued, however, to search with dogged determination. A nearly imperceptible glint of reflected light caught the attention of one of the officers. About 14 inches from the victim's body, at her chest level, he saw a small object almost obscured by the mud and water. Cautiously probing into the mud, the officer pulled out a small pair of manicure scissors that had been stabbed into the ground. He carefully placed the scissors into an evidence bag.

Detective Hooper took a close look at the scissors. Incredulously, he asked, "Can this be the weapon? Would anyone use this to inflict so many wounds on her?" The object looked so small, so harmless, so benign. The scissors were quite flimsy and less than four inches long. If this was a murder weapon, it would be the most bizarre and unusual one ever seen by Hooper.

Flashes of bright light illuminated the gray afternoon as one of the forensic specialists began to photograph the crime scene. He took color shots of the victim from various angles and multiple pictures of the scissors, clothing, and surrounding terrain.

Despite their prodigious efforts, the team was unable to find any fingerprints, footprints, or any other clues that might point to a suspect or help identify the victim. There were not even any tire tracks to suggest whether the perpetrator had walked or driven into the field. Nor were there any marks to tell whether the victim had been dragged to the spot or killed where she lay. If the killer had left any such evidence, the rain had long since washed it away. Detective Hooper realized this was not going to be the easiest case of his career.

The immediate challenge facing Hooper was to identify the victim. The clothing found near the body contained nothing to help accomplish this task. He could recall no missing-person report matching her description. In the absence of any other clues, Hooper hoped that her fingerprints might lead to her identity. Since death had occurred just a few hours before discovery of the body, decomposition would not be a problem. A forensic specialist obtained a full, clear set of the victim's fingerprints.

On the following morning, Thursday, the first piece of the puzzle fell into place. Hooper received a telephone call reporting that the fingerprints had, indeed, revealed the victim's identity. Her name was Beverly Alexandria Holzmiller, age 47. Her most recent address was less than two miles from Hooper's office.

Wasting no time, Detective Hooper drove to the listed address. Neighbors in the apartment building informed him that Holzmiller had relatives living in Huntington Beach.

One of the most difficult duties of a police officer is to notify the survivors of a family member's death, especially in the case of a homicide. There is no easy or comforting way to do it. But it is an integral part of the job, and Detective Hooper accomplished it with the smooth professionalism that comes with experience.

When the victim's relatives had recovered from the shock and were able to answer questions, they provided Hooper with information that helped develop a profile of the victim.

Beverly Holzmiller's last few years of life were somewhat troubled. Her husband had died in the mid-1970s, and her recovery from the emotional trauma was slow. She sometimes lived with relatives, including three grown offspring and six grandchildren, for brief periods. Recently, she had moved from the nearby community of El Toro to an apartment in Huntington Beach. She bounced from job to job and was last known to be working for a sales firm doing telephone solicitation.

Beverly Holzmiller, according to family members, believed that liquor helped ease her pain, and sometimes she consumed more than was prudent. Social activity became important to her. If there was a party to go to, Beverly went. It was fun to dance and laugh. And she attracted men. But her family members hastened to emphasize that Beverly was not promiscuous. On the contrary, she often became loud and belligerent when overly amorous men became too aggressive. Her behavior dampened the attentions of some men, but infuriated others. One close friend commented that Beverly's lifestyle, even though she probably didn't realize it, made her a perfect candidate for a brutal crime.

Detective Hooper learned that on Wednesday, December 17th, Holzmiller visited a close family member in Huntington Beach. When she left, she mentioned that she was going to a nearby liquor store. No one had seen her since.

But another close relative remembered that Holzmiller had telephoned him on Wednesday night. She said she was at a fast-food restaurant on Pacific Coast

Highway and called to ask if he could give her a ride home. He apologetically told her that he was unable to do so. Then a man's voice replaced Holzmiller's, saying that his name was Jerry and that he was with Beverly. Jerry reiterated the request for a ride, and the relative again explained that he was not able to accommodate them.

After answering a few more of Detective Hooper's questions, the relative suddenly said, "Hey, wait a minute! She recently had a roommate named Jerry!" Hooper felt the flush of excitement that comes with success. Quickly, he ascertained Jerry's full name and his address.

Meanwhile, Beverly Holzmiller's body had been taken to the Orange County coroner's laboratory. Dr. Joseph Halka, a forensic pathologist, performed the autopsy. Through the clinical methodology of his profession, he was able to develop important facts about the victim's death.

With meticulous precision, Halka counted the puncture wounds. There were 120 of them. Carefully, he measured the depth and configuration of each one. He established that they were consistent with the size, depth, and shape of the manicure scissors found at the crime scene.

The brutality of Beverly's attacker was further revealed when Dr. Halka discovered that the victim had several broken bones. Her sternum, two ribs, and a cervical vertebra were fractured by blows that required "a great deal of force." He formed the opinion that Beverly had been forcibly raped.

But the most disturbing finding by Dr. Halka related to the circumstances surrounding the stab wounds. He would later testify that the wounds were delivered over a period of 10 to 30 minutes and that Beverly had survived the first 80 stab wounds. Those 80 wounds had bled profusely because Beverly had still been alive while they were being inflicted. Halka stated, "My estimate would be that of the one hundred and twenty wounds, there are approximately forty that would have been delivered after or around the time of death."

Dr. Halka, like Detective Hooper, was puzzled and disturbed. Why would anyone be so violently brutal?

Hooper had obtained a photograph of Beverly Holzmiller from a family member. He arranged for it to be published in local newspapers with a request for anyone with information about her to contact Hooper.

On Saturday, December 19th, the newspapers ran the article and photograph of Beverly Holzmiller. In another section of the papers, they happily announced that the prolonged rainstorm was over and that Huntington Beach could look forward to fair, sunny days.

Lawmen found out the "Jerry" identified by Holzmiller's relative was Jerry Gelner, who indeed had been a roommate of Holzmiller's. On the same Saturday that the picture of Beverly Holzmiller was carried in the newspaper, Jerry Gelner was brought to the Huntington Beach Police Station to be interviewed. While waiting for the report that would describe any criminal history on Gelner, Detective Hooper was at his desk finalizing the list of questions he planned to ask Gelner.

As Hooper rose to walk to the room where Gelner waited, his telephone rang. A little irritated at the interruption, Hooper answered. A male voice on the other end said, "I have some information about that lady in the newspaper. I was at a party Wednesday night, and she was there with a guy named Robert."

Hooper quickly sat back down and gave his full attention to the caller. He learned that "Robert" was Robert Carter, a local resident. He had been seen by three witnesses leaving the party Wednesday night with Beverly Holzmiller.

Now there were two potential suspects: Jerry Gelner and Robert Carter. Which one was the more likely killer? Hooper wouldn't dismiss either of them without thorough investigation And a good place to begin would be with their respective criminal histories, if any existed.

The rap sheet on Gelner had arrived, and Hooper requested a rush on the one for Carter. When he scrutinized the two, he immediately knew which one would receive priority investigation. Jerry Gelner had no criminal history. But Robert Carter was a different story.

Twenty-year-old Robert Allen Carter had been arrested in Illinois for burglary. There was an outstanding warrant from that state for violation of probation. In addition, there was a warrant for Carter's arrest from nearby Long Beach, California, for arson. Police in Arcadia, California, were also interested in questioning Carter.

So was Detective Hooper. With the help of the witnesses at the party, Hooper learned Carter's address and telephone number. Armed with the warrants, Hooper and his team raced to Carter's apartment, which was only a few blocks from the site of the party and a short walk from the oil field where Holzmiller was found.

A strategic telephone call made by Hooper quickly established that Robert Carter was at home. But when Hooper and his partner knocked at the door of the apartment, there was no answer. They loudly announced who they were and knocked again. Risking a quick peek through a window, Hooper saw curtains moving and knew someone was there. Without any further hesitation, the sleuths kicked the door open. Inside, the probers were greeted with silence and a closed, locked bedroom door.

Once again, they announced their presence and demanded that Carter surrender himself — and again, silence. Using shoulders and feet, they smashed open the bedroom door. Robert Carter was crouched behind a bed in a vain attempt to hide.

Hooper arrested Carter on the warrant charges, handcuffed him, and locked him in the backseat of the car. Detective R. Howell drove the suspect to the Huntington Beach Jail. He was booked at 7:25 p.m.

Many circumstances pointed to Carter as Beverly Holzmiller's killer, but the investigation team still had no hard evidence to link the young man with the crime. He had been seen leaving a party with the victim on the night she was killed, but that certainly did not prove that he was the killer.

Law enforcement people have known for many years that there is no reliable way to identify a criminal by his appearance. Robert Carter was no exception to that rule. He had just turned 20 years old two months prior to his arrest, and his face looked even younger. His skin still bore the red acne dots of adolescence. His hair was relatively short, neatly styled, and parted in the middle. It would have been difficult to distinguish him from the hordes of youths, mostly surfers, who inhabited Huntington Beach.

One feature of his, however, was inconsistent with the typical look of wholesome youth. His upper left arm was garishly tattooed with an eagle, wings spread, its talons grasping a serpent, with a lightning bolt in the background.

Detective Hooper entered the room where Carter sat. He knew he had to proceed cautiously, because he had no evidence to connect Carter to the killing. Hooper began by ensuring that Carter understood his Miranda rights. Then he casually told Carter that he would like to have permission to search his bedroom at home. Carter didn't seem worried and readily signed a standard Huntington Beach Police Department consent form to search the room.

While Carter was signing the document, and during the interview, Hooper carefully watched the young man's right hand. He saw what he suspected would be there. Two small circular bruises in Carter's palm looked as if they could have been made by the finger holes of the manicure scissors found at the crime scene.

Hooper asked, "How did you get those bruises?"

Carter casually replied, "I was removing some floor tiles with a screwdriver. The screwdriver must have caused the bruises."

Detective Hooper left the room for a few moments to have a video camera set up to record any subsequent conversation with Carter. The detective knew that he had to have a confession from Carter or else he could forget any charges of homicide. And to get a confession, Hooper was going to have to convincingly pull a colossal bluff.

Back in the interview room, Hooper decided to start the interrogation by reviewing the charges against Carter. He said, "You know you are under arrest for a warrant. There is one in Illinois, one in Long Beach, one in Arcadia, and one in Huntington Beach."

Carter mumbled. "I'm sorry. . . ."

Not entirely sure what that meant, the detective decided to start again. "Okay, you know you are under arrest for a warrant. There is one in Illinois. . . ."

Carter interrupted, ". . . Yeah, and one in Long Beach and one in Arcadia and one in Huntington Beach." His voice was cold and arrogant.

"Okay, you know all that," countered Hooper. "I'm also conducting a homicide investigation."

With no change in expression, Carter said, "All right."

Quickly, Hooper gambled, "I want to talk to you about that. Any problem?"

Very cool and unperturbed, Carter responded, "No problem. None . . . none at all."

Now it was time to put all of his chips down, so Hooper began the bluff. His voice level and firm, he told Carter, "I know you killed Beverly Holzmiller!" Furthermore, he added, Carter's bloody fingerprints were on the body and on the scissors. Hooper continued to bore in by informing Carter that witnesses had seen him go into the oil field with the victim.

The convincing bluff worked to perfection. Robert Allen Carter began to waver, show doubt, and then completely caved in and agreed to confess to the killing. For the next two hours, Carter was videotaped giving his version of the bloody events on the previous Wednesday.

According to Carter, he had met Beverly Holzmiller in a liquor store early Wednesday evening and invited her to a party. They walked the few blocks to the party, which consisted of just four or five people. After quite a few beers, he said, Holzmiller started to get loud and belligerent. So they left the party at about midnight and went to an apartment where a friend of Carter's lived. The friend agreed to let Carter stay there, but said that the woman could not stay.

Without showing any remorse, the youth continued his story. He said that after leaving the friend's house, he and Beverly walked up Alabama Street to an unoccupied house where they thought they could get in out of the rain, but locked doors and windows prevented their entry. So they continued to walk a short distance until they found a place between two buildings where, according to Carter, Holzmiller agreed to have sex with him.

From there, he said, they went into the oil field, where they again had sex. At this juncture in his story, Carter began to show anger. In the oil field, he claimed, the victim began to taunt him about his inadequate sexual performance. His voice grew more strained, and he blurted out, "Then she told me that she gave me AIDS!" That enraged him, so in a blind fury, he found the scissors in her purse and stabbed her "four or five times." Then he left her in the oil field.

That was the reason for the violent, brutal killing of Beverly Holzmiller. She had taunted him and told him that she had given him AIDS. At least, that was Carter's version of the reason. Detective Hooper suspected that the youth's explanation might contain considerable self-serving rationalization.

When Hooper mentioned that Holzmiller had telephoned someone fron the fast-food restaurant on Pacific Coast Highway and had been with a man named Jerry, Carter was amused. He laughingly admitted that he was Jerry! He had used the phony name as a lark. No big deal.

Detective Hooper marveled at the suspect's coincidental selection of a false name. It had cast suspicion on a totally innocent man, Jerry Gelner.

The detective wanted to know more about the purse from which Carter had taken the scissors. No purse had been found in the oil field. He asked Carter where it was. Carter admitted that he had taken it with him when he left the victim alone in the field and had subsequently put it in a plastic bag and thrown it in a large trash container near his apartment. Confident that he had convinced Detective Hooper that Beverly Holzmiller had provoked her own death, Robert Carter figured that it would be to his advantage to cooperate. He even agreed to show Hooper where he had tossed the bag containing the purse.

Not wanting to risk a change of heart by Carter, Detective Hooper immediately accepted the offer. Even though it was well past 10:00 p.m., Hooper and two of his partners took Carter to the apartment complex where the trash containers were located.

Digging through piles of garbage in the middle of the night is not the most pleasant task in the world. But it comes with the territory in police work, so, as Carter stood by, the officers plowed through the trash and found the plastic bag containing Holzmiller's handbag.

Carefully removing the contents of the large shoulder bag, the investigators inventoried the last pitiful possessions of Beverly Holzmiller. A California Department of Motor Vehicles identification card bore her picture. There were assorted photographs of her family members and a few personal documents. The underpants she had worn that fatal night were also stuffed into the bag. The only cash consisted of three pennies lying loose in the bottom of the bag. And, among assorted cosmetics, there was another pair of manicure scissors, this one with curved blades.

The peculiar thing about the contents of the victim's purse was that Carter had used the scissors to cut many of the photos and documents into small pieces.

Detective Hooper asked if there was anything else that Carter had thrown into the trash. Remarkably, the youth led them to another large container and admitted that he had thrown the boots he had worn that night into the receptacle. He said, "I took my boots and I threw them away because I was afraid they were evidence." Carter apparently didn't consider that the rain had washed away any trace of footprints.

The group's next stop was the oil field where the killing had taken place. Standing near the evergreen shrubs, Carter raised his manacled hands and pointed to the spot where he had left Beverly Holzmiller. But, of course, he had stabbed her only "four or five time," and "she was still alive" when he left her.

About 60 yards away from the shrubbery, in a large culvert, Carter pointed to where he had thrown a beer bottle when he had been there with the victim. The officers found the bottle and dusted it for fingerprints. The prints were Carter's.

Detective Richard Hooper had obtained the confession he wanted. There was no doubt that Robert Carter had killed Beverly Holzmiller, but despite the cold brutality of the homicide, the confession did not guarantee that Carter would be convicted of murder. His recital contained comments that a clever defense attorney might use to convince a jury that there were mitigating circumstances. Potentially, that could lead to a conviction that carried very little prison time. The callousness of this killing, in Hooper's opinion, deserved no less than a sentence of life in prison.

But that is the domain of the district attorney's office, and Hooper passed the case on to them.

A preliminary hearing was conducted to determine if there was enough evidence to even try Carter on murder charges. Defense Attorney Michael Horan argued Carter's case and made a strong effort to convince the court that a lesser charge than murder should be applied. He focused on Carter's story that Holzmiller had provoked him into a frenzy by taunting him and telling him that she had infected him with AIDS. But with information provided by Dr. Joseph Halka, who had performed the autopsy, the counsel finally agreed to stipulate that an analysis of the victim's blood showed that she did not have AIDS.

Halka testified about the many injuries sustained by Holzmiller. The curved linear wound on her left breast was referred to as a "tease" wound, suggesting that it had been inflicted as an overture to the bloody orgy of stabbing that followed.

The court ordered Robert Carter to stand trial for first-degree murder.

In California, as in most states, the legal process for major crimes is painfully slow. Wrangling over fine legal points and postponements of trial dates can cause delays of months or even years.

On June 12, 1990, well over two years after the death of Beverly Holzmiller, Robert Carter finally went to trial. Five days prior to that, his defense attorney had made a motion to have his confession suppressed so that it could not be used as evidence, but the judge ruled against him.

The responsibility for prosecuting Carter fell on the broad, square shoulders of Deputy District Attorney Patrick Donahue. A no-nonsense ex-officer in the United States Marine Corps and a military history buff, the tall, slim Donahue was a formidable prosecutor. But when he examined the challenge of trying Robert Carter, he could see some serious obstacles.

First, there were the self-serving statements in th

154

confession that the defense attorney could possibly manipulate. Second, there had been three witnesses who had seen Robert Carter leave the party with Holzmiller, but in the ensuing two years one of the witnesses had died. It was not going to be easy to prove beyond a reasonable doubt that Carter had, with premeditation, murdered Holzmiller.

Carter's confession described how the sex with Holzmiller had been consensual and rationalized an enraged response to her taunting him. It seemed far more probable to D.A. Donahue, as it had to Detective Hooper, that after Holzmiller had left the party with Carter and telephoned for a ride home, Carter had made sexual advances toward the woman. She had probably refused, and Carter had raped her at the site between the two apartment buildings. If any discussion of sexual performance or AIDS had really taken place, Holzmiller had probably used it in desperation, trying to ward off the rape. After he raped her a second time in the oil field, the prosecutor and detective surmised, Carter cold-bloodedly searched her purse for money and possibly a weapon. They reasoned that when Carter found the scissors, he decided to use them to kill Beverly so that she could not identify him as her attacker.

D.A. Donahue had the additional task of convincing the jury that the crime had been committed with "special circumstances." In order to ask for the death penalty or life in prison without the possibility of parole, California law requires that special circumstances be proved. This includes murder while committing rape and murder involving torture of the victim.

When the trial began, Defense Attorney Michael Horan, in his folksy, charming manner, did not deny that Robert Carter was responsible for the death of Beverly Holzmiller. But he hammered on the mitigation of the crime, emphasizing a scenario in which the defendant had responded in an emotional frenzy to

155

the woman's taunting him about sexual performance and AIDS.

D.A. Pat Donahue, in his deliberate, logical manner, argued the improbability of Carter's statement that the sex acts were consensual. He asked the jury if they could really believe that this woman had consented to having sex with Carter outside in the mud, once between two apartment buildings during a driving rainstorm and again in an open oil field.

Horan countered, pointing out to the jury that the yellow sweat shirt had been found underneath the victim's back, as if she had placed it there to be comfortable when lying down on the ground.

It was an interesting point, D.A. Donahue privately conceded. But he argued that there was no way to know who had placed the shirt there, or when. It could just as well have been thrown there by Carter prior to his wrestling the victim to the ground or placed there by Holzmiller under threat by Carter.

Donahue called the two surviving witnesses from the party to the stand. He asked, "When Mr. Carter and Mrs. Holzmiller left the party, were they kissing, or holding hands, or generally affectionate to each other?"

On the contrary, both people testified, Carter and Holzmiller were angry and were arguing loudly when they were last seen. Donahue pointed out that this was not the behavior of two people who were about to have consensual sex.

The two attorneys continued to lock horns for nine days. Robert Carter did not testify in his own behalf.

Finally, on June 21st, at 11:35 a.m., the case was given to the jury. They deliberated for less than three hours, including 50 minutes for lunch. At 2:29 p.m. they filed into the jury box and the verdict was announced.

Robert Allen Carter was found guilty of first-degree murder. The jury also found that special circumstances did apply to the crime. They rejected the alle gation of torture, saying that they had not had enough evidence to prove that Carter intended to torture Holzmiller. But they did agree that Carter had raped her.

On July 27th, while Carter hung his head and refused to look up, Superior Court Judge William Bedsworth sentenced him to life in prison without the possibility of parole. "This is the hardest thing that I do, having to send someone to prison," the judge stated. "This case, however, was as cruel and heartless an act [as] I've seen. . . . The law provides a sentence, and I will impose it."

D.A. Pat Donahue summed it up. "He's a bad guy. I just never want him out of prison."

Detective Richard Hooper put it even more succinctly. "He's a stone cold killer."

EDITOR'S NOTE:
Hal Ibison and Jerry Gelner are not the real names of the persons so named in the foregoing story. Fictitious names have been used because there is no reason for public interest in the identities of these persons.

"FINICKY FELINE FEASTED ON THE FOXY LADY'S FLESH!"

by Philip Westwood

Flakes of snow swirled around the main street of the North Wales village of Higher Kinnerton. It was a little after 10:30 a.m. on a morning in the early part of February 1991, but the lights were still on in the shops and houses that lined each side of the narrow roadway. This was one of those wintry days when the dark of night seemed loath to give way to the brightness of morning, and the sun was too weak to dispel the thick layer of cloud that clung like a shroud to the countryside. A mile away to the east, a thick carpet of snow obliterated the border that separates the country of Wales from England.

In the center of the village, one building displayed more lights than any of its neighbors. It was an imposing structure, built, like all the others, out of gray Welsh stone. To the casual passerby, it looked like a large old house. Only the blue lamp that hung over the entrance indicated the building's purpose. Etched into the lamp glass in big, white letters was the single word "Police."

Inside the station, Sergeant Andrew Hunter had been looking forward to his daytime shift. He knew that it would have been a quiet night. There would be little—if anything—to follow up from the work of the night staff. The crime rate tended to fall with the temperature, and the previous night had been really cold. On such nights, burglars were as fond of their own firesides as anyone else. And with everyone at home, muggers and petty thieves found little scope on the snow-covered streets for their activities.

Sergeant Hunter had been correct. Nothing had been reported the previous night. The station's crime book was blank. With luck, nothing would happen during the day. Everything would remain as it had been, nice and quiet.

But then the woman came in. She was a young woman, in her early 20s. She seemed worried — very worried. Hunter got an uneasy feeling. His plans for a peaceful day were not going to work out after all.

The woman had called in to report that a relative of hers was missing. She had not seen the relative for over two weeks and that was unusual. The relative lived only a mile away. The woman usually saw her nearly every day.

Hunter ascertained from the woman that the missing relative was named Arminda Perry and that she was 26 years old.

"Unusual name, Arminda," Hunter remarked.

"She's from the Philippines," the woman explained. She went on to explain that Arminda was married to John Perry. They had met while Perry was on vacation in the Philippines back in 1984. From her tone, Hunter detected that the woman's opinion of John Perry was not particularly high.

"She's his third wife," the woman went on. "The first two divorced him."

"Do you know why?" Hunter asked.

The woman nodded her head. "They got tired of being beaten up for the least little thing," she said. "He's a very violent man. And that's why I'm so worrierd about Arminda. I'm dreadfully afraid that he may have done something to her."

Asked to explain further, the woman said that Perry

was jealous—obsessively so. If another man so much as looked at Arminda, he would fly into a rage.

"And is there any reason why he should be jealous?" Hunter wanted to know.

"Yes, there is," the woman replied.

Arminda was very pretty, she explained. She had the face and figure that would turn any man's head. Perry was twice her age. And the years had not been kind to him. He looked every one of his 52 years, and some more besides.

After the woman left the station, Hunter meticulously entered his report in the incident book before conferring with his superior, Inspector Ross Duffield.

"I'd better go and check it out," Sergeant Hunter concluded, after informing Duffield of everything the woman had told him.

"All right," agreed the inspector, before adding, "I'll come with you. There's nothing much doing here."

The ice-covered road meant that it was almost a half hour before the officers had covered the two-mile journey to John Perry's home.

"It's just routine," Duffield told the tall, stockily built man who answered the door and identified himself as John Perry. "May we come in?"

Perry showed them into the living room, where Duffield explained that they had received a report that Mrs. Perry appeared to have gone missing. The lawmen were somewhat surprised by Perry reaction.

"Yes, she has," the husband replied in a casual, almost nonchalant, manner. "She's been gone for about ten days."

"You don't seem to be particularly concerned," Duffield remarked.

"I'm not," the husband replied in the same couldn't-care-less way. "She'll have gone off with some man. It's not the first time. She's done it before. After all, she's just a slut. But I knew that when I married her."

It was such an unusual opinion for a husband to express about his wife that Inspector Duffield asked him to elaborate.

Perry confirmed what his wife's relative had already told Hunter; namely, that he had met Arminda while on vacation in the Philippines back in 1984. "I met her in the bar of the hotel where I way staying," Perry said. "She was there every night, always on her own. She looked lonely and in need of company. And I was alone and also needed company. So on the third night, I went over and started talking to her. We got on well and I asked her for a date. She agreed, and after that, we were out together every day and every night."

"And where did you go?" Duffield wanted to know.

"Everywhere," Perry replied. "Clubs, shows, bars. We did the lot."

"And you became fond of her?" the detective pressed.

"Yes," agreed Perry. "I suppose I was flattered. You know what it's like. I had a girl young enough to be my daughter hanging on to my arm and hanging on to my every word.

"Anyhow, as the days passed, she became sort of withdrawn and thoughtful," Perry continued. "I asked her what was the matter, and she said that my vacation would soon be over and I would be going home. That made her sad because it meant that she would never see me again. She said that she had fallen in love with me."

A wistful look came into Perry's eyes, as if he were remembering those far off days in that faraway place. "And I had fallen in love with her," he said softly.

"Had you?" remarked Duffield. The inspector was not entirely convinced by Perry's last comment. It was said in a manner that seemed more at home in the unreal world of a bad television soap opera than in the reality of an austere Welsh cottage.

"Yes," continued Perry, oblivious to the incredulity on the inspector's face. "So we got married."

Duffield raised his eyebrows and looked toward Sergeant Hunter. He had expected to see an expression similar to that which he was experiencing. But Hunter

161

was not really paying attention. His mind seemed to be on other things. His nose twitched, as if he had sensed a bad smell and was trying to track it down. It was the kind of twitch that was infectious. Duffield found himself doing it, too. He sniffed a couple of times. There *was* something fishy in the air. He didn't know what it was, but it wasn't a pleasant odor. In fact, it was so bad that Duffield felt his stomach beginning to turn. So he stopped sniffing and turned back to Perry. Hunter could continue with his bloodhound work alone.

"Go on, Mr. Perry," Duffield invited.

"It might seem a bit rash, getting married like that," Perry said, "but I suppose I was on the rebound."

"On the rebound?" inquired Duffield. "What do you mean by that?"

"I'd just been through a divorce," explained Perry. "It was a very painful experience. It shook me up badly. After it was over, I felt that I needed to get away. That's why I went on vacation. And I felt that I wanted to get right away from everything and everyone that I knew. I wanted a complete change. That's why I went to the Philippines. But I was vulnerable, particularly to a girl like Arminda."

Duffield raised his hand to his mouth, and hoped that it got there in time to mask the smile that came to his lips. The idea of the burly, middle-aged Welshman being easy prey to a Filipino girl barely out of her teens was somehow ridiculous. He allowed himself another glance in the direction of his sergeant. Hunter's nose was now twitching furiously. He was concentrating his efforts in the direction of a closed door at the far end of the room.

A large cat uncurled itself from its place on the sofa, stretched, yawned, and jumped noiselessly down onto the floor. With an easy, loping action, the animal padded silently across the carpet and over to where the inspector was standing. It rubbed itself against the leg of Duffield's trousers, closing its eyes and purring contentedly as it did so.

"Katie! Stop that and go away!" Perry snapped, emphasizing the instruction by propelling his hand firmly against that part of the animal's anatomy where the underside of its tail met its back legs.

"It's all right," cut in Duffield. "I like cats. I've got two of my own." He bent down and picked up the animal. "But they're not as big as you are," he said, looking the cat straight in the face. Katie closed her eyes and turned her head away.

"This cat's really heavy," Duffield remarked to Perry in a conversational manner. "What do you feed her on?" It was an honest inquiry since Duffield was genuinely fond of cats.

"Only the best meat for my Katie," John Perry replied. "None of that canned cat food from the supermarket. She gets top quality steak. And she deserves it. She's the only female I can trust."

"That's a strange thing to say," observed Duffield. "What about your wife?"

"Her!" replied Perry with more than a hint of bitterness in his voice. "There's no way that I can trust her."

Asked what he meant by such a remark, Perry went on to explain. "That's what I meant by being vulnerable," he said. "It was only after I had married Arminda that I found out why she was in the hotel bar every night."

"Why?" Duffield wanted to know.

"Because she was a prostitute!" Perry shouted. "And she only married me so that she could escape from the poverty of the Philippines and have a better life over here."

Inspector Duffield studied Perry closely. What he saw was a man consumed by anger. It was a disturbing sight.

"And what did she do when she came here?" Perry stormed on. "Was she grateful for her new life? Was she happy to be out of the poverty and squalor that she had known? Was she prepared to settle down here with me? No, she wasn't. She wasn't at all."

163

"So what did she do?" Duffield inquired.

"She was a hooker," Perry replied. "She had always been a hooker. And old habits die hard."

"You mean that she continued to work as a prostitute?" the inspector suggested.

"No, not exactly," Perry replied. "You see, she didn't need the money any more. She got enough of that from me. So she did it for free."

"There were other men?" Duffield asked.

"Oh, yes," Perry agreed. "There were other men. Plenty of them. Of course, I never knew who they were. She managed to keep their identities secret. But I know that she had other men."

Duffield had already formed the impression that Perry was virtually paranoid about his wife. Perry was almost certain to be worried that he would be unable to hold Arminda's interest and attention for very long. The age difference between them would increase disproportionately with the passing years. She was young when he was middle-aged. She would still be young when he was old.

"But I fixed her," Perry went on. "She won't be a leech on me any more."

"What exactly do you mean?" Duffield wanted to know.

"I'm divorcing her," Perry replied. "It's in the final stages now. I shall soon be a free man."

It would have been a normal arrangement in a divorce for the family home to be sold, and the money divided equally between the couple. But Perry explained that he had been anxious to keep the house. He had lived in it for many years, long before he ever met Arminda. He was very fond of it and didn't want to lose it. So in order to avoid selling the home, he had agreed to give Arminda a cash settlement. Asked by Duffield how much he had to pay, Perry replied that the sum involved was £15,000 (about $25,000).

"That's a lot of money," Duffield observed. "Do you have it?"

"Of course I don't," Perry snapped back. "How would I come to have £15,000?"

"So what are you going to do?" the inspector wanted to know.

"I'm borrowing it from a bank," Perry replied. "It's going to cost me a fortune, but it'll be worth it just to be rid of her."

During the latter part of Duffield's conversation with Perry, Sergeant Hunter's insistently twitching nose had drawn him to the door at the far end of the living room. Neither man had noticed the sergeant as he made his way toward the door. Only Katie had seen him. And she was as anxious as Hunter to see the room that lay beyond.

Hunter reached out, took a hold of the door handle, and turned it. The door opened easily. It swung back noiselessly on well-oiled hinges when the sergeant gave it a push. Katie leapt forward and was through and into the room beyond in an instant. The pungent odor that had initially attracted the sergeant to the room grew in intensity as the door was opened. As Katie leapt forward, Hunter recoiled back. The smell was almost too much to bear. Hunter gave himself a moment to get used to it, gathered his composure, and followed the cat through the door.

The sergeant found himself standing in the kitchen of John Perry's home. It was a particularly untidy room. In the center was a large wooden table. Its scrubbed surface was cut and scratched by years of food preparation. A blood-stained knife lay on the table. There were further bloodstains on the tiled floor beneath and around the table. In one corner of the room, an electric drill, its cable still connected to the power supply, lay on the floor.

In the opposite corner were two large plastic bags. Sergeant Hunter went over to them and looked inside. Each bag contained a quantity of chopped-up meat. The sergeant could not make out what type of meat it was, but he knew one thing — it definitely didn't resemble anything that his wife had ever given him for his evening meal. And the smell from the meat was something else. Perhaps, Hunter thought to himself, it was some kind of pet food. Katie seemed to like it. She was purring loudly and doing her level best to get into one of the bags.

Hunter pushed the cat away and folded over the tops of the bags so that their contents were no longer visible. The odor subsided a little. Katie had retreated under the table, from where she watched the sergeant with suspicious and unfriendly eyes. Hunter walked slowly around the kitchen, looking closely at everything in the squalid little room. The more he looked, the more strongly the feeling came to him that the place was more like a slaughterhouse than a domestic kitchen.

He became aware of more bloodstains. It seemed that everywhere Hunter looked, there were spots and splashes of the substance. At the side of the sink was a large screwdriver. Its blade was stained by something that looked like blood. By the side of it was a hacksaw, also bloodstained. Nearby, on a small table, was a book. Hunter saw that it was a medical encyclopedia. It was opened to a page headed "The Skeletal System." The page bore a diagram of the structure of the human skeleton. The text informed the reader that there are 206 major bones in the human body, before going on to detail their biological and anatomical composition. Hunter shuddered. It was not his kind of reading material.

A sudden thought occurred to the sergeant. It was not a pleasant thought and he hoped that he was way off the mark. He looked again at the book and the picture of the reclining human skeleton. Then he looked at the bags on the other side of the room. Could it be that the strangely pungent meat that he had been unable to identify was human flesh?

Hunter made his way back into the living room. "I think you'd better take a look in the kitchen, Inspector," he said to Duffield, without any trace of emotion.

166

in his voice. It was the first time that he had spoken since the two officers arrived at the house.

Duffield broke off from his conversation with Perry, looked at Hunter, and then turned back to Perry. "Any objections?" he asked Arminda's husband.

"No, none at all," replied Perry.

Howard led the way back into the kitchen. Duffield and Perry followed behind. The sergeant pointed out various items — the knife, the screwdriver, the drill, the book, the bloodstained table and floor. He left the bags until last. "Take a look in there," he invited the inspector.

Duffield did as he was asked. He stared at the rotting meat for several minutes, though the time he spent sniffing at it was rather less. "What is this?" he finally asked Perry.

Perry seemed nervous. He bit his bottom lip and wrung his hands together. It seemed to Hunter that Perry was trying desperately to think of a plausible reply.

"It's just meat," Perry eventually responded. "I took it out of the freezer a few days ago, but I never got around to eating it. It started to go bad, so I put it in those bags. I was going to throw it out with the trash."

"Your cat seems quite fond of it," remarked Hunter.

"Yes, she is," replied Perry. Perry's nervousness had been heightened by a strange little laugh that had crept into his voice. "I told you she likes fresh meat, though I think that this is now a little past its best."

The two police officers were unimpressed by Perry's sudden outward demonstration of chatty friendliness. They were becoming more and more convinced that its purpose was to hide something sinister and evil.

"Do you mind if we take a look around the rest of the house?" Duffield suddenly asked.

The question seemed to trigger a total change in John Perry's attitude. Gone was the futile attempt at geniality. In its place was a defensive aggression that only served to enforce the officers' growing suspicions.

167

"Yes, I do mind!" stormed Perry. "You have no right to do that."

"Yes, we do," cut in Duffield. "If we have reason to believe that a crime has been committed here, we can get a search warrant and turn the place over." Perry became quiet. "Do you know where your wife is?" Duffield asked, calmly and deliberately.

"No," replied Perry.

At that, Duffield instructed Hunter to go to the car, radio in their findings to headquarters, and arrange for a search warrant to be issued. "I'll wait here with Mr. Perry," he concluded.

Ten minutes later, Hunter was back. "It's all in hand," he told Duffield. "Detectives are on their way. They'll bring the warrant with them. Forensics experts are also coming." Perry's face turned a delicate shade of white.

Before long, the little cottage was a hive of police activity. Forensics men, on their hands and knees, took samples of the tiny bloodstains on the kitchen floor. Detectives directed uniformed officers in a thorough search of the house. And in the middle of the living room, overseeing all that was going on, stood the tall, imposing figure of Detective-Superintendent John Cooke.

Cooke sniffed at the odor that pervaded the room. He looked thoughtful. Some officers thought that he looked unwell. "The smell that met us when we entered the room is something that will stay with me forever," he would later tell reporters.

"Check out the garage," Cooke told Duffield and Hunter. "Perry may have stashed her in there."

The inspector and the sergeant did as they were instructed. When they opened the garage door, the two officers noticed the same smell that was present in the house. But in the garage, it was stronger. They made their way over to what seemed to be the place from where the odor was emanating — two large, green wine fermenting bins. Duffield lifted the lid of one of the

168

bins and looked inside. Immediately, he dropped the lid on the floor and reeled back, clutching at his stomach.

Hunter's approach to the bin was more cautious than that of Duffield, but his reaction was the same.

The bin, like the bags in the kitchen, contained what appeared to be meat. Some of it had been cooked, while some had been overcooked and burned. Other pieces of the meat, darkish red in color and encased in white fat and gristle, were raw. All of the meat stank with an intensity that was totally overpowering.

Pathologist Sarah Brownhill would later identify human intestines, liver, and kidneys as being among the debris found in the bin.

It was when Duffield and Hunter staggered back into the living room to report on what they had found to Cooke that Perry decided there was no use in holding out any longer.

"All right, I killed her," he blurted out. "But I didn't mean it. I lost my temper. She was standing right here and taunting me about her boyfriends and I just lost my head. I put my hands round her throat, and before I knew what had happened, she was dead. I didn't mean to do it."

"And then you cut her up?" Cooke asked.

"I was in a panic," answered Perry. "I didn't know what to do. I thought that if I disposed of her body and said that she had gone away with a boyfriend, everything would be all right. Nobody would suspect anything."

"And where are her remains?" the detective wanted to know.

"All over the place," Perry replied calmly.

He was not exaggerating. Detectives found blood and other remains in the bathroom, two bedrooms, the living room, and the kitchen of the house, as well as outside in the garage and the garden, and in the trunk of Perry's car. The cooker was caked in the fatty residue that was the result of it having been used for cooking human flesh. Moreover, much of the flesh and several of the internal organs were missing. Apparently, Perry had fed them to the cat and Katie had feasted as she had never feasted before.

But none of the pieces of flesh and bone that the detectives did find were immediately identifiable as what they had been when Arminda was alive. Only two instantly recognizable items were recovered, part of a tooth, which was found in the bathroom, and Arminda's false teeth, which Perry had in his pocket.

Superintendent Cooke did not believe Perry's story about the killing being an accident, a provoked assault that had gone too far. He was convinced that it was cold-blooded, deliberate murder. But proving it was something else. So, with Perry held in custody to await trial, Cooke and his team set about finding the evidence that would put the accused man behind bars for life.

The pathologist faced the most daunting task. Arminda Perry had been cut up into so many pieces that establishing the cause of death was impossible. Her flesh had been diced and removed from the bones in order to make disposal of the body easier. But the pathologist kept at it, and, eventually, the results started to come.

Over many weeks, Dr. Brownhill was able to piece together a sufficient amount of the bone fragments to reconstruct most of the skull. She was then able to obtain a match with the dental plate recovered from Perry's pocket and state that the victim was definitely Arminda. Although she was still unable to establish the cause of death, she was pretty sure Arminda had not been strangled. Some of the bone fragments indicated that Arminda had been hit over the head. There was also evidence that she had been scalped.

Forensics experts were able to disprove John Perry's original story about Arminda having been killed during an argument in the living room. She had been killed in the bathroom. An attempt had been made to clean the room, but sufficient traces of blood, flesh, and hair re mained to establish beyond doubt that the woman was killed while taking a bath.

"Now we're getting somewhere," Cooke told his colleagues. "I've never before come across a case of a person taking a bath whilst indulging in a violent argument with someone standing over them."

Other evidence in support of the murder theory was turned up by detectives involved in the routine questioning of Perry's friends, relatives, and acquaintances.

Friends and relatives described Perry as a Jekyll-and-Hyde character. He could be warm and loving, but he also had a violent temper. Women with whom he had had a relationship reported that he had often beaten them up for no other reason than that they had prepared a meal that was not exactly to his liking.

One woman told detectives that Perry had tried to strangle her while they were sitting in a restaurant. It took six men to drag him off.

"He liked to beat me up," she told the detectives. "After a while, I got used to it. But what he enjoyed most was looking at the wounds he had caused me. After he had finished beating me, he would sit and stare at my injuries for hours. He was morbid like that."

But the most useful information came from colleagues at the factory where John Perry worked. Several of the men said that Perry was disgruntled at the thought of having to pay Arminda a divorce settlement of £15,000. He discussed at length news stories about the murder and dismemberment of a prostitute in the English city of Manchester. He followed the case with great interest.

Another colleague—a trained butcher—reported that Perry had questioned him about cutting up bodies. "How long would it take to butcher a carcass?" he had wanted to know. The man had replied that it would not take very long with good knives. Perry had also inquired about human flesh. What did it look like? What did it taste like? The man told Perry that he could not say for certain, but he believed that it was similar to pork. He also believed that it would be difficult to distinguish cooked human flesh from cooked pork. The man said that Perry seemed inordinately interested by this particular piece of information.

Prosecutor Alex Carlile, Q.C., detailed all of the evidence to the jury when Perry stood trial at Mold Crown Court in November 1991 on a charge of murdering Arminda. "There was a deliberate and violent attack with a weapon, and it was intended to kill Mrs. Perry," he said.

For the defense, John Rodgers, Q.C., maintained that the killing was as Perry had described, a spontaneous reaction to Arminda's constant taunting. He produced as evidence a letter written by Arminda to a man with whom she had had an affair. In the letter, Arminda described the man as "the best sex instructor I have ever had."

But the jury was not impressed. On Tuesday, November 26, 1991, John Perry was found guilty of murdering Arminda. The judge, Mr. Justice Scott Baker, sentenced him to life imprisonment.

Detective-Superintendent John Cooke was extremely pleased with the outcome. "Had we not followed up the initial missing-person inquiry so quickly, Perry might have gotten away with it," he told reporters. "There was evidence to show that he was planning to dispose of all of the remains the following day. He was going to take them to the place where he worked and dissolve them in a bath of acid."

As for Katie the cat, latest reports from the cats' home where she now resides indicate that she is more than happy with a simple diet of milk and meat — meat, that is, that comes from a supermarket can, and not from a plastic bag in the corner of the kitchen.

"BIZARRE LOVE BITE
MURDER CASE!"

by Lenore Nir

On Friday, October 19, 1984 Masha Efrati went to
pick up the mail from her post office box in the Jerusalem suburb of Bet Hakerem. It was a short, pleasant
morning walk among the attractive apartment buildings of Jerusalem stone.

She bumped into her closest friend May and they
stopped to chat. Both worked in the public health department of Jerusalem's municipality. Masha was a
dental nurse, May was a clerk.

Masha and May lived near each other. Masha's
apartment was above the parking area but at the rear
of the building on the ground level. She had lived on
this quiet one-way street for 14 years.

Masha was a 62-year-old widow who had no family
in Israel. She asked May to visit her on Saturday,
which happened to be a Succoth harvest holiday, as
well as the Sabbath.

May didn't know if she would have time. "I'll phone
you if I can come," May said. She didn't phone and
she never spoke to her friend again.

On October 21st—Sunday is a working day in
Israel—Masha didn't show up at the dental health
clinic where she'd been a nurse for 20 years.

The dentists and other nurses were sure Masha

would phone to explain her absence. They knew she took her work seriously and was very reliable. But there was no call from Masha.

That morning, May herself phoned Masha's apartment, but there was no answer. She decided to stop by on her way home from work.

When May reached Masha's apartment around three o'clock, all the shutters were tightly closed. This was not unusual. Masha was afraid of burglars because she lived at ground level and she kept everything closed. Two strong locks were also on the door.

May rang the bell. No answer. She kept ringing. Where could Masha be? Gingerly, she touched the door handle and, to her great surprise, it opened at once. This was really unusual, as Masha always locked her door.

May was afraid to enter the apartment alone so she asked a neighbor to go with her. He agreed and the two of them carefully opened the door.

It was dark inside. Only a speck of light came from the bedroom where the shutters were open slightly, just enough to reveal a body on the floor.

The neighbor turned on a light and with mounting horror they walked closer. Masha lay dead, beaten and stabbed in a large pool of blood. Her purse was nearby.

They hurried to phone the police as this was clearly murder. When it was discovered that Masha was a very active member of the Communist party in Israel, two of the most senior officers in the Jerusalem area arrived on the scene.

Southern District C.O. Commander Avraham Turgaman and Jerusalem Police Deputy Commander A. Alvadas decided to place an experienced detective. Inspector Solomon Amir, in charge of the investigation team. Deputy Inspector Danny Ben-Menachen would assist.

The first thing that impressed Amir was how sparkling-clean the apartment was. The furniture was polished to a shine. He had rarely seen such a spotlessly clean apartment.

It was clear that robbery wasn't a motive. Nothing had been touched. Everything was neat. Masha's purse was in her bedroom. No money had been taken.

There were also no signs of breaking and entering. Masha had opened the door to whoever killed her. It had to be someone she knew.

Amir brought criminal identification experts to search for evidence in the apartment. He sent the body to pathologists at the forensic lab to discover the exact time and cause of death.

In the meantime, he'd have to find out what sort of a person Masha Efrati was in order to find out who could have killed her. He would question friends, neighbors, people she worked with.

He learned that Masha was born to a Christian family in Russia who lived on a kolhoz, a collective farm, south of Moscow. Masha married before she was 20 to a man who was also a Christian.

When Germany invaded Russia in 1941, Masha and her husband fought with the partisans. Her husband was killed. Masha, who was pregnant at the time, lost the baby. Doctors told her she'd never again be able to give birth.

After the war Masha fell in love with a Jewish doctor who wanted to move to Israel. She married him, converted to Judaism and came to Israel. She kept close to her family on the kolhoz.

Her husband wanted children, which Masha couldn't give him. A few years later, they divorced. They lost touch and Masha made a new life for herself. A lively, round-faced woman with short black hair, she soon married again — a businessman named Efrati.

This marriage was a happy one, but unfortunately her husband died. He left her in comfortable circumstances with one apartment in pretty Bet Hakerem and another in a town called Natanya on the Mediterranean coast.

Masha was all alone, however. Her family in Russia begged her to return, but she stayed. On long holiday weekends when Israeli families were together, she was very lonely.

Masha had been an ardent Communist in Russia and now became active in Rokach, the Israeli Communist party. She attended the meetings of the Jerusalem branch.

Many leading Communists, among them the parliamentary leader who was head of the party, came to her house. She visited Russia several times with other party members and saw her family again.

She was still lonely, however. And now she took a step that would change her life. She placed an ad in a lonely hearts column. It wasn't romance she was seeking, but rather someone to share her life.

A number of men answered the ad. One was a 66-year-old welder from Turkey named Shmuel Brooks who lived in a suburb of Haifa, a city about 95 miles away.

Inspector Amir found Brooks' name among the 80 names in Masha's small address book next to the telephone. He and his team called every single person in that book.

Before he contacted Brooks, two men came to see Amir — Eliezer Ramat, chairman of the Jerusalem branch of Rokach, and Haim Dunsky, another Communist and old friend of Masha's. They offered to arrange her burial. If Rokach didn't do it, they said, who would?

Amir asked these men, both of them prominent local citizens, to give him the Jerusalem Rokach membership list. He thought this murder might have been politically motivated.

"That's confidential information," Ramat said.

"If you don't give me that list, I'll have to arrest you," warned Amir.

Ramat contacted the head of the Rokach Party, who

told him to stick to his guns and not surrender the list. When Amir heard this, he arrested Ramat.

Although nothing linked the official to Masha's murder, Inspector Amir informed the press that a suspect connected to Rokach was being held. The Communist party appointed Felicia Langer to defend Ramat.

Langer, a tall, elegant attorney and a leading figure in civil rights cases, quickly arranged his release.

Police now had the report of the pathologist, Dr. Bezalel Bloch, who said Masha died of loss of blood. Bloch was unable to fix the exact time of death, but he said it was between Friday night and Sunday morning. The report also indicated the victim had been hit on the head with a blunt instrument and stabbed 17 times. Her assailant also left five teethmarks on her back and saliva on her blouse.

Masha had put up a strong fight.

Her friends, Anna and Haim Dunsky, told Amir that Masha was a tough fighter. She knew karate and had been a partisan. It would not be easy to overcome her, even though she was 62.

Criminal investigation experts had a difficult time finding fingerprints in the immaculate kitchen and elsewhere. Finally, after much effort, 13 prints were found in the kitchen. Most were hers; three on the wall belonged to someone else.

Neighbors told police that Masha was an obsessive housekeeper who went around the flat with a towel in her hand. She opened drawers and cupboards with a cloth in her hand, so as not to leave prints.

She often had visitors; she was a good hostess. But as soon as people left, she wiped everything they'd touched. Neurotic about cleanliness, she made guests walk in stockings if their shoes were dirty.

Masha never let dust gather. Everyone told police that once a week she did a thorough housecleaning using strong cleaners and DDT. Once a month, she hosed down the tile walls in the kitchen and bathroom.

Neighbors told police that many men, some of them Arabs, others political friends, or the men who answered her ads in the personal column, visited Masha in the evenings.

Masha was a good-hearted woman who fed many neighborhood cats. She also fussed over the children who lived in the building, offering them sweets or little gifts.

Politics was close to Masha's heart. She was always ready to argue with people she worked with about government policies.

"If you don't like it here, why don't you go back to Russia?" asked the other nurses, who didn't like her much. They knew she wasn't born Jewish and had no real ties to Israel.

"I won't give you that pleasure," she would retort. But it wasn't true. For years, her family had been asking her to return and even found an apartment for her. Now she was ready to go.

Masha planned to retire and return to Russia, but the clinic didn't want to give her a pension. She postponed leaving until she could get the money she was owed. She was a fighter.

She had already begun to fill her tidy closets with presents she would take to her relatives. Now she would never distribute these gifts.

At first, Inspector Amir concentrated inquiries on the political level. He thought she was killed because of her Communist views, but May and several Jerusalem Communists heard her speak of a man named Shmuel, who'd threatened her.

Shmuel was one of the men who had answered Masha's ad nearly a year before. A relationship had developed and they were lovers. They would spend weekends together, either at his place or hers.

May knew the affair had broken up in February. Masha told Dunsky and other party members that Shmuel wanted to marry her and threatened her when

178

she refused. She never asked anyone for help, however, nor did she inform the police.

Shmuel was in her address book. The telephone company gave Inspector Amir his full name and address. The sleuth went to Kirat Yam near Haifa to call on the man, whose last name was Brooks.

The small, ground-level row-house was locked and the shutters were closed. The neighbors said the place had been closed on Friday and Saturday, too. He had only returned on Sunday.

Inspector Amir decided to call on Brooks when he was sure he'd be home. He arrived with Deputy Inspector Danny Ben-Menachem at two o'clock in the morning and knocked loudly.

Brooks shouted: "Who's there?" He lived alone. He was a widower who had remarried, but his wife later divorced him. They had quarreled bitterly and were on very bad terms.

"Police. We've come about Masha," Amir explained.

When Brooks opened the door, he said something very strange, "When did she commit suicide?" he asked.

Nobody had mentioned that she was dead.

Brooks, a small wiry man with gray hair, stated that he knew Masha but hadn't seen her for eight months. He said they weren't in contact any more and that he had been at home all weekend.

Brooks had worked as a welder for many years. About 15 years earlier, he'd been in an accident and now lived on his pension. His only family was a married son and one grandchild.

The police officers took him to Jerusalem to fingerprint and question him at the Russian Compound, Jerusalem's detention center. While Amir was waiting for the tests to begin, the police received an urgent call concerning a terrorist bomb in a supermarket.

It was a big attack with many victims and Inspector Amir had no time to deal with Brooks. He was released and told to return next week. When things calmed down, Amir discovered that the fingerprints on Masha's wall belonged to Shmuel Brooks.

Now Brooks was arrested and brought to Jerusalem. He claimed that the prints were left the last time he visited Masha, eight months before.

Amir found this hard to believe. He knew how thoroughly Masha scrubbed her apartment. Brooks also insisted he was in Haifa that weekend, although neighbors told Amir they hadn't seen him and all the windows of his little apartment were closed.

Israeli police have the right to take fingerprints, but can't take blood samples or teeth impressions. Since saliva can be identified by blood type, Amir wanted a blood sample and bite prints, too, but Brooks refused.

While Brooks was in detention in Jerusalem, his married son approached the well-known Jerusalem criminal lawyer Yair Golan to take the case. A handsome blue-eyed man in his late 30s, Golan had an excellent reputation.

Golan urged his client to take these tests to prove his innocence. Brooks wouldn't hear of it. He refused completely.

Police had no motive for the crime and hadn't found a weapon, either. The fingerprints at the crime scene and testimony about Masha's cleanliness were enough for Amir to build his case.

Amir still needed the teethprints. By now he found out that Brooks' upper teeth were false and he obtained a court order to take these from him.

He sent them to Dr. Yona Sela of the Hebrew University dental school. Dr. Sela, a dentistry lecturer, has identified hundreds of war and accident victims by their teeth.

He made a cast of the teeth and compared the bite marks with those on Masha's back. In his opinion, they were identical, yet he still wanted to get the prints from Brooks' lower teeth.

Sela said that if he had a piece of yellow cheese that

180

Brooks had bitten into, it would be sufficient. But how could Amir get this? The prisoners ate by themselves.

Amir discussed the matter with his senior officers, Turgaman and Alvadas. Together they came up with an unusual plan. It would begin with the police being nice to Brooks.

Guards at the Russian Compound would invite him to eat with them one morning, a regular Israeli breakfast with fresh bread, eggs, tomatoes, cucumbers, various cheeses and coffee.

This was better than the breakfast prisoners usually had, so Brooks was delighted to accept. When Brooks bit into the cheese a guard would grab it from his mouth and rush it over to Dr. Sela.

The men laughed and joked with Brooks as he sat down to eat. He filled his plate with everything on the table, then unsuspectingly bit into a triangle of cheese.

The policeman who had been joking with him a minute earlier reached over at once. With one hand he held Brooks' jaw open and with the other he extracted the cheese and hurried to Dr. Sela.

From the marks on the cheese, Sela attempted to make a model of Brooks' lower teeth. This didn't work out too well. Nevertheless, Seal was certain that only upper-teeth marks were on the body.

As the police gathered evidence, Brooks, who still refused to cooperate, asked to talk with Deputy Commander Alvadas, the senior officer for the Jerusalem district.

"What do you want?" asked Alvadas.

"I want to offer a reward of $20,000 to anyone who can help me find the murderer," he answered.

"I think we already have him," Alvadas answered. Brooks said nothing, and the matter was dropped.

The fingerprints and teethprints were sufficient evidence even without a motive, murder weapon or blood sample. The district attorney's office prepared to bring charges against him.

In November 1984, there were several hearings to extend Brooks' arrest. Finally, on December 4, 1984, Counselor Orit Son charged Shmuel Brooks with the murder of Masha Efrati. She wanted Brooks held until the trial ended, but defense counsel protested.

On December 12th, there was to be a final hearing on this matter. But Brooks never made it to the courthouse. The night before, he suddenly had terrible pains. A prison doctor examined him and sent him to the Hadassah Hospital emergency room.

He was taken in handcuffs to the hospital, where doctors diagnosed a prostate problem and prepared to operate immediately. Naturally, it was necessary to take blood samples. Brooks couldn't object. His illness was a lucky break for Amir.

A nurse agreed to hand over a few drops of blood to Amir. He found that Brooks' blood type, matched that of the saliva left on Masha. This strengthened the case for the prosecution.

After Brooks recovered from surgery, he again appeared before a Jerusalem judge. This time, Golan didn't object when prosecuting attorneys Shimon Dolan and Orit Son asked that Brooks be held till the end of the trial. The judge agreed.

In the spring of 1985, the trial opened at Jerusalem District Court before three judges—Eliahu Noam (president of the court), Zvi Tal and Shalom Berner.

This was to be a very long trial with a great many sessions. Over 15 months would pass before the judges reached a verdict. There are no jury trials in Israel and the sentence for murder is always life imprisonment.

Defense Attorney Golan knew he had a difficult case. Police now had Brooks' fingerprints at the scene of the crime, his blood type matched the saliva on Masha's back, and an expert claimed that his teethmarks were on the victim's back and shoulders.

Golan would have to bring experts to refute this evidence. He began looking for the expert in forensic dentistry. This was a man named Dr. E.J. Simms of England.

Golan wrote to Simms to find out if he would come to Israel to testify for the defense. He sent copies of the relevant photos and Dr. Sela's opinion. The fee would not be high, since Brooks and his son had little money.

Simms agreed. He had already appeared in many important cases, including the famous dingo case in Australia that was made into a movie. He lectured to British police and had a worldwide reputation.

This would be Sela's first appearance in a criminal case and there was no Israeli precedent for this type of dental evidence, especially as regards false teeth.

Even in the United States, England and Australia, where forensic dentistry has been crucial in trials, there's no consensus on false teeth among the experts.

The police pathologist, Dr. Ben Bloch, described the cause of death and condition of the body when discovered. He couldn't determine the exact hour; some time between Friday evening and Sunday morning was all he could say.

Golan seized upon this point in cross-questioning, trying to establish the time of death as Sunday morning. Brooks was seen in Haifa on Sunday morning. He had an alibi but no one had seen him on Friday evening or Saturday.

In fact, neighbors testified that they knocked on his door on Saturday and there was no answer. Others said the shutters were closed the entire day, a sure sign he wasn't at home.

From time to time, Brooks screamed "liar!" hysterically when witnesses testified, and he eventually had to be silenced by the court. It was not the sort of behavior that made a favorable impression.

Staff Sergeant Major, Albert Shmia, a fingerprint expert, took the stand to describe his findings. He found two prints on one of the kitchen wall tiles and one on the sliding door to the victim's storeroom. No other prints were found.

Shmia found them after he'd dusted all the surfaces leading from the kitchen to the bedroom with a dark aluminum spray and then cleaned the area with a small brush.

"When prints are old," he told the court, "the surface has to be brushed several times. These prints were seen after the tiles were just brushed once."

Only these prints showed. The only other fingerprints in the apartment belonged to Masha. The tile and the door were then taken to the police lab.

When these prints were found to match Shmuel's, the defendant claimed the prints were eight months old. Shmia insisted they were new. To be absolutely certain, he made a comparison control test.

A policeman who had extremely clear prints touched the tile and the sliding door. When these were examined a few days later, the prints were already fainter than the prints Shmia had found. After several weeks, these prints had almost disappeared.

The defense attorney didn't accept this testimony. He called an expert of his own, Avraham Levi, a former policeman who worked in fingerprint identification for 30 years.

Levi claimed it isn't possible to fix the exact age of a fingerprint if it's more than two days old. Moreover, he argued, the comparison test wasn't accurate because climatic conditions weren't the same.

Under optimum conditions, a print can stay up to a year. In a kitchen, Levi noted, steam from cooking can keep prints fresh a long time, whereas the sun will dry prints after a few days. Attorney Golan said the police test therefore had no scientific basis.

But there were other factors to consider. Many witnesses testifying for the prosecutor spoke of Masha's obsession for cleanliness, emphasizing the unlikelihood that Masha hadn't hosed down this tile wall for eight months.

The location of the prints also played into the hands of the prosecution. They were situated at chest height, just above the chair where Masha had been sitting at the time of her death. Shmuel, Dolan claimed, placed his left hand against the wall as he struck her with his right. It was as if the murderer had left his calling card.

Next, the prosecution turned to the bite marks, calling Professor Sela to the stand. This was the first time an expert in forensic dentistry would testify in a criminal trial in Israel.

The professor came armed with a shelfful of books and with a slide projector. He spoke so smoothly, it almost seemed as if he had rehearsed what he was going to say. He showed full command of the subject.

Describing the uniqueness of a person's bite, Sela explained how the marks from upper teeth differ from those of the lower. He quoted from the textbooks he had brought with him.

A person's upper plate has two large incisors and four smaller teeth, two on each side, which bite the food. Lower teeth have four smaller teeth in front, and larger teeth on each side.

Using the courtroom wall as a screen, he showed slides of the marks on Masha's back. He compared them with photos of bite marks made by Shmuel's teeth, both his own and the false teeth.

Sela confirmed he made a cast of Shmuel's upper teeth based on the false teeth he had obtained through a court order. In his lab at Hadassah Hospital he'd filmed marks made by these teeth on human flesh and showed this film in court.

He covered the cast with cloth and then with special paper and photographed the marks. He compared these with the bite marks on Masha's back. This film showed that the marks were alike.

Sela's conclusion was that the bite marks had come from Shmuel's false upper teeth. At present, testimony concerning false teeth is a new field and the ex-

185

perts don't always agree.

This detailed testimony took several days. When Golan cross-questioned him, trying to find flaws in his argument, Sela replied in a confident manner.

The defense attorney called his own expert to the stand, Dr. E.G. Simms of London, England. A Hebrew-English translator stood by to translate all the questions and replies, since Hebrew is the language of the court.

Unlike Dr. Sela, who was testifying for the first time, Simms had often appeared in criminal trials. His version was in complete contrast to Dr. Sela's.

He claimed that the bite marks on Masha's back were made with the lower teeth, not uppers, and Brooks had refused to give his lower-teeth prints. Simms also said it was impossible to determine whose teeth had made these bite marks.

The judges listened to the two experts whose opinions were so different and had to decide which expert they would put their trust in. This decision would be crucial for Brooks.

An unexpected witness for the prosecution was Shmuel's ex-wife, whom he had divorced a few years earlier.

She told the court that her ex-husband was lying when he claimed he broke up with Masha eight months before. She said she had seen Masha and Shmuel on the street in Haifa only two months before the murder.

She declared that Shmuel was a habitual skirt-chaser. He had been throughout their marriage and continued to be even though he was in his 60s.

During her testimony, Shmuel shouted aloud that she was lying. Knowing this behavior made an unfavorable impression on the court, Defense Attorney Golan urged him to calm down and restrain himself. Brooks, it seemed, was unable to do so.

Nothing could have been more detrimental to his case. By shouting out angrily, Brooks showed himself to be a person who was easily inflamed. In answer to a question when testifying, he spoke of how a woman can "drive a man out of his mind."

Was he referring to Masha Efrati? Was this what had happened? Perhaps he'd gone to Jerusalem to talk to her and when they quarreled he suddenly struck her and stabbed her. Or was this premeditated?

The court would never know, since Brooks never confessed. The blunt instrument and knife were never found. On circumstantial evidence alone, the judges would have to reach their decision.

Their decision would also be influenced by his behavior, his refusal to give blood samples and teeth-prints, and his outbursts. Also by the conflicting testimony of forensic dental experts who agreed on one point: teeth-prints can be a basis for conviction.

In their summary, Prosecutors Dolan and Son cited eight cases in the United States in which a murder conviction rested on evidence of the killer's teeth-prints. Golan agreed—there had been cases, he said. But there wasn't enough scientific data to base a definite identification on teeth-marks in this case.

Golan claimed there were errors in Dr. Sela's methods of work, but even if there weren't, it was impossible to say for certain that no other person would have the same teeth-prints.

Dr. Sela had stated this was a minority opinion. Experts now believed that prints from only four or five teeth were enough to make a positive identification of an individual.

On July 8, 1986, the three judges reached their verdict. They found the defendant guilty on the basis of circumstantial evidence alone.

They described in detail the reasons for this decision.

Concerning the fingerprints (sufficient evidence to convict a man), the judges accepted the prosecution's claim that these were new prints. They based their opinion on Sergeant Shmia's testimony and on the reports by witnesses of Masha's fastidiousness.

Furthermore, the location of the fingerprints, just above where Masha was sitting, and the signs of blood supported the conclusion that the struggle started in the kitchen and ended in the bedroom, said Judge Noam, who read out the decision.

Other evidence supporting the prosecution's claim included the lies told by the accused, which were contradicted by his ex-wife's testimony and Brook's refusal to give teethprints and blood samples.

In tendering their verdict, the judges referred at length to the forensic dental testimony. Regarding the conflicting testimony of the experts, the judges ruled that it's clear to the eye that the marks on Masha's back were the marks from Brooks' upper teeth.

However, this alone didn't secure Brooks' fate. "To be careful," wrote the judges, "we wouldn't rely on this identification alone as clear evidence for a conviction, but this lesser identification definitely joins the other proof, such as the fingerprints at the scene of the crime."

The judges added that they accepted Defense Attorney Golan's claim that there must be stricter rules on deciding what criteria are acceptable for teeth characteristics.

The judges sentenced Brooks to life imprisonment. In Israel, this is always the sentence for a murder conviction. Shmuel Brooks heard the sentence in silence.

Brooks decided to appeal his case, claiming the fingerprints were eight months old and the teethprints weren't acceptable as evidence. Golan represented him again.

In August 1989, three Supreme Court justices handed down their verdict, rejecting Shmuel's claim and accepting in principle the findings of the district court. As for the acceptability of teethmarks as evidence, their answer was in the affirmative.

Because of Masha's housecleaning, Brooks was convicted by his fingerprints, and it's ironic that the teethmarks on the back of a woman who was a dental nurse also led to his conviction.

EDITOR'S NOTE:
May is not the real name, of the person so named in the foregoing story. A fictitious name has been used in order to comply with Israeli police regulations.

"CORPSE LOVER'S UNHOLY RITUAL"

by Alva Busch

The fields of corn were standing tall, their browned tassels the only break in the green walls that lined the county roadway. The warm summer sun rose lazily over the farmland and reflected off the windshields of the vehicles parked on the streets in town. School vacation in Beckemeyer, Illinois, was in its sixth week, allowing youngsters time to visit friends and relatives during the weekday.

Sandra Shelton's relative returned home after spending some time with other family members. Upon entering the residence, the relative became aware of the strong odor of natural gas. When she walked into the kitchen, she found that gas was emanating from the kitchen stove. The knobs on the stove were in the "on" position. The girl quickly turned the knobs counterclockwise to shut the gas off. Still unaware of what had occurred in the residence, the girl walked into the living room, where she noticed candles burning in glass holders on the wall. On the floor of the bedroom, in the doorway to the living room, she could make out a figure of someone under a blanket. She bent down and lifted up the blanket. For a moment the girl stood frozen with fright and choking back tears. The corner of the blanket fell from her hand. She ran to the front door screaming for another family member, who met the tearful girl on the front porch.

The family member instructed the girl to go across the street and have a neighbor call an ambulance and the police. In the doorway of the bedroom the lifeless body of Sandra Shelton lay on the floor. She had been brutally murdered.

Medical personnel from the Beckemeyer Fire Department responded to the Shelton residence, as did the East Clinton Ambulance Service. Unfortunately, their quick response time was in vain. The victim had been dead for several hours.

The Beckemeyer fire chief entered the Shelton residence through the front door. The heavy odor of natural gas still permeated the kitchen and living room. The fireman quickly noticed the two candles burning on the south wall of the living room. Chancing the possibility of being caught in an explosion, he entered the living room and extinguished the candles. Firemen placed large exhaust fans in the doorway, to draw the gas from the interior of the residence.

Sheriff Don Krohn and Captain Jim Hummert of the Clinton County Sheriff's Department arrived at the murder scene. They walked into the living room that opened into the bedroom where the body lay. It was 11:15 a.m., Wednesday, July 12, 1989. After viewing the deceased, Sheriff Krohn turned to Captain Hummert and said, "Have the dispatcher call the crime lab for a crime scene man to process this scene. I'll wait here and secure the crime scene until he gets here. You take a couple deputies and do a neighborhood canvass."

Captain Hummert summoned the additional manpower and began the neighborhood canvass.

The Clinton County Sheriff's Department had received a strange call earlier that morning, around 8:30 a.m., from the Christian County Sheriff's Department, who had received the information from the

Pana Police Department. Captain Hummert contacted the police dispatcher at Pana. He soon learned that an unidentified male caller had telephoned the Pana Police Department around 8:25 a.m. to report that a woman had been murdered in Beckemeyer, adding that she drove a Chrysler Cordoba.

Captain Hummert and Clinton County Deputy Roger Deteman drove to the town of Beckemeyer, Illinois, which is located in Clinton County. Beckemeyer is a small farm town located about 60 miles east of St. Louis, Missouri, on the Illinois side of the Mississippi River. There had never been a murder in Beckemeyer, but the detectives were determined to check out the area and look for the Cordoba.

They arrived in Beckemeyer around 9:00 a.m. The town looked quiet and peaceful that sunny Wednesday morning. They drove up and down the town streets. After an hour of searching for the car described by the mystery caller, the detectives returned to the sheriff's department to attempt a license plate check for the car. Within the hour, Sandra Shelton's body was discovered in her home by her relative.

At 12:35 p.m., Inspector Alva W. Busch of the Illinois State Police, Bureau of Crime Scene Services, arrived at the Shelton residence. The hot noon sun had already pushed the temperature up into the high 80s as Inspector Busch walked onto the front porch of the two-story residence. Sheriff Krohn met the crime scene specialist there. He began to brief the investigator on the case. Krohn told Busch about the mystery phone call received by the Pana Police Department.

"The caller described the car as a Cordoba, and that is the type car Sandra Shelton owns. It's parked around back," stated Sheriff Krohn.

"Pana! That's way up north of here, at least sixty miles," exclaimed Busch.

"We had men out in this area earlier this morning, but we didn't locate the Cordoba," advised Krohn as the two men walked to the back of the Shelton resi-

192

dence, where the victim's car was parked under the carport.

"These six-foot hedges that encompass the house on the street side would make it hard to spot her car," reflected Inspector Busch, who was now checking the exterior of the house for any signs of forced entry.

Busch took charge of the crime scene. He told the sheriff that it would take several hours for the initial phase of the scene processing before the body could be removed. Busch photographed the exterior and interior of the crime scene. He detected no signs of forced entry into the house, which suggested that the victim may have allowed her killer inside the house. The victim's black-over-silver 1975 Chrysler Cordoba was parked under the carport at the rear of the residence. Busch peered through the open window on the passenger side of the vehicle. The keys to the car were still in the ignition. The sliding glass doors at the rear of the residence were unlocked. Taking notes as he examined the exterior of the residence, Inspector Busch now entered the house to begin processing the interior.

The body of the 32-year-old woman lay in the doorway between the bedroom and living room. The blanket now covered the nude body only from the waist down. A light green shirt was tied around the victim's neck. She had sustained multiple stab wounds to the left side of her chest. Several linear injuries were present across her abdomen. During the examination, Busch spoke with Sheriff Krohn.

"This guy is a bad actor," stated Busch, referring to the killer. "He will probably kill again if we don't catch him soon. He took his time while he was here. Most of this was done after her death."

"What do you think went on here?" inquired Krohn. "There isn't anything that would make you think there was a fight."

Busch said, "She has shoestrings tied to her right wrist, with both ends of the shoestrings tied together. Her hands were probably tied together at some time.

Judging from the bruises on her face, I would think she was probably rendered unconscious before she was strangled. These superficial incisions across her abdomen were done after death," reflected Busch.

"Why is her skin so shiny?" asked the sheriff.

"I don't know," replied Busch as he knelt next to the body to examine it closer. "Damn! It's oil. Someone poured oil all over her. It's all over the carpet around her body. Now I have it all over the knees of my pants," Busch said.

"There is an empty bottle of vegetable oil on the kitchen floor. It may have the guy's prints on it," remarked Krohn.

"Look at this, there are little pinkish patches on the surface of her skin. It's candle wax droplets. The bastard poured candle wax on her after he killed her," stated Busch in disgust.

The two men found a red candle lying on the living room floor next to the woman's foot. Her clothing, lying inside out on the living room floor suggested that someone had stripped her. Her bra was ripped in half. The physical evidence was collected by the crime scene expert. Busch was confident that he would be able to obtain a shoe print of the killer on the kitchen floor. Deductive reasoning by the investigator revealed that the killer had to cross the kitchen floor at least four times — once during entry into the house, the second time to obtain the vegetable oil from the kitchen cabinet, the third time to deposit the empty container after pouring the oil on the victim, and the final time to turn on the gas at the kitchen stove after he lit the candles on the north wall of the living room.

The total surface of the kitchen floor was processed using a fingerprint brush. This procedure took Busch several hours to complete, but the end result netted him several latent shoe patterns and a bonus clue.

Meanwhile, Captain Hummert had developed vital information about Sandra Shelton's activities prior to her death. The divorced widow had stopped at a local bar in Carlyle, Illinois, only 10 miles east of Beckemeyer. She had entered the establishment just before midnight on Tuesday and sat at the bar. She ordered a beer. A few minutes later a stranger walked into the bar, sat down beside her, and asked the bartender for a beer. The young stranger began to talk with Sandra. The bartender overheard him ask the woman customer, "What's there to do in Carlyle?" Thirty minutes later, the two left the bar together.

Another witness was located who put the stranger and Sandra in a bar in Beckemeyer at 12:45 a.m. on Wednesday. There, they apparently sat at a table in the corner of the room. Sandra asked the barmaid for an ink marker to write on the wall, a custom most townspeople followed when drinking there. She wrote on the section of paneling, "Sandy Shelton, 10-29-56." The stranger took the inked marker and wrote on the paneling, "Rockin Dobbs was here." The barmaid told investigators that when Sandy went to the restroom, the stranger walked back to the wall and wrote, "Bob Todd Rockin Dobbs was here July 11, 1989." After Sandy returned from the restroom, the stranger purchased a six pack of beer. Sandy and the husky man then left the tavern.

Special Agents Craig Koehler and Charles Brueggemann from the Division of Criminal Investigation (DCI) of the Illinois State Police arrived in Beckemeyer to assist Sheriff Krohn in the case. They made contact with the sheriff at the Shelton residence.

"We came over to see if you needed any help on this," said Agent Koehler after greeting Krohn and Busch.

"I'm going to be tied up here, and this puts a strain on our manpower. I could use the help," replied the sheriff.

"What do you want us to do?" asked Agent Brueggemann.

"Get with Captain Hummert. He has some leads on a stranger who was seen with the victim early this morning," Krohn informed him.

The body of Sandra Shelton was removed from the crime scene. Local newspaper reporters and photographers had gathered outside the residence to get a story and photographs on the case. Sheriff Krohn was swamped with reporters when he walked outside the residence. He had been a lawman a long time. He knew that if the media knew everything about the case, it could weaken the investigation. Therefore, he did not tell the reporters about the brutal death of the woman.

"It appears to be a homicide, and the case is being investigated," was all Sheriff Krohn would tell the reporters. Reporters then scurried off to interview neighbors and relatives of the slain woman.

Sheriff Krohn rejoined Inspector Busch inside the crime scene.

"Well, how did it go with the news media?" teased Busch.

"They weren't too happy with my news release," replied the sheriff, a smile on his face.

"They'll get over it. Too much information printed in newspapers has ruined other cases in the past," replied the inspector.

"What do you have here?" asked Sheriff Krohn as he looked at the now-blackened kitchen floor.

"I dusted the entire kitchen floor and found several footwear patterns. There is one pattern that goes in front of the stove and the kitchen cabinet and goes to and from the entranceway out the back door. I think that one, with the small diamond and circle design, is the killer's shoe print. We also have a barefoot impression in front of the kitchen cabinet where the vegetable oil container was kept," advised Busch.

The investigator continued to collect physical evidence at the scene. At 6:00 p.m., the crime scene was secured and the investigators attended the autopsy of the victim. The cause of death was strangulation. By 9:30 p.m., the investigative team regrouped at the

Clinton County Sheriff's Department for a briefing. By this time, the probers had learned the name of the stranger seen with Sandra Shelton. His name was Robert Todd. He was a construction worker who had moved to Carlyle several weeks earlier.

Lawmen tracked down the location of Todd's apartment. When they arrived at the apartment complex, he was not home. Two witnesses at the apartment complex told investigators that during the early morning hours they observed a beat-up-looking car enter the parking lot and jump the curb. The car pulled to a halt on the sidewalk outside the building, and a man ran from the vehicle into the apartment. A short time later, the man was seen making several trips from the apartment to the car, carrying items to the car. The witnesses stated that the man then raced off at high speed.

The team of sleuths returned to the Clinton County Sheriff's Department and contacted Clinton County State's Attorney Dennis Middendorff. Middendorff met with the investigators at the sheriff's department and was apprised of the situation. The detectives wanted a search warrant for Robert Todd's apartment. Middendorff quizzed the lawmen on what items of evidence they were searching for.

"The killer poured candle wax on the victim after he killed her," replied Busch to Middendorff's question. "I know he didn't wash up at the crime scene. I checked the bathroom and kitchen there. If he washed up at his apartment, there will probably be wax droplets or oily clothing there. We may be looking at a man who is into necrophilia."

Captain Hummert prepared the complaint for the search warrant from the information the investigators had uncovered. A search warrant for Todd's apartment was issued. The lawmen then divided their manpower into two teams. The first team would execute the search warrant while the second team would follow leads on locating their prime suspect.

197

At 10:30 p.m., team one, composed of Krohn, Hummert, Busch, and Carlyle City Officer Kent Newkirk, arrived at Todd's apartment. On the floor of the apartment lay a white mesh shirt with blue lettering. It matched the description of the shirt worn by the stranger who witnesses in the bar had seen leaving with the victim. Busch checked the bathtub. In the bottom of the tub lay wax droplets. Additional wax droplets were observed by the investigators on a bar of soap.

The second team of investigators consisted of Clinton County Deputies Roger Detterman, Troy Spaul, Mike Dall, Mike Burton, and Mike Kreke, Carlyle Police Chief Paul Spaur, and DCI Agents Koehler and Brueggemann. Their task was to locate Robert Todd. Agent Brueggemann was selected as leads coordinator. He would have the nonglamorous but vital job of assigning leads to the other members of the team to investigate. Brueggemann suggested that all police departments north of Clinton County be contacted to determine if Todd had any prior arrests. They reasoned that if he had been arrested before, there might be addresses listed and possibly the license plate number of his car.

Investigators took to the street knocking on doors to interview witnesses. They had worked nonstop since the investigation had begun. With every tick of the clock, the sleuths were getting closer to tracking down the brutal killer.

During the early-morning hours, probers contacted the utility company at which Todd had applied for service for his apartment. That interview netted probers the address of the suspect's girlfriend's residence, which was located 100 miles north of Beckemeyer.

The lawmen were able to obtain a license plate number for Todd's car. Additional information uncovered by the probers revealed that Todd had relatives who lived near Decatur, Illinois. Agent Brueggemann, through the DCI higher command, contacted Zone

Commander George Nuxoll in Zone 10, near Decatur. Brueggemann requested assistance from the commander to check for Todd's vehicle at the two addresses they had obtained in the Decatur area.

While Brueggemann worked with Commander Nuxoll, the first team of investigators that had executed the search warrant at Todd's apartment in Carlyle returned to the sheriff's department. The discovery of the wax droplets and white mesh shirt was relayed to Clinton County State's Attorney Dennis Middendorff, who had been burning the midnight oil waiting for the outcome of the search warrant. At 1:30 a.m., on the morning of July 13, 1989, Agent Koehler and Captain Hummert received an arrest warrant for Robert Todd. The charge was murder.

Commander Nuxoll assigned Special Agent Michael Mannix to drive by the two addresses to see if the suspect's vehicle was there. He drove past the first address, but the driveway was empty. At 2:00 a.m., the agent drove his unmarked car past the second location. There, in the driveway, sat Robert Todd's Oldsmobile. Driving past the location, the agent radioed the information to the dispatcher and then parked down the street. Special Agents Greg Fernandez and Dave McLearin arrived to assist in the surveillance.

The investigative team received information that Todd's vehicle had been located at his girlfriend's house and a surveillance team was staking out the car. Koehler, Brueggemann, Kreke, Busch, and Spaur were en route to Decatur. The two-car convoy headed north to meet with the stakeout team. Busch, the senior investigator of the group, sat in the backseat of the van. He'd worked several hundred homicides in his 13 years with the state. He was impressed with the way Agents Koehler and Brueggemann were working this homicide case. They had only been in DCI for three years. Koehler, a young agent, was seated on the passenger side of the van. He reached over and turned the music up on the radio. This brought a response from the backseat area.

"Did we pass through teentown? Have you lost your hearing and your mind?" quizzed Busch in a sarcastic tone.

"Hey, this is a good song, what do you have against some tunes, old man?" teased Koehler.

"You want to hear some good tunes? Stick your head out the window and listen to the bugs impact on your forehead," replied Busch with a grin.

Deputy Spaur, the driver of the van, chuckled at the exchange of insults between Koehler and Busch as they approached the stakeout area. The five-man team met with Commander Nuxoll and assisting personnel in the parking lot of a shopping mall near the suspect's girlfriend's residence. A plan was drafted by the officers to lure Todd from the residence to avoid the chance that hostages might be taken or officers and civilians injured.

Agents learned that Todd, a construction worker, had called his boss earlier that morning inquiring about any work that would be available, since he had finished his last job in the Carlyle area. They contacted Todd's boss and explained the situation to him. He placed a call to Todd and requested that he meet him at his office in town. A location with open fields on both sides of a highway was selected for the site of the arrest. The officers were very much aware what could happen in these types of arrest situations. An agent with DCI, earlier in the year, had been slain during an arrest attempt of a suspect from a vehicle.

The surveillance team radioed the arrest team that Todd had exited the residence and was entering his vehicle. The surveillance team of unmarked vehicles held their position in the neighborhood of the residence until the suspect's vehicle had passed them. One unmarked unit from the surveillance team pulled out onto the highway a short distance behind Todd's vehicle. The driver's job was to keep Todd's vehicle in sight while he reached the arrest location.

As Todd drove down the road, Illinois state troopers in marked units pulled alongside the suspect's vehicle. Before Todd realized what was occurring, the three marked units were in place. One unit pulled in front of him, the second unit beside him, and the third unit behind him. He was blocked in, with nowhere to go except to the side of the road. When the red lights of the troopers' vehicles flashed, Todd pulled to the side of the road. He was taken into custody without incident.

Inspector Busch walked up to the squad car where Todd was seated. He asked the sandy-red-haired man to show him the design on the soles of the tennis shoes he was wearing. Todd lifted his foot for the investigator. There were small diamond and circle designs on the sole of the tennis shoe. Busch walked over to Agents Koehler and Brueggemann, who were standing on the shoulder of the highway.

"Well, are they the same kind of shoes?" asked Brueggemann.

"They're the same design as the shoe patterns in front of the stove, cabinet, and doorway. So, there you have it," replied Busch.

Todd was returned to Clinton County and incarcerated at the Clinton County Jail. The investigative team, having put in over 25 straight hours on the case, now took time to catch a few hours of rest before beginning their follow-up investigation.

Early the following day, Deputy Mike Kreke put together a photo lineup that included a photo of Robert Todd. He started traveling along the route he thought Todd might have taken when he left town on the night of the murder. This was a long shot and a lot of miles for the investigator to cover, but Kreke was determined to play out his hunch. He had driven for 40 miles and stopped at several gas stations and restaurants on his way north. Kreke stopped at a small restaurant and handed the waitress the photo lineup. She studied the photos for a moment and then pointed to the picture of Robert Todd. She told the investigator that the man in the photo had come into the restaurant early in the morning and had ordered a large breakfast. He had also made a call from the pay phone while in the restaurant, she recalled.

Deputy Kreke's next stop was the town of Pana, Illinois. He was around 100 miles north of the murder scene, but this was the town from which the killer had called the police to report the murder. Kreke went into a small restaurant in town and showed the photo lineup to the waitress. She pointed to the photo of Robert Todd. She recollected that he had been in the restaurant for change to make a phone call.

Kreke then returned to the sheriff's department. His longshot had apparently paid off; investigators now had two more witnesses in the murder case.

Investigators next checked the phone records of Todd's girlfriend's phone. She had received a collect call from him when he was at the restaurant eating breakfast earlier that morning. The waitress at the restaurant in Pana told investigators that the man in the photo had made a call around 8:25 a.m. The Pana Police Department had received the report of the murder in Beckemeyer from a male caller at 8:25 a.m. The Pana Police Department is across the intersection from the restaurant where Todd got change to make a phone call.

Over 90 items of evidence had been collected during the investigation. Several hundred miles had been traveled by the investigative team during their pursuit of the man who had killed Sandra Shelton. Now they had to wait for the forensic work to be completed.

Inspector Busch had collected the bedroom door at the Shelton residence. There was an oily forearm impression on the door and the doorknob was covered with oil. This item and all other items of physical evidence in the case were submitted to the Illinois State Police Metro-East Forensic Laboratory. Forensic Scientist David Peck of the Latent Print Section examined the items. After weeks of work done by the forensic expert, he found a fingerprint in oil on the bottom side of the doorknob of the bedroom door. Peck compared the fingerprint on the doorknob to the fingerprints of Robert Todd. Todd's left ring finger matched the fingerprint in oil on the doorknob.

Peck compared the tennis shoes that were worn by Todd when he was arrested to the shoe patterns collected on Sandra Shelton's kitchen floor. Todd's tennis shoes were positively identified as the shoes that had left the shoe patterns at the murder scene. The examiner also matched Todd's bare foot to the bare footprint on the kitchen floor.

Forensic Scientist Cheryl Cherry of the Trace Chemistry Section performed analysis on the wax droplets collected from the victim's body and suspect's bathtub. This would be the first case for the forensic laboratory where candle wax was evidence in a murder case. Analysis revealed that the wax droplets were composed of paraffin with a red dye. After experimentation and research, it was determined that there are differences in the dyes of red candle wax. Through the use of gas chromatography, stereomicroscopy, and thin-layer chromatography, the trace chemist was able to determine that the wax droplets collected from the victim's body and the suspect's bathtub were similar in composition to the red candle collected near the victim's body.

In December 1989, while incarcerated in the Clinton County Jail, Robert Todd bragged to a cellmate about the Shelton murder. He told of the events of the fatal night. He said he met the woman in a bar and they each signed the wall. They then went to the woman's home, where he attempted to recruit her into a satanic cult he was forming. After she refused to join the cult, he attempted to rape her. Angered by the woman, Todd began to slap her around. He strangled her with her shirt. Before he left, he lit candles and turned on the gas stove.

This information was relayed to the Clinton County

Sheriff's Department by Todd's cellmate. One new piece of evidence was gleaned from this information. The cellmate told investigators that Todd had told him that on the night of the murder, Shelton and Todd had listened to a Bob Seger tape on her tape player. The tape player was examined, and the Bob Seger tape was inside.

On May 16, 1990, Robert Todd went on trial for the murder of Sandra Shelton. Todd chose to have a bench trial, waiving his right to a trial by jury. Circuit Judge Dennis Huber presided over the trial in the Clinton County Circuit Court. Clinton County State's Attorney Dennis Middendorff, assisted by Assistant State's Attorney Robert Matoush, had covered every item in the case in their four-day presentation of witnesses and evidence.

During his closing argument, Middendorff stated to the trial judge, "The evidence in this case is so strong, it is hard to know where to begin. Taken altogether, the evidence of this defendant's guilt is overwhelming."

On May 22, 1990, the stocky, six-foot-tall defendant stood in front of Judge Dennis Huber, who read the verdict to Todd. "From the strong evidence that the state had presented, there is no doubt at all in my mind that the defendant is guilty of murder on counts one, two, and three."

On July 2, 1990, Judge Dennis Huber sentenced Robert Todd to the death penalty. Todd, a one-time student in a Bible college, now awaits an execution date.

"TRYSTING DRAG QUEEN AND THE CAT MAN KILLER"

by Marc Gerald

PITTSBURGH, PA.
MARCH 29, 1989

It was getting very late. It was also getting pretty cold. And it was getting just a little bit scary. But the dark, seedy streets on the tough north side of Pittsburgh, Pennsylvania, are always bad and they've been known to be worse.

There could be no question that if he had his way, David "Toni" Lowry would've rather been just about anywhere else. Ideally, in a warm, comfortable bed . . . in Acapulco by the beach . . . in his favorite tavern with a drink in front of him and a few friends by his side — even, as the saying goes, in Philadelphia.

Surely there. Not here.

David swung his hips back and forth, then side-to-side. No reaction. He hiked up his skirt, providing a quick, almost too revealing view to passing motorists — would-be tricks. Still no takers. David then struck an affected, exaggerated pose, based on but scarcely resembling the photos of models he had seen in the fashion magazines when he was a child. An "A" for effort, an "F" for results.

Dejected, David — as he stubbornly continued to call

himself, though to all concerned he was now just "Toni"—stared blankly, absently, hopelessly, waiting and wishing for his next meal ticket.

Once, he might have expected a knight in shining armor to appear, a Mr. Right, a sugar daddy who'd care for all his wants and needs, but now David had learned to set his sights considerably lower. Two hundred bucks? Wishful thinking. A hundred and fifty? Guess again, buddy! A C-note? When hell freezes over!

Well, he had to admit that even $10 or $15 in his pocket would be a good deal better than nothing, which was all he had now.

Courageously, resolutely, David struck another pose, this time a parody of a Playboy centerfold. He sucked in his already gaunt cheeks and hiked up his skirt so high that there was really no point in his wearing it at all. Cars honked, young suburban kids out late on the town in their parents' cars yelled obscenities at him, but no one stopped to pick David up.

With downcast eyes, he smoothed down his skirt to its original, slightly more modest position and closed his coat against the cold. Mentally scolding the world for its lack of good taste, David looked down at his wrist to check the time, then remembered he wasn't wearing a watch, only a bracelet. It just doesn't matter, David thought to himself. A watch wouldn't do him much good anyway. Whether it was two o'clock in the morning or four o'clock in the afternoon, his circumstances would be just as bleak.

All the same, it was getting late. If David had been in any other business, he would have packed it in for the night, writing off these lost hours as a simple operating loss. But in his present occupation, David knew the importance of waiting. Somebody was going to come around somehow, sometime. Someone always did.

But at the age of 28, David Lowry had become too experienced to just stand around half the night, waiting in a dead location, hoping that someone would pick him up. So, as quickly as his tired legs would carry him, he walked a couple of blocks to a gas station at the intersection of Fort Duquesne Boulevard and Ninth Street, where he hoped he would have better luck.

When he got there, it appeared that the gas station would hold no more opportunities for short-term employment than had the streets earlier. For five minutes, maybe longer, David perched himself beneath bright lights and a sign that said "Gas." Still looking to drum up some business, he flaunted legs which had been the envy of many a woman for all they were worth. That gets them every time, David thought, adding in the same internal breath, just not tonight.

Now walking over to the bathroom, David caught the eye of a man who was shutting the door and stepping back outside. He had seen, solicited and had even gone out on "dates," as he liked to call them, with some pretty strange men. Who in this business hadn't? What David had never seen before, however, and surely not two weeks before Halloween, was a dude dressed like this.

To start with, this man was wearing a tuxedo with tails. This in itself wasn't so unusual. But combined with a long brown and black wig, and a face painted silver and black — well, that added up to a pretty bizarre picture!

Thinking back, David recalled having seen an outfit like it in an advertisement for the Broadway musical "Cats." It wasn't every day you saw something like that in Pittsburgh.

Seizing the opportunity, David squealed in his most seductive falsetto, "Yo! Do you wanna dance? Hey, honey, honey!"

The man looked closely at David's face, sized him up from head-to-toe. David was well accustomed to such scrutiny. If you were going to buy a watch, a secondhand garment or a 16-inch color TV, you'd examine it closely, checking it out for its features and flaws. Why should this be any different?

Smiling, apparently pleased with what he saw, the

man nodded a yes.

Together, David and the "Cat Man" stepped into a 1974 white Thunderbird and sped off into the dark Pittsburgh night, out of view of two gas station attendants who had witnessed the transaction with a shrug.

Some nights, sleep doesn't come easy. Barbara Simmons had tried everything she could think of to keep her tired eyes closed for the night. She had tried to read herself to sleep, but that had failed. She'd tried counting sheep, but had just grown bored, not sleepy. She'd even tried different forms of self-hypnosis, but at roughly 3:20 in the morning on October 20, 1988, Barbara Simmons was still awake and not terribly happy about it.

Suddenly, she heard someone screaming outside her apartment in a deserted parking lot on a closeby street near the Allegheny Center Mall. Damn, Barbara thought. What does an honest, hardworking citizen have to do to get some shut-eye?

The screams persisted and Barbara's resentment soon gave way to genuine concern. She couldn't hear any words now, only the terrible sound of someone being hurt or dying.

Barbara Simmons threw the covers off, jumped out of bed and looked out her bedroom window. She saw nothing and that comforted her none the more. Wondering where the sounds might be coming from, then running as fast as she could into her daughter's room, Barbara immediately witnessed the frightful cause of the commotion.

Peering out the second-story window, Barbara saw what seemed to be a man and woman engaged in a violent struggle. Through sleepy but transfixed eyes, Barbara noticed that the man had a painted face and wore a tuxedo with tails, while the woman appeared to be wearing a dress.

The woman, Barbara would later report, "was trying to back away and he (the man) was sort of holding on

208

to her clothing."

Realizing this dream material was actually for real, Barbara quickly retreated from the window and called 911 to report the fight.

Mentally and physically exhausted from the nightmare of witnessing the brutal scuffle, Barbara returned to bed and fell into a troubled sleep.

It was still quite early in the morning. The crew members on the night shift of the Pittsburgh Police Department probably would've rather been at home, asleep with the wife and kids. They had a tough job to perform, however. Within a matter of minutes after being alerted about the fight, a small detail had roped off the area around the Allegheny Center Mall parking lot in approved crime scene manner.

David "Toni" Lowry lay dead at the scene, awash in a mass of blood. He'd died clutching a piece of green shrubbery which, no matter how you looked at it, was clearly not weapon enough to ward off his relentless attacker.

A subsequent autopsy report issued by Katherine Jasnosz, the pathologist on the case, would indicate that Lowry had succumbed to several stab wounds inflicted by a single, sharp-edged knife. These included a four-inch-wound that had penetrated Lowry's heart, and a six-inch-wound that had pierced his liver. Lowry had also sustained at least six "defensive" wounds to his right hand, Jasnosz would later report, indicating that the victim had desperately tried to fend off his assailant.

As the sun began to rise over Pittsburgh, forensic and homicide specialists tirelessly canvassed and combed the grounds of the mall's parking lot, hoping to find meaningful bits of evidence, anything to help draw them closer to understanding what exactly had transpired.

Most important to the sleuths' search, of course, was the recovery of the murder weapon. But this turned out to be more easily said than done. As days passed, and even after the suspect was apprehended, the killer's knife was not found.

Meanwhile, officers raced around the city, hoping to find somebody who might have seen something or somebody who could be connected to the puzzling killing.

Barbara Simmons, the witness who had watched the grisly crime from her window, was able to provide detectives with a description of the suspect's "Cats" costume upon reawakening. This lead was extremely useful and sleuths expressed their deepest appreciation to Simmons.

Armed with this bizarre account, officers believed that apprehension of David Lowry's killer could not be too far off. After all, how many people could be seen answering this sketch 300 miles or so from Broadway, and still two weeks away from Halloween?

Their predictions were soon confirmed.

Late in the day of the killing, a report was received that a man answering the suspect's description had been seen the preceding evening, barhopping from a popular nightspot in Green Tree to a hotel bar in downtown Pittsburgh. Then he was seen at a swank nightclub in the Strip District, and finally at the gas station where he and the victim were reportedly seen together.

All along the way, the suspect had made quite an impression on patrons and club owners alike in his authentic costume from "Cats."

According to several witnesses whom police managed to locate, Lowry's killer supposedly told them he worked in New York as a production assistant for the show "Cats." His costume and story were so convincing, in fact, that people thought he was a cast member.

Said one witness: "His makeup was so very well done. I naturally assumed that he was a member of 'Cats.' He convinced me and the rest of us sitting at the table."

As the probe unfolded, sleuths learned that the suspect was not a member of "Cats," as he had led people to believe, but was known to tell more than one tale.

Said another witness: "He was a likeable fellow but he told stories. He once told me that he was a pro football player and that he was a pro golfer on the circuit, neither of which turned out to be true."

Upon additional questioning of witnesses, detectives learned that the freaky-costumed suspect was one David Neal, a 29-year-old from Seven Fields in nearby Butler County. The sleuths learned considerably more about Neal when, still late in the day of the killing, they examined his lengthy rap sheet.

For starters, Neal had been arrested for possession of a small amount of marijuana in Chicago, Illinois, in 1978.

Neal's trouble with the law escalated in 1980, when he was arrested on assault charges in Zelienople, Pennsylvania.

Neal reemerged in 1987, when police in Campbell, California, filed burglary and auto-theft charges against him for allegedly stealing his Volkswagen Beetle from a repair shop when he did not have the money to pay for nearly $500 in repairs.

In December of the same year, Neal had been questioned by an FBI agent in California about his possible involvement in a bank robbery in Zelienople.

Up until 1988, there was nothing in Neal's record to differentiate him from thousands of other small-time criminals. His crimes were relatively minor and hardly noteworthy. In scanning his record, however, cops noted that since September 1988, Neal's criminal activities had taken a somewhat bizarre turn . . .

That September at Riverside High School in Pennsylvania, Neal posed as a senior transfer student by the name of Micky Accardo, from Los Gatos High School in California. Los Gatos is Spanish for the cats. To gain admittance, he produced a birth certificate from the former Rochester Hospital, immunization records and a transcript of grades.

Neal easily made friends, impressed teachers with all he knew, practiced with the football team, and then disappeared a mere four days after enrolling, to the regret of numerous girls who found him good-looking.

Neal's reasons for enrolling in school were sketchy. But it was believed that he had done it to test the security of local schools after learning about a woman who had entered an elementary school in Chicago and killed several students with an automatic rifle.

No criminal charges had been filed against Neal in this case.

All of this was a bit strange, cops reasoned. Judging from his record, David Neal did not seem like a man predisposed to murder. He did not have a particularly long history of violent crime. There had been no indication that robbery was a motive. And barhopping around all night dressed as a member of "Cats" didn't seem consistent with the behavior of someone who was disposed to commit a criminal act, or at least, someone who wants to get away with it.

More reason, detectives felt, to pay David Neal a little visit.

Darkness had enveloped Pittsburgh by the time officers led by homicide Detective Terrence O'Leary reached Neal's residence. When they entered and informed the suspect of the reason for their call, Neal denied any involvement in the slaying of David "Toni" Lowry.

The police, however, suspected otherwise and told Neal so. They informed him that they had a videotape of him dressed in a "Cats" costume as he'd entered the Vista International Hotel only hours before Lowry died. They also told him that he had been spotted at the gas station with Lowry, and that a man in a similar costume had been seen in the deserted parking lot. Was it merely a coincidence, officers pointedly asked, or . . . ?

Within 15 minutes after the interrogation began, the officers had a recorded confession in hand. They also had a story which was vastly different from what was indicated by the evidence they had gathered and the testimony they had received.

Said Neal: "I was solicited by what I thought was a female prostitute and I reacted by, you know, saying yes and she asked me if I would like her friend to accompany us."

Upon his acceptance of the offer, Neal said, the three climbed into a 1974 white Thunderbird owned by Neal's girlfriend and drove to the parking lot. There, a scuffle broke out before Neal offered Lowry and his friend $15 for services rendered.

Apparently infuriated by the offer, the prostitute whipped out a knife and held it to his throat, Neal claimed. Neal then made a wrestling move, which he said he had learned as a wrestler at Seneca Valley High School during the 1970s, bending Lowry's arms down and trying to reach for the knife.

Lowry's life was cut short, Neal explained, when the young transvestite prostitute made a mad dash and ran into the knife which was being held by Lowry's companion.

"My reaction was to defend myself and that's what I did," Neal told disbelieving detectives. "I defended myself and as God is my witness, I had no intention, or pre-planned this to set out and stalk someone."

As the interrogation was winding down, police officers asked Neal for the clothes he was wearing earlier that day. That, Neal explained, would be impossible, since he had burned them immediately after watching a newscast about Lowry's killing. "It was just a reaction I had. I wasn't sure until I saw the newscast."

Detectives were not at all impressed by David Neal's story and his self-defense plea. They told him that he might do well to save it for the judge and jury.

David Neal was booked on a murder charge and was subsequently taken to the Allegheny County Jail, where he was held in lieu of $250,000 bail.

* * *

Neal's trial began on March 29, 1989, before Allegheny County Court of Common Please Judge Jeffrey A. Manning. The courtroom was jam-packed with spectators who had come to hear all the startling testimony and the defendant's riveting confession.

Few were left disappointed.

Deputy District Attorney Anthony Krastek began the case by telling jurors that David Neal was not to be believed, that despite what he might contend, he acted alone, aggressively and not in self-defense. Evidence found at the scene and eyewitness testimony, Krastek continued, would prove Neal's guilt beyond the shadow of a doubt. "That was Toni Lowry's last trick," he said, facing the jurors. "That's also his last trick — David Neal — the defendant in this case."

Defense Attorney Michael Healey took another tack. Said he: "The issue in the case isn't that should Mr. Neal have been out that night in a 'Cats' costume. My main plea at this point is for you to keep an open mind. If you do that, I believe the verdict will be just in this case."

The jurors did keep an open mind. After nearly five hours of deliberation, the jury reached their verdict. David Neal was found guilty of third-degree murder.

Said one juror at the trial's conclusion: "There was no doubt in everyone's mind in the room that Neal was guilty of murder."

As of this writing, David Neal is being held in the Allegheny County Jail and faces a maximum prison sentence of 10 to 20 years.

EDITOR'S NOTE:
Barbara Simmons isn't the real name of the person so named in the foregoing story. A fictitious name has been used because there is no reason for public interest in the identity of this person.

"REJECTED ROMEO FED THE BARMAID TO THE PIGS!"

by Philip Westwood

John David put his finger on the bell push and pressed. A muffled ringing noise from the hallway beyond the door told him that the device was working. After a few seconds, he took his finger off the button, put his ear to the door and listened for the sound of approaching footsteps that would tell him his call had been answered.

But on the other side of the door, there was only silence. Nobody was coming to see what he wanted and yet someone must be at home. He decided to try again. So he pressed the bell once more, only this time he did not remove his finger from the button.

Inside the house, the woman put aside the newspaper she was reading, looked at the clock and sighed. It was 8:30 on the morning of Thursday, April 9, 1987, and whoever was leaning on the doorbell of her house on the quiet street in the English town of Reading, 40 miles to the west of London, seemed to be in a pretty determined mood.

With that feeling of irritation experienced by someone who is being thrown into the events of a day that, for them, has not quite begun, the woman eased herself out of her chair and slowly made her way towards the incessant monotone of the ringing bell.

"All right, all right. I'm coming," she shouted wearily in the general direction of the door at the end of the dark hallway. Her slippers flip-flopped on the carpet as the dull ache in the back of her legs told her brain of her body's unpreparedness for any form of activity at that hour of the morning.

All the while the bell kept ringing.

It was still ringing as the woman flicked up the catch on the lock and withdrew the bolts at the top and bottom of the door. "All right," she shouted again. "For heaven's sake . . ."

With something of an effort, the woman pulled the door open. A shaft of bright morning sunlight streamed into the hallway and instantly dispelled the darkness that had previously wrapped the place in a sort of soft, but strangely comforting, gloom.

"Oh God!" the woman exclaimed, cupping a hand to her face as the unaccustomed light hit her square in the eyes.

After what seemed like an eternity, but was, in reality, no more than five seconds, the woman felt that her eyes no longer needed quite that degree of protection. Slowly, she removed her hand from her face and squinted in the direction of the man on the doorstep.

"Oh, it's you," she said with a voice that made no attempt to conceal the level of disappointment and disapproval she felt as she recognized her caller. "Well, what do you want?"

The woman had known John David for several months—and she didn't like him. That was not unusual. There were quite a few people whom she knew and of whom she was not particularly fond. But David was different. What bothered her was that she didn't know why she so disliked him. There was no obvious reason. It was just a gut feeling, irrational but insistent.

To all outward appearances, John David was a very likeable person—far more so than many of the young men who frequented that neighborhood. A good looking 25-year-old, he was quiet and polite and his manners were impeccable. Those who knew him even described him as charming.

He had no regular job, even though he was a skilled motorcycle mechanic. But such a situation was not unusual in the economically depressed Britain of the 1980s.

David had shown that he was not afraid of hard work. He had a part-time job as a laborer at a local hog farm. It was not pleasant spending most of his time knee-deep in slurry as he tended to the needs of the animals in his charge. But at least it enabled him to earn enough money to maintain his motorcycle and to have a reasonable social life.

Women were particularly attracted by David's good looks and quiet charm. Over the years he had had many girlfriends. But he was not promiscuous. There was never more than one girl in his life at any given time. Each affair had, however, been shortlived. The steady and lasting relationship that he so desperately sought had always eluded him.

Maybe it was David's apparent success with girls that contributed to the woman's dislike of him. After all, his latest liaison had been with her own daughter, Miriam. It was an off-on affair of which the woman did not really approve.

The real trouble was that Miriam was married. True, she was separated from her husband. But Miriam's mother always hoped that Miriam and her husband would get back together again, if only for the sake of their child. They had a little girl who, the woman felt, needed the steadying influence of a stable home and David's association with her daughter was doing nothing to help bring that about. In fact, it could be said with some assurance that it was doing quite the opposite.

"Is Miriam here?" David asked in a soft, cultured voice.

"No, she's not," the woman replied. She started to

close the door when a sudden feeling came over her. It was a feeling of doubt tinged with mild panic. She opened the door again.

"Why should she be here?" she asked David, a quizzical expression on her face. Miriam lived with the child in a dingy, one-room apartment on Wantage Road, near the center of town. Occasionally, men would spend the night with her, though Miriam's mother didn't like to think too much about that. Miriam's life-style and the people with whom she mixed, often left much to be desired.

"She asked me to do some babysitting for her last night," David explained. "She was going out somewhere but she didn't come back all night. And she still isn't back this morning. I was wondering what I should do about the baby. It isn't like Miriam to just go off and leave her."

"Where was she going?" the woman asked.

"I don't know. She didn't say."

"Well, who was she going with?"

"I don't know that either. I'd better get back and see to the baby."

Telling David to do just that and that she would be along shortly to take over if necessary the woman closed the door and went back to the living room. She was now wide awake. The day had really begun, and if its first few minutes were any indication, it wasn't going to be a very pleasant one.

Over the years, the woman had managed to come to terms with Miriam and her wild ways. As a teenager, the girl had been rebellious and had mixed with the sort of people with whom her mother would have preferred her to stay away. She had even married one of them and had his child.

But Miriam was not a bad girl. She knew just how far she could go before wild and unconventional behavior spilled over into that area where it became socially unacceptable and attracted the attention of the authorities.

218

Daniel Kimball testified in court that "accidents do happen" and claimed the victim, Rosemary Kleinsmith, "was a good friend of mine."

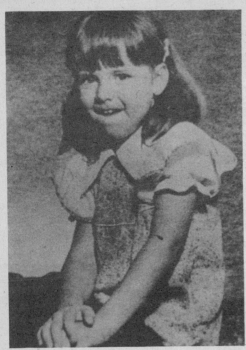

Angel Halstead, 4, was last seen walking towards the woods in search of a lost kitten.

Angel's killer, Brooks Bellay, 14, sits at the defense table while attorneys debate his fate.

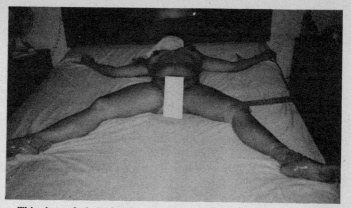

This photo of a bound and apparently drugged Diane Casora were on a roll of film belonging to the murder suspect.

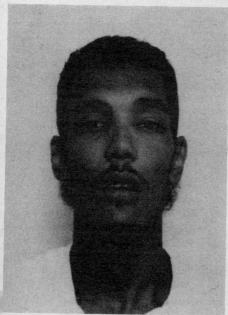

Mark Cadiz, Diane Casora's killer. Police are still searching for another woman whose picture was on the roll of film.

Her husband and child found beautiful Lynea Kokes, 28, horribly mutilated.

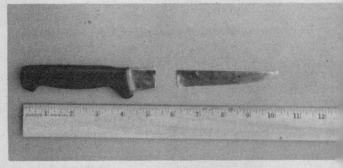

Lynea's killer was so violent he broke his weapon in two inside the victim.

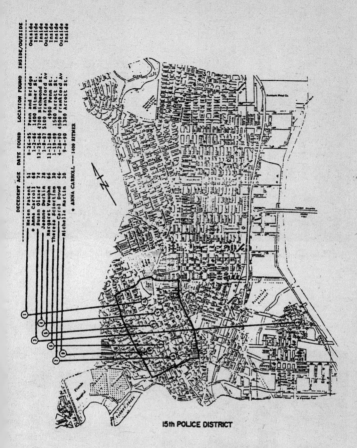

Although six of eight apparently related murders took place within a few blocks of each other in Philadelphia, the time between each killing made it hard to see a pattern.

The split-open body of one of the victims was found in this alley behind a fish store.

An employee at the seafood market became the prime suspect in the brutal serial slayings.

Katie the cat was the unwitting partner in crime of John Perry, who killed his wife.

Arminda Perry.

Some of Perry's instruments of dismemberment.

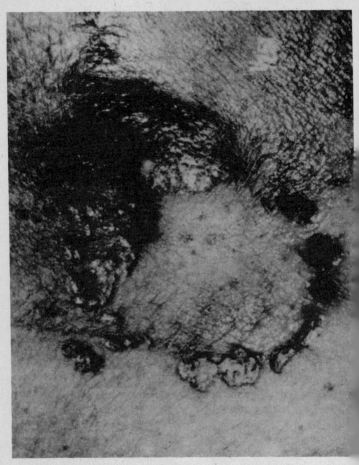

This bizarre "love bite" on dental nurse Masha Efrati's back helped
convict her killer.

Police search the pig farm where the body of Miriam Jones was dumped.

Imitating a Stephen King movie, the killer used Stanley Detweiler's blood to write REDRUM on the wall of his apartment.

Michael St. Clair and his brother Robert, below, boasted "We're kin to Jesse James on one side of the family," but Michael's arrest for his uncle's murder divided the family.

On entering Clifton Ellis's house, investigators saw this clean, undisturbed living room.

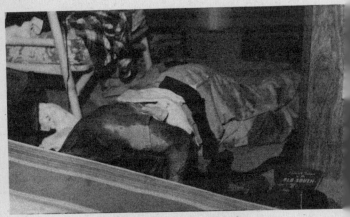

Ellis's body in the ransacked bedroom.

And whatever else she was, nobody could deny Miriam Jones was a good mother. She thought the world of her little girl. She might go out in the evening and leave the child in the care of a babysitter whom she knew and trusted but she would never stay away all night. If nothing else, she knew that to do so would mean that she risked losing the child. Leaving a child for so long, especially overnight, was against the law. The authorities tended to take a dim view of such behavior. She would be regarded as an unfit mother and the child would be taken into foster care.

Even though Miriam had been missing for only a short time, her mother felt strongly that something was wrong—dreadfully wrong.

The two officers who came to see her in answer to her call to the local police station tended to agree. It was a matter that seemed to warrant further investigation, they told Mrs. Jones.

The officers' report landed on the desk of Detective Superintendent John Birbeck, who studied it closely. He, too, felt that some rapid action was called for. So he assigned two detectives to do some groundwork and turn up everything on Miriam Jones' background and life-style, along with details of her friends and acquaintances.

Since her teens, pretty, dark-haired 25-year-old Miriam Jones had been fascinated by motorcycles and the men who rode them. She had mixed with the local Hell's Angels and knew several of them very well.

Four years earlier, she had met her husband—also a motorcycle fanatic. From the outset, the marriage had been a tempestuous affair. Miriam had been unable to settle down and had tried to pursue the life-style she had enjoyed in her single days. Arguments were a nightly occurrence. Even the arrival of a child provided only a temporary lull in the stormy proceedings.

Eventually, it all became too much and the pair split up.

Miriam took the apartment on Wantage Road and

219

went out to look for a job in order to support herself and her child. She found one at a pub called the Cider House in the nearby village of Winkfield where she was taken on as a barmaid.

The Cider House was used as the main venue and meeting place of the Windsor chapter of Hell's Angels. Every night, the Angels would gather, enjoying themselves, drinking mind-bending cider cocktails with names such as "Brain Damage" and "Hand Grenade."

One of the pub's regular customers was John David. He was not one of the Angels, though he would like to have been. He tried to get himself accepted, but the Angels regarded him as being too soft to ever become one of them.

But Miriam liked him. Soon the two of them became friendly and then more than just friendly. David would occasionally spend the night at Miriam's apartment, and at one point it seemed that their relationship was becoming serious.

Then someone else started using the pub on a regular basis—someone to whom Miriam had once been very close, and for whom she still felt great affection. The new customer at the pub was Miriam's husband.

Away from the pressures of married life, the couple found that they still had a great deal in common. The laughter that had been so obviously absent when they were living together returned to their relationship. They started to talk about a reconciliation. The talking developed into definite plans. Miriam's affair with John David started to cool an he was pushed abruptly into the background.

"Yes, we were getting back together again," Miriam's husband told the detectives who questioned him.

"Did you know where she is now?" they asked.

"No, I don't," the husband replied.

"Well, do you know of any reason why she would want to disappear?" the officers wanted to know.

"On the contrary," Miriam's husband told them. "There is every reason why she would stay around."

The detectives looked puzzled. Miriam's husband explained.

"We had settled all of our differences and had decided to make a new start. We were very happy about how things had worked out, and we were confident that the future would be good. To celebrate, the three of us — Miriam, the baby, and I — were going off to Spain for a vacation. We were due to leave tomorrow. Now I've got this awful feeling that I'll never see her again."

Up to that point, the detectives felt that Miriam Jones may have simply gone away with some new boyfriend, though the fact that she had left her child behind cast grave doubts over such a theory.

But after talking to Miriam's husband, the detectives were more concerned than ever. They now were convinced that she had either been abducted, or worse. Detective Birbeck ordered a full scale search of the area. Among the search party that combed the fields and hedgerows was Miriam's husband and her one-time boyfriend, John David.

David was just one of several men who were eventually pulled in for questioning. The unemployed motorcycle mechanic told the detectives that he was aware of Miriam's reconciliation with her husband. How did he feel about it? he was asked.

"It's one of those things," David answered with a shrug of the shoulders. "It was always on the cards."

The officers wanted to know where Miriam was going on the evening David agreed to act as babysitter.

"I don't know," David told them.

"Was she going to meet her husband?" they persisted.

"I've told you, I don't know," David replied with some irritation. "She never told me where she was going."

The detectives were not happy. There was some-

221

thing about John David that did not add up. But events were about to take a turn that would change their suspicions into absolute certainty.

During the course of the routine interrogation, David sat at a small table in the center of the interview room. The room was illuminated by the lamp of a single electric light positioned directly above the table.

One detective sat opposite David and took notes, while a second officer paced around the room firing off questions.

Suddenly, the officer handling the questioning looked at David, stopped walking around the room and looked at him again. He moved closer and bent down so that his face was only inches away from that of the suspect.

"How did you get that?" he asked.

"Get what?" David inquired.

"That," the detective responded, reaching out with his finger and touching a small cut on David's cheekbone. It was a blemish that had gone previously unnoticed because of the shadow cast by the small light.

"I cut myself while shaving," David replied unconcernedly.

The detective studied John David's face closely. He noticed the edge of his beard line. The cut was way too high to have come from a razor. The detective had a flash of inspiration.

"Get your shirt off," he ordered.

"Why?" David asked, his composure rapidly evaporating.

"Just do it!" snapped the officer.

The detective's tone meant obey, and David did. Slowly, he unbuttoned his shirt, removed it and placed it on the table in front of him.

Both officers let out that soft, involuntary whistle that comes when one is confronted by a sight that is totally unexpected. For John David's chest and stomach were covered by dozens of small cuts, just like the one on his face.

222

"I suppose you got those from shaving," the detective standing over him sarcastically observed.

"I got them at work. I use a lot of wire. It's sharp you know," David replied with equal sarcasm.

"They don't look like cuts to me," the detective remarked dryly. "They look more like scratches. Still, forensics will be able to tell if they are cuts made by wire or scratches made by nails — human nails, that is, not iron ones. Now, once more, where is Miriam Jones?"

"I keep telling you. I don't know."

The circumstantial evidence against John David was far too strong to warrant his release. The officers decided to detain him overnight while further investigations were made.

The detectives were now convinced that Miriam Jones was dead and that John David had killed her. But proving it was another matter. All the information the officers had gathered indicated that he was an even-tempered man not given to outbursts of violence.

One friend of David's had told police who questioned him, "John is the kind of man who wouldn't hurt a fly. If there was a spider in his path, he would sooner pick it up and move it out of the way than tread on it."

Hell's Angels who were questioned told officers that David had asked many times if he could become one of them, but they had always turned him down. "He wasn't our type," they said. "He was not hard enough."

Detective Birbeck felt differently. From his observations, he regarded David as a pleasant enough character who could turn on the charm when it suited him. He had a mild manner which was deceptive — and dangerous.

Birbeck's problem of proving his involvement in the disappearance of Miriam Jones was solved the following morning — by John David himself.

A night spent locked up alone in a police cell had

given David plenty of time to think. He realized that it was only a matter of time before the evidence stacked up against him became irrefutable. So he decided to save everyone a lot of trouble by making a full confession.

Shortly after dawn, John David was back at the small table in the interview room, telling his story to Detective Superintendent John Birbeck.

John David had a strong and abiding fear of rejection. His mother had abandoned him when he was only six weeks old and he had been brought up by a couple who had eventually adopted him. But being adopted had given him a deep inferiority complex.

Through his late teens and into his 20s, he had never had any trouble getting girlfriends. But none of them had wanted a steady and lasting relationship. All he had wanted was to marry, settle down and raise a family. But his girlfriends weren't interested.

Then he met Miriam Jones. He knew she was separated from her husband. He knew she had a child, but he didn't mind that at all. The idea of a ready-made family was rather appealing to him.

Their relationship blossomed. Miriam even talked about getting a divorce so she and David could get married. Everything seemed to be working out perfectly. Everything he had always wanted out of life seemed to be within his grasp — finally.

But then Miriam's husband returned to the scene. At first, it had all been pretty innocuous. Their conversation had been confined to chatting about everyday matters over the bar at the Cider House. David had not gotten involved. He had simply stood aside and hoped that things would not develop between Miriam and her husband. Maybe if he had been more assertive from the start, things might have been different.

But he had been passive. The relationship between Miriam and her husband had grown to a point where they were talking of getting back together again.

David was being pushed out. He tried to get himself back into Miriam's favor but it was no use. Things between Miriam and her husband had gone too far.

David decided to make one last effort to win Miriam back. On the evening of April 8th, he called round to see her at her apartment. He only wanted to take her out to dinner and have a little talk.

But Miriam was not interested. She had already decided to return to her husband she told David. They had a vacation in Spain and were to leave in two days time. David begged her to reconsider, but she was adamant. Her affair with David was over.

David decided to try a different angle. Sexually, things between him and Miriam had always been more than satisfactory. So he tried to rekindle the passion of their early days.

He tried to kiss her but Miriam turned away. He tried to touch her but she pushed him off. He tried to force himself upon her but Miriam fought him off like a wildcat. He had a deep hatred of rejection and now he was receiving the ultimate rejection from the woman he loved. It was too much. Something inside David snapped.

Roughly, he grabbed Miriam, turned her towards him and put his hands around her throat. He pressed. He noticed the look of sheer terror that filled Miriam's eyes. He pressed harder. Her mouth was open. She was trying to talk but only strange gurgling noises came out. He maintained his hold and the gurgling noises stopped. Miriam's eyes rolled and her body went limp. When he was sure she was dead, he let got of her throat.

"What did you do with the body?" Birbeck asked, without emotion.

"I got rid of it," David replied.

"How?"

"I destroyed it."

"Explain what you mean," coaxed Birbeck. David did.

As part of his plans for a romantic evening, David had borrowed a friend's car. He was going to drive Miriam to a fancy restaurant for a romantic candlelit dinner. Now he was going to take her for a rather different drive than the one he originally planned.

He wrapped Miriam's body in a bedsheet and carried her down to the car. Placing the body in the trunk, he drove to the hog farm where he worked. It was isolated, there would be nobody around to see what he was doing.

At the farm, he syphoned some gasoline from the fuel tank, threw it over Miriam's body and put a match to it. But the fire failed to destroy the body and David had to resort to other measures.

The farm housed over 100 hogs. And hogs will eat anything — absolutely anything. So David tipped the body over the fence and into the area where the hogs were kept. After a few seconds there were grunting and snorting noises in the darkness as the animals came out to investigate their midnight visitor.

As David got back into the car, the noises coming from the hog pen told him that the animals were completing the job that the fire had failed to do. That night, the hogs had a real feast.

When David finished his story, he put his head in his hands and wept. Birbeck stared at the ceiling. He was an experienced officer. Murder investigations were not new to him, but this was the first time he had come across a killer who had gone to such gruesome lengths to get rid of the body.

Distasteful as the task was, Birbeck knew a search would have to be made of the hog pen where David had disposed of Miriam. So later that morning, a team of six officers began what had to be the most unpleasant job they had ever undertaken.

For three days, the officers waded knee-deep through the slurry of the hog pen. With long poles, they probed and prodded the depths of the slimy substance. If the poles struck something that was not instantly recognizable, then the officers had no alternative but to reach down into the slurry with their hands and pull out the mystery object.

At the end of the three-day search, all that remained of Miriam Jones had been recovered. It was a pitiful collection, consisting of a fragment of her dress, part of her suspender belt and four small pieces of chewed bones.

Everything else — flesh, hair, teeth, bones, clothes and shoes — had been consumed by the voracious hogs.

John David was charged with the murder of Miriam Jones and was remanded to prison to await trial.

Given David's character and his attitude towards women and rejection, Birbeck got the idea that maybe — just maybe — Miriam was not the first girl to have pushed him over the edge. Perhaps some other woman had tried to ditch David when she tired of him and had paid the ultimate price.

So Detective Birbeck decided to look at the files of unsolved murders involving young women in the south of England going back over five years. One case proved to be particularly interesting.

On the evening of December 23, 1984, in the nearby town of Maidenhead, 22-year-old Jacqueline Cheer was found dead at the home she shared with her parents. Her parents had been out for the evening. Jackie had decided to stay home because she was suffering from a viral infection and did not feel well.

When her parents returned home, they found Jackie lying on her bed. She was wearing a nightdress, her bra, panties and suspender belt being neatly laid out beside her. At first, her parents thought that she was sleeping. They realized the awful truth only after they tried to wake her for her evening medication.

An initial medical examination concluded that Jackie had asphyxiated during a convulsion brought on by her illness. But in the cold, clinical atmosphere of the autopsy room, more sinister forces were found to have caused the young girl's premature demise.

Tests showed that Jackie had engaged in sexual intercourse immediately before her death. And from external bruising at the top of her thighs and internal injuries to her sex organs, it was clear that she had not succumbed willingly to such intimacy.

Jackie's death had been due to strangulation. Cracks in the hyoid bone—that bone in the neck that supports the tongue—indicated that manual pressure had been applied in a manner very similar to the method that John David said he had used when he strangled Miriam Jones.

But the most significant factor, as far as Detective Birbeck was concerned, was that, at the time of her death, Jackie had reached the end of an affair with a boyfriend. It had been a passionate liaison. Friends had thought that a wedding was in the air. But it was not to be. For some reason, the affair had cooled and the couple had drifted apart. The boyfriend's name was, of course, John David, which seemed like quite a coincidence to sleuths.

In the 18 months that John David spent waiting for his trial, police built up a strong case against him concerning the death of Jackie Cheer. But the Crown Prosecution Service decided not to proceed with it before the Miriam Jones case had been concluded.

At Reading Crown Court, jurors and spectators alike looked decidedly ill as Prosecutor Nicholas Purnell, Q.C., detailed the sickening events surrounding Miriam Jones' death.

"Two days before Miriam was due to get back with her husband for a holiday to Spain, she was murdered," Purnell told the court. "In her Reading bedsit, the defendant, knowing his relationship with Miriam was over, killed her."

On Tuesday, December 6, 1988, after a four-day trial, the jury found John David guilty of murdering Miriam Jones. The judge, Mr. Justice French, sentenced him to life imprisonment.

After David had been sentenced, Purnell announced that, in view of the verdict, the prosecution would not be proceeding with the case concerning Jackie Cheer.

In England, as in the United States, a life sentence rarely means exactly what it says. In about 15 years time, it will probably be deemed that John David has paid for his crime and he will be released. But there is a strong possibility that his freedom will be shortlived. He could be rearrested to stand trial over the death of Jackie Cheer, such things often happen.

Hell's Angels have a reputation—rightly or wrongly—for unruly behavior, often involving a high level of violence. John David wanted to join them, but they turned him down because they thought him too soft and too weak. Ironically, events proved he was far tougher and more violent than any of them.

"KILLER STOLE HER FALSE TEETH FOR A SOUVENIR"

by Gary C. King

It was truly a winter to be remembered by the thousands of people who ski on Mt. Hood every year. The snow was late again, which was becoming more and more the rule rather than the exception. When it did start snowing, however, it came down hard and heavy and produced a thick white blanket of covering for the ground that satisfied not only the skiers, who had been anxiously awaiting its arrival, but brought a sigh of relief from the resort owners as well. People would soon be pouring into Timberline Lodge from all over the Northwest, eager to turn the mountain into their winter vacationland.

The majestic beauty of the mountain is, indeed, an awesome sight. It is inconceivable to think that anything short of a volcanic eruption could spoil the beauty and the splendor of this magnificent peak.

But, in December of 1979, a ghastly murder was committed on the slopes of Mt. Hood that would take a heavy toll by leaving an indelible mark in the minds of those who love the mountain so dearly.

It was December 4th, the third day of an intensive effort by a ten-member search team from the Clackamas County sheriff's department to find the body of a young woman who had reportedly been shot to death in the area of High Rock, which is located about 10 miles from Timothy Lake in the Mt. Hood National Forest.

The heavy snowfall and cold wind made the search a miserable one for the deputies, who were searching for the body as a result of a tip they had received, a body that they were not sure really existed. There were snowdrifts that were nearly thigh-deep in places. The deputies were tired and cold, yearning to return to the warmth and comfort of their homes and families. Many wanted to call the search off entirely, wondering just how reliable, if at all, their tipster really was in directing them to the body site.

The search team was at the 4,200-feet elevation level of the mountain and were about to call off the search when one of the deputies yelled that he might have found something. There, mostly covered by snow, was the form of a human body protruding through a drift of snow. It seemed, at first glance, to be attached somehow to the trunk of a tree.

As the day pressed on, the search team awaited the arrival of the crime lab technicians and homicide detectives, a prerequisite to removing or disturbing a homicide victim. When they finally arrived, photographs were taken and samples obtained, and the digging out process was allowed to begin.

When the body had been dug out of the snow, it could not yet be moved, for it was bound securely to a tree. The body was badly decomposed, indicating that it had been there before the first winter snow had fallen. It was difficult to estimate the age of the victim, although the body was clearly that of a female. It was also plainly obvious how she had died. There were several wounds to her head, and it was evident that the wounds had been inflicted by gun shots fired at close range.

The woman had been thumb-cuffed to the tree, and releasing her from her bound position proved to be somewhat difficult, due to the frozen condition of her

231

body. It was clear to everyone present that she had been deliberately murdered in cold blood, execution style.

The next day, Wednesday, December 5th, an autopsy was performed by Dr. William Brady, the medical examiner for Oregon State. He was assisted by the deputy state medical examiner, Dr. Larry Lewman. The results of the autopsy revealed that the woman was believed to be in her mid-to-late twenties, was 5'9" tall, weighed about 115 pounds, and had brown hair. According to the medical examiner's conclusions, she had been dead approximately two months, and was probably killed in early October. The cause of her death was four gunshot wounds to her head, which were inflicted at nearly point-blank range. One bullet entered the back of her head, one below the left eye, and two bullets entered on the left side of her head. Any one of the bullets would have probably resulted in the woman's death, and the presence of multiple shots was a clear indication that the murderer was a calculating, cold-blooded killer who found great pleasure in what he did.

Days passed, turning rapidly into weeks, weeks into months, and no suspect was in custody and no identification had yet been made of the victim.

It was beginning to look as if this case would go into the state's unsolved homicides book.

And then, on Thursday, February 21, 1980, more than two months after the woman's body had been found, Lt. Winston R. Brady, chief of Clackamas County's sheriff's detectives, made the announcement that his office had determined the identity of the murder victim.

Lt. Bradshaw said that the woman had been identified as one Kittie Coy, 34, a Portland resident who had moved there from Chico, California. Bradshaw said that Ms. Coy's death was definitely being investigated as a homicide, but he refused to comment on whether a suspect had been identified. Bradshaw did say, however, that Ms. Coy had been using several aliases, one of which was Mary Ellen Donnelly, and he indicated that the use of the aliases had hindered his department's investigation and delayed identification of the body.

"At this point," Bradshaw said, "we have some pretty good leads in the case, and we should be getting pretty close to a conclusion." He did not reveal any details of their leads.

Now according to John Bennett, Multnomah County deputy district attorney, Ms. Coy had been charged with being a member of a very smooth and sophisticated forgery ring operating in the Portland area. It was when Ms. Coy had failed to appear at her arraignment in Multnomah County that the pieces of the puzzle began to come together. Through the cooperation of Multnomah County and Clackamas County police officials, identification of Ms. Coy's body was made possible.

The investigation surrounding Ms. Coy's alleged involvement in the Portland forgery ring led police to connect her with two other people who were known to be involved, Dennis Richard Brooks, 26, and Frederick E. Hazeem, 21, both residents of the Portland area.

Hazeem was already in custody in the Multnomah County jail after pleading guilty to his involvement in the forgery ring by obtaining $35,000 worth of goods and cash through the use of stolen checks and credit cards in August, 1979. Brooks, who was formerly employed as a security guard in Portland, was serving time in the Oregon State Penitentiary after being convicted for assault, forgery, theft, and receiving stolen property.

Meanwhile, on April 10th, a Clackamas County grand jury returned a murder indictment against Frederick Hazeem for the shooting death of Kittie Coy.

The case seemed, at this point, to be all wrapped up, airtight, open and shut. Until Hazeem decided to make a deal with the District Attorney's office, in which case he was allowed to plead guilty to first-degree manslaughter in return for being a witness for the prosecution against Dennis Brooks. In Oregon, a conviction of murder could have brought the death sentence while, on the other hand, a conviction of first-degree manslaughter would bring a maximum of 20 years. Also included in the deal was a recommendation by Judge Howard Blanding for Hazeem to serve his sentence elsewhere than in the Oregon State Penitentiary.

It was feared that his life would be in danger from other inmates, angry that he would turn state's evidence.

Thus, an indictment was handed down against Dennis Richard Brooks, charging him with murder-felony murder, and first-degree kidnaping in the death of Kittie Coy.

Felony murder is a charge that involves a person who was a participant in a felony crime, such as kidnaping, when a murder was committed, whether or not the person charged actually committed the murder. Brooks pleaded not guilty to all the charges.

The morning of July 28, 1980, jury selection began in the trial of Dennis Brooks in the Clackamas County Circuit courtroom of Judge Dale Jacobs. Judge Jacobs issued a warning to prospective jurors not to dwell on the possibility of a death sentence in the event that Brooks was convicted of murder. Jacobs also told the potential jurors that the trial might be a lengthy one, taking anywhere from ten days to two weeks. The jury selection process took nearly two days to complete.

The reason for taking so long in selecting a jury in this case was outlined by Deputy District Attorney Andrejs Eglitis.

"The prosecution and the defense, in a case of this nature, have to be very careful," said Eglitis. "In the South they can take up to a week to pick a jury and, in places like Chicago or Los Angeles, the defense and prosecution talk to people who know the potential jurors, such as friends and relatives."

Defense Attorney Dale Liberty told a prospective juror that he expected the prosecution to call as many as

40 witnesses, while the defense expected to call only a few, including the possibility of Brooks himself.

After a brief opening statement by Eglitis that chronicled the events which allegedly led to the death of Kittie Coy, the jury was taken to the High Rock area in the Mt. Hood National Forest where the alleged shooting occurred. They went to the spot where Ms. Coy's body was found and viewed the tree to which she had been thumb-cuffed.

When they returned to the courtroom later that day, Eglitis pointed out to the jury that Brooks and Hazeem first met Ms. Coy in Chico, California.

"Brooks and Hazeem first met Coy," Eglitis said, "when they traveled to Chico to help a friend who had escaped from jail, and who, by the way, has since been recaptured. Coy and a friend returned with the two men to Oregon.

"Coy was an artist in using and forging credit cards and checks," said Eglitis. He went on to charge that Coy, Brooks, and Hazeem went on a fling of taking cash, credit cards, and checks from shoppers in stores. He said that the men were, however, getting only the checks and credit cards and began to get suspicious about where the cash was going, since they were getting very little of it.

"Mistrust built up until October 7th," said Eglitis. October 7th was the date that Ms. Coy allegedly was shot to death.

Frederick Hazeem was called to the stand and was asked why he told a policeman about the death of Kittie Coy.

"It was bugging me," he told the jury. "I was fed up to here (indicating his neck with his hand) worrying about it every time I saw a policeman." He further stated that he told Portland Police Detective Tom Jacobs about the shooting while Jacobs was bringing him back to Oregon from Wyoming, where he had been arrested.

Hazeem went on to testify that he and Brooks told

Ms. Coy that they were going to a restaurant called the Safari Club in Esticada, which is on the way to Mt. Hood. The excuse they gave her was that they were to meet a businessman there, and had planned to take his money and credit cards.

But, instead, according to Hazeem, they drugged Ms. Coy and took her to the High Rock area and thumb-cuffed her to a tree. Hazeem said that he returned to the car and, a short time later, heard three shots. He said Brooks then returned to the car and they drove back to Portland. Hazeem also stated that he and Brooks returned to the scene of the crime a week later and took a ring from Ms. Coy's hand, then gave it to another girl.

"There are at least three people who know that I didn't shoot Kittie," Hazeem told the jury. He was directing his attention to the people who administered a polygraph test to him, and his statement could have, and nearly did, cause a mistrial.

"The results of a polygraph test are not admissible as evidence," said Circuit Judge Jacobs, who instructed the jury to ignore that portion of the testimony.

On the fourth day of the trial, Jan Leonard, a female witness for the prosecution, told the court that Kittie Coy wanted to leave California because of numerous bad checks she had written. Thus, the two women left for Oregon with Brooks and Hazeem, after Ms. Coy had stolen three guns from the home of a friend in Red Bluff, California.

The witness also told the jury that she and Kittie had been living with Hazeem and his roommate but moved to a motel after an incident involving some money that Ms. Coy had stolen from Hazeem's roommate. She said that distrust had built up between them and Hazeem, and that is what prompted them to move into the motel.

The next day the jury was shown color photographs of Ms. Coy, after she had been shot, by Deputy State Medical Examiner Dr. Larry Lewman. As the photo-

236

graphs were being viewed, Lewman explained to the court that it was four bullet wounds to the head, fired at close range, that killed her.

Brooks did not display any noticeable emotion when he saw the photographs of Kittie Coy's badly disfigured, decomposed face, photographs of a face that displayed the blueness of death, which were taken two months after she had died.

Lewman commented on the gunshot wounds to Ms. Coy's face, pointing out one that was below the left eye, which he said was inflicted from a distance of six inches to two and a half feet. He also pointed out two wounds on the left side of the woman's head, and another in the back of her skull.

This brought forth an objection from the defense attorney, Dale Liberty, who contended that Lewman was not present during the entire autopsy, which was actually performed by Dr. William Brady, the state medical examiner. Liberty also objected to the photographs being introduced as evidence, and Judge Jacobs made the jury leave the courtroom several times during Liberty's objections. Liberty also moved for a mistrial. Judge Jacobs denied the motion.

"You're going to deprive this defendant of a fair and impartial trial," Liberty complained to Jacobs.

With Liberty's objections overruled, Dr. Lewman was allowed to continue by displaying additional photographs of Ms. Coy's thumbs, which showed damage which was caused by something with a serrated or grooved edge having been firmly connected to them.

Later that same afternoon, a manager of a Portland gun shop was called to identify some rifles he had purchased in September, 1979. He identified two of the three rifles but, when asked to identify the man from whom he had bought them, he could not.

Frederick Hazeem continued his testimony to the jury by stating that Brooks had told him he had shot Kittie Coy only three times. He said Brooks could not understand how the medical examiner was able to get four bullets out of her head.

Hazeem went on to say that Brooks had threatened the lives of several other people involved in the case, and that Brooks had bragged about taking Ms. Coy's false teeth, after her death, to keep as a souvenir. At this statement, members of the jury stirred uneasily in their chairs.

The next day Judge Jacobs dropped the charges of felony murder and kidnaping against Brooks, at the request of the alternate defense attorney, Tim Lyons. Lyons argued that Kittie Coy accompanied Brooks and Hazeem of her own free will and, as a result, the case did not involve kidnaping.

"I'm going to withdraw the charges of felony murder and first-degree kidnaping," Judge Jacobs said, "because the state has not shown sufficient evidence that it was kidnaping."

That same day Dennis Brooks took the stand as the only witness in his defense, contradicting the testimony of Frederick Hazeem and shifting the blame to Hazeem. Brooks, high-strung and jittery, said that Hazeem told him to go back to the car and get Kittie's purse. He said that as he was walking back from the car to the tree where Kittie was thumb-cuffed, he heard three gun shots.

"At first I didn't think that he had done it," Brooks said. Brooks also said he did not go all the way back to the tree and that Hazeem had met him half way, and that they then left together. Brooks denied that he even had a gun that day, and vehemently protested that he was not the one who shot Kittie Coy.

Deputy District Attorney Eglitis, in cross-examination, brought the defendant's previous convictions out into the open. He pointed out to the jury that Brooks had been convicted for assault, forgery, theft, and for receiving stolen property; also that Brooks used several aliases and fictitious birthdates.

When asked about throwing Ms. Coy's personal belongings from the car in order to destroy evidence,

Brooks' replied: "I was scared."

Brooks also made a confession in open court about how he lied to a grand jury and to Doug Peterson, a Portland police detective.

"Today is the first time you've told this story to anyone, right?" Eglitis asked him.

"Yes, sir," was Brooks reply.

Brooks testified that he had agreed with Hazeem only to thumb-cuff Kittie Coy to a tree as a means of scaring her, and that they planned to release her after he and Hazeem had a few drinks at Timberline Lodge.

With the testimony over, the jury could return a verdict of guilty or not guilty of murder. They could also, however, take the option of finding Brooks guilty of a lesser charge, such as manslaughter.

In the event of a guilty of murder verdict, the judge would have the option of sentencing Brooks to death or life imprisonment. Life imprisonment would bring a minimum of 25 years to be served before he would be eligible for parole.

The six-man, six-woman Clackamas County Circuit Court jury found Dennis Richard Brooks guilty of intentional murder on August 7, 1980, after five hours of deliberation, in the execution-style shooting death of Kittie Coy.

Brooks remained calm and resigned, showing little emotion as the verdict was read. As he left the courtroom, however, he broke into tears, and could be heard sobbing as he was being escorted away by Clackamas County officials.

The prosecution decided to seek the death penalty for Brooks, and, according to state laws, Judge Dale Jacobs had to take several things into consideration before imposing sentence.

First, Jacobs would have to decide if Brooks caused Ms. Coy's death "deliberately and with the expectation of death," and whether or not Brooks was reformable. That is, would he continue to "commit criminal acts of violence that would be a threat to society?" And, finally, Jacobs had to decide if the killing was "unreasonable in the response to the provocation."

If Jacobs could not agree to all three of the issues, he would have to sentence Brooks to life imprisonment. On the other hand, if he did agree to all three issues, he would have to sentence Brooks to death.

Before Jacobs made his decision, he would have to hear testimony at a sentencing hearing from Dr. Jack Seidler, the chief psychologist at the Oregon State Penitentiary, and he would hear additional testimony from Frederick Hazeem.

Hazeem, who was given 20 years for his role in the death of Kittie Coy—the maximum sentence for first degree manslaughter—testified that "Brooks had a history of violent behavior."

"I've known Brooks for about seven years and I've never known him to be without a weapon unless he didn't have access to one," said Hazeem.

Dr. Jack Seidler, the state psychologist, told Judge Jacobs that Brooks had "an anti-social personality with psychopathic proportions."

And then, on Tuesday, December 23, 1980, Judge Jacobs sentenced Dennis Brooks to death, after nearly three days of hearings. Brooks became the fourth man to receive the death sentence under Oregon's 1978 statute re-establishing such a sentence.

But in January, 1981, the Oregon Supreme Court overturned the state's death sentence statute, claiming that it was unconstitutional under its current wording.

As a result of the State Supreme Court ruling, Dennis Brooks and the three other men who were condemned to death in Oregon can now expect to face life imprisonment behind bars.

"STRANGLED MAN IN THE BLACK NEGLIGEE!"

by Tom Basinski

On May 13, 1986, the members of San Diego homicide team IV sat in the cramped cubicle that the administration loosely termed an "office."

Each of the four desks was against a different wall. When the men who occupied these desks turned in their chairs to face the middle of the room, their knees almost touched.

Team IV had drawn a homicide two days before on May 11th. It was not a homicide that would attract headlines. In fact, local crime buffs found the 12-line story on page six.

In spite of the low profile of the incident, the members of team IV were waging a terrific battle against the clock. If they did not solve this one in two weeks, it was unlikely that the case would be solved at all.

Each of the members of homicide team IV, except the leader, Sergeant Hank Olais, was being transferred in two weeks.

Easygoing, slow-moving Detective Fred Dreis would be moving across the hall to Missing Persons. Dreis was a 23-year veteran who said little, but whose mind never stopped working.

The pace of working homicide for the past eight years was beginning to tell on Fred Dreis. Too many

241

call-outs in the middle of the night were starting to get to Fred. He sometimes lamented, "Why can't they kill each other at nine in the morning?" The overtime was weighing him down. The four San Diego homicide teams were "on call" one week a month.

All of the teams were under a great deal of pressure to get their cases solved during the first few days. If a team drew more than one homicide during their "up" week, they usually handled whatever they drew.

Even a simple domestic homicide with a suspect in custody meant there was still a great deal of work to do. The families of both the victim and suspect had to be contacted and interviewed. Often the murders were seemingly motiveless. The follow-up work was necessary for uncovering clues as to motive.

Sometimes search warrants had to be obtained for bank records of the deceased or the suspect. After passion, money ranked up near the top in establishing a motive for a killing.

Then there was court. It seemed that the homicide cops were always either on "standby" for a homicide trial, or they were sitting in the courthouse hallway or on the witness stand for a trial.

More than once a detective would be at a crime scene collecting physical evidence on a homicide and the detective's beeper would go off summoning him to court.

It was a rough, grinding job. Fred Dreis would be easing out in a few weeks and he was not sorry.

Dreis' two partners, Dick Thwing and Jim Shively, would also be moving on. Thwing would be going across the hall to homicide team II and Shively would be in Missing Persons.

Thwing was 6 feet 7 inches tall and had a booming voice. He had an uncanny memory for names, dates and addresses.

On one occasion, a homicide detective from Chula Vista mentioned to Thwing the name of a person he was looking for. The San Diego homicide cop put his head back in a thoughtful gesture, took a drag on his cigarette, wrinkled up his face, and said, "He's twenty-six years old, lives at twenty-four thirteen First Avenue and works at the Job Corps. We interviewed him two years ago as a witness in the Holmes killing. He gave us some information, but held a lot back."

The Chula Vista detective, John Stewart, was skeptical and looked up what Thwing had said. Thwing was right.

Since Thwing's partners were leaving, he decided a change of scenery was in order. Team II had an opening so Thwing decided to go.

Jim Shively was on his way for the same reasons as Dreis. He was tired too. For some unknown reason, team IV had drawn more than its share of "border bandit" homicides.

Illegal Mexican aliens often crossed into the United States from Tijuana in search of the good life of hard labor in California's agricultural regions. The aliens would carry their life savings in their pockets in order to pay a smuggler for transportation past immigration checkpoints along the coast.

The "life savings" often consisted of about $200. The "border bandits," as they were called, would rob the aliens, who often traveled in groups of five to 10. After robbing the aliens, the bandits would frequently and wordlessly assassinate them right there on the moonlit trails.

The lucky ones would scatter into the night, sometimes back to Mexico. Seldom was anyone in authority told of the murders. Many times it was days before the body or bodies were discovered. The homicide team would arrive at the crime scene and notice that it had been trampled by other illegal aliens who kept on heading north.

There were virtually no clues and no witnesses who would ever come forth. Very often the victims were never identified.

Team IV drew a lot of these cases and it was a disheartening experience. Dreis, Thwing and Shively were all looking for a change from the grind. But, before they left, they had one more case they wanted to crack.

On the morning of May 11th, Aubrey Willis went over to the second-story condominium of Gerald Anderson, his good friend.

Willis found the front door ajar, which was unusual. Anderson lived on "B" Street in the Golden Hills section of San Diego.

This area was once a showcase for San Diego, 30 years before. Lately, however, Golden Hills was covered with gang graffiti. Narcotics officers did a lot of work in Golden Hills. The majority of residents were law-abiding and hardworking. The gang members and dopers, although in the minority, made it tough on the rest of the residents.

Willis knocked on the open door and it opened farther. Willis called out, "Gerald! Gerald! You in there, boy? Hey Gerald, it's Aubrey. What you doin'? They gonna steal you blind leavin' yo' door open. Hey Gerald!"

Willis took a few steps inside and saw that a fight had taken place there. Willis walked to the bedroom and stopped at Anderson's bedroom door. Willis froze in horror and disbelief.

The curtain had been torn from the west window. A lamp was shattered. There was blood on the walls, floor and bed. An empty drawer had been left on the floor, its contents strewn about.

On the other side of the bed Willis saw a body lying on its stomach. The hands and feet were tied and something was wrapped around the person's neck. Willis thought the person was Gerald Anderson, but he was not sure.

Willis ran from the building and dialed 911 from a pay phone. Within minutes the police were there. The patrol officer looked through the house quickly for more victims and then backed out to call for a sergeant and the homicide team.

Sergeant Hank Olais, Fred Dreis, Dick Thwing and Jim Shively showed up an hour later to begin their grim tasks.

The body was that of a slim, 6-foot-tall black male. He was clad in a black silk negligee with red trim.

Thwing rubbed the flimsy black material between his thumb and forefinger and said, "Nice. Do you like it, Fred?" Dreis was speaking into a tape recorder, noting the temperature of the room and which lights were on.

Dreis grinned at Thwing and shook his head, but never dropped a phrase as he continued his description of the disarrayed room.

A video cassette recorder wire was still plugged into the wall, but the VCR was gone. A suitcase had been dragged from the closet and left in the middle of the floor.

There was a photograph of Gerald Anderson on the table in the living room. The picture was of the same person that was dead in the bedroom.

The homicide detectives would have to wait for the autopsy, but their best guess at the time was that Anderson died from a beating and/or strangulation.

The detectives were not encouraged by the feminine-looking black nightgown the dead man was wearing. The sleuths knew that any case involving a homosexual or a transvestite contained inherent complications.

In many of the transvestite cases, the homicide victim would pick up a stranger in a bar and bring him someplace for a night of unbridled sexual passion. Very often the person accompanying the victim would be unaware of the true sex of his partner.

When the foreplay was at its zenith and the real gender was discovered, the passion would change from erotic to violent and the results would often be fatal. These cases were seldom solved.

Team IV completed its crime scene work late that afternoon. In spite of Anderson wearing the nightgown, there were no other women's clothing found in the victim's bedroom.

Sergeant Olais thought this was odd. A true transvestite usually had scads of exotic, clinging apparel. Yet Anderson had none.

Another bedroom contained a closet full of women's clothing. This collection was practical, and did not have the flair of the standard drag queen.

The surroundings showed that a woman actually lived in the apartment with Anderson. Shively (jokingly) wondered if the woman resident came home and found Anderson wearing her nightgown. Maybe the woman became enraged and killed Anderson.

This was a highly unlikely possibility as Anderson, although thin, was wiry and muscular, probably able to fight off an average woman.

While the detectives were still there, the female roommate, Naomi Smith, arrived home and incredulously wondered what the police were doing there. She was allowed to look around and tell the officers what was disturbed or missing.

She was taken to police headquarters and interviewed at length. Naomi Smith was married to a sailor who was away on a cruise. She lived with Gerald Anderson on a rent-only basis. There was no romantic involvement whatsoever.

Smith told sleuths that Anderson worked as a singer in a nightclub. He was hoping to catch on with a recording company and make it big in show business. Thwing asked her if Anderson sang well enough to make it big. Smith lowered her head and replied, "Not really. He was okay for the bars he sang in, but not good enough to cut a record."

Smith never knew Anderson to be either a homosexual or a transvestite.

Additionally, Smith said that a video cassette recorder was missing from the apartment along with two suitcases and some of her jewelry.

Thwing finished interviewing Smith and drove her

246

back to the house in the 2700 block of "B" Street. The crime scene work had been done and the entire place had been photographed and dusted for fingerprints, both inside and out.

Thwing and the others wanted to get this case wrapped up soon.

Meanwhile, the meeting back in the cramped homicide quarters continued. Sgt. Olais looked at his notes and asked questions. All witnesses had been interviewed.

The autopsy revealed that Anderson had died of asphyxia by strangulation. He had been hog-tied with a telephone cord that had been wrapped around his neck and tied to his hands and feet.

Anderson had been beaten severely, but not enough to cause death. Sgt. Olais gave each detective another set of things to do on the case. He reminded them that they would be scattered soon and he wanted the case cleared up before they left. They all agreed.

This was not to be, however. The transfers came, the detectives went, and the case of Gerald Anderson seemed to be at a standstill.

Enter the new homicide team IV.

Frank Martinez was an 18-year police veteran who had done five years in patrol. He was thorough, aggressive and smart. After patrol, Martinez pulled assignments in vice, and later in robbery.

Martinez stood 5 feet 8 inches tall and he weighed about 250 solid pounds. He had a massive chest and arms, and virtually no neck. Martinez was a lineman on the San Diego police football team that played the sheriff's department in a charity game every January.

Martinez did not play fancy football, nor did he do fancy police work. On the other hand, he was very smart and thought things through, both on the gridiron and in the police car. Martinez had been a good vice cop, working undercover and investigative assignments alike. In robbery, he had earned a reputation for being fair and tough.

Martinez welcomed his new assignment in homicide.

The other new members of team IV were Bob Lopez and Vince Villalvazo, both from the gang detail. These two detectives had been part of a new squad of officers that monitored and prosecuted the growing gang population of San Diego.

Heading up the squad was suave Hank Olais. He had been a homicide detective for several years before deciding to take the sergeant's test. Olais scored high and made sergeant right away. After a short stint in patrol, Olais applied for homicide and was soon back, this time in charge of team IV.

Olais was smooth and good-looking. Except for a crooked nose and a scar from a ratchet handle wielded by a Hell's Angel in 1974, Olais had a flawlessly handsome face.

As soon as the new team IV was formed, it drew its share of homicides. Sgt. Olais rode the new sleuths hard and their clearance rate was high. Team IV worked quickly and thoroughly and took their new cases to the district attorney for prosecution.

When team IV was caught up on its cases, Sgt. Olais pulled old cases that were still open and had the detectives do more follow-up.

One morning in mid-July, two months after Gerald Anderson's body was found, Sgt. Olais began passing out assignments on the Anderson case. There were witnesses who had to be re-interviewed.

Also, Olais had received a phone call telling him the name of a person who supposedly knew someone who knew who had killed Gerald Anderson.

The person with the knowledge of the case lived in a seedy hotel in the inner city. Olais handed the case folder to Frank Martinez and said, "Frank, I have somebody named 'Bo Peep' who should be interviewed. He lives in a sleazebag hotel. You will fit in there quite nicely. Go to it."

Martinez and Lopez drove to the hotel that rented

usually by the month, but sometimes by the hour.

They interviewed Bo Peep, a young man who looked to be about 26 years old, wearing flashy clothing and gold chains. The man had large, tobacco-stained teeth and watery eyes.

At the beginning of the interview there was a lot of stalling and denying on the part of Bo Peep.

Martinez started off by being nice. "I know you know about the case. I want to give you the chance to help us out and help society out to stop a killer from going free."

Bo Peep said, "I don't care 'bout no damned society. They ain't never did nuthin' for me. Screw 'em. I don't know nuthin'. Screw it, man."

Detective Martinez closed his notebook. His beefy fingers drummed slowly and lightly across the edges of his folder. He said nothing. The silence was uncomfortable.

Finally, Martinez spoke. "A man is dead. Several people know who killed the man. Bo Peep, you know the name of a person who knows the name of the killer. You are now involved as an accessory whether you like it or not. You have no choice."

Bo Peep sniffed and turned his head. "There ain't nuthin' you can do to me. This is some humbug jive you layin' on me."

Martinez continued, unperturbed. "I will arrest you as an accessory. We will have a trial. I will bring in the person who gave me your name. The person will testify. The jury will deliberate. You will be found guilty. You will got to jail for one year. The killer will remain free. Is that what you want, you in jail and the killer on the street laughing? Is it worth it?"

Bo Peep sat there unblinking. Finally, he took a king-size Kool from a pack and lit it. "Gut damn," he said. "I ain't did nuthin' and I'm the sum bitch who's goin' to jail. Gut damn. Justice, my ass."

Then, he gave Martinez the name of a woman who supposedly knew the killer. Martinez and Lopez thanked the witness and left.

Once inside the detective car that was parked at the hotel curb, Martinez looked at Lopez and grinned. "Close, wasn't it?" Martinez asked.

Lopez said, "Sure was. You can tell he's been to jail before."

Martinez started up the car. Martinez's eyes narrowed. "Yeah, and I would've put him there again. He can play games with somebody else."

It took two days to find the woman whom Bo Peep had told them about. As expected, she did not want to say anything.

Her reason was fear. She wanted justice done, but was afraid. She was separated from her husband, a small-time dope dealer. She had three children and was afraid.

Martinez came on real soft during the interview at police headquarters. They talked about her background. Martinez and the woman had grown up in the same neighborhood, only a few blocks apart. They knew a lot of the same people. They had gone to the same high school.

Martinez talked and talked. It was not working. Martinez reasoned with her. Nothing. He told her that her kids were heading in the same direction as her husband. The burly detective asked if she wanted more for her kids than the life she and her husband knew.

Martinez could see the wall of resistance starting to weaken, maybe just a little. He told her how serious the case was.

For a moment the woman's strength rallied. She would not talk. Martinez began to plead with her. He begged, stopping just short of getting down on his knees in the tiny interview room. Later, he said he would have done just that if necessary.

Then, the woman's eyes filled up. Martinez watched her until her eyes overflowed and a single tear rolled down each cheek. Once the first tear escaped, the rest came easily. Soon she was sobbing, her shoulders and

250

chest heaving. Finally, it came out: "Bobby Gray."

That was it. Martinez slumped back in his chair, his shirt soaked with sweat, his forehead and face glistening.

The woman related how Bobby Gray had told her he had picked up someone who he thought was a girl in a bar. They went to the girl's apartment and Gray found out soon enough that the girl was really a man.

A fight ensued and Gray tied the man up. Then, Gray left.

Martinez made arrangements to have the woman driven home from police headquarters. Martinez walked into the homicide office and told Hank Olais, "Bobby Gray is our man."

Olais said, "That wasn't too bad, was it?"

Martinez did a double-take and replied, "About as easy as doing oral surgery with a paring knife and pliers."

Detective Martinez went to the police computer and did a work-up on Bobby Gray, who turned out to be Bobby Ray Gray, 35 years old, small-time thief and burglar.

Gray had a lot of entries in the county computer. Many of the entries were for hanging around with a bunch of do-nothing guys in the parking lots of local liquor stores, drinking malt liquor out of a tall can that was inside a paper bag.

He did have a few arrests for theft. The best part was that Bobby Ray Gray was currently in the county jail for being caught burglarizing a business at night.

Martinez told Sgt. Olais the search for Gray would be a short one. Lopez looked at his watch and told Martinez that the jail inmates were probably eating dinner now, as it was about 5 p.m. Lopez suggested the cops get something to eat and then interview Gray in the early evening.

Martinez agreed. After deli sandwiches and coffee, the two homicide sleuths checked into the Central Detention Facility at 222 West "C" Street in downtown

251

San Diego.

The cops filled out the pink card which contained the name and inmate number of Bobby Ray Gray, along with the tank he was being held in. They also had to put down their names, identification numbers, agency name and phone number.

Martinez and Lopez were admitted through a barred door which led to a weapons locker where they deposited their guns, cuffs and bullets. They walked through another mechanically operated steel bar door and stood in front of the jailer, who asked to see their police identification cards.

The jailer kept the cards and handed them a yellow laminated jail identification card with an alligator clip that fastened onto the lapel.

The officers sat down on the wooden bench in the hallway and waited about 10 minutes before Gray was led to them by a young, beefy deputy.

Unlike in the bustling daytime hours, all of the jail interview rooms were empty. Martinez picked one at the end of the hall.

They sat down and Gray asked the detectives for a cigarette. Neither Martinez nor Lopez had one. Gray reached down into his sock and pulled out a pack of menthol filtered cigarettes. Martinez stared at Gray, who merely shrugged and looked away.

Martinez said, "Bobby, you're in here for burglary. Detective Lopez and I are not burglary detectives."

Martinez paused to let that sink in. Gray smoked. His eyes went from Martinez to Lopez and back to Martinez. "So?" Gray shrugged.

Martinez said, "We're homicide cops, Bobby." And he paused to let that one sink in. Same effect. Smoke. Eye movement. Another shrug and another, "So?"

Martinez continued. "We want to talk to you about a case we're working."

"Go ahead. I don't know nuthin' 'bout no homicide," Gray said.

Martinez explained to Gray that before they talked

252

they had to advise him of his rights. Martinez did so and Gray said he understood his rights and agreed to talk with the officers.

Outwardly, Martinez remained impassive. Inwardly, he could not believe that Gray had agreed to talk with him.

Gray said, "Okay dudes, here's the way it happened."

Gray explained that he was in a bar on Market Street in eastern San Diego. A woman came up to him in the bar and bought Gray two or three drinks in about an hour and a half. The woman suggested they go to her place. Gray agreed. Gray said they took a cab to a place on "B" Street.

Gray said the woman told him to go get in bed while she took a shower. Gray took off his clothes, except for his underwear. He lay on his stomach and soon fell asleep.

Martinez and Lopez exchanged glances, but said nothing. Martinez continued taking notes.

The next significant thing Gray recalled was someone lying on top of him and a sharp object up against his neck. Gray thought it might be one of the woman's fancy acrylic fingernails. Martinez silently recalled that Gerald Anderson had normal fingernails.

Gray could feel his underwear being pulled down and some type of lubricant being applied to his anal region. Gray turned his head enough to see that the sharp object against his neck was a knife.

Gray said he thought he was soon to become a dead man so he rolled over and grabbed the hand that held the knife all in one motion. The fight was on. During the struggle a wig fell off of Gray's assailant and Gray knew he was fighting a man.

Gray and Anderson rolled onto the floor. They got up. Punches were thrown. Gray picked up a lamp and smashed it over the victim's head. Gray then picked up a telephone and rammed it against Anderson's head. When Anderson went down Gray hog-tied him with

253

the telephone cord. When Gray knew Anderson was sufficiently under control, he took a shower to clean the blood off and then got dressed.

Gray called a relative to come and get him. By now the time was between 5 and 6 a.m.

While waiting for the relative, Gray helped himself to a video cassette recorder and a jewelry box. He ransacked the place and put some selected items in a suitcase he found in the closet.

Gray said he gave his relatives some of the loot from the victim's apartment and traded the VCR for some cocaine. That was it.

Gray pushed his chair back, lit up another cigarette and said, "And that's the way the thing went down. That dude be alive when I left."

Martinez asked for the name of the cab company that took him from the bar to Gerald Anderson's apartment and Gray told him.

Martinez asked where the knife was that Anderson held at his neck. Gray explained that he had thrown it away, and could not remember where. Gray insisted that Anderson was alive and hog-tied when he left. "I didn't kill nobody," were Gray's last words during the interview.

The next day Lopez and Martinez briefed Sgt. Olais. Everyone agreed that Gray's statements were self-serving at best and outright lies at worst.

However, if a jury believed Gray, he would go free for committing a homicide in self-defense.

Martinez's first task was to see if Gray's statements withstood scrutiny.

The detectives checked with the cab company and found that no cab picked up anyone near the bar from where Gray said he and Anderson had left. The time lapse was so great that finding witnesses who remembered Gray and a "lady" on that night was not successful. It may have been that no one could remember. It also could have meant that Gray was lying.

Also, sleuths believed Gray's knife story was ludicrous. No knife was found at the crime scene. Why did Gray dispose of the best piece of evidence to give credence to his self-defense story?

Even if Gray had thrown the knife away he should have been able to remember where he had thrown it. It was not as if he was grief-stricken and in shock, since Gray had taken time to shower and ransack the place.

Martinez and Lopez checked with Gray's relatives and retrieved an empty suitcase and jewelry box.

Naomi Smith, the woman living with Anderson, identified her jewelry box, but could not identify the suitcase.

A wig was found at the crime scene. The wig belonged to the roommate, and was found in a different room from where she had left it.

Martinez and Lopez went to the bar where Gerald Anderson sang. They were told that Anderson never dressed in drag when he performed and that he had never been seen dressed in drag at any time. Nor was Gerald Anderson known to be a homosexual.

Martinez and Lopez were confused about where the nightgown came from. It did not belong to Naomi Smith and Anderson did not own any other trappings that could be termed "feminine."

Even though a lot of questions were unanswered, Martinez was convinced that Gray was lying about the majority of the evening's events.

The entire investigative package was assembled and presented to the district attorney's office. Deputy D.A. Patricia Cookson was assigned to prosecute the case. She filed murder charges against Gray and various dates were set for arraignment, preliminary hearing and trial.

Somewhere along the line, Gray sized up his chances in this case. Perhaps his appointed lawyer, or maybe even a jailhouse lawyer, detailed what the prosecution would try to prove. They would also assess what his defense sounded like. In short, Gray's defense sounded pretty lame.

Prior to the preliminary hearing, Bobby Ray Gray pleaded guilty to second-degree murder. He is now serving a 15-year-to-life sentence in the California prison system.

Frank Martinez has been promoted to sergeant and is now working in the patrol division on the graveyard shift. He keeps reminding himself that it was indeed a promotion.

During periods of down time, Sgt. Olais continues to pull inactive cases from the files and assigns them to his detectives.

EDITOR'S NOTE:
Aubrey Willis, Naomi Smith and Bo Peep are not the real names of the persons so named in the foregoing story. Fictitious names have been used because there is no reason for public interest in the identities of these persons.

"BIZARRE SCRAWLS BESIDE THE BEHEADED BACHELOR"

by Bruce Gibney

The Shining was a hugely successful horror novel by Stephen King turned into a high-budgeted, blood-drenched, horror film starring Jack Nicholson.

The movie opened to mixed reviews, but was something of a campy hit once it came out on video cassette and cable TV.

In July 1987, *The Shining* was all that people of Reading, Pennsylvania, could talk about — the hideous, blood feast of a movie, and an even more shocking real life murder that occurred in their otherwise pristine community. It was a classic case of life imitating art.

The main player in this sanguinary police drama was Stanley Detweiler, a quiet, 42-year-old bachelor who lived modestly in a five-room apartment on South Fifth Street.

Dark-haired and slender with sensitive, large brown eyes, Detweiler enjoyed a fulfilling but unpublicized lifestyle. That, likely, is exactly how he wanted it.

Born in Sellersville, Pennsylvania, and educated in nearby Souderton, Detweiler was a talented musician and a primary organist for his church. He practiced endlessly with the high point being every Sunday when he played the organ for the Silverdale Brethren in

Christ Church, where he also served on the church board.

When not playing, Detweiler enjoyed listening to one of the hundreds of recordings he had in his extensive music library.

Unfortunately, organists are like poets — their skills are in demand and widely appreciated, but rarely can they make a living at their art.

Stan Detweiler was no exception; he lived for his art, but to pay the rent, he waited tables at the Holiday Inn, in Muhlenburg.

He had no complaints. The hotel treated him nicely and paid him handsomely. Management had no complaints either. Detweiler was punctual, hardworking and friendly. The hotel was happy to have him.

Detweiler was scheduled to work the night shift on Friday, July 24, 1987. He spent the day listening to organ music and going over the sheet music he would play at the church on Sunday. Later in the afternoon, he showered, dressed and got ready for work.

Before leaving, he chatted with his roommate Brad Clark, 22.

Clark was not working Friday night.

"Anything planned?" Detweiler asked his roommate.

"Not much," Clark replied. "Hit a few clubs. Maybe head down to the Rooster Cafe later on."

Detweiler knew the club. It was a smoky, artsy place that catered to the homosexual crowd.

Leaving, Detweiler said, "See ya later."

The call that came into the Reading police station at 3:30 Saturday morning was typical. It came from a paperboy who was delivering the *Reading Times*.

The newsboy said a man had staggered out of an apartment on South Fifth Street screaming for help. "He said someone had killed his roommate," the newsboy told the dispatcher.

A police cruiser with two beefy officers inside sped through the sultry July night and stopped in front of the apartments at 201 South Fifth Street.

They raced inside. An enormous blood pool greeted the officers as they pushed open the door to the ground-floor apartment.

The officers gingerly stepped over it into the living room and were greeted by the ghastly sight of a man sprawled in another blood pool. Laying next to him was his head, with the face pointed toward the floor.

Above the head in two-foot high letters was written the word "REDUM."

The lead officer stayed in the living room, wondering what the word REDUM meant, while his partner checked the other rooms.

"Hey! In here," his partner shouted.

The officer ran into the other room where his partner stood. On the wall was another word, in huge letters. This time the word was "REDRUM." In small letters was painted "LSD."

The lawmen stayed only long enough to make sure there were no other victims before they retreated. One officer stayed at the front door to keep spectators out while his partner notified headquarters.

A team of detectives under the direction of Lieutenant William D. McGuire arrived. They were followed by a deputy coroner and a crime lab team.

A veteran cop, McGuire personally inspected the crime scene. It was one of the bloodiest and most gruesome experiences of his career.

The victim's body was sprawled chest up on the living room floor about two feet from the front door. The head was lying on the floor at the left side of the corpse, near its elbow. Near the head was a blood-smeared bread knife, the long thin blade bent almost into a knot.

The blood was so thick that it was seeping through the floorboards into the basement. There was also blood on the light switch plates, and bloody footprints tracking through the flat. In the bathroom near the kitchen area toward the rear of the apartment, detectives found bloody towels stuffed in the toilet. They also found traces of blood in the shower and on the shower curtain.

On a chair in the living room, police found a wallet about 20 feet from the body. The wallet contained $20 in cash and identification for Stanley Detweiler. The photo on the ID matched the victim.

The man who came rushing out into the street screaming was Detweiler's roommate, Brad Clark.

Clark had been taken to the hospital where he was being treated for shock. A detective went to the hospital to question him.

Clark told the sleuth that he returned home to the apartment at 3:30 a.m. and found the door ajar. He pushed it open and that's when he saw the blood in the vestibule and then the body of his roommate with his head laying next to it. He said he screamed and ran out of the apartment.

Clark said he didn't know who could have done such a grisly thing or why. "Stan is one of the nicest guys in the world," he told the detective. "He didn't have an enemy in the world."

Somebody apparently didn't like him, however.

At the autopsy, performed later Saturday, pathologist Neil A. Hoffman discovered that there were bruises on Detweiler's body and some broken ribs and cuts in the facial area which indicated he had struggled with his assailant. The cause of death, however, was listed as decapitation.

"He was alive when his head was cut off," Hoffman said.

According to the report, Detweiler was beaten and likely unconscious when the killer went to the kitchen and returned with a bread knife to cut through his neck.

The knife cut through the muscle and tissue but was not strong enough to cut through the neck bone, according to the autopsy findings, so the attacker finished the job by gripping the victim's head and twisting it off the neck stem.

The savagery of the attack absolutely astounded the weary-eyed detectives, who thought they had seen just about every hair-raising example of human cruelty possible. Nothing less than a monster had pushed his way through the front door and turned the five-room, nicely furnished apartment into a house of carnage.

But why? And, equally important, why Stanley Detweiler?

Investigators assembled in the stationhouse. It had been a long morning, and everyone was tired, but there was a lot more to do.

Two of the most puzzling aspects of the case were the meanings of the words "REDUM" and "RED-RUM," and why they were written in blood on the apartment walls.

This was solved when an investigator said "REDRUM" was murder spelled backward. He said the word was written in blood on a wall in the horror movie *The Shining*, which had been released as a movie several years earlier and had been shown on cable TV on Thursday night.

"Go down and get a copy from the video store," Lieutenant McGuire instructed. "Maybe it will tell us something about this killer."

The motive for the slaying was apparently psychological. Robbery didn't seem to be it — the victim's wallet with cash inside was found on a chair just 20 feet from the body.

"Probably somebody completely stoned on drugs," one detective offered.

That seemed a plausible theory.

But why Detweiler? According to his roommate and neighbors, the 42-year-old churchgoing organ player was one of the nicest, most pleasant persons around. What could he have done to prompt such a hideous bloodbath?

Employees at the Holiday Inn were questioned. According to them, Detweiler had arrived promptly for work at six, worked a full shift, and then left the hotel for home shortly before midnight.

"He seemed in a very happy mood," his boss recalled. "He didn't say anything to me about being in trouble."

Co-workers said pretty much the same thing. "He wasn't into drugs or anything," one employee said. "I can't think of a single person who disliked him."

Detweiler's passions centered around organ music and activities at his church — hardly activities that would incite mayhem.

Detectives contacted the crime lab and asked if there was anything to report. A crime technician said that they had tested the bloodstains and determined that they had all come from the victim. The tech added that they had lifted prints from different areas of the victim's apartment and were in the process of identifying them.

While waiting for a response from the lab, detectives searched through boxes of clothes, papers and personal items that been confiscated from the apartment. They also checked out dozens of leads that were phoned in. The murder was one of the most shocking in recent memory and there was no shortage of callers.

There was also no shortage of media coverage. Once reporters learned that a man had been decapitated in a murder almost identical to one in a popular movie, they converged on the South Fifth Street apartment. Police denied entry to the first-floor apartment, but one enterprising photographer climbed a ladder and shot a photo (through a side window) of the huge letters written in blood on the wall.

At a news conference on July 26th, Police Chief Rodney E. Steffy told reporters that detectives had so far interviewed 30 persons in connection with the slaying but as yet there were no suspects.

"What's the motive?" a reporter asked.

"We don't really have one," the chief admitted. "At this time we don't know why the victim was murdered."

He explained that police were working on a number of theories but nothing he cared to comment on right now.

One reporter asked if the murder was part of a blood ritual and if a satanic cult was involved.

The chief responded that police initially considered that because the victim was murdered in such a gruesome way, suggesting a satanic cult might have been involved, "But we didn't find any signs of evidence of cult activity," he said, "so we don't consider that theory a possibility."

Another reporter asked if police had figured out the importance of the words scrawled on the apartment wall.

"We don't know if the killer was trying to mimic the movie *The Shining* or if this was his sick idea of a joke," Chief Steffy said.

Investigators watched the movie for possible clues that might help them learn more about the killer. However, investigators learned that if there were clues in the movie, they were so subtle that only the killer could identify them.

Running short of leads, investigators contacted the FBI office in Philadelphia and requested information as to how to acquire a psychological profile on the killer.

The agent in charge said he could provide a specialist who might be able to help them. He explained that they would need to fill out a 48-page questionnaire detailing facts about the victim and the murder. The questionnaire would ask if the victim was black or white, if he or she was found inside or outside the apartment and how the person was attacked.

Investigators returned to the field and re-interviewed everyone for any possible new information that might have occurred to them since the killing. The search took sleuths to bars and clubs and back to the church where Detweiler had spent so many joyous hours playing the organ.

The interviews turned up nothing new — everybody liked Stanley Detweiler. He simply didn't have an enemy in the world.

"Well someone didn't like him," grumbled Detective Dennis Carl. A big man with a stoic demeanor, he had been working nonstop since early Saturday morning.

"If not Detweiler, how about the roommate?" Lieutenant McGuire asked.

"You mean did Clark kill Detweiler?"

The lieutenant shook his head. Clark had been initially viewed as a suspect. He was repeatedly questioned over the weekend and detectives were certain he had nothing to do with the crime.

"Maybe Clark was the intended victim," the lieutenant said. "He didn't get home until after three o'clock. By then Detweiler was already dead."

"Why would anyone want Clark murdered?" the detective asked.

"Let's ask him."

Clark was still shaken from his ordeal but agreed to talk. He still couldn't believe that his roommate was dead. "He was just the last person in the world you would expect this to happen to," he said.

Asked if he might have been the intended victim, Clark just shook his head. He wasn't involved with drugs. He didn't dabble in witchcraft or strange cults. He didn't have any enemies.

He told detectives that he left the apartment shortly after Detweiler went to work and saw some friends. He stayed with them until about nine o'clock and then went to a nightclub. He met some more friends, had a drink and then went to another club. It was a typical evening.

He said he didn't get into any arguments and he was pretty sure he wasn't followed.

"What about Thursday night?" McGuire asked.

"Pretty much the same," Clark replied.

"Did you come home alone?"

"Yes."

"What clubs did you go to?"

Clark then named the Rooster Cafe.

"I know the place," the lieutenant answered. "It's a gay joint. Did you meet anyone there?"

"Just some friends."

"Anyone else?"

"No."

Then pausing, Clark said, "Wait a minute. I did."

He explained that while in the cafe on Thursday night he had struck up a conversation with a teenager who was playing an arcade game. He said they went outside and ran into another teenager.

"The guys weren't doing anything and I suggested they come back to the apartment," Clark said. "Stanley has a great sound system and we could listen to music and drink beers."

He said they started to head back for the apartment when a girl stopped to talk. The teenagers decided to go with the girl but made arrangements to see Clark at a later date.

"That was the last I saw of them," Clark said.

He said the teen he met at the cafe was named Michael. His buddy was Ned. Clark didn't know their last names or where they lived.

He described Michael as 16 to 18 years old, 5 feet 10 inches tall, 140 pounds with blond hair worn over the collar. Ned was about the same age, 5 feet 8 inches tall and 125 pounds with curly dark brown hair and a slight mustache. He said he was sure he could identify them if he saw them again.

"Did you give them your address?" the lieutenant asked.

Clark nodded. "I told Michael," he said. "He said he was on foot and wanted to know if we could walk there."

It wasn't much of a lead, detectives admitted. A couple of teenagers met casually in an after-hours joint who traipsed after a girl didn't fit the profile of blood-crazed maniacs. Still, it had to be checked out.

A detective went back to the Rooster Cafe and pestered bartenders about the two teens. One of the waiters said he knew a kid named Ned who fit the description given by Clark.

"He hangs around here," the employee said.

Ned was quite popular at the cafe and it didn't take detectives long to come up with a last name or an address.

That evening they paid Ned a visit. He appeared startled to open the door and find two plainclothes detectives on the stoop seeking him.

"What is this about?"

The detectives identified themselves and told him they were investigating a murder case. "What were you doing Thursday evening?" one detective asked.

Ned remembered the evening well. The young girl in the tight leather dress, high heels and silk blouse was actually a hooker. She was sweet, but all business.

"Too bad," Ned said wistfully. "I really liked her."

Impatient, one of the detectives asked, "Who was your blond-haired buddy?"

"Oh, Mike," Ned said. "You mean Mike Boettlin. I see him outside the cafe all the time."

"What did you do after you met the hooker?" the detective asked.

Ned said that he and Mike chatted with the girl before she slinked off to do the night trade and they went to play pinball. Ned said he bid Mike goodbye and went home.

The next time he saw Mike was Monday. He said they played some games at a game room and drank a couple of sodas.

Mike was his old good-natured self, Ned said, except for one thing.

"He asked me if I heard about that murder on South Fifth Street," Ned recalled. "I told him I had. He said that was the place we were going to go Thursday night."

Sleuths learned that Michael Boettlin, 16, lived on Walnut Street in suburban Reading. He didn't have a police record and his name didn't appear in police files. As far as the cops were concerned, Michael Boettlin was just a nobody.

Anthony Miccicke is a Reading patrol officer and by coincidence he knew Michael Boettlin and lived just a couple of doors down from the Boettlin home.

At 9:30 Tuesday morning, July 28th Miccicke went to the Boettlin home and asked to see Mike.

When the teenager appeared, Miccicke explained that detectives wanted to talk to him about a police matter and he was taking him downtown.

When Mike asked what the police wanted to talk to him about, Miccicke said he didn't know. Pausing, Boettlin said, "Well, I bet I know what they want. It's probably about that murder."

And it probably was.

Michael Boettlin was only 16 and not very good at keeping a secret. In a confession made during a five-hour interrogation, he told police everything about the Detweiler murder. It was one of the most shocking statements detectives could remember.

The youngster said he was looking for something to do on the night of the murder when he ran into a buddy, John Calvaresi.

Calvaresi, 22, described later by friend as "a guy who went in and out of crowds but was not a psychopath who cut off heads," had spent most of Friday, July 24th, playing pool at a game room.

Boettlin said they were both broke and wanted money for beer and arcade games. He said he told Calvaresi about the man he met the night before and the roommate who was supposed to have the great sound system.

"We decided to go see what they had," Boettlin said.

"You mean that you wanted to see what he had so you could take it," one detective clarified.

"That's right," Boettlin said.

Before leaving, the teen said they exchanged shoes, and after the trade each was wearing one boot and one sneaker.

"It was John's idea," Boettlin said. "I thought it was a little screwy, but he thought it was neat."

After switching shoes, they continued to the apartment on South Fifth Street that Boettlin had only heard about and had never been to.

The youth said they knocked on the door and when a man answered they forced their way inside. Boettlin said the man who answered the door wasn't the same one he had met the night before.

Not that it mattered. Boettlin said they kicked and beat the victim to the floor then continued to beat him until he was unconscious. Boettlin said he then went looking through the apartment for items to steal while Calvaresi remained in the living room with the victim.

Boettlin said when he returned to the living room Calvaresi was holding a long, thin knife in his hand and was sawing the man's neck.

"He was cutting and cutting and blood was going everywhere," Boettlin recalled. "There was so much blood."

He said Calvaresi put down the knife and began twisting the victim's head in his hands until it came free. He continued playing with Detweiler's head until it was completely covered with blood and spillage from the head.

According to Boettlin, Calvaresi then dipped his hands in the blood and wrote "REDUM" and "RED-RUM" on the walls. He also scrawled LSD in blood.

Calvaresi, Boettlin said, gave no reason for ripping off the victim's head or scrawling the ghoulish messages.

"I guess he thought it was a neat thing to do," one lawman remarked.

Boettlin said that after writing the words, the two took separate showers to wash off the blood and tossed the towels into the toilet. Afterward, they searched the house and took a checkbook, two shirts and a watch, along with some money that was on the dresser.

They kept the money — seven dollars a piece — and disposed of the rest in a park pond. Those items were later recovered by the Reading Search and Rescue Team.

Boettlin insisted that the motive for going to the house was to steal the expensive stereo equipment and other valuable items that might be there and not to kill anyone.

"I don't know why it happened," he said.

"Were you on drugs like LSD?" one investigator asked.

Boettlin shook his head. "I wasn't high and as far as I know neither was John."

He said he did not participate in the murder or the beheading. "I only wanted to steal," Boettlin insisted.

John Calvaresi had a lengthy juvenile record. Most recently he had been arrested on charges stemming from a street fight. To authorities, however, he was known as more of a nuisance than a hard-core delinquent.

Investigators went looking for him. They got a tip that Calvaresi was aware the police were looking for him and he was hiding out at a relative's home on North 10th Street in rural Reading.

Two officers went to the house which was set back from the curb and surrounded by a forest. After checking the house, one of the officers pulled out a pair of binoculars and scanned the woods.

After several minutes, the officer spotted a head pop out from behind a tree. "Let's go John," one of the detectives yelled.

Flanked by police, John Calvaresi was physically escorted past a mob of reporters into the police station where he was interrogated. Afterwards, he was arraigned on 26 counts of criminal homicide, murder, voluntary manslaughter, burglary, aggravated assault, robbery and conspiracy.

On July 30th, Calvaresi appeared on a bail hearing before Judge Calvin E. Smith.

Dressed in jeans, a camouflage T-shirt, a black leather jacket and white sneakers with no socks or laces, he appeared confused by all the attention being given him.

The bail hearing was brief.

"Have you ever posted bail in the past?" Judge Smith asked.

"Yeah, but I jumped bail," Calvaresi replied, thrusting his hands into the pockets of his jacket. "After my bail was paid, I went to another state."

He explained that he moved to California, where he worked in a carnival from June 1986 until March 1987. He said he then returned to Pennsylvania and was arrested.

"Tell me about your family," Smith said.

"They split up," Calvaresi replied.

"Where have you been living?"

"On the streets."

"Have you ever had any mental problems or been treated for mental conditions?"

"Do I have to answer that?"

"No."

"Fine."

Judge Smith ruled that because of the severity of the crimes and the defendant's past criminal record, bail would be denied.

Calvaresi was returned to the Berks County Jail and ordered to be kept isolated from Michael Boettlin, who was being held as an adult.

Trials were scheduled for both men with Calvaresi to appear first. However, on March 25th, 1988, in a plea-bargain agreement, Calvaresi pleaded guilty to first-degree murder and was sentenced to life in prison without the possibility of parole.

Michael Boettlin went on trial in August 1988. He claimed the gruesome slaying was Calvaresi's work and that he had not participated. He said he did not try to stop his friend from his grisly mission or call police because he was terrified that his head would be next.

Calvaresi, however, testified as a prosecution witness. He said Boettlin had willingly participated in the crime and had held Detweiler's hand down with his foot so he could cut off the victim's neck.

Jurors agreed and found Boettlin guilty of first-degree murder. He was sentenced to life in prison.

Both men are currently serving their terms in the Pennsylvania prison system.

EDITOR'S NOTE:
Brad Clark and Ned are not the real names of the persons so named in the foregoing story. Fictitious names have been used because there is no reason for public interest in the identities of these persons. The Rooster Cafe is also a fictitious name.

"ANIMALS FEASTED ON HIS ROTTING CORPSE!"

by Patricia Harrell

The baying of the hounds in pursuit of a raccoon echoed through the trees in the cool darkness of that spring night, filling the hunters with exhilaration as they urged on their mules in the rugged timberland of southeastern Oklahoma's Pushmataha County. Even as the thrill of the hunt came upon the five mounted men, each of whom wore a miner's wheel-lamp helmet, their cunning quarry darted ahead of the howling dogs like the black-masked bandit he resembled, and soon gave his canine pursuers the slip in the forest's dense undergrowth.

As the hounds yelped in confusion and began circling about, trying to pick up the elusive coon's scent again, the mounted hunters became separated from each other in the dark woods. The huge pine forest, with its tall trees, thick brush, and deep ravines, was a familiar stomping ground to four of the men, but the hunting party's fifth member, Juan Sanchez, was a newcomer. Finding himself alone with only his helmet light offering limited illumination amid the deep, shadowy darkness, Sanchez began to feel an almost atavistic fear of the night tightening its grip on him.

Beyond the limits of his beam, Sanchez could see only blacker shadows within the deep darkness—

shadows that took on sinister shapes and summoned nameless horrors to mind. Then, suddenly, his ears picked up the sound of voices and laughter. Relieved that his hunting companions were not too far off, he reined his mount toward the sounds and urged it forward.

The mule took a few tentative steps and then stopped short. Sanchez gave it a few kicks, but the animal stubbornly refused to move. Man and mule remained motionless in a shallow ravine.

As Sanchez pondered how he could get the balking beast to move, he slowly became aware of a foul stench. Wondering if a dead animal was lying nearby, he aimed his helmet light toward the ground directly in front of the mule. What Sanchez saw then raised the short hairs on the back of his neck and he let out a cry of sheer horror.

The beam of the hunter's lamp was illuminating the skeletal remains of a decomposing human corpse.

Scant moments later, Sanchez's cry brought his companions riding up. Their combined lamp beams immediately gave the other hunters a start as they saw, very clearly now, what had terrified Sanchez.

On the ground before the five mounted hunters lay a portion of a human torso with a leg covered by the tattered remnants of a pair of blue-denim jeans. The skeletal foot was in a brown, lace-up boot, misshapen by long exposure to the elements. Clinging to the bones were strips and bits of foul-smelling, desiccated flesh.

Justin Haws, one of the other hunters, got off his mule and picked up a long, thin piece of broken-off branch lying nearby. Holding his nose, he used the stick to pry open one of the pockets of the frayed jeans. He could barely make out the dull metal sheen of some coins and what looked like a set of keys.

As the riders glanced around, one of their headlamp beams picked up an oval, grayish-white object lying about 20 feet from the group. Barry Davis, another of the hunters, reluctantly went over to check it out. When he reached the spot, he found himself staring into the empty eye sockets of a human skull.

Suddenly, the hunters became aware again of their hounds' baying. The dogs were still trying to latch on to the coon's scent. Now the baying of the hounds took on an ominous tone, chilling the hunters' blood.

With all thoughts of coon hunting banished, the hunters began calling their dogs to heel. After attaching a handkerchief to a nearby tree to mark the spot of the grisly find, the five hunters beat a hasty retreat.

The shaken men were relieved to find that they were less than 100 feet from a gravel road. Stopping just long enough to tie a beer can to a tree at the point where they emerged from the woods, they rushed to where they had left their pickup trucks. Only after loading the mules into the horse trailers did the men pause to discuss their next step. It was 10:30 p.m., Sunday, May 27, 1990. Less than an hour had passed since Sanchez made his grim discovery.

Three of the hunters had driven some distance to join the hunting party, so they were reluctant to get mired in the delays involved in an investigation of the mysterious corpse. The consensus was that those three would return to their homes, which were in a neighboring county. The two locals, Juan Sanchez and Justin Haws, would wait until daylight to notify the Pushmataha County authorities.

On Monday, May 28th, Don Henley, an investigator with the Pushmataha County District Attorney's Office, sprang awake to the early-morning jangling of his telephone. The caller was a casual acquaintance — Justin Haws, one of the coon hunters. Haws was calling to inform Henley about the skeleton found by the hunting party in the timberland near Sobol the previous night.

The call quickly dashed Henley's holiday plans for a leisurely Memorial Day. He immediately reported what he'd just heard to the Pushmataha County Sheriff's Office and the Oklahoma State Bureau of Investigation (OSBI). Then, after quickly getting dressed, Henley headed for the OSBI's regional office in Antlers, where Senior Agent Chuck Jeffries would be waiting for him.

A few minutes later, the two investigators were driving southeast through the rolling forestland toward the wide spot along State Highway 3 where a general store and a weathered Baptist Church are the only visible signs of the existence of Sobol, Oklahoma.

Waiting at the Sobol store with Justin Haws and Juan Sanchez was a contingent of law enforcement officers, including OSBI Inspector George McFarland, Agents Reanae Hamm and David Seals, and Pushmataha County Deputy Lee Ayers. The convoy of cars led by Deputy Ayers and the two coon hunters soon turned north onto a lumber road designated as Weyerhauser Road No. 80,000.

The huge Weyerhauser Lumber Company has carved more than 5,600 miles of such roads out of the vastness of the 900,000 acres of timberland it cultivates in Oklahoma. The group of official vehicles followed the narrow meandering road — traveled primarily by lumber trucks hauling logs to the mill — for about 11 miles before Justin Haws spotted the beer can tied at eye-level to one of the trees.

Five minutes later, Juan Sanchez and Justin Haws led the officers to something which, in the brightness of day, was even more offensive to the senses than the macabre partial skeleton that had frightened them in the darkness of night.

The foul smell hit them hard as the group, following a dry creekbed that ran perpendicular to the road, came upon a heavy plastic tarpaulin. Weaker stomachs tightened at the sight and sound of the large green flies hovering above the tan sheet of plastic. Almost hidden by the cloud of flies — whose persistent buzz reverberated through the forest — was a decomposed human corpse.

"It was hard to tell that it was a human body," Agent Jeffries later said. "There was just a few bones, but the tarp was probably an inch thick, with decomposed matter and fatty tissue."

At one edge of the tan plastic shroud lay a brown, lace-up workboot. A few clumps of dark hair and large fragments of a once colorful flannel shirt could be seen among the decaying bits of flesh.

Leading away from the tarp, down deeper into the ravine, was a trail formed by clumps of hair and bits of blue denim material. The macabre trail, apparently made by a wild animal dragging a portion of the corpse deeper into the woods, led to the partial skeleton found by Juan Sanchez on the previous night. The skull lay midway between the two body sections.

Mindful of the need to preserve, uncontaminated, any evidence that had survived the passage of time and exposure to the elements, Inspector McFarland dispatched an officer to escort Justin Haws and Juan Sanchez away from the scene, back to their vehicles.

Now the homicide team swung into action. Agent Hamm measured, photographed and sketched the crime scene, while Agent Seals slowly and methodically searched the surrounding area for anything unusual. Agent Jeffries donned surgical gloves and checked the contents of the dead man's pockets.

The right front pocket yielded a pocket knife, some coins, a set of keys, and five rounds of live bullets. The left pocket relinquished a wallet containing some money and a Texas driver's license. The license was issued to a 35-year-old white male named Robert L. Dunigan. According to other documentation in the wallet, Dunigan currently resided in Mesquite, Texas.

Could this Robert Dunigan have suffered a heart attack or a fatal accident while he'd been out alone in the woods? The investigators thought it unlikely. The plastic tarp strongly indicated that the victim was killed elsewhere, then wrapped in the tarp and transported to the forest.

The agents wondered why anyone would go to the trouble of hauling a body to this remote area and then fail to remove the victim's identification. No matter. They were grateful that such lapses of logic seemed to be part and parcel of criminals' thought processes. The criminals' deficiencies certainly made the sleuths' job easier.

By midday, the scattered remains had been gathered and zipped inside a body pouch, and placed in an ambulance to be taken to the medical examiner's lab in Oklahoma City. Agent Hamm, now in charge of the investigation, watched the ambulance move slowly down the lumber road and fought back her fears that the case might go unsolved.

Inspector McFarland had told her, "This will be a good case for your first whodunit." On hearing that, Reanae Hamm's youthfully flawless complexion had turned pink with enthusiasm. Now, the young woman's enthusiasm was tempered by anxiety. Hamm had served the bureau as a forensic chemist for four years, but she'd been with the investigative unit only three months. Her peers in the male-dominated field of law enforcement had been helpful but reserved. This was her chance to become a bona fide member of the team—to prove her worth as an investigator.

Agent Hamm knew the odds were against finding the killer. Already long past were those all-important 24 hours immediately following the crime—those hours in which, statistically, most homicides are solved. This victim had been lying in the woods for weeks—perhaps months. Time and the elements had done their work.

The detectives found almost nothing that could be considered a clue. The skull bore no indication of trauma—no bullet holes and no evidence of bludgeoning with the proberbial blunt instrument. The method used to kill often links the perpetrator to the victim, but in this case, the agents found themselves left wondering *"whatdunit?"* The sleuths had been unable to determine the cause of death and doubted that even the forensic experts could do so. Without the identification found in the victim's wallet, the investigation would already have run into a dead end.

"What if we find Robert L. Dunigan alive and well and living in Texas?" one of the other agents asked.

"We'll ask how it happens that we found his personal papers on a corpse in Oklahoma. There's got to be *some* connection," Hamm responded.

As it turned out, Robert L. Dunigan was *not* alive and well and living in Texas. Family members in Mesquite — a suburb of Dallas — told the authorities that they had not seen or heard from the young husband and father since the middle of March.

By the time Agent Hamm, accompanied by Special Agent Perry Unruh, made the trip to Texas to talk with the bereaved relatives, dental records had proved beyond a reasonable doubt that the skeletal remains were indeed those of Robert Dunigan.

It was when the agents entered the working-class home where Dunigan had lived and worked and loved, that the victim in Reanae Hamm's "first homicide" turned into a real person. Described as a devoted son and a loving husband and father, Robert Dunigan smiled at Hamm from a photograph.

As she looked at the husky, good-looking man in the photograph, Hamm was struck by a sudden mental image of scattered bones and decaying tissue. She felt the full weight of responsibility. Her job, she clearly saw, was to reconstruct the series of events that had led to Dunigan's death. What random twist of fate had led the smiling young man to the pine forests of Pushmataha County? Or — what fatal error in judgment?

The innate decency of the grieving family made a deep impression on the investigators, but — mindful that crimes of violet passion are often committed by those nearest and dearest to a victim — the sleuths took particular note that Robert was last seen in the com-

278

pany of a male relative. That relative, an individual named Rusty, had driven Robert to Durant, Oklahoma, where Robert was to stay for two or three weeks "doing some work for a friend."

Robert had been wearing blue jeans, a flannel shirt, and brown workboots when he kissed his wife and children goodbye and drove off with Rusty.

When the officers contacted him, Rusty told then, "When I left Robert in Durant, he told me he'd see me in three to four weeks, but he never showed up. I drove back up there a couple of times, but his buddy said he hadn't seen him since that first day."

A background check revealed that both Robert Dunigan and Rusty—in spite of an upbringing that stressed the values of hard work and faith—had allegedly succumbed to the lure of the quick money associated with narcotics. Both had once been charged with carrying a concealed weapon and both were suspected of low-level involvement in the drug-culture that flourished in and around the grungy bars of east Dallas.

With little difficulty, the officers obtained Rusty's admission that the purpose of Robert's trip to Oklahoma was to set up a drug lab "somewhere in the backwoods." With visible trepidation, Rusty divulged the name of Robert's friend and co-partner in the proposed enterprise. When the officers learned that the "friend's" name was Richard St. Clair, they understood Rusty's apprehension.

Richard St. Clair was a member of a large Bryan County group alleged to be key distributors in a drug-dealing network that operated throughout an area of southeast Oklahoma and north Texas that surrounds Lake Texoma.

Richard's older brother, Michael St. Clair, was presently incarcerated in the Bryan County Jail facing two first-degree murder charges in the double-slaying of his uncle and a hired killer (See "Drugs, Deception, and Double Death," in *True Detective*, June 1992).

279

On May 11th, just weeks before the discovery of Robert Dunigan's skeleton, the bullet-riddled body of Ronnie St. Clair was found on a lonely road in Bryan County. The next night, May 12th, an individual named William H. Kelsey Jr. was gunned down under remarkably similar circumstances.

The subsequent investigation revealed that it all began when 33-year-old Michael heard that his Uncle Ronnie was planning to cut him out of the "family business" — that business being the alleged drug-dealing operation.

Perhaps acting on the premise that a good offense is the best defense, Michael secretly engaged the services of Kelsey, a known killer, to take Ronnie out of the picture. Then, to keep the family from learning of his involvement in his uncle's death, Michael shot down his own hired killer and boasted to his kin that he'd avenged Ronnie's death. He'd planned — in one fell swoop — to put an end to internecine warfare over territorial drug turf and to "inherit" the business.

Perry Unruh — a veteran OSBI agent gifted with subtle powers of persuasion and an uncommon understanding of the vagaries of human nature — assisted in the investigation that put the stock-built Michael St. Clair behind bars. Unruh was still actively engaged in helping the Bryan County authorities strengthen the pending court case and was investigating the accused man's possible involvement in two unsolved Choctaw County murders.

When the agent realized that Michael's younger brother might be connected to Dunigan's killing, he felt a surge of adrenaline. Putting a cap on his excitement, however, Unruh turned his attention back to the questions Agent Hamm was asking Rusty. Despite the young man's apparent grief at Dunigan's death, the agents knew that they could not discount Rusty as a suspect.

Rusty said he couldn't believe that Richard St. Clair had harmed Robert. "They were good friends," he declared. "Lottsa times when Richard come down to Mesquite, he had visited with Robert and his family." Rusty said that both he and Robert visited Richard's home on a number of occasions.

Agent Hamm suspected that those visits had not been purely social in nature. She knew that when thieves — or drug-dealers — fall out, friendship means next to nothing.

Elated with their new lead, the agents headed back to Oklahoma for a word with Richard St. Clair.

St. Clair, well versed in the rights of a suspect, would not talk with the investigators. At 31, Richard was more slender than his brother Michael. His long brown hair framed a narrow face that was alternately menacing or boyishly ingratiating — depending on the expression in his gray-green eyes. Beyond flatly denying Rusty's story of the proposed drug-lab partnership with Robert Dunigan, Richard refused to answer any questions posed by the sleuths.

The investigators suspected that Richard St. Clair was involved in the murder of Robert Dunigan, but they had no physical evidence linking him to the crime. The task before them — tedious interviews with anyone and everyone who might have a small bit of information to contribute — would be made a little easier by the recently completed investigation into the Ronnie St. Clair-William Kelsey murder.

With Michael's arrest for his uncle's murder, the family had become a house divided. Loyalties were strained. The sleuths felt certain that the faction eager to avenge Ronnie's death — angry with those who supported his killer — would not hesitate to tell what they knew about Richard's association with Robert Dunigan.

The trouble was — could they be believed?

The sleuths' fears were soon realized. In the subsequent interviews, Agent Hamm found contradiction piled upon contradiction; guns changed hands; words were spoken first by one mouth, then another. The young investigator often turned to more seasoned officers, drawing on their years of experience with criminal behavior, for help in determining the truthfulness of any particular version of a story.

The first real lead came from a woman named Kathy Reser. A relative of Richard's, Reser told Hamm that "sometime back in March," Richard had said to her, "I took care of the big boy from Dallas." The woman then gave an account of the killing that involved another character well known to southern Oklahoma lawmen.

"Red Leopard saw what happened," Kathy said. "He was there when Richard accused the Dallas boy of beatin' him out of some of the chemicals they was usin' to cook up the drugs. Richard told me that him and Robert got into this big argument and that he 'had to kill him.' Richard said that Red Leopard helped him haul off the body."

Edmond Leon "Red" Leopard, a resident of nearby McCurtain County, had a record that included convictions for armed robbery in Oklahoma County, burglary in Greenville, Texas, and involuntary manslaughter in Denton County, Texas. If Reser's story was true, a murder charge could now be added to the long list of crimes credited to 58-year-old Red Leopard. The lawmen, acknowledging the unpleasant fact that many crimes would go unpunished without the aid of informants, wondered if they might eventually persuade Red Leopard to turn state's evidence in return for a reduced charge.

First, however, they sought corroboration of Kathy Reser's statement. Having given conflicting statements in the investigation of the St. Clair-Kelsey murder case, she was accused by other relatives of fabricating the story. A younger female relative later testified in court that she and others in the family "never knew whether Kathy is lying or telling the truth."

Fortunately, information gleaned from others who

were interviewed not only linked the victim to Richard St. Clair and Red Leopard, but also led the sleuths to a third man—a lay minister who lived on a country road about a mile north of Sobol—who would be a witness in the case.

The self-proclaimed preacher saw no conflict in his practice of two widely divergent professions. On Sundays he preached the gentle tenets of Jesus Christ. The rest of the week he devoted to raising and selling game roosters for cockfighting.

The inhumane blood sport of equipping game roosters with razor-sharp metal spurs, then watching them fight to the death in an arena, is illegal in all but five states. In Oklahoma it is legal, and is practiced—almost furtively—by an avid group of followers. Some of them bet—illegally—large sums of money on the outcome of each fight.

"I don't fight 'em myself—I just raise 'em and sell 'em," the preacher was heard to offer by way of justification.

The professed man of God resorted to the same rationale when he was confronted with reports that he had rented Richard St. Clair space for use in "cooking up" drugs.

"Richard was a good friend of mine and I didn't think he used drugs hisself. I told Richard that them drugs killed people." The man then sactimoniously added, "We talked about it and I more or less blessed him."

Seemingly ignorant of the legal and moral responsibilities implicit in the Christian faith, the minister claimed to be "a religious man who didn't want to judge anyone." Finally, while admitting his fear of being "dumped out in the road like that guy who was murdered," he gave the officers a somewhat self-serving version of the events of March 15, 1990.

Denying that drugs were involved, the preacher said, "Richard and the other two guys come by real early that morning to look at some roosters and I told

283

'em to go on up to the barn. When I went up there about seven-thirty to feed the chickens, Richard and that Robert fellow was arguin'." The preacher described Robert Dunigan as "a big youngster — over 250 pounds," and added, "Richard was wavin' around one of them carbines that has a long clip to it. Red Leopard had a pistol stuck in his hip pocket, but he was standin' off to one side."

The preacher said he had "blessed" the two angry men as he passed them, but when his back was turned, he heard a shot. "When I turned around all three of them was scufflin'. Robert run off down through the woods and the other two run after him. In just a few minutes, somebody yelled, 'Drop that gun!' and I heard another shot. I don't know who was doin' the shootin'."

The preacher, who was visibly frightened by the events surrounding the recent double-murder in Bryan County, said he had watched Leopard and St. Clair drag Robert Dunigan's corpse back up through the woods and load it into a "dark-colored" blazer.

"I just stayed quiet," the preacher said. "I didn't want to wind up in a ditch somewhere with a bullet through my head."

While the OSBI and Pushmataha County authorities continued their tedious series of interviews, the Oklahoma State Bureau of Narcotics and the Federal Drug Enforcement Administration (DEA) pursued an unrelated investigation into the illegal activities of Red Leopard.

Within days of the coon hunters' discovery of Dunigan's skeletal remains — but weeks before the name Red Leopard would be connected to the killing — Red was arrested in Broken Bow, Oklahoma. It was there that he had purchased enough chemicals and lab equipment to manufacture 41 pounds of methamphetamine. One DEA official said that when Leopard was arrested, he had in his possession sufficient chemicals and equipment to produce a quantity of "speed" with an estimated street value of more than $4 million.

"Edmond Leon Leopard is not one of your up-standing-type citizens," the DEA representative said. "He wasn't playing games, and he carried a gun with him."

Leopard was subsequently tried and convicted in federal court on charges of attempting to manufacture methamphetamine, possession of chemicals used for the manufacture of methamphetamine with intent to distribute, unlawfully carrying a firearm during the commission of a felony, and possession of a firearm by a convicted felon.

As anticipated, the investigators found Red Leopard willing to bargain when they informed him that he faced first-degree murder charges—and possibly a death sentence—for his role in the Robert Dunigan murder. In return for immunity, he gave a surprisingly articulate account of the events leading up to the killing.

Leopard told the authorities that he, along with Richard St. Clair and Robert Dunigan, had gone to Sobol on March 14th to rent space in a barn behind "the preacher's house." Leopard said that the space was used in the manufacture of "crank." St. Clair had allegedly made the deal with the preacher and left the two men there overnight.

"Robert and I worked independently of each other," Leopard said. "His pots were on one side of the room and mine were on the other side. It came a hard rain that night. Some of the water came up in the barn and caused one of Robert's pots to tip over."

The man went on to say that when St. Clair returned the following day and heard the Dunigan had accidentally tipped over one of the pots and spilled its valuable chemical contents, he became very upset. St. Clair accused Dunigan of faking the accident to cover a theft of chemicals.

"Richard was of the opinion that Dunigan had once cheated him in a prior arrangement," Leopard said.

"He started yelling and making threatening gestures with an AR-15 rifle. I wasn't part of the initial argument, but when Robert grabbed the German Mauser I had in my hip pocket, I threw some waste water in his face."

Then, Leopard went on, Robert Dunigan — eyes stinging from the lye water — ran into the woods, with Richard St. Clair in pursuit.

"I followed them down to the fence row behind the barn," Leopard said. "Dunigan still had my gun, but both his hands were in the air — he wasn't doing any threatening."

Red Leopard told the officers that he yelled for Dunigan to drop the gun. After some hesitation, Dunigan laid the pistol on the ground.

Meanwhile, Leopard said, St. Clair "kept hollering and throwing down with the gun" to emphasize his point that he would not be cheated. "Then he threw down with the gun and it went off. When Robert dropped to the ground, Richard just said, 'The S.O.B. got what he deserved.' "

Leopard did not deny that he had helped St. Clair dispose of Dunigan's body. "We wrapped him up in a tarp, put him in Richard's blazer and drove north on the lumber road. We put him in a ditch and covered the body with some brush and stuff," Leopard said. "Richard told me that his brother would come back with him and help bury the body."

What Red Lopard said next caused Agent Hamm to again reflect on the lack of logic in a killer's thought processes. According to Leopard, Richard St. Clair — who had left his victim's wallet, complete with identification, in his hip pocket — fleetingly considered cutting off the dead man's hands to prevent fingerprint identification!

In late August, officers bearing an arrest warrant descended on the Bryan County home of Richard St. Clair. But he was nowhere to be found. When his family denied all knowledge of Richard's whereabouts,

Bryan County Sheriff B.J. Moore made an appeal to an older female relative who was believed to wield considerable influence inside the clan.

"Running won't make the charges go away," Moore told the woman. He pointed out that since Richard was assumed to be armed and dangerous, she should be concerned for his safety.

"If he's stopped, he'd better be sure the first thing he does is put his arms up in the air and step out," Sheriff Moore warned. "The officers out there know he's wanted for murder, and they'll act accordingly."

Despite the sheriff's warnings and an OSBI offer of a $1,000 reward for information leading to his arrest, Richard remained in hiding for several weeks.

On Saturday, September 12, 1990, a reporter with *The Durant Daily Democrat* received a call from Richard's relative.

"Richard wants to turn himself in," she said. "But he won't turn himself over to anyone but B.J. Moore . . . and he wants the newpaper there when he does it. He's afraid the law will shoot him on sight." The woman said that she had spoken with Richard, who told her he would call at eleven o'clock on Sunday morning to tell her where he wanted Moore to pick him up.

Shortly after 9:00 a.m. on Sunday—two hours before the scheduled time—the woman called to tell Moore, "Richard is ready to get it over with—he don't want to wait."

Following instructions to come alone, the sheriff drove his personal pickup truck to the parking lot of a convenience store where the woman was waiting. Moore later admitted to some trepidation as he drove behind her vehicle to a remote wooded area north of Durant.

"You never know if these people would like to see you dead," he later told a reporter. "But it's part of the job—a man's gotta do what a man's gotta do."

Sheriff Moore followed as the woman pulled into

287

the driveway of an abandoned house and then honked her horn. From the woods came a responding whistle. Moments later, Richard St. Clair suddenly appeared at the side of Moore's pickup.

"He kept his hands where I could see them," the veteran lawman said. "He didn't give me any trouble—just climbed into the pickup and I brought him in."

Following his arrest and subsequent transfer to the Pushmataha County Jail, Richard St. Clair, who had arranged to retain the services of an attorney while he'd been a fugitive, maintained a stubborn silence regarding Robert Dunigan's death.

At the suspect's preliminary hearing, Kathy Reser now testified under oath that she had lied in her earlier statement to OSBI Agent Hamm. "I was mad at Richard because he was always threatening to kick my ass," Reser explained. Now, she said, Richard had told her of returning to the Sobol drug-lab to find Red Leopard and Robert Dunigan fighting. According to this scenario, Red Leopard was the one who fired the fatal shot into the man from Mesquite.

But Richard St. Clair, who subscribed to the brand of machismo common among his ilk, had boasted to others of "taking care of the big boy from Dallas." The testimony of those witnesses led to his being bound over on charges of second-degree murder in Robert L. Dunigan's death.

Agent Hamm could rest on her laurels for a moment. She had not only reached a professional milestone—she'd solved her first "whodunit"—but she had also reached a personal milestone. Her determined resolve to fulfill her potential as an effective investigator had not interfered with the fulfillment of her romantic potential as an attractive young woman. In October 1990, Reanae Hamm became Mrs. Keith Childers.

Reanae's new husband, at that time a deputy with the Pushmataha County Sheriff's Department, shared his bride's enthusiasm for law enforcement.

The St. Clair saga continued. And the new Mrs. Childers would add many pages to her already voluminous file on the St. Clair-Dunigan murder case.

In the months preceding the separate trials of the two brothers, various persons allegedly tried to bribe and intimidate witnesses. The investigators had to employ skillful persuasion to convince the frightened witnesses that it would be safe for them to testify.

Agent Perry Unruh, working with local officers, ferreted out evidence that linked Michael St. Clair and one of his relatives to the unsolved double-murder in Choctaw County. The two now faced first-degree murder charges in the 1987 deaths of Mary Smith and Edward Large, who had been found shot to death inside a car parked alongside U.S. Highway 70.

Slumped behind the wheel, Edward Large had been shot twice with a small caliber handgun—once between the shoulder blades and once in the mouth. Mary Smith, seated upright in the backseat, had been shot in the forehead, cheek, and jaw.

The moment came when the authorities found themselves faced with a unique situation: there were so many witnesses, relatives, and others involved in the five murders, that it was getting hard to keep them all separated. Richard St. Clair was held in the Pushmataha County Jail; the relative charged in the deaths of Smith and Large was incarcerated in the Choctaw County Jail; a material witness who was unable to make bond was lodged in the Atoka County Jail; another material witness who also faced drug charges was placed in the Bryan County Jail, where Michael St. Clair was awaiting trial.

One investigator in the case commented, "We're just about to run out of county jails that are conveniently located."

In September 1991, Michael St. Clair was sentenced to life without parole in the deaths of Ronnie St. Clair and William Kelsey. While awaiting transfer to the state prison, Michael and a fellow inmate escaped from the Bryan County Jail.

After his escape, the convicted killer telephoned a reporter with the *The Durant Daily Democrat* and threatened the lives of those responsible for his arrest and conviction. While Michael swore he would never be taken alive, the reporter could hear the theme music from an old TV series, *The Dukes Of Hazzard*, playing loudly in the background. The message was clear: *The Dukes Of Hazzard* featured a pair of "good ol' boys" who always managed to outwit the corrupt and dimwitted lawmen who pursued them each week.

After the phone call, one lawman referred to Michael as "a legend in his own mind." Bryan County District Attorney Theresa McGeehee made a news-media appeal to those in the community who seemed to be giving "folk hero" status to the escaped killer.

"If you think he isn't dangerous, you are wrong," she said. Subsequent events would bear out her statement.

Michael and his companion eventually escaped the area and reportedly embarked on a multistate robbery and killing spree. The authorities believed that Richard St. Clair, who was free on $50,000 bond, played a key role in helping his brother evade capture.

On Wednesday night, September 25, 1991, a reserve officer in the area of Madill, a small town west of Durant, noticed a blue 1980 Oldsmobile weaving back and forth on a rural road. When the officer tried to stop the vehicle, it lurched away at high speed. In the ensuing chase, the Oldsmobile failed to negotiate a curve and plowed into a ditch. The two men inside jumped out and fled on foot. The Madill lawman did not get a good look at the driver of the car, but he believed that the passenger, who was briefly illuminated by a beam of light, strongly resembled St. Clair's companion in the jailbreak.

The sighting set off a manhunt that mobilized the resources of serveral city, county, and state agencies. Agent Reanae Childers and her OSBI colleagues joined local law officers who were combing the densely wooded area. Search dogs from a state prison facility sniffed their way through the underbrush. Highway patrol helicopters equipped with infared scanners hovered above. But the two men, who had bolted in opposite directions, managed to elude their pursuers. The search wound down about 10:00 p.m., Thursday, with no confirmed sightings of the escapees.

Concerned area residents, alerted by the media that both men should be considered armed and dangerous, nervously bolted their doors and windows. Those who owned firearms kept them close at hand, hoping they wouldn't need them.

Around noon the next day, a resident of a rural community between Madill and Ardmore notified his local sheriff that a dark, slender man, "who looked like he'd been trompin' through the woods," had walked up to his mobile home and requested a glass of water. After thirstily consuming the water, the stranger tried to hire the man to drive him into nearby Ardmore.

"When I told him no, he just walked on down the road," the resident said.

Less than an hour later, that unarmed man — a tired and hungry Richard St. Clair — was taken into custody by Carter County officers.

When Richard denied having been in the company of his brother Michael, some officers believed him. "I think Richard and whoever was with him were acting as decoys so Michael could get plumb out of this part of the country," one lawman remarked.

Did Richard and his unknown cohort purposely attract the attention of the reserve officer? Had they made themselves the objects of an extensive manhunt to give Michael a better chance to get clear of the Durant area?

Though the authorities were unable to prove that Richard had aided the fugitive from justice, they recognized that it was a "double danger" for both brothers to be on the loose. Richard was held as a material witness and on charges related to the drug-lab caper in Sobol. He was returned to the Pushmataha County Jail, where bail was initially set at $1 million. It was later reduced.

Three months later, on December 19, 1991, Michael St. Clair was recaptured in the home of another brother in Hugo, Oklahoma. The brother was arrested and charged with harboring a fugitive and with various drug-related crimes. He and his wife are currently under indictment for a later alleged attempt to solicit the murder of the Hugo police chief. Of course, in accordance with their constitutional protections, they must be considered innocent of the charges until and unless proven otherwise by a jury under due process of law.

Michael St. Clair's flight to freedom brought himself and his siblings widespread notoriety. Smiling for the TV cameras, he proudly declared, "We're kin to Jesse James on one side of the family." In another media statement, Michael said that he and his brothers were "just good ol' boys who don't mean no harm."

Bryan County District Attorney Theresa McGeehee did not agree. She told reporters that Michael and various family members had, through threats and intimidation, virtually "held Bryan County hostage" during the three months of Michael's freedom.

In February 1992, Richard St. Clair was brought before the bar of justice in Pushmataha County. Throughout the trial, Assistant District Attorney Larry Grant was a study in frustration. Grant's frustration stemmed from the fact that the prosecution was barred from presenting certain evidence that had been unearthed subsequent to the preliminary hearing. The defendant had been bound over on charges of second-degree murder, and a court ruling prevented the presentation of the new evidence that alleged premeditation.

Certain members of the local drug culture were prepared to testify that the crime was not committed "in the heat of passion," but was cold-blooded, premeditated murder.

The new evidence alleged that in early 1990, Robert Dunigan and Richard St. Clair had been business associates in a drug-lab setup located just across Lake Texoma in Grayson County, Texas. Informants said that Dunigan had left the lab to get something to eat just minutes before it was raided by Grayson County authorities. When Dunigan returned to find his companions being led away in handcuffs and the drug-making paraphernalia being carted off by authorities, he had chosen discretion over valor and faded into the background.

It would have seemed the height of foolishness for Dunigan to step forward, proclaim his association with the illegal enterprise, and share in the punishment to be meted out to his cohorts. His escape from arrest—which at the time must have seemed a stroke of good fortune—was alleged to be what had marked him for death.

According to the informants, Richard St. Clair did not believe that his partner's absence at the crucial time was coincidental. He branded Dunigan a snitch and reportedly said in the presence of witnesses that he [Richard] was going "to kill Robert for it."

More evidence came from another relative, described in the words of one official as "particularly believable since he lacked the sophistication to lie." The relative now proclaimed his willingness to testify that he had heard Richard speak of his intent to kill Robert Dunigan.

The prosecution believed that Richard St. Clair had invited Robert Dunigan to share in the Sobol drug enterprise with a dual purpose in mind: first he would capitalize on Dunigan's expertise in the manufacture of drugs, and then he would impose a sentence of death for Dunigan's alleged treachery in Grayson

County.

But things had not gone according to Richard's plan. On that day in March 1990, when St. Clair returned to the drug-lab and found that valuable chemicals had been lost through spillage, he apparently fell victim to his own volatile nature. Described as being unable to control his temper, Richard shot Dunigan ahead of schedule — in the presence of witnesses who could — and later did — testify against him in a court of law.

In a courtroom pervaded by an aura of fear, the Sobol lay preacher testified to witnessing an altercation and hearing a gunshot; Red Leopard gave his eyewitness account of Dunigan's murder; Kathy Reser took the stand and testified under oath that Richard St. Clair had indeed boasted to her of "taking care of the big boy from Dallas."

Reser swore that she had recanted her original statement and lied at the preliminary hearing, because repeated threats and intimidation by Richard and certain other family members had caused her to fear for her life.

Hampered by the inadmissibility of the evidence alleging premeditation, Prosecutor Larry Grant still managed to win a verdict of "guilty as charged" against Richard St. Clair. Acting on the evidence that was allowed to be presented, the jury convicted the defendant of second-degree murder.

Richard St. Clair was sentenced to life in prison for the murder of Robert L. Dunigan and was given a second life sentence for manufacturing a controlled dangerous substance.

His brother, Michael St. Clair, is currently serving two life sentences for the double-slaying of Ronnie St. Clair and William Kelsey in Bryan County. In the fall of 1992, Michael St. Clair, along with the relative named as his codefendant, will face trial in the Choctaw County murders of Mary Smith and Edward Large. Michael St. Clair is also a suspect in several slayings that occurred in Colorado, Kentucky, and Tennessee following his jailbreak. In accordance with their constitutional guarantees, the pair must be considered innocent of the pending charges until and unless proven otherwise through due process of law.

Edmond Leon Leopard was granted immunity in the slaying of Robert Dunigan, but he is currently serving a 32-year sentence on various drug charges.

Officials in all branches of southeastern Oklahoma law enforcement are quick to emphasize that most members of the St. Clair brothers' family are God-fearing, law-abiding citizens who agonize over the violence wrought by their convicted kinsmen. Some have courageously risked lives and property to bring to justice those who have not upheld the honor of the family name.

EDITOR'S NOTE:
Juan Sanchez, Justin Haws, Barry Davis, Kathy Reser and Rusty are not the real names of the persons so named in the foregoing story. Fictitious names have been used because there is no reason for public interest in the identities of these persons.

"THE HAIRY, TOOTHLESS 'MAD PADDLER' "

by Bill G. Cox

The perversity of human beings has long puzzled and intrigued the mind doctors of the world. Such mental wizards as Sigmund Freud and Richard Krafft-Ebing tried to put their analytical fingers on what makes men and women drift into the twisted, kinky offshoots of the libido. Krafft-Ebing pursued the catalogue of sexual perversions in his *Psychopathia Sexualis*, his famous text on the deviate states of mind that the hormones can produce.

Among the centurions of today—those who pack badges and guns—nothing much surprises them anymore when it comes to the kinky bents of the violent sexual criminal. In fact, most of the habits and preferences of the sexual psychopaths are indexed by M.O. in the computerized, state-of-the-art Violent Criminal Apprehension Program (VICAP) of the FBI.

One has to wonder if all those electronically stored bad memories of the twilight world of the perverse do not put those finely tuned crime-fighting computers in need of an electronic psychiatrist to avert a system nervous breakdown.

It's all there on the microchips—fetishism, masochism, sadism, bondage, torture. If some weirdo happens to kill while dabbling in his deviation, VICAP has recorded it for the law enforcement agencies of the world.

But in the late 1980s, something happened in and around Fort Smith, Arkansas, that cast some new shadows over the distorted realm of sexual psychopaths who become serial murderers. To this day, the motivations of one of the strangest of this violent breed remain a mystery to those who put the brakes on his heinous deeds.

Fort Smith, lying just east of the Oklahoma-Arkansas line, gained historical recognition in the late 1880s from the legendary "Hanging Judge" Isaac Parker, whose attentiveness to dispatching convicted killers kept the gallows rope jerking in the breeze. Parker ordered some 80 hangings in two decades. Since then, there have been those who have longed for a return of Judge Parker's brand of justice, especially in light of the terrible happenings that started to come to light on Tuesday, February 17, 1987.

At 7:15 p.m. that evening, a 15-year-old Fort Smith boy, William Eric Domer, was sent on an errand by his mother. Given $10 to buy several items, the teenager left his home to walk to a neighborhood grocery store.

When the boy didn't return from the errand, William's mother thought he might have been temporarily sidetracked by friends. As time passed with still no word on his whereabouts, the worried mother called the Fort Smith Police Department to ask for help in locating him.

But it wasn't until five days later that the youth was found. On Sunday, February 22nd, three small boys were playing near Leard Cemetery on the southwest edge of Fort Smith. It was shortly after 1:30 p.m. when the youngsters, who were playing around a farm pond, made a gruesome discovery.

Lying face down in about six inches of water in the shallow end of the pond was the fully clothed body of a boy, obviously dead. The terrified youngsters ran for help.

The Fort Smith Police Department was the first agency to be notified of the discovery. Officers who went to the scene, a fishing pond about 150 yards south of the cemetery along Texas Road and less than one mile from Interstate 540, determined the site was outside the city limits. Police passed the call along to the Sebastian County Sheriff's Department.

Deputies who arrived at the pond saw that the boy, who was clad in blue jeans, a pullover knit shirt, and an insulated jacket, appeared to have two gunshot wounds below the left shoulder blade. It was estimated that the body had been in the water at least 24 hours, but probably longer.

The boy and his clothing matched the description of the missing William Domer, who had vanished without a trace while walking to the grocery store. A relative later confirmed the identification. As the investigation continued, it became apparent that the slaying scene was barely over the state line on the Oklahoma side. Thus, the LeFlore County, Oklahoma, Sheriff's Department and the Pocola, Oklahoma, Police Department joined the Arkansas authorities at the scene.

Some possible evidence found on the Arkansas side near the death site was turned over to the Oklahoma investigators. The nature of the evidence was not revealed immediately to the news media.

That evening, officers from the two states met in the Fort Smith office of Sebastian County Sheriff Bill Cauthron to exchange the known details of young Domer's disappearance and subsequent murder. Present was Kenneth Ballew, an investigator for the LeFlore County District Attorney's Office, who took charge of the evidence.

The youth's body was sent to Tulsa, Oklahoma, for an autopsy to determine the exact cause of his death.

Sheriff Cauthron issued an appeal in the local papers and on television for anyone who might have possible information on the slaying to contact his office, especially persons who might have been fishing in the pond within the previous 72 hours. No pertinent information was forthcoming, and as the months passed, the Domer murder remained unsolved.

Almost four years later, it happened again. Another area teenager boy was reported missing for no apparent reason.

Fourteen-year-old Mark Anthony McLaughlin, who lived in Van Buren, Arkansas, not far from Fort Smith, disappeared under circumstances eerily similar to the case of William Domer. It was about 7:00 p.m. on November 11, 1990, when Mark rode away from home on his bicycle to purchase some bread, lunch meat, and cigarettes for his mother. His destination was a store only a few blocks away.

When Mark hadn't arrived home two hours later, his mother started a search for him. She held out hope that he still would be home, but at midnight she became desperate and decided to notify the police department.

Police searched along the route the boy would have taken, but could find nothing to explain what might have happened to him.

Nor was any trace found of the bicycle Mark had been riding when last seen.

On the following morning, about 10:30 a.m., a fisherman found the McLaughlin boy's body in the same pond near Leard Cemetery where William Domer's corpse had been discovered in 1987. The marked similarities in the two murders continued when an examination of the McLaughlin boy disclosed that he had been shot in the back just below his left shoulder blade with a small-caliber gun.

An autopsy revealed the single bullet had pierced the heart and lung of the teenager and had lodged just under the skin of his chest. The pathologist reported to officers that the shot had been fired at close range.

The autopsy also revealed something else: Contusions were apparent on the boy's buttocks and thighs, as if he had been whipped with some object. Although he was fully clothed, his pants were unzipped. This was another similarity to William Domer's death, the officers recalled when they met to discuss the latest case that had such a chilling likeness to the child murder of four years earlier.

Were the two slayings of teenaged boys linked? the officers wondered.

The two victims, in addition to being about the same age, were both of small stature. Was a killer selecting similar-looking young boys for some unknown motive? The autopsies had not shown any sexual assaults on the two teenagers.

No weapons that could have been used in the two shooting deaths were found in either case. In fact, evidence of any kind was lacking. Again, officers appealed to the public to come forward if they had any information on the last known activities of either boy. Working on the two murders at this point were Oklahoma and Arkansas authorities, the state police of both states, and the FBI. The officers awaited the results of ballistic, toxicology, and other tests run by the Oklahoma State Bureau of Investigation (OSBI).

Twelve days later, a third young boy from the area was reported missing under suspicious circumstances. Alonzo Don Cade, 12, a Fort Smith boy, had last been seen at a basketball game at Westark Community College. His mother reported him missing when he had failed to return home that evening after the game.

At first, it was thought the boy might have run away because he and a relative had argued before he left for the game. However, Fort Smith Police Sergeant Bob Hicks didn't think the earlier family dispute was the reason Alonzo had not come home.

Alonzo's relative admitted they had argued briefly, but said, "He settled down and apologized and gave me a hug [before leaving for the game]." And any time he had a problem in the past, the youngster always went to a friend's house, police learned.

Sergeant Hicks was extremely concerned because Alonzo had not been in touch with any of his friends, who had last seen him at the basketball game. The police detective had known Alonzo personally for about three years and recalled it would not be like him to run away from home.

When his friends had seen Alonzo after the game, he had left riding his bicycle, which was described as purple and white and having a green seat.

The youth was wearing blue jeans, a multicolored T-shirt, and black tennis shoes. He weighed about 95 pounds and was 4 feet 9 inches tall.

On Sunday, December 9, 1990, 18-year-old Dale Markam, a student at Westark Community College, had finished work at a grocery store in Van Buren, Arkansas, a town adjacent to Fort Smith. At 5 feet 2 inches tall and weighing 120 pounds, Dale appeared to be younger than he was. He got into his truck and was preparing to drive to his girlfriend's home in Alma, a nearby small community, when a four-door automobile pulled directly behind his pickup. The driver, dressed neatly in a blue suit and wearing semi-thick horn-rimmed glasses, approached the driver's side of Dale's vehicle.

The man flashed a badge and identified himself as a policeman from Booneville, Arkansas. He asked to see Dale's driver's license.

After examining the license, the bespectacled "officer" told him to get out and lock up his truck.

The man then handcuffed Dale and fastened leg irons on him before placing the college student in the car. As the man drove south on Interstate 540, Dale noticed that the car was not equipped with a radio or emergency lights found on most police units. He was growing suspicious and anxious about his welfare.

"Why am I being arrested?" the youth asked the driver.

"You think it's all right to rob others?" the man replied.

As best Dale could determine by the earlier conversation with the "officer," he was accusing Dale of stealing something from a grocery store in Booneville, a place where the youth had never been.

The minutes passed as the car zipped along the interstate. Then the driver pulled off onto a dirt road and guided the vehicle into a clearing.

"How long has it been since your father whipped you?" the man asked. As the spoke, he took hold of a smooth, rounded stick resembling a broom handle about one and a half feet long and climbed into the backseat with Dale.

The man with the wooden handle ordered the college student to turn onto his right side. Then he unfastened and pulled down Dale's pants. Pain knifed through the young man's body as the abductor beat him on the buttocks for several minutes.

Apparently tiring, the assailant stopped, pulled up Dale's trousers, got out, and stood in front of the car for a moment. He returned and pulled Dale from the backseat. Still handcuffed and in the leg irons, the youth was led to a trail at the edge of a ridge.

At first the man walked beside him on the left, then dropped behind him. At this point Dale felt certain that the strange man was not a police officer and that he probably intended to kill him, perhaps shoot him in the back of the head and shove his body over the cliff. The stories of two other teenagers who had been shot and dumped in a pond flashed through Dale's mind. He tried to stay calm.

Suddenly, Dale heard the man reach inside his coat. Thinking he was pulling out a gun, the abducted youth whirled around and yelled, "Are you going to shoot me?"

The man told Dale he was not going to shoot him and pulled back his suitcoat to show that he did not have a gun. The abductor ordered Dale to keep walking.

All of a sudden Dale felt sharp, stinging blows

striking him in his back. Dale dropped to the ground, pretending to be dead. He went limp and tried to hold his breath. The attacker grabbed Dale's left leg and dragged him face down on a downward sloping hill to the edge of a nearby pond. The man stopped three times to catch his breath.

At the pond the assailant began to remove the handcuffs and leg irons from the apparently unconscious youth.

Dale could feel wetness on his back. He realized the sharp blows he felt had probably been stabs with a knife. As the man picked up his legs and unshackled the leg irons, Dale kept his legs limp and let them fall to the ground.

After the abductor unlocked and took off Dale's handcuffs, the man, breathing hard from the exertion, rolled the boy over, unzipped his pants, and pulled down the youth's shorts. The realization that he was suddenly exposed drove the youth into action.

Dale lunged to his feet and knocked down the surprised attacker, who was caught off guard. As he struck out, Dale shouted, "You son of a bitch!" The man suddenly looked as if he had suffered a heart attack. His eyes widened in disbelief.

The attacker grabbed Dale's right arm, but Dale pulled away and ran back up the hill. Growing weak from his wounds, the youth stumbled and fell twice. The kidnapper was gaining on him, even though the older pursuer was breathing in loud gasps.

Dale made it to the car, fell inside, and was locking the last door as the kidnapper reached the vehicle. Luckily, the keys had been left in the ignition. Starting the motor, Dale tried to hit the assailant with the car as he roared away from the spot.

As investigators would pinpoint it later, the site to which Dale was driven is east of Greenwood, near the Washburn community. Escaping in the abductor's car, Dale Markam drove at high speed up Washburn Mountain, honking the car's horn all the way to attract attention. At the mountain's top he pulled up before a house, where the family inside came to his aid. Police and an ambulance were summoned for the bleeding youth.

As the alarm was broadcast with a description of the knife-wielding assailant and the area in which he was thought to be afoot, Sebastian County sheriff's officers converged on the Washburn community.

It was 8:55 p.m. when Sebastian Chief Deputy Sheriff Frank Atkinson sped along Highway 10 and spotted a man in a blue business suit walking along the road. The chief deputy turned his unit around and pulled up beside the man. He jumped out with his revolver drawn and leveled it at the disheveled figure, who had bloodstains on his hands, neck, and suit jacket.

The officer ordered the man to lie on the ground face down and radioed for a backup that arrived shortly thereafter. The man was identified as George Kent Wallace, a part-time truck driver who resided in Fort Smith.

The suspect explained to the officers that he had been in a fight with a boy who stole his car and fled with it. He gave his identity but did little talking otherwise as he was driven to the Sebastian County Sheriff's Office in Fort Smith.

As Dale Markam was being loaded in the ambulance, an officer opened the door and told him, "They got him." At the hospital, it was found that the youth had been stabbed five times in the back and once in one arm. Luckily, the thrusts of the sharp instrument had not pierced any vital organs. Though Dale had lost a large amount of blood, the boy would recover.

The mild-mannered and softspoken Wallace, who was difficult to understand because he had no teeth or dentures, stuck to his story, saying he had fought with a boy who was stealing his car and had stabbed him in the struggle. The officers noticed that Wallace had powerful arms.

Uppermost in the minds of the Sebastian County sheriff's officers because of the nature of the attack on Dale Markam—his having been whipped on the buttocks by an abductor who had taken him to a pond—were the unsolved murders of William Domer and Mark McLaughlin, whose bodies had been recovered from the pond near Leard Cemetery. Had he not outwitted the man who stabbed him repeatedly, Dale undoubtedly would have ended up dead in a pond, the investigators believed.

Wallace's arrest for the attack on the Markam youth was like a bright light suddenly turned on the earlier teenage boy murders.

There had been nothing in the meager evidence at the scenes to point suspicion in the direction of George Wallace. He did have a criminal record locally, but the offense for which he had gone to prison wasn't the kind indicative of a serial murderer of young boys.

Local files on Wallace revealed that he had moved to Fort Smith in the fall of 1986 and set up a mail-order business. Wallace was not the most scrupulous businessman. He got in trouble with the law for inflating the dollar amounts on his customers' credit card slips. For this he was charged and convicted of a felony theft by deception. He received a 10-year sentence and entered the Arkansas Department of Corrections on June 2, 1989. He was released on April 20, 1990. Fort Smith Police Captain David Chapman recalled that Wallace had made restitution for the credit card thefts. He had been a model prisoner while confined, prison authorities reported.

The investigators noted that Wallace's prison term for the credit card scam had occurred after the 1987 murder of the Domer boy and that Wallace was free again when Mark McLaughlin was abducted and slain.

At the time of his latest arrest, Wallace was renting a two-room apartment in the downtown section of the city and was working part time for a trucking company. Those who knew him on the job were shocked at his arrest for the attack on Dale Markam.

But, as far as could be determined, Wallace had made no friends and had no relatives in the area. Born in Steubenville, Ohio, he lived in West Virginia before moving to North Carolina during his adolescence. After graduating from high school, he served in the U.S. Navy from 1959 to 1963. Both of his parents were deceased, and he had few living relatives.

As the investigators checked further into George Wallace's criminal record, they learned it went back to 1966. Wallace had been living in North Carolina before he came to Arkansas. It was in that state where his past showed the tendencies toward violence that seemed so unbelievable to those who knew him in Fort Smith, Arkansas.

According to the records, Wallace had prior prison convictions stemming from crimes committed in and around the Winston-Salem, North Carolina area. His first conviction was on August 20, 1966, on two counts of kidnapping, which included the abduction of a police officer. He was sentenced to 15 years and served nine years before being paroled.

On January 13, 1977, Wallace was convicted of kidnapping and assault with a deadly weapon, which brought him a sentence of 8 to 10 years. After three years, he was again paroled.

From Forsyth County Sheriff Department officers in North Carolina, it was learned that Wallace's convictions in that state involved the abduction of boys by a man who impersonated a police officer and assaulted the youngsters with a paddle. The crimes had earned the perpetrator the nickname of "The Mad Paddler." The victims had been approached by a man who displayed a detective's badge to get the victims into a four-door car that resembled an unmarked police vehicle, the North Carolina authorities recalled.

Moreover, the Arkansas officers learned that in the early 1980s, a George Kent Wallace had been a suspect in the deaths of two teenage boys in the Winston-Salem area. The victims, who were abducted and killed under circumstances similar to the cases in Arkansas, included Jeffrey Lee Foster in 1976 and Thomas Stewart Reed in 1982. The two homicides were unsolved, and Wallace was still a suspect in the slayings, although there had been insufficient evidence to link him to the cases, according to North Carolina officers.

As they continued to interrogate Wallace in the kidnapping and stabbing of Dale Markam (he was charged with kidnapping and attempted murder in this incident), Arkansas' Sebastian County Sheriff's Department launched an intensive search for evidence in the Washburn Mountain area. A special posse composed of 37 officers and volunteers combed the terrain.

Walking side by side, the searchers had progressed through 100 yards of the woods and grassland at the stabbing site when Mansfield Police Chief Butch McGhee spotted a black leather knife sheath partially covered with leaves. The police chief called for Chief Deputy Frank Atkinson, who was directing the search, and a team of deputies secured the area against intruders.

Nearby they found handcuffs, leg irons, and a police badge. The evidence was found about one mile east of the location where Wallace had been arrested Sunday night as he walked in a ditch along Highway 10. The items were placed in evidence bags by Sheriff's Investigator Stan Hall.

Still missing were the keys to the handcuffs and a flashlight, but Sheriff Grimes commented, "That's okay. We're in good shape with what we have."

The recovered weapon was a survival knife that had a compass in the handle. It was encased in a black leather sheath about eight inches long.

Meanwhile, the publicity surrounding the case brought new information to the sheriff's department

307

and prompted the filing of another felony charge—attempted kidnapping—against Wallace. A 19-year-old Fort Smith man named Manuel Romero notified police that a man believed to be Wallace had tried to abduct him on November 10, 1990.

The witness related that a man fitting Wallace's description had stopped him on a Fort Smith street and flashed a badge, attempting to arrest and get him into his car. The vehicle was a blue Chevrolet Celebrity, Romero said. The ruse hadn't worked that time, however, because Romero told the man to get away and leave him alone. Encountering resistance, the man drove off.

Since he hadn't been harmed, Romero had not reported the incident at the time, but he did so when he learned of the kidnapping and stabbing of Dale Markam.

Because they knew Wallace didn't own an automobile, sleuths checked the records of local rental agencies and discovered that the suspect had rented a car on the same weekend Manuel Romero was accosted by the phony detective. Wallace's rental was of the same make and description as the one Romero said the stranger was driving. Earlier, the investigators had found that Wallace had leased a 1981 Chevrolet on the weekend that he attacked Dale Markam.

The hunt for more evidence continued. The pond to which Markam had been driven was drained by the authorities, but nothing linked to the probe was found. However, an additional search by 15 officers turned up the missing flashlight and also Dale Markam's driver's license near where the knife, badge, cuffs, and leg irons were retrieved.

The charges continued to mushroom against George Wallace as information on past unreported cases surfaced after the suspect's arrest. The newest to be reported was the abduction of an 18-year-old Fort Smith youth named Steven Clarke. Clarke told detectives that he was walking along a city street near a park in late October or early November 1990 when a man in a car stopped, flashed a badge, and said he was going to take the youth to a detention center. The "officer" handcuffed him and attached leg irons and drove the shackled prisoner to the pond near Leard Cemetery, barely over the Oklahoma line.

But the youth began kicking and screaming to the point that the abductor said he would return him to town if he would be quiet. The restraints were removed and Clarke was driven into town and freed at a shopping mall. As he left, the "officer" told the youth he would be checking on him.

Ironically, a few minutes later, the youth was questioned at the mall by police who mistook him for a shoplifter. He was released after questioning, and Clarke never reported the earlier abduction to the officers because he thought his quizzing at the mall was part of the "checking up" promised by the "cop" who had released him.

Clarke did report the kidnapping, though, after Wallace had been nabbed in the Markam stabbing. Clarke identified the badge found in the Washburn Mountain area as the one Wallace had shown him.

The Wallace arrest and publicity brought other developments.

Police in Van Buren, Arkansas, were comparing the details of the April 9, 1986, murder of a teenage boy whose body was found in a culvert in that town. Clad only in socks and a T-shirt, the youth had been stabbed numerous times and his throat had been cut. The boy had been employed at a grocery store.

Meanwhile, the search for the missing Alonzo Cade swung to Springdale, Arkansas, after a piece of mail bearing the name and Fort Smith address of George Wallace was found on a resident's property. Police conducted dragging operations in three ponds on the man's land but found nothing.

Six days later, the mystery of the missing 12-year-old came to a tragic end. Alonzo Cade's small body was discovered in a gas well drilling pond located on Fort Chaffee land. The pond was in an isolated area of the fort used by the Army for training. A gas company worker made the discovery on Thursday morning, December 20, 1990.

On hand when the boy's body was pulled from the pond were FBI agents, since the site was on federal land, and sheriff's and police officers from Sebastian County, Fort Smith, and Van Buren. Because of the similarities in the cases, the officers sought a link with the other teenage boys' murders.

The Cade boy had been stabbed in the back numerous times, it was reported.

From the time of his arrest on December 9th for the Markam kidnapping-stabbing, 49-year-old George Wallace had become a prime suspect in the murders of the two teenagers whose bodies were found in the pool near Leard Cemetery, in Oklahoma, just across the state line from Fort Smith, Arkansas.

The day after Wallace's arrest, Sebastian County Sheriff's Investigator Stan Hall filed an affidavit in county court requesting search warrants for both Wallace's apartment and the car he had rented and used in Dale Markam's abduction. In the affidavit, the investigator listed the similarities between the assault on Dale Markam and the murders of William Domer and Mark McLaughlin.

All of the victims were teenagers who looked about the same age. All had been taken to ponds—all but Markam to the same pond. All had been abducted in the vicinity of grocery stores. All three victims' pants had been unzipped or entirely removed. Domer and Markam had both been dragged face down at some point during their assaults. McLaughlin and Markam had both been abducted at about 7:00 p.m. on a Sunday. Markam had been handcuffed and leg irons locked on his ankles, and the autopsy on McLaughlin showed bruises on his ankles and wrists that the pathologist said were caused by his having been bound

310

or restrained in cuffs and leg irons.

It was also noted on the affidavit that George Wallace was driving vehicles rented from the same agency in Van Buren on the days of the McLaughlin murder and the Markam kidnapping.

After the officers obtained the warrants, they searched Wallace's home and the Chevrolet that he had rented to use in Markam's abduction. They found some telling evidence.

One item removed from the rented Chevrolet was an object similar to a paint roller handle, which Dale Markam had said his abductor had used to beat him on the buttocks. The Oklahoma Medical Examiner's Office had reported that the autopsy on Mark McLaughlin showed bruises on his buttocks that "were consistent with the use of an object similar to the handle" taken from Wallace's car.

Inside Wallace's apartment, the officers found the rental agreement for the car driven by the suspect, a new pair of handcuffs and the box it came in, and other boxes for handcuffs and leg irons. Also found in the apartment were three copies of the Fort Smith newspaper, the *Southwest Times Record*, two of which had page-one stories about the search for evidence in Mark McLaughlin's death and an interview with one of his relatives.

The third edition had an interview with a relative of Alonzo Cade's. At the time, Alonzo was still missing.

Sheriff Grimes and his investigators felt certain from the time of the suspect's arrest for the attack on Dale Markam that Wallace was involved in the murders of William Domer and Mark McLaughlin and probably others — considering the prior investigations by North Carolina authorities, who had reopened those investigations after learning of the Arkansas arrest.

Even as they dug for the evidence to prove their belief that George Kent Wallace was a serial killer of peculiar bent, sleuths had to admit that every time they looked at him and talked with him, his appearance and mannerisms belied the enormity of the "Mad Paddler" slayings.

Standing 5 feet, 8 inches tall and weighing around 150 pounds, George Wallace was not a large man, although his arms looked muscular and powerful. He spoke quietly in a low and coarse voice, his words muffled further by the absence of any teeth. He wore his graying dark brown hair short, neat, and tapered to a slight widow's peak on his high forehead. His eyebrows were heavy. His dark eyes behind the semi-thick lenses of his horn-rimmed glasses were attentive. His arms, in addition to being powerful, were covered with thick hair.

Wallace was courteous and his demeanor meek. If you looked closely, however, the hardness of years spent in prison was written on his face.

Sheriff Grimes talked with the demure suspect more than a dozen times. Finally, made aware of the strong evidence that was mounting against him, Wallace volunteered to make a statement to Grimes and Investigator Stan Hall. Before making the statement, he had been warned of his legal rights, had consulted with his attorney, and had decided to confess against the wishes of his lawyer. To the public defender representing him, Wallace expressed a desire not to live any more.

The dutiful attorney on December 21st petitioned a judge to try to stop his client from making a statement, saying he doubted Wallace's mental competency to defend himself. At a hearing that day, Circuit Judge John Holland denied the motion and permitted Wallace to talk to Grimes and Hall.

Also present were representatives of the Fort Smith Police Department and LeFlore County investigators. The attorney once more, with the tape recorder running, advised the suspect not to talk, but Wallace dismissed him as his lawyer and proceeded with his statement.

Wallace made two separate statements, which he signed later when they were transcribed, admitting to the abductions and slayings of the Domer and McLaughlin boys. The two statements, which filled 17 pages, were dated December 21 and December 26, 1990.

Wallace related how he had first spotted William Domer in February 1987 as the boy was walking along the street.

"I drove past him, stopped, confronted him. I identified myself as a law officer. Told him to put his hands on the car . . . and then put handcuffs and leg cuffs on him."

The suspect said he showed Domer an Arkansas law officer's badge, saying he'd obtained it from a firm in New Jersey or Rhode Island. During the confession, Wallace said he never told the boy why he was being arrested. He put him in the backseat of a rented two-door car.

"Where did you go?" Wallace was asked.

"I went to the cemetery beside Leard Pond and parked at the far right-hand side. Close to the pond. Well, I guess it would be just as much distance from the road as the pond." After pulling the car into the cemetery, said Wallace, he took down the boy's pants and tried to spank him. He said, "He wasn't going for it, and I gave up on that and got him out of the car and shot him in the back." Then, Wallace backtracked and said he got the boy out of the car and pulled up his pants.

Continuing, he said he took Domer "a little ways down the hill, where I shot him several times."

The boy was still in handcuffs and leg irons, Wallace said. He said he was behind the youth when he shot him with a .25-caliber automatic pistol.

"What happened after you shot him?" Wallace was asked.

The suspect replied calmly, "I drug him to the pond and threw him in."

Wallace recalled that he took off the handcuffs, which he had bought at a local firm after shooting the teenager, adding, "I dumped them into a Dempsy dumpster." Asked what he did next after killing the boy, Wallace answered simply, "Went home."

In the suspect's signed statement about the slaying of Mark McLaughlin, Wallace said, "When I first saw him, he was riding a bicycle from a grocery store. When I encountered him he was walking." Wallace said he was driving from Fort Smith on U.S. Highway 71 when he spotted the youth at a store. He continued:

"I watched him ride the bicycle to a building . . . just in front of a street which he apparently was going up. So I drove on up to the end of that street to wait on him. And when he reached where I was, he was walking. And that's where I stopped him. I had him put his hands on the car. I patted him down and then put handcuffs and leg cuffs on him."

Wallace added as an afterthought, "I flashed a badge at him before I shook him down." He said that badge was an "Oklahoma security badge."

Wallace said he placed the McLaughlin boy in the back of the car and ordered him "to sit there quietly." Then, "I took him to the far side of Leard Pond. There's a driveway into or beside Leard Pond, that's where I took him. . . . Go past the cemetery, past the pond, and then there's a little drive-in."

Still inside the car, Wallace said, "I told him I was going to take his pants and underpants off and spank him. Which I did."

He related that he spanked the youth with a "plunger handle" and then pulled up his pants. He continued in the signed statement to police:

"After I spanked him, I got him out of the car, walked him toward the pond, and then I pulled the .22 out and shot him, one time." After removing the handcuffs and leg irons, which Wallace kept, he threw the body into the pond, the suspect related.

"What took place after that?" an officer asked.

"I went home," Wallace replied.

Wallace cleared up other details in the confessions. He said that he took home the .25-caliber pistol used to kill William Domer and concealed it in some laundry. When he was sentenced to the Arkansas prison on the credit card theft by deception charge, he gave the pistol to an acquaintance to keep, Wallace said. Later, the investigators recovered the gun from a person the acquaintance had sold it to.

Wallace told sleuths that he tossed out the .25-caliber weapon used in the McLaughlin boy's slaying in a wooded area near Seminole, Oklahoma, while on one of his truck runs after the murder. On December 26th, he led Sebastian County sheriff's officers to the area and a brief search recovered the discarded gun he'd used against McLaughlin.

Wallace explained that he rented cars for his weekened forays because he didn't own a private vehicle. Apparently, the only time he dressed up in a suit was on the weekends also, when he planned to impersonate a police detective to pick up young boys for the purpose of paddling them.

As for his motive for the paddling attacks, the investigators were puzzled. Wallace offered no explanation for his strange conduct. His sexual assaults apparently went no further than spanking.

"He has a thing about ponds, about impersonating police officers, and paddling," one detective said.

Wallace told the investigators that he had had psychological and psychiatric evaluations and treatment for 20 of the last 30 years. He added that he had previously been found competent in a criminal court and that he didn't want to undergo any more psychiatric examination.

Captain David Chapman of the Fort Smith Police Department told reporters, "People stereotype these kind of people as people who live in a cave or something like that. In this case, nothing could be further from the truth."

Authorities said speculation that something in Wallace's past caused him to abduct and beat young boys is just that — speculation.

"He refuses to talk about his early childhood life," said one investigator. "He made it clear up front that he did not care to discuss his motivating factors."

The suspect was described as a model prisoner during his confinement in the Sebastian County Jail, asking only for western adventure novels to read.

On December 31, 1990, 12th Judicial District Prosecuting Attorney David Saxon called a press conference to disclose to the news media that Wallace had given confessions to the slayings of the Domer and McLaughlin youths. Saxon said that after Sebastian County and Oklahoma authorities followed up leads given by the suspect, Wallace was charged with kidnapping in two cases. LeFlore County District Attorney Ray Edelstein said murder charges would not be filed until results of forensic tests and other phases of the investigation were complete. In addition to the new kidnapping charges, Wallace also was charged in both Arkansas and Oklahoma courts with being a felon in possession of firearms.

The charges alleged that he was in possession of a .22-caliber pistol when he abducted Mark McLaughlin and a .25-caliber automatic when he kidnapped William Domer four years earlier.

Wallace already was charged with attempted first-degree murder and kidnapping in Dale Markam's abduction and knifing and attempted kidnapping in the unsuccessful try to force Manuel Romero into his car. Another charge of being a habitual criminal was also added.

Two days later, when the heavily guarded Wallace was approaching the judge's bench to enter a plea, a female relative of Mark McLaughlin's suddenly lunged at him shouting, "I want to kill the bastard!" She was restrained by officers.

She later told reporters, "I wanted to kill him — I

316

still do—but I won't go after him again." She claimed that the accused kidnapper had grinned at her as he sat at the counsel table.

"I would have killed him with my bare hands," she told reporters. "I didn't have any weapons. I never have. I don't need any." The enraged relative and others in the courtroom were watched closely by officers during Wallace's appearances.

Sheriff Grimes said that security would be a priority whenever Wallace was moved outside the county jail to court or elsewhere. He said he thought officers should search anyone attending a public proceeding where Wallace was present.

"Security is important," the sheriff said. "So many families are involved and tensions are running high."

Another example of the rising animosity in the area occurred on the day that 12-year-old Alonzo Cade's body was discovered in the oil well drilling pit on Fort Chaffee land. Fort Smith Police Chief Don Taylor confirmed to reporters that some people mourning the youngster's death had tried to get arrested so they could get to Wallace. Officials had announced that there was no evidence so far to link Wallace to the Cade homicide, which was being investigated by the FBI. But apparently the publicity given the other boys' deaths to which the suspect had confessed were enough to arouse the wrath of persons mourning the Cade boy's slaying.

An ambulance had been called to take the distraught mother of the slain boy to the hospital after his body was found. The ambulance crew had called for police backup because of actions of some people milling in the street.

One man asked a police officer, if he hit the policeman, could he be put in the cell with Wallace? The police chief said there had been a minor shuffle, but no one was arrested. Sheriff Grimes said it was an idle threat because Wallace was confined in isolation away from other prisoners.

On the same day that Oklahoma authorities announced they were ready to file capital murder charges against George Wallace in the slayings of the Domer and McLaughlin boys, Wallace chose to enter guilty pleas to the kidnapping charges filed in the Arkansas abductions of the two youths, as well as to the other charges pending against him.

The accused kidnapper changed his earlier innocent pleas to guilty, against the advice of his attorneys, who told the judge he was not competent mentally to enter a plea and should be given extensive psychiatric tests. But when the judge asked Wallace what he wanted to do, the defendant said, "I wish to proceed, your honor."

Prosecuting Attorney Saxon said he believed Wallace was mentally competent to enter the pleas. Sheriff Grimes, called as a state witness, testified that based on numerous talks he had with Wallace, he believed him to be mentally qualified to enter the pleas.

The sheriff said that during interviews he had with the suspect, Wallace "had specific answers, no wandering. If he was confused by a question we asked, he put thought into his answer and gave a specific answer." Also, the sheriff said that Wallace "had shown concern over the well-being of the families [of the victims]."

Circuit-Chancery Judge Don Langston on January 2, 1991, accepted Wallace's pleas of guilty to seven felony charges and sentenced him to three life terms — two of them to run consecutively and the other concurrently to the two — for the kidnappings of William Domer, Mark McLaughlin, and Dale Markam. He was given another 60-year sentence, to run concurrently, on the attempted murder charge in the stabbing of Dale Markam.

Another concurrent 60-year term was meted out for the attempted kidnapping of Manuel Romero, and Wallace was given 10 years each on the two charges of felon in possession of a firearm, also to run concurrently.

The next day, the Oklahoma authorities filed two capital murder charges against George Wallace in the deaths of the Domer and McLaughlin boys. Newly elected LeFlore County District Attorney Mike Sullivan announced that he would seek the death penalty in the two cases, which are pending trial at this time.

As this was being written, the FBI investigation into the murder of Alonzo Cade was continuing, but no new developments had been announced. FBI agents did talk with Wallace early in January.

Authorities said they were still looking for Alonzo's purple and white 24-inch boys' model bicycle with a green seat, which he was riding on the night of his disappearance. Officials said anyone who might have information about the missing bicycle should contact the FBI. They said no theft charge would be pressed against the person who might have the bike.

On January 10, 1991, George Wallace was moved to the Arkansas Department of Corrections facility at Pine Bluff, Arkansas from his Sebastian County Jail cell. Sheriff Grimes said that Wallace had remained a model prisoner at the jail, but that threats on his life made from outside the jail created a security problem. Deputies commented that Wallace was quiet and somber on the early-morning drive from Fort Smith to the state prison diagnostic unit.

Still lurking in the shadows of the whole ugly story of George Kent Wallace is the question, what made him the mad paddler he turned out to be? Were his often-fatal assaults on boys at the edge of ponds reenactments of some primal experience buried deep in his subconscious mind?

As one investigator summed it up, "There will be a lot of psychologists and others who say why they think he did it, but how can you be sure? There may be something in his past that triggered this or he may just be a mean guy and likes to do it.

"There are people out there that just like to kill

319

people."

"KINKY CLUES SURROUNDED THE SLAIN GAYS"

by Julie Malear

March 31, 1987, dawned crisp and bright in Okeechobee, Florida, a small town located on the north bank of its name sake, the biggest US inland lake.

Except for the tourists who came to fish, and the passers-through who stopped for gas or a catfish dinner before traveling from Palm Beach to St. Petersburg, or from Miami to Disney World on Routes 70, 98 or 441, everyone knew about each other in Okeechobee.

Gazing through a downtown restaurant window as she served her customers, Della Stanton had a queasy feeling in the pit of her stomach. Most of the people who dined at her place of business were "regulars." She thought of them as family, and when one of them didn't show up she worried.

Della Stanton wondered where Joseph C. Ellis was. Was he sick? The 66-year old man was so punctual, such a person of habit, the uneasy waitress couldn't recall a single weekday morning he hadn't appeared for breakfast.

After preparing another pot of coffee and serving ham, biscuits and gravy to a newly arrived customer who'd taken the last seat at the counter, the concerned woman wiped her hands on her apron and hurried across the restaurant to the phone.

When a deputy in the Okeechobee County Sheriff's Office answered, Della reported Joseph Clifton Ellis a "missing person."

Responding to the call, Deputy Eddie Bishop drove to 1209 Park Street, a residence edged with tall ficus and palms that sat back off Route 70 but could be seen from the highway. Ellis, whom Bishop knew was a retired warehouse worker, had lived there for years. The deputy knocked on the door but when no one answered and he saw that Ellis' car was gone, the lawman departed. As noon approached, he tried again with similar results.

Meanwhile, as soon as the luncheon crowd reduced at the restaurant, Della Stanton slipped out of her apron and went to the Ellis house to check on Cliff, herself. There was a car parked outside but it didn't belong to Ellis. Pounding on the door, Della called his name until at last, a sleepy-looking, dark-haired man appeared.

She recognized him as Tom Derby, a railroad employee who lived away but stayed at the Ellis home when he was in Okeechobee. "Where's Cliff?" she demanded.

Not here, he replied, indicating that his host's car was not parked in the yard. Derby told the waitress he had dropped by the afternoon before. At that time, he'd rented the room from Ellis, then gone to nearby Clewiston to visit a cousin. From there he'd worked the night shift. When he got back to Ellis's house to go to bed at 7 a.m., Ellis's car was gone and he was obviously not at home. In fact, Derby added, he'd taken a quick glance through the man's bedroom door and saw sheets and blankets heaped on the floor as if Ellis was starting to change the bed.

Still worried, Della walked over to the next-door neighbor's home to talk to her. The two women had scarcely begun a conversation, however, when they heard Tom Derby yelling as he ran toward the house.

Out of breath, he told the two women to call the police, that there was a body in the house!

First to arrive at the scene at 2:30 p.m. were Deputy Eddie Bishop and Sergeant David Brough of the Okeechobee Sheriff's Department (OSD), with Jason Winer and Charles Collins of the Okeechobee Emergency Medical Services right behind them. None of them touched the corpse; it was obvious the man was dead and they waited until Officer Bill Saum and Detective Gene O'Neill of the Okeechobee City Police Department (OPD) reached the house moments later.

Deputy Bishop told the police officers about the missing person's report and assured them that neither he nor the paramedics had disturbed the body or crime scene. He indicated tire marks in the yard made by his car and the ambulance and also pointed out a blue baseball cap inscribed with an oil company emblem lying on the grass.

Lead Detective Sergeant Gene O'Neill, a short-haired, strongly built 19-year law enforcement veteran who'd been with the Okeechobee police for a decade, was the first to enter the northwest bedroom where he quickly viewed a man's inert body lying beneath bedclothing. Splattered over the floor was a large amount of blood. As soon as the scene was secured, Sergeant O'Neill radioed the dispatcher to notify the medical examiner, assistant state attorney, chief of police and Captain Buck Farrenkopf, of the death.

This done, O'Neill spoke briefly with Della Stanton, the waitress, and Tom Derby, the railroad worker and roomer. Derby said that he'd seen the blue baseball cap with the oil emblem on it lying in the yard when he came home at 7 a.m.

O'Neill sent Della and Derby to the police station for more interviews, advising Captain Farrenkopf to keep them separated until they gave their statements. After conferring with Chief Larry Mobley of the OPD, O'Neill sent for Detective Sergeant George

Miller from the sheriff's office to work the crime scene. Miller and Detective Dale LaFlam arrived soon after, as did Detective Allen "Bingo" Levin. Throughout the case, the two law enforcement agencies worked together as a team. A BOLO was issued for the victim's 1983 white and blue Olds Cutlass.

Examining the scene, O'Neill noticed the porch light on; he also saw signs of forced entry on the Western front window. Closer inspection, however, uncovered cobwebs stretched over the area which told him the marks were from an earlier burglary. Actually, according to reports he saw later, the victim had been burglarized several times in the past.

Trying to picture what had happened, the detective decided Joseph Ellis might have been relaxing on the couch. Bed pillows indicated someone was resting his back while in a sitting position. A pair of shoes sat by a nearby footstool. On a small end table near the couch, a black telephone rested, its cord neatly snipped as if to prevent a call for help.

As Miller, LaFlam and O'Neill examined the house, they noted one inside light burning in the bathroom adjoining the victim's bedroom. There they found blood and dirt rimming the raised toilet seat. Nearby, a pair of men's briefs, flung on a section of newspaper on the floor, revealed possible bloodstains. The light switch also bore a blood smear.

Stepping back into Ellis's bedroom, they saw blood splatters and smears on the wall behind a shelf unit that held a TV and VCR. The room appeared to have been searched. Drawers had been pulled out of a four-drawer bureau and from a vanity. Socks from the bottom nightstand drawer were on top of the body and had been put there prior to the bedclothes being rolled from the bed onto Ellis's body. The drawer, so handy to the bed, would have been an ideal place for Ellis to have hidden a gun.

Detective Sergeant O'Neill went outside to question the neighbor about whether the victim owned a gun.

"He recently bought one," she told O'Neill. "I believe it was a twenty-five. He bought it after the last time he was burglarized."

Ferreting further, the detective concluded that the perp had probably found and taken the gun from the nightstand drawer which had obviously been ransacked. O'Neill re-entered the room and continued his search.

Walking to the end of the bed, the lead detective and his co-workers saw a footlocker-type box standing open on the floor. Delving into its contents, they discovered that it held a number of porno films and magazines, mostly dealing with homosexuality. O'Neill had been aware of Ellis's reputation as being gay. This discovery merely confirmed what he, and most of the town, already suspected.

Detectives Miller and O'Neill put in a call to the Broward County Sheriff's Office for Detective Charles Edel of their forensic services unit. They wanted him to interpret "the blood splatters and cast of blood." They agreed to keep the body undisturbed until he could arrive to make an examination.

While the crime scene team was taking photographs and videos as well as checking for latent prints, particularly in the bathroom, Dr. Leonard Walker, chief medical examiner of the 19th Circuit, arrived. Detective Miller guided him around the house and into the master bedroom where the shocking sight awaited him. Blood drenched the rug in huge pools around Ellis's body which lay on the floor beside the bed with only his feet sticking out from the crimson-stained bed linens covering him.

The covers—a pale green and white sheet, a white throw with a multicolored square pattern and a brown blanket—were removed from the body by Detective Miller and preserved as evidence. There were multiple stab wounds to the upper body and head. The victim had on a short sleeve, button-up shirt, light gray-colored work pants, green socks, jockey shorts and his zipper was open.

Splattered on the north wall above the body and beginning at the foot of the bed were a number of bright scarlet droplets. Higher on the wall were blood smears. A silver-colored, bloody, single-blade kitchen knife was found under the bed. A wallet, empty of money and credit cards and partly covered by some clothing, lay on a chair by the nightstand. It appeared to have been tossed there carelessly.

The sleuths found two paperback books on the floor nearby. When the officers held a flashlight at a low angle and let the beam cross the blue cover of one of the books, they saw a bloody shoe print. Detective Miller found another bloody shoe print on the fitted sheet which still covered the mattress. This print stood at the foot of the bed pointing towards the head of the bed where another bloody print stained the sheet.

Miller noticed a distinguishing feature to these prints—a small section of the shoe sole had been sheared off, probably by accident while the suspect was wearing the shoes. Excited at the discovery, Miller realized that with such an identifying mark, they might be able to match the perp's shoes to the prints.

The crime scene sleuths had a theory. "The suspect walked on the sheet covering the mattress after stepping in the victim's blood on the bedsheet. This occurred while the suspect was en route to cut the telephone line."

Actually the perp had cut wires on both phones. The one Miller referred to, hung on the wall on the left side of the bed, its wire dangling.

Detective Bobby Kelly of the OSD, called for forensic specialist Detective Charles Edel who arrived on a flight between 8 and 8:30 that night. After examining the body, he explained his findings on the blood splatters to the other lawmen.

The attack on Mr. Ellis, he said, took place on the right side of the bed. While Mr. Ellis was in a sitting position there, his attacker stood in front of him thrusting a knife at Mr. Ellis's upper body, creating the stab wounds. Afterwards, according to the findings, Ellis fell to the floor from the bed. At some point after that, the suspect moved Ellis's body around to its present position.

When they lifted the victim to carry him into the living room where there was more room to examine him, the lawmen found two .25-caliber shells and a pair of scissors lying in the blood beneath his dead body.

Delving into the facts, they now knew that Ellis had a .25 caliber gun which the perp had stolen along with the victim's car.

After his crime scene work was completed, Detective Miller stated his ideas. Since there was no sign of forced entry, it was his opinion that "the perpetrator was let into the house by the victim, possibly in good faith. I believe in the time prior to the killing of Mr. Ellis, that very possibly Mr. Ellis and the suspect were viewing TV."

He based the fact that the victim may have been watching TV when the suspect arrived, on the position of Ellis's shoes in front of the couch as if he'd just slipped out of them. When the lawmen arrived, the TV was off and the changer was in the bedroom.

Detective Miller concluded that "the suspect either asked for the use of the bathroom or made some excuse to go into the other room, the bedroom. Probably after an extended period of time, Mr. Ellis maybe got curious and walked into the bedroom, very possibly caught the suspect going through a nightstand drawer or even possibly going through Mr. Ellis's wallet. . . .

"I believe," Miller continued, "the suspect knew Mr. Ellis kept a weapon in the nightstand drawer. Mr. Ellis came in and caught the suspect by surprise. The suspect hit him in the mouth one time, either stunned him or knocked him back on the bed, and I believe Mr. Ellis was in a semi-sitting position on the edge of the bed when he was stabbed and killed. After which, I believe in all sincerity, the suspect cleaned himself up, possibly washed himself off, hands, arms etcetera, in the bathroom, came back out of the bathroom—an extremely wet towel was found at the foot of the bed—cut the lines of both phones, took the keys to Mr. Ellis's car and left."

Seventy miles east of Okeechobee, a seeming coincidence was occurring. That very day, about the same time that Della Stanton had become alarmed because Joseph Clifton Ellis had not dined at the restaurant, co-workers of Thomas Sisco, a well-known lawyer in West Palm Beach, began to worry about his whereabouts. When the unusually reliable man didn't come to work that morning, two office people and his business partner drove to Sisco's house to see what was wrong.

After no one answered their knock at the Sisco home, they walked around the house and peered in windows. To their horror, they saw a person, perhaps their friend, lying on the floor near the kitchen door. One of them ran immediately to a phone and called authorities.

The paramedics and road Patrol Officer Chuck Pearsall responded, entering the attractive home on 36th Street and affirmed that the man was dead. Actually Sisco had been dead for some time. His body was quite cold.

Fifteen minutes later, lead Detective Sergeant Guillermo Perez, a pleasant, literate, dark-haired man with a mustache, arrived at the house with assistant lead Detective John Johnson. Moving quickly through the neat, artistically furnished living room, they found the victim in a kneeling position, face forward on the floor. A heavyset man with reddish-blonde hair, Sisco was wearing a bracelet and a heavy thick gold chain with a medallion. He'd been shot in the back of his head and was lying in blood.

Finding no signs of forcible entry, the detectives assumed that Sisco knew his assailant. His house was in perfect order except the bedroom which was slightly mussed. Noting the jewelry, as well as many fine art pieces, the sleuths felt at first that robbery was not the motive. They altered their first opinion, however, when they learned Sisco wore a $5,000 Lucien Piccard wristwatch. It was missing along with some of his credit cards. Detective Sergeant Perez quickly put out a BOLO on the expensive timepiece.

Deducing that the attorney was first shot near the front door, they concluded that the first .25 caliber bullet grazed his head and ricocheted onto the ceiling at a spot where they found a mark. As he fled towards the back of the house, the second shot probably missed him. Then, when Sisco fell and lay bleeding by the sliding doors, the third bullet found its target, killing him.

Although the detectives had no suspect, they began by questioning Sisco's co-workers. The two women and one man knew a great deal about the victim and told the investigators what they could. Sisco was gay, they said; he frequented a lot of gay bars. Often, he advertised in gay publications for contacts and stayed very busy in that respect. They knew of 20 or 30 people who had stayed with him. Some stayed a day, others two days, still others hung around a couple of weeks. Gay bars afforded Sisco another way of picking up friends.

As Sergeant Perez delved further into the prominent attorney's life, he learned that the 46-year-old man was wealthy, politically active, and had a passion for fine art. He was a popular man with a booming law practice. He had a record of helping abused children and a reputation for assisting people who were down on their luck.

"He was extremely intelligent, one of the smartest people I ever met," the woman who'd been his law partner told Perez. "And he was very caring, very giving."

Perhaps because of his sexual preferences, however,

Thomas Sisco was a lonely man, so lonely he was almost reckless in his choice of companions. According to his former law partner, Sisco was so starved for companionship that he sometimes advertised for "houseboys" in the gay magazines.

The officers tracked down a favorite bar the victim had frequented. They learned, in fact, that Sisco had been at that bar on March 30th, the night on which he was later killed. He was last seen at 11, leaving alone. At midnight, a male friend drove by Sisco's house. The lights were on; he saw nothing unusual.

Examining the bedroom and noting that the bedcovers had been turned down, Sergeant Perez and Detective Johnson determined that the lawyer was in bed reading when the knock occurred. A gay publication lay on the sheet as did a cordless phone. Sisco's co-workers told the lawmen that their friend always had a cordless phone so he could walk around.

Oddly enough, the battery cover was stuck to the blood on his forehead.

"Apparently," Perez observed, "he answered the knock on he door with the phone in his hand . . . and the phone had been picked away from him . . . apparently so he couldn't call anybody." The lawmen discovered the phone on the dining room table with blood on it.

Following usual policy procedures, they checked with neighbors, finding one who'd heard something after midnight. Shortly after Sisco presumably let someone he knew into his house, a neighbor heard an argument and gunshots.

However, with no gun, no obvious prints, no witnesses, and no known enemies, the detectives knew they would be spending most of their time tracking down and interviewing the many people who had stayed with Sisco or even had relations with him.

Meanwhile, on the following day, April 1st, Detective Sergeant O'Neill in Okeechobee, contacted Joseph Ellis' bank regarding check activity, and called the phone company to determine if any long distance calls had been made on the victim's phone on March 30th and 31st.

Detective Miller attended an autopsy performed by Leonard Walker. The medical examiner found 15 stabs on Ellis, including defense wounds on both of his hands.

Soon afterwards, the owner of a nearby lounge came to headquarters, advising that he's seen Ellis' blue and white car in his parking lot around 8:30 a.m. When his other employee came to work an hour later, they decided to move the vehicle. He got in the car, touching a picture frame and the glovebox. Detective O'Neill sent him to the sheriff's office to have a set of elimination prints made.

Detective Miller and Captain Farenkopf, in processing the vehicle for blood and latent prints, found a bloody shoe impression on the floor mat on the driver's side. Later, O'Neill joined the men to further process the victim's car. On the backseat, they found a checkbook of Ellis' with no checks missing and a balance of $12,639.72 in the account. They also found an expended .25-caliber shell casing, a case for a Walkman radio, and a token from a West Palm Beach saloon on Congress Avenue.

The trio spotted a Sprite soda can on the front floorboard, which had been converted to a cocaine rock smoker by crushing it and punching holes in it.

Meanwhile, Della Stanton notified O'Neill that a friend was telling a story around town that one of her son's friends had seen a body which was missing a head, wrapped in a sheet. The lawmen immediately backtracked the story and decided it was a passerby at the scene who'd observed Ellis' corpse being brought out of the house by the ambulance people.

On April 2nd, O'Neill checked local gun dealers until he found one who claimed that on September 29, 1986, he'd sold Ellis a Raven .25-caliber automatic, model MP-25 which was nickel plated. A few days

331

later, Detective O'Neill entered the missing gun into the computer and sent teletypes to area departments to search local pawnshops for the weapon.

He and Captain Farrenkopf visited the Moose Club where Ellis belonged, only to find out that he hadn't been there for a couple of months. He'd lately been involved in a local singles club, a witness said.

When the detectives attended the funeral home viewing of the body, they saw one known gay, Robinson Lee Courtney, at the service.

Speaking to Della Stanton later, the Okeechobee lawmen ferreted out that Clifton Ellis had been friendly for years with his accountant, Dell Wilson, and thought the victim had a safe deposit box in the accountant's name.

Digging further, the sleuths learned that the victim's tendencies leaned toward young males aged 15 to 25. Over the years these youths would go to him, perform services and receive money. Sergeant O'Neill knew there was no file on Ellis' homosexual activities. Instead there was a file of different burglaries, different thefts and incidences where he had been ripped off because of the nature of his activities.

The detective compiled a list of the victim's acquaintances. Because the town was small and so many people knew Ellis, Sergeant O'Neill commented that "everybody in Okeechobee" was a suspect in the investigation. "Probably ninety-five percent of the people that visited Clifton Ellis were not gay. They went to Clifton Ellis and received favors from him in exchange for money." O'Neill was referring mainly to oral copulation done by Clifton to them.

"A lot of the youths went to him if they needed five bucks, or in later years," the lead detective continued, "when crack got to be ten dollars a hit, they probably went to him and got ten or fifteen bucks from him. A couple of them did live with him for a length of time and took him for a lot of money."

On April 3rd, a young white drifter was brought

332

into the police station from beneath the Taylor Street Bridge when it was learned he had recently burnt up a pair of tennis shoes. The wino was permitted to leave, however, when an investigation revealed the incident had happened prior to the homicide. The drifter had been drying out his shoes by hanging them over a campfire. Disgusted when he accidentally dropped one, he tossed the other into the flames. Later he was given a better pair from the local mission.

Sergeant O'Neill and his captain went to an adult book store where they spoke with the one gay person they'd recognized from Ellis' funeral—Robinson Lee Courtney. This man agreed to come to the station and make a statement.

Ellis was gay, too, he told the lawmen. He would "pick up hitchhikers who might stay a night or for weeks." As far as Courtney knew, Ellis was not fooling around with anyone steady at the time of his death. He'd known Ellis for 20 years, he said. Courtney admitted being gay himself, but said he never had sex with Ellis. He occasionally visited, however, and at one time did watch gay videotapes with the victim.

He told his interrogators that teenagers would often visit Ellis for the purpose of sex for money and Ellis would often be ripped off by these kids. He named three people Ellis had had problems with. Two had vandalized his home. Another, George School, had lived with Ellis a long time until his host grew tired of supporting School's beer habit and told him to leave.

Courtney said Ellis didn't get his books and movies locally but he would travel to West Palm Beach. He verified Della Stanton's story about the accountant, Dell Wilson. The victim had recently put Dell on his checking account as an authorized signer. Sean Wilson, Dell's brother, was a good friend of Ellis and was gay. But Dell Wilson was not.

The latter information was again confirmed when the lawmen interviewed Ellis' next-door neighbor who had also been his tenant. She said Sean Wilson often took Ellis to West Palm Beach to pick up videotapes which she thought were of a gay nature. The two brothers would then join Ellis to view them.

The victim had one room set aside to rent to railroad men, the neighbor said. Young men often visited Ellis and he had one young man who lived with him for some time.

The woman added that she'd paid her rent of $180 in cash on Friday or Saturday. The last she'd seen of her landlord was when he'd been working in his yard on Sunday.

Sergeant O'Neill's next interview was with the victim's accountant, Dell Wilson. The man said he'd known Joseph Ellis for 30 years and handled his affairs for the last six or seven. Worrying that by living alone he'd have no one to help with his accounts should something happen, Ellis put Dell Wilson as a signer on the checking account.

"I am not gay," the accountant told O'Neill. He knew of course, that Ellis was. He spoke of his friend being a "creature of habit and very time-oriented."

"The person you are looking for," Dell Wilson prophesied, "will be a young male wanting something for nothing, and possibly on drugs or alcohol."

Recalling some of the "young males" who visited Ellis, Dell Wilson mentioned knowing George School, whom the victim had kicked out for excessive beer drinking. In fact, while School was living at Cliff's home, the accountant told his inquisitors, the two men had come to his office for him to fill out their income taxes. School was returning to the Midwest and Ellis was loaning him the money to make the trip, the victim had explained to the accountant that day. The arrangement was that School's income tax return check would be sent back to Ellis to repay the loan he was making to School.

The next interview in the homicide took place in Belle Glade, Florida, where the lawmen tracked down the oil company whose name was on the baseball cap found in Ellis' yard. The owner of the business told Sergeant O'Neill that although some of the hats had been "given out as advertising," they were primarily for employees. Scanning a list of workers' names the owner handed him, the detective recognized no one, nor did he see a single Okeechobee address for any of those listed.

Continuing with his interviews, O'Neill uncovered information from Sean Wilson, the brother of Ellis' accountant, Dell Wilson. Sean confirmed that the victim was a "very routine person" but had gotten to be "such a gossip," that the two of them hadn't been together for some time.

Sean said he'd passed the Ellis residence at dark on March 30th, and noticed a living room lamp was on. The following day, while visiting Ellis' next-door neighbor and hearing that his friend was missing, he noticed Ellis' car was gone and a white railroad truck was parked in the yard. He also saw the blue baseball cap in the grass. He walked over to the house, touching nothing. The cap, he was sure, did not belong to Ellis. It was soiled and old looking, not something his friend would wear.

It had been "about two years" since Ellis had picked up any hitchhikers, Sean continued. Due to frequent burglaries and thefts, the victim had become choosy about his contacts.

The investigator probed for names of anyone who'd been with Joseph Ellis in the past. Thinking deeply, Sean mentioned an ex-con from Colorado who'd rented a room from the victim in December of '85, and another man who used to visit and watch films. Other frequent visitors, he recalled, were Donnie Craig and another young man. Sean Wilson finally remembered a number of other possible suspects who'd stayed with Ellis, including one who'd been convicted of armed robbery in nearby Indiantown. Listening carefully, O'Neill copied down their names, each of whom he planned to investigate.

Sean brought up the name George School. George, he said, "stayed with Ellis for three or four weeks, possibly more," then continued his relationship by mail and collect calls up to a few months before he was due to get out of prison. From what Sean Wilson was saying, Sergeant O'Neill felt he must find out more about this George School.

When he finished interviewing Sean Wilson, the sleuth received a stack of letters from one of Ellis' out-of-state relatives who'd come in for the victim's funeral. There were 60 letters, all written by George School, the man whose name kept coming up. O'Neill read every page, finally digesting the last one April 8th.

In discussing the case with another lawman, O'Neill said, "It is obvious that School has taken advantage of a friendship and played upon the emotions of Ellis and begged hundreds of dollars out of Ellis." He noted that School continued to stress that upon his release from prison he'd return to Okeechobee and he and Ellis would continue from where they left off. School didn't actually admit to a gay relationship, but O'Neill felt it was obvious. As the letters continued, however, a discord appeared between the men which seemed to be initiated by Ellis.

In the last two letters, School told Ellis he was getting married and he wanted Ellis to buy him a pickup truck as a wedding gift. He and his wife would then come and live with Ellis.

Delving further into this information, O'Neill contacted corrections authorities and learned that George School had been released in August 1986, his current whereabouts unknown. Until he could be found, sleuths decided to look into other clues.

Trying to track down the shoe which made the bloody prints, the detectives found a similar pair at a store. They purchased the pair and turned them over to Detective Miller for test purposes.

The following day, Detective LaFlam had a hot

clue; a stolen truck from Okeechobee was found in Gainesville after an aborted burglary of a gun store. The local team immediately investigated but the lead fizzled when it turned out the truck was stolen four days after the homicide.

On April 12th, Robinson Lee Courtney informed the detectives that he had called home the day before to speak with his live-in friend, and the phone was answered by Donnie Craig.

"I became very upset that Donnie was in my house," Courtney told the lawmen. "I don't like him! Donnie had no business being there." The investigators could see how intense the man's feelings were.

"Take a close look at Donnie," he told Sergeant O'Neill. "Donnie was a frequent visitor at Ellis' and he ripped Ellis off in the past."

Following this tip, the detective ran a records check on Donnie Gene Craig. Sure enough, they learned that the 23-year-old man's past contained arrests for burglary, robbery, auto theft, kidnapping and sexual assault. Currently outstanding were three warrants for violation of probation.

Actually, O'Neill had personal knowledge of Craig, for he'd worked a burglary on him in 1983 in which Craig had broken into Ellis' house and stolen items from him.

Phoning the Okeechobee Sheriff's Office, the detective learned the warrants were still active. He requested the last known address of Craig. O'Neill was told it was in a trailer park which O'Neill realized was the only close residential area to the lounge where Ellis' deserted car had been found.

The sleuth then contacted Detective Miller and asked him to pull Craig's fingerprints and compare them with latents lifted during the investigation. He and Captain Farrenkopf rushed over to the Okeechobee Sheriff's Office and met with Miller who excitedly told them he had "a match." He'd identified the latent print they'd picked up on the rear view mirror of Ellis'

Cutlass.

No sooner had Miller given them that news than Detective LaFlam announced that he had recently worked a case on Craig and knew the whereabouts of his family and girlfriend.

Without wasting a moment, the four lawmen sped to the trailer park where they found Sheila Wynn, Craig's girlfriend. Somewhat older than he, Sheila told the men she was "close friends" with Donnie but that Donnie hadn't stayed with her since his arrest around the first of the year—the one worked by Detective LaFlam. She and her son hadn't even heard from him for two months, she said, not until Donnie had called her from an unknown location about a week before.

"A friend dropped him off last Saturday," she said. "He stayed a couple of hours and left." She assured the detectives she did not know where he was living now.

After leaving Sheila's trailer, the men, except for Miller, drove to a dairy where Detective LaFlam knew family members of the suspect were working. The relatives told the men the Donnie was working the night shift at another dairy and living in Playland Park with other family members.

Leaving quickly, they raced to Playland Park, where the police officers identified themselves to a relative of Donnie's who owned the home there.

"We need to talk with Donnie," O'Neill said. "Is he here?"

The family member told the men Donnie was asleep. He allowed the lawmen to enter, however, and pointed to the bedroom at the end of the hall. After awakening the suspect, Detective LaFlam told him, "You're under arrest for violation of probation."

When they told Donnie Craig to dress, a family member brought in a pair of his pants which were checked by LaFlam before being given to the suspect. Still barefoot, Donnie asked a family member for his

338

shoes. When she told him they were "still wet," he told her he wanted them anyway as he had no others. She brought them in and handed them to LaFlam to pass on. LaFlam looked at the bottom and showed the shoes to Sergeant O'Neill. Both men noted that the design was the same as those of the bloody footprints at the Ellis murder scene.

"Donnie, we're confiscating the shoes as possible evidence in a case we're working," they told him before transporting him to the police department for questioning on the Ellis homicide. Once at the station, they were joined by Detective Miller who quickly took the shoes to the lab for examination.

Sergeant O'Neill advised Craig of his rights. Waiving his right to an attorney, he agreed to answer questions. Craig stated that he'd been back in Okeechobee since around March 16th and stayed with Sheila Wynn until the 25th or at which time he returned to his relatives' Playland Park home.

He was currently working at the dairy, and had been there for about three weeks. "Since being at the dairy I've worked seven nights a week except for last Friday." This, of course, would give him an alibi for the time of the homicide, sleuths realized.

He told them it had been a month and a half since he last saw Cliff Ellis, and he had never driven Cliff's car—although he had been in it once, about a year and a half earlier.

He agreed that the shoes were his. "I bought them about two months ago in West Palm Beach." He hadn't loaned those shoes to anyone, he told probers.

Answering the investigators' questions about previous work, Craig told them he'd been living and working in West Palm Beach. He gave them a catering service and a restaurant where he'd been employed. As for the death of Clifton Ellis, he claimed he knew nothing.

After speaking with Craig, Sergeant O'Neill checked with Craig's boss at the dairy. Contrary to the suspect's statement, Craig hadn't started work there until April 3, 1987, several days after Joseph Ellis' murder.

Detective Miller arrived back from the lab with the report that the shoe pattern was indeed the same, but due to the washing of the shoes and their wetness, it could not be determined at that time whether there was any blood on the shoes.

A search warrant was secured. All the involved officers met at the sheriff's office to go to Craig's home and collect evidence. Before they could do so, however, the family brought all of Donnie's possessions to them and turned them over. His family members signed a "consent to search" form and gave the officers a gray duffel-type bag. The lawmen drove to Playland Park where they searched the residence with negative results.

Returning to the county jail, O'Neill arrested Donnie Gene Craig for the murder of Joseph Clifton Ellis. That done, the detective released the arrest information to the press at a news conference on April 14th.

Meanwhile, to the detectives in West Palm Beach, it seemed as if they'd been spinning their wheels for two weeks regarding the homicide of the popular attorney, Thomas Sisco.

With no results from his earlier BOLO on the Lucien Piccard watch, Sergeant Perez began going through every individual pawn slip in town. It was a last ditch sort of thing but it paid off when he found a watch at a pawnshop on Clematis Street in downtown West Palm Beach that seemed identical to the one that was stolen. Somehow the pawn slip had previously gone unnoticed.

Checking the slip, Perez found that a white male named Teddy Baer had pawned it. Investigating Baer, Perez decided he was just a "street person" with no type of job and it would seem highly unusual that such a person would be pawning a $5,000 watch — for which he got $250. After picking up the watch from the pawnshop, the detective started checking through the phone book for jewelers who had knowledge of, or would sell that type of watch.

Locating one likely jewelry shop in the yellow pages, Sergeant Perez spoke to the owner. By lucky coincidence, the shop owner had sold that very watch to Mr. Sisco. Another fortunate occurrence was that the owner, himself, had sized the Lucien Piccard for the victim and had placed his jeweler's mark on its back. As a result, he could positively identify the watch from the pawnshop as the one owned by the murdered attorney.

Now that the property was known to be Sisco's, the detective team started to backtrack Teddy Baer, the street person who had pawned it. On the same day that the Okeechobee detectives were taking Donnie Gene Craig into custody, the West Palm Beach officers finally located the street person.

"A guy named Matt gave me that watch," he said. It took Sergeant Perez, and assistant Detective Johnson about a day to identify a male who was actually Matthew Runner. Now the street person said that he'd gone with Runner to the pawnshop. Since he had some identification, he was the one who pawned the watch. The street person indicated that Matt Runner claimed some dude had traded the watch to him on March 31st for a couple of cocaine rocks—about $20 worth. He'd gotten a "good deal," Sergeant Perez noted, a $5,000 watch for $20.

The next day, the lawmen located Matthew Runner but found the interview difficult because he was doped up. In fact, he was so rocked from smoking cocaine all night, he kept falling asleep while he was talking to the two detectives.

The statement they finally got was that on the night of the 30th, Matt was partying at 330 Pembroke Place in downtown West Palm Beach, an apartment house where everyone was basically a drug user. A male known only as "Dean" arrived at the party. He had plenty of money, the fancy watch, and several other items he soon began trading for cocaine.

Along with Matt, Dean partied with a nice-looking woman and her 16-year old strawberry-blonde daughter, as well as the woman's male cousin.

Helpful, Matt Runner led Sergeant Perez to the group. In order to get the interviews, however, the detective had to completely convince the four that he would absolutely not pick them up for drugs. Once these street persons understood that he merely needed information, they were very cooperative. All four lived together in a one-room apartment.

These people who'd been partying that night each told the same story. They described Dean as what they'd call a "Loxahatchee red-neck type." He was short, baby-faced, and young and told the group at the party that he'd come from Okeechobee. They'd seen him immediately as a meal ticket or chump, and although they seemed to go along with him, they were actually ripping him off. He would buy $20 worth of cocaine and they would give him $10 worth, keep the rest of the money, and help him smoke the rocks.

Dean had about $200 on him, the street people told Perez. But in a period of a few hours, they had bilked him out of all of it. Then, when the money was gone, he started showing the watch and later the gun. That was when, Matt told the officers, he got the expensive timepiece and gave Dean the rocks.

The four street people all described the gun as a .25 Raven automatic. Dean had a gold lighter, too, they recalled. He gave that to the young strawberry-blonde. During this time, Dean was bragging to them that he was on his way to Tennessee and had a load of marijuana in his trunk. He did his best to get the teenager to come along. Since Matt Runner was her boyfriend, however, she resisted.

"If she'd gone," Sergeant Perez remarked back at the police station, "she'd probably be dead as well."

That night, Dean bragged that his father was a "rich

dairy farmer" who had bought him a new car. While the group partied and smoked crack, Dean let his hostess and her male cousin use the vehicle. As the couple drove around in the blue and white Cutlass a couple of times, they noticed a checkbook on the backseat. Curious, and rifling through the glove case, they saw that the name on the checks matched that on insurance papers found in the glove compartment.

As Sergeant Perez probed further, the woman and her cousin said that they had thought seriously of stealing the car to sell it but gave up the idea because Dean was so nervous. They searched the trunk while he was inside the apartment. Although they did not find the marijuana he claimed he had, they did spot the gun. Later, he took it out to show them. Dean offered to see it to them and carried it in to the party.

Shortly afterwards, while he was messing around in the drug house and buying a great deal of cocaine, the four dealers distracted Dean's attention and hid the gun under a couch. For some time they played with their "chump," passing the weapon from one partier to another. Each of them noted Dean's extreme nervousness. He would jump every time a car passed the house. They ended up stealing the gun from him. They also stole the shells.

It was Matt Runner, the group agreed, who took it to Third and Rosemary Streets, an anything goes area, and traded it for cocaine the next day. So, although the police didn't have the actual gun, they knew the suspect had been in possession of a Raven automatic. The casings they'd gotten at the homicide scene were consistent for just such a gun.

At some point in the early morning hours, according to the dealers, Dean went to a pay phone right beside the apartment house and made a long distance call. The woman overheard him telling someone he'd be "home in the morning." Perez ferreted out that he left just before daybreak.

But trying to find this redneck Dean was another

question. Where was he? In the Okeechobee area as the street people hinted? Or had he gone to Tennessee as he claimed was his plan?

Then came a stroke of luck for Sergeant Perez. On April 17th, Thomas Sisco's law partner saw an article in a local paper regarding the arrest of Donnie Gene Craig in Okeechobee for the murder of Joseph Clifton Ellis. Noting a similarity in the two deaths—both gay men with many contacts, both homicides occurring the same night, both men robbed—the detective wondered if the dealers were actually saying "Gene," as in Donnie Craig's middle name, instead of "Dean" as he and his team had believed. Could this Craig have killed an old man in Okeechobee then driven 70 miles to West Palm Beach and killed Sisco in the span of a few hours? If so, Perez felt he'd better find out.

Assistant lead Detective Johnson contacted Detective Sergeant O'Neill to tell him about the attorney's murder and to ask some questions. The answers made Johnson feel that Craig was their perpetrator. First of all, the east-coast sleuth learned, the arrested man fit the description of Dean, "a young white male, late teens to early twenties, about 5'2" to 5'3", weighing 130 to 140 pounds, who told the dealers he was from Okeechobee. He was wearing a casual shirt, jeans, and white Reeboks, and was driving an 82/83 blue Oldsmobile in cherry condition.

Second, a .25-caliber automatic had been stolen, as well as a vehicle and cash. This fell in line with Perez's and Johnson's knowledge that the perp was driving an '83 Cutlass, had cash when he arrived at the dope house in West Palm Beach, and had committed the murder with a .25-caliber Raven automatic. The detectives agreed to get together on April 21st.

Before that meeting, the Okeechobee detectives re-interviewed Sheila Wynn, Donnie Craig's girlfriend. "I was not entirely truthful," she admitted during the second interrogation. She had "a soft spot for Donnie," she now told the lawmen. Besides, she didn't know the seriousness of the charges against him when she'd been questioned before.

As she talked, Sergeant O'Neill wrote Sheila's story in a report: ". . . on 3/29/87 Craig came over from West Palm, that he had a car, but that it had gotten a flat tire and was parked alongside the road by Nubbin Slough, that she took him down there, he changed a tire, and then drove the car into the Nubbin Slough area and parked it. He took the battery out and the license tag off. They then returned to the Wynn trailer. Wynn described the car as being an older model, beat-up, silver gray in color . . . Baracuda. On Monday, 3/30/87, she took Craig back to get the car, it was gone. They checked the local towing compounds and didn't find it. She dropped Craig off in Playland Park, she returned home. Craig called in the early afternoon and said he and a family member had located the car in Indiantown, that the police had had it towed there. He told Wynn that he and his relative were going to Indiantown to get the car.

"She didn't hear anymore from him until about one o'clock on the morning of 3/31/87 when she got a collect call from him. He said he was in West Palm Beach, that they couldn't get the car because it was still registered in the other guy's name. He then advised her that he would call her or would see her later. . . ."

Sergeant O'Neill continued to probe, ferreting out that Donnie had awakened Sheila around nine or ten that morning. Apparently his normal self, he was wearing a short sleeve, button-down shirt, white jogging shorts and white high-top tennis shoes. On his wrist he wore a gold wristwatch. The sleuths delved into this but Wynn claimed she'd seen Donnie wearing the watch before the homicide. He stayed with her several days before she took him back to Playland Park on April 3rd.

O'Neill requested a toll drop on Sheila's phone. He then went with Detectives Miller and LaFlam to the crime scene where they recovered paneling and a chair. Miller took both these items to Ft. Lauderdale for examination.

When the lead detective told LaFlam about Sheila's story regarding Craig's car being towed, the latter checked it out. It was partly true. The sheriff's office took it all right, but they'd left it at a garage in Okeechobee.

On April 21st, Detectives Johnson and Perez drove from West Palm Beach to Okeechobee to meet with Detectives O'Neill, LaFlam and Miller of the two co-investigating agencies there. After exchanging a multitude of information, including the number of the phone booth outside the dealers' house, they came to the conclusion that Donnie Craig had gone to West Palm Beach, committed the murder, slept at the apartment, then driven back to Okeechobee and dumped the car.

Apparently when he'd stolen the Cutlass and was on his way to West Palm Beach, he had test-fired the gun out the window and the casing had ejected in the car. Sergeant Perez carried the shell back to check it with the casings from the Sisco homicide. According to Gerald Styers of the Palm Beach Sheriff's Office, the casings matched perfectly. The same gun that was test-fired in the car had also killed the lawyer. The only problem was, probers didn't have the gun. They did, however, get the gun's serial number from the Okeechobee police.

Also, when the sleuths returned to West Palm Beach, they took with them photos of Craig and the car. The detectives would see if the dealers could identify either.

That same day, O'Neill received a message that Craig wanted to talk. O'Neill went to jail. The suspect spoke of trivia, but when the lead detective probed further, Craig asked to see his lawyer before saying anything else. Attorney Michael Sullivan arrived and spoke with the suspect alone. Later, the attorney said

346

his client might give another statement "sometime down the road."

On April 22nd, Sheila Wynn gave Sergeant O'Neill the phone bill she'd received the day before. Significantly, there was a collect call received by her on March 31st at 1:15 a.m. That call had been made from the booth near the drug house. When the detective called West Palm police to advise them of the phone match-up, he learned that Johnson and Perez had gotten four positive IDs both on Craig and on Ellis' vehicle.

Detective Miller positively matched up characteristics from the confiscated shoes to the bloody prints left at the scene.

The following day, Detectives Perez and Johnson drove over to Okeechobee to speak with the suspect. Craig admitted knowing Sisco and having lived with him for a couple of weeks. He denied being in West Palm that night and denied killing the attorney.

On April 27th, Sergeant O'Neill interviewed a woman from the Okeechobee Office of Probation. "On February eleventh," she told him, "Craig had been sent to a center in West Palm to work off his restitution." He would work at a restaurant, then spend the night at the center. On March 28th, she said, he left and never returned. "The warrants were issued on April sixth," she told O'Neill.

While speaking with O'Neill, she noticed the homicide photos pinned to the project boards on his office wall and asked if she could look at them. Stopping at one photo, she said, "That hat looks familiar to me."

Shown a closeup of the blue baseball cap from the oil company, she exclaimed, "This is Donnie's hat. I saw him wearing it when I interviewed him October 28, 1986. I remember the hat because I asked him if he was working at the oil company."

At that time Donnie had told her it was "just a hat he'd found laying around," the probation officer recalled. She initialed the back of the photo for O'Neill.

Two days later, a man in West Palm Beach struck a woman and was arrested for aggravated assault. He had in his possession a .25-caliber Raven automatic, probably the gun Runner claimed to have traded the day after getting it from Craig. When officers checked its serial number, lo and behold it matched the Ellis gun. Elated, Sergeant Perez phoned the news to the Okeechobee team.

Then, although Craig continued to deny being in West Palm Beach the night of Sisco's murder, Sergeant Perez found a co-worker of the victim who had met Craig at the gay lounge frequented by Sisco. The same bartender on that night identified Craig as being there on the murder night as well.

It was a circumstantial case on the Sisco homicide, Sergeant Perez realized. Nonetheless, in both cases, Donnie Gene Craig was found guilty. His lawyer, Michael Sullivan, tried to prove that one of the street people, not Craig, had committed the murder—that Craig was in a crack house smoking cocaine when the murder occurred.

At one time, the suspect told a detective while being driven to prison, that the son of his girlfriend, Sheila Wynn, had accompanied him to Sisco's home and did the grisly deed.

Prosecuting Attorney Mary Ann Duggan was allowed to bring in details of the Ellis homicide in Okeechobee since the property of the first victim— gun and car—was seen in West Palm Beach, and shells and casings of the Raven Automatic gun were found to be a perfect match not only to those lying under Ellis, and dispensed in his car, but to those used to kill Sisco. The two cases were so intertwined, the judge ruled that some evidence from the first case was not only admissible but necessary.

In Okeechobee, the young defendant was given a death penalty.

In West Palm Beach, minutes before the judge was to hand down a sentence, Craig's attorney asked Judge

James Carlisle not to impose the death penalty because his client was "retarded." Carlisle rejected the motion, sentenced Donnie Gene Craig to death in the electric chair, then asked if the defendant had anything to say.

Clad in jail blues and a gray sweatshirt, Craig stood and said, "I ask for mercy from the court." He is now on Death Row.

EDITOR'S NOTE:
Della Stanton, Tom Derby, Sean and Dell Wilson, George School, Robinson Lee Courtney, Sheila Wynn, Matt Runner and Teddy Baer are not the real names of the persons so named in the foregoing story. Fictitious names have been used because there is no reason for public interest in the identities of these persons.

"THE CAPED 'COUNT' AND THE SEXY TEEN"

by Don Lasseter

Black, silver-studded pumps with two-inch heels and a long black skirt—not exactly mountain-climbing attire, but 18-year-old Lisa Ann Mather was not concerned about that. Lisa had dressed specifically for a night of fun on Hollywood's notorious Sunset Strip. But now that the drinking was over, she found herself climbing a steep hillside through heavy brush, far above the glitz and twinkling lights of Los Angeles. And she was game for adventure.

Lisa Mather was a beautiful young woman with shining blonde hair and a taste for sexy black clothing. To enhance her already shapely figure, Lisa had wiggled into a black bra and girdle and attached garter straps to her patterned dark hose. Her ensemble was completed with a tight, green blouse, several strands of gold-plated chains around her neck, a black Marcel watch, and white metal earrings.

Yes, on the cool winter evening of January 12, 1985, Lisa Ann Mather was in the mood to party.

The Sunset Strip, on the west end of Hollywood's world famous Sunset Boulevard, has long been a magnet for seekers of fun, thrills, and provocative entertainment. Popularized on the 1950s television show, 77 *Sunset Strip*, it became a haven for hippies

350

and teenage runaways during the '60s. Later, the one-mile stretch turned into a center for nightclubs featuring go-go dancers clad in fringed bikinis. In the '80s, the clubs evolved into discotheques.

Multicolored neon signs, noisy bars, loud music, young men and women wandering the sidewalks in various stages of dress or undress—everything about "The Strip" attracted a partying crowd. But some of them had more than partying in mind.

Lisa and her friend danced, drank, and talked to several men by the time 1:00 a.m. rolled around. When her girlfriend and a male buddy last saw Lisa, she was talking with a man dressed in black who looked considerably older than her.

It was the last time anyone ever saw Lisa Ann Mather alive.

Hours later, frantic family members and friends reported to the police that Lisa was missing. The reports were dutifully processed, but no law enforcement agency in the world is adequately staffed to search for every missing person. This is especially true in an area like Hollywood, where thousands of young people deliberately run away to seek excitement, glamour, and a life free from parental control.

Days passed, then weeks, then months. The intense pain felt by Lisa's family and friends turned into a dull ache mitigated by a clinging hope that she would be found alive and safe.

On December 3, 1986, nearly two years after the young woman had vanished, a homeless transient looking for a place to camp overnight climbed a trail on a North Hollywood hillside. He had followed the winding Coldwater Canyon Avenue up into the hills for several miles and had noticed the steep trail leading to a wooded area. At the top of the path, he threaded his way among the trees along an animal trail to a small clearing.

Near another steep incline, the transient started to

351

make his way around a large tree, but when he casually glanced down, he froze in his tracks. Staring at him vacantly from the base of the tree were the hollowed-out eye sockets of a human skull! Other large bones lay close to the skull. The remnants of a rope that was looped around the trunk still clung to other skeletal remains.

When the initial shock wore off, the transient became curious and picked up some of the large bones and the skull. He attempted to place them in a semblance of human form, but soon gave up. He decided he'd better call the police and made his way back down the steep trail.

Detectives Theodore Ball and Kevin Harley of the Los Angeles Police Department's North Hollywood branch exited the Ventura Freeway at Coldwater Canyon Avenue. They slowed as the two-lane road began winding upward through the Hollywood Hills, about eight miles from the Sunset Strip. They had no trouble locating the steep trail that led to the grisly discovery. Three black and white police cars were parked near it alongside the twisting highway, and traffic cones channeled curious motorists into a single lane from which they gawked at police officers as they climbed up and down the steep path.

Theodore Ball, a 15-year veteran, and his partner, Kevin Harley, who had almost as much service, struggled up the trail to where other officers had secured a clearing with yellow crime scene tape. They learned that the transient who had found the disarticulated skeleton had moved some of the bones. They knew that his curiosity and carelessness certainly wouldn't make their jobs any easier.

The two detectives grimaced as they looked at what was left of a human being. The skull, spinal column, and long leg bones were at the base of the tree. Other bones were still entangled in the rope that drooped in circles around the trunk. A pair of

352

rusty handcuffs dangling from the rope suggested that the shackled human remains were of someone who had met a horrible death.

With the help of forensic specialists, the detectives searched every square inch of the clearing and the immediate periphery.

Detective Ball kneeled to scrutinize the rope in more detail. What appeared to be frayed filaments, he found, were actually strands of blonde hair caught in the fibers. There were also some disintegrating shreds of black cloth entangled in the rope.

Within a yard of the tree, the detectives found more tattered pieces of black material and green cloth.

One of the searchers summoned the others, "Over here," he beckoned, as he pointed at the ground where he had pushed some topsoil and brush away. "It looks like what's left of a camping tent."

The remaining dirt was scooped out, and the decayed tent was pulled from its hiding place for examination. When it was stretched out, the investigators could see that it was large enough to accommodate at least two people. Apparently, it had been buried rather hastily and not very effectively.

With precise care, the investigating team began to remove brush from a nine-foot semicircle north of the tree and to inspect the brush and topsoil. Like archaeologists at the excavation of an ancient civilization, they carefully strained scoops of dirt through a screen in search of clues.

Less than a yard from the tree, the detectives uncovered a black girdle with garters. Not far away, they found a yellow metal chain with a heart-shaped pendant, green fabric attached to another piece of rope, two white metal earrings that were separated by about two feet, and a black skirt.

More shreds of fabric showed up as the investigators continued to sift the area. The remains of a black bra and additional pieces of jewelry chain turned up. Several shocks of blonde hair were uncovered.

A black, Marcel brand wristwatch was found north of the tree. Incredibly, it was still running!

Encroaching darkness halted the search for that day. Detectives Ball and Harley didn't have much to go on, but there was something gnawing at the back of Ball's mind. Something about this set-up was maddeningly familiar, but he would have to sleep on it to figure out what.

On the following morning, December 4, 1986, forensic anthropologist Charles Cargill climbed the steep trail to the site of the bones, which had been left where they were found. A security officer had guarded them overnight.

Cargill carefully charted the location of each bone, all of which were found within a radius of 6 to 10 feet from the tree. Then he began to assemble them. He decided that they were the remains of a female Caucasian between 16 and 23 years old and between 5-foot-6 and 5-foot-9 in height. The scapula, or shoulder blade, had sustained a puncture wound. Cargill concluded that the victim had been naked when she was tied to the tree.

After examining the earth around the skeleton and the skull, Cargill formed the opinion that the body had not been buried. That is, no grave had been dug. There was no dirt in the nasal aperture, indicating that the skull had not been covered with dirt. It was his opinion that the body had probably been covered with brush, and some dirt had been shoveled over the brush. There were clear shovel marks on the ground.

It was evident to the anthropologist that death had occurred about two years before the skeleton was discovered.

When Cargill was finished, the bones were trans-

354

ported to a laboratory for a more intensive examination. Joseph Anselmo, deputy coroner, was a specialist in forensic dentistry. He took 18 X-ray photos of the skull and began the tedious process of comparing the pictures to X-rays of missing persons on file.

Forensic specialists often do not receive much public recognition for the important contributions they make in solving crimes. Neither do they come up with the magic solutions like those portrayed on the old crime show, *Quincy*. They must generally be satisfied with the personal feeling of a job well done.

Joseph Anselmo had that feeling when he found the match for the X-rays of the unknown skull. Nearly two years earlier, a dentist had provided X-rays of a patient who was missing.

Lisa Ann Mather had been found at last.

Something was still gnawing at Detective Ted Ball's memory the next day when he resumed the investigation of Lisa Mather's death. One of the first steps in such an investigation is to interview family members and friends of the victim. Still trying to pin down just what was in the back of his mind, Ball started the interview process.

A close relative told the detective that Lisa did not drink, never used drugs, and rarely went out or dated. "She would never go up there to Sunset Boulevard," the woman told Ball.

However, a completely different picture of Lisa Mather emerged from the story told by the girlfriend who had accompanied her on what became the last night of Lisa's life.

"We wanted to dress sleazy and go up to the Sunset Strip and get drunk and act wild," the friend told the investigator.

A male crony of the girls, who had seen them on "the strip" that night, described an evening in which

355

the two girls had been sexually propositioned by at least one passerby. "Before Lisa disappeared," he said, "her girlfriend got on the back of a truck, started dancing around and drawing attention to herself." He added that he had last seen Lisa outside a local discotheque talking to a tall, white male with long brown hair.

Detectives Ball and Harley interviewed Lisa's girlfriend again, this time asking more pointed questions.

"Were you two sexually active?" the detectives asked.

"Sometimes we got kind of wild," the friend said. She gradually added details, telling them about a man whose nickname was Pierre and who liked to take nude photos of her and Lisa. The three of them, she reluctantly admitted, had engaged in group sex. Once, she claimed, she and Lisa met Pierre at a popular nightspot on Sunset Boulevard. They left together, went to a room, took a "threesome shower," and took photographs in a lot of different sexual positions.

The girlfriend knew where Pierre lived, and she told Detectives Ball and Harley. They expedited the processing of a search warrant. Numerous photos, just as the victim's friend had described, were recovered. However, Pierre was quickly cleared as a suspect in Lisa Mather's death.

The gnawing at Detective Ball's memory finally broke through the wall of oblivion. He remembered talking to colleagues and reading reports describing two rapes that occurred on Coldwater Canyon Avenue about two years earlier, close to the same time Lisa Mather had vanished. One had occurred in October 1984 and one on December 28th of the same year.

Digging into the records, Ball found the report of the October rape. It had occurred almost exactly where the skeleton of Lisa Mather was found.

Quickly flipping through the report pages, Detective Ball read the details of the rape: In mid-October 1984, Karen Shields, an attractive 20-year-old woman, had met a man in front of a popular Sunset Strip bar. He invited her to a party and she agreed to go. He didn't have a car, he told her, so they used her silver Datsun. En route to Coldwater Canyon, where he said the party was, the two stopped at a liquor store and bought a bottle of 151-proof rum. They drank most of the bottle, along with two cola drinks. Karen had already downed three or four rum drinks earlier at the bar.

The couple arrived at a wide space in the twisting canyon road, where Karen parked her car. There were no houses around, and the man told Karen that they had to climb up a trail to get to the party. She started willingly, but she soon became frightened as they climbed the steep hill in the dark. He then started pulling her up the trail.

Karen Shields later told the police that she never consented to have sex with the man. When they arrived at a tent in a clearing at the top of the hill, he invited her in for a drink. Afraid to refuse, Karen went in with him. Inside, she said, she became confused and suddenly found herself on the ground, handcuffed and bound around the ankles with chains. The man ripped off Karen's skirt and underclothes and raped her. The assault lasted for an hour.

Afterwards, Karen said, the rapist unshackled her, and she climbed down the trail, crying. When she arrived at her car, she discovered that she had lost her keys somewhere. Karen walked to the nearest house, asked to use the phone, and called the police to report the rape. But later, she decided not to prosecute.

Detective Ted Ball located the second report. It de-

357

scribed the rape that occurred just two weeks before Lisa Mather disappeared from the Sunset Strip. This report was far more detailed:

Three days before Christmas 1984, 22-year-old Sherry Thomas had gone to the same bar where Karen Shields had met her attacker. Sherry drank with friends until the bar closed at 2:00 the following morning. While walking to her car, a man approached her. He seemed interesting, and he said he was a drummer with a well-known band.

Sherry was feeling her booze and was in a friendly mood. When the young man told her he was going to a party at the home of another famous band member and invited her to join him, Sherry agreed to go. As they were walking, two other young women drove up. They seemed to know the man and announced, "There's no party tonight."

"No problem," the drummer said. "We can go to my place for champagne."

Sherry and the man got into the car with the two girls. One of the young women said that she needed to go home, so the driver dropped her off. The man then directed the driver to go up Coldwater Canyon, to where, he said, he "lived with the daughter of a world-famous singer."

At 2:30 a.m., Sherry and the stranger got out of the car at a wide spot on Coldwater Canyon Avenue and said goodbye to the woman who was driving.

"This path going up the hill is a shortcut to my place," the drummer told Sherry. She thought it was kind of weird, but she started up the path with him. Halfway up, however, Sherry became suspicious and told him she didn't want to go any further. But he was very convincing, and she agreed to continue up the trail.

Finally, the couple came to a tent in a clearing. "I just need to go in there to rest a minute," the man said. "You sit out here and wait for me, I'll be right back."

"I don't want to sit out here, I want to leave," Sherry replied, her alarm growing as the liquor began to wear off.

Without warning, the man grabbed Sherry around the throat with both hands and pushed her to the ground, shouting, "Don't leave!" Sherry later told the police that she was so frightened, she twice lost control of her bladder.

The man stopped choking Sherry long enough to rip a scarf from her waist and use it to tie her hands behind her back. He rolled Sherry over on her back and yelled, "I'm going to go get the machete!" Then he added, "Look, I'm not going to hurt you as long as you do what I say."

Grabbing Sherry's sequined vest, the attacker ripped it open, then pulled her unitard down to her ankles. "I have a fantasy about tying a girl up and raping her," the man whispered hoarsely to Sherry.

After raping her for several minutes, the attacker sat up and removed one of Sherry's boots and one leg of her unitard. "I won't hurt you as long as you do what I say," he repeated. "Otherwise, I will kill you." He then began to rape Sherry again.

Sherry began to beg for the rapist to stop, saying that she was cold and wanted to go in the tent to get warm.

"No," he replied. "I'm going in there to get the machete." The rapist left Sherry lying on the ground, stepped into the tent, and instantaneously returned with a wicked-looking blade. Jamming the point into the ground, he growled, "I could chop your head off! If you don't do what I say, I'll kill you!"

"But people at the club saw us leave together," Sherry pleaded. "If you kill me, they'll know it was you."

"As long as you do what I want, I won't hurt

you," the rapist responded.

Once again, Sherry begged to go into the tent where she could shake the effect of the chill night air and maybe convince her brutal attacker to stop. The rapist grabbed Sherry's arms, pulled her to her feet, hands still tied, and walked her into the tent.

It was a spacious interior for a camping tent. It contained an "outdoor-type chaise lounge." The rapist forced Sherry down onto the lounge and untied his shoes. He pulled out the laces and used them to tie Sherry's hands tighter and to bind her ankles.

The rapist then began to sodomize Sherry. In agony, she pleaded for him to stop and managed to roll off the lounge. On the ground, he raped her again. When he was finished, he stepped out of the tent, ordering her to untie herself and to give him his shoelaces. Sherry managed to comply.

"I'm tired and I'm going home," he told her. "You'll have to find your own way back." Without another word, the vicious rapist stepped out of the tent and disappeared into the darkness.

Nearly hysterical, Sherry tried to rearrange her torn, dirty clothing as much as she could and scrambled down the steep path. Stepping in front of the first pair of headlights she saw, Sherry flagged down a motorist who took her to the Beverly Hills Police Department. There, she reported the rape.

Investigating officers climbed the path on the following day, having been directed there by Sherry Thomas and the Good Samaritan motorist. The tent was just where Sherry had described, but it was unoccupied. Just outside the unzipped front flap was a pair of white tennis shoes without shoelaces. Inside was a machete with a 24-inch blade, a battered chaise lounge, a wet sleeping bag, a battery-powered lantern, and a lot of trash. There were also parts of Sherry Thomas' clothing. The rapist, however, was missing.

A thorough search of the area turned up something else. Along the path leading to the tent, the investigators found a sketch pad containing drawings and writing. It also contained the name Edmund Matthews.

The tent was kept under surveillance for several days, but no one showed up, so the watch was discontinued. But all local police agencies were alerted to arrest Edmund Matthews on suspicion of rape.

On January 28, 1985, just 16 days after Lisa Mather had disappeared, a woman who lived a short distance from the trail on Coldwater Canyon Avenue reported that a suspicious-acting young man had borrowed a shovel from her. Within an hour, LAPD Officer George O'Connor arrested Edmund Arne Matthews, age 27, while he was walking on Coldwater Canyon Avenue, carrying a shovel, less than a mile from the steep mountainside trail.

When investigators interviewed "regulars" along the Sunset Strip, they found that Edmund Matthews was not unknown. Many of them recognized photos of him as someone they knew as "The Count." Apparently, Matthews' interest in young women was well known, and his vampire-like habit of wearing a black cape while searching for female companions had caused him to be christened with the nickname.

Detective Ball continued to read the report of the arrest and trial of Edmund Matthews. Matthews was charged with rape, tried, and convicted. He was sentenced, on September 23, 1985, to serve 10 years in the state penitentiary.

So the primary suspect in the death of Lisa Mather, Detective Ball discovered, was already in state prison and had been behind bars all but 16 days since Lisa's death. Ball made immediate arrangements for Detective Kevin Harley to accompany him to San Luis Obispo on the central California coast where Edmund Matthews was incarcerated to talk to the prisoner about Lisa Mather.

When the two detectives faced Matthews in the interview room of the prison, they saw a handsome man with light hair and brown eyes who weighed nearly 200 pounds and stood one inch over six feet. He was certainly large enough to manhandle young women.

With a tape recorder rolling, the interview began. At first, Edmund Matthews was reticent, then evasive. Finally, he began to tell the two detectives that he could barely recalled the evening he met Lisa Mather on the Sunset Strip. He had been drinking a lot that day, he said, and everything was pretty fuzzy.

Gradually, his recollection seemed to sharpen under the questioning of Detectives Ball and Harley. Yes, he said, he remembered that he and the girl had taken a cab to his campsite. He kept blacking out, he claimed, and he vaguely remembered stumbling down the hill thinking he might have hurt someone with a rope.

"I might have tied her up, but I just can't remember," Matthews said. "Later, I think I went up there and covered her up with bushes."

As the investigators coaxed him on, Matthews recalled more. "About three days later, I went up there to bury her. I saw the body of a naked girl with a rope tied around her neck and it was tied to a tree. I looked her over closely, but I didn't see any stab wounds. I tried to untie the rope around her neck but I couldn't do it."

"Did you have sex with her?" Harley wanted to know.

"Probably," came the terse reply.

"Maybe it would help if you could write out everything you remember," Harley suggested.

On January 8, 1987, Edmund Matthews wrote out his statement. In it, he revealed that he had been drinking all evening when he met a young woman in front of a well-known nightclub. They "picked each other up" and went across the street to have a drink. After a while, they decided to go swimming and took a taxi to a high school where he knew he could get into the pool. He kissed her at the pool and they had sex on the diving ladder. He then invited her to go to his place on the hill.

At his campsite, Matthews wrote, he found a rope and suggested to the woman that he tie her up and make passionate love to her. He wound the rope around a tree and around her neck. Then, as he went into his tent to get the lantern, he hears a squeal outside.

"So I rushed over to her," he wrote, "and she was on her back, coughing and choking. I started crying and panicking, trying to untie her as she coughed. She stopped breathing while I was crying and trying to untie her. I felt her pulse; no pulse . . ."

Matthews described how he ran down the hill to a friend's apartment, but he did not tell the friend what had happened. Later, he went back to bury the girl with sticks and debris. Again, he was unsuccessful in his attempts to untie her. About two weeks later, he borrowed a shovel to bury Lisa. He was arrested when he was walking with the shovel down Coldwater Canyon.

In another discussion with the detectives, Matthews said he liked to pick up "party girls" along Sunset Strip. "They came up the hills to get laid," he bragged. "I was introducing my bondage techniques. It's really fun because your sex partner is totally at your whims. It got out of hand with her because I was drinking heavily."

The taped discussions and the written narrative, along with circumstantial evidence, made a strong case for the investigators. But they hoped for something more. They finally got it, in the form of a jailhouse snitch. The jailbird, who was in a position to handle inmates' mail, intercepted a letter that Edmund Matthews had written to a relative. The snitch turned it over to authorities.

The letter was in Matthews' handwriting and ended with his signature. Matthews wrote, "I didn't want you to worry so I didn't tell you about one of the girls, but her name was Lisa. And one evening her and I were playing by the high school pool and we were getting drunken [sic] drinking so she didn't want to go swimming so we went up the hill where I was camping and we took the rope that they used for water polo [at the school] so we could tie up each other when we got to the tent. . . . We started to make love and I said, 'Let me tight [sic] you to a tree and we'll pretend I captured you and I'll make love to you.' So she laughed and said, 'It's like a fantasy I once had.' "

Matthews' chilling account continued. "I started winding her around the neck, not tightly, but loosely and when I finished I told her that I was going to get my lantern, so when I came back her foot had slipped in the mud and she had fallen intangled [sic] in the rope coughing. So I rushed to try to untie the rope but I couldn't untie her, so she layed [sic] there coughing. Then she stopped breathing and died as I tryed [sic] to help her. So I felt her heart and it had stopped."

The letter concluded; "And the next day I buried her. I wept and never went back. I never told anybody except God. . . . That's what happened because we were drunken [sic]. They have me in the hole in a separate cell. Could you write me? Keep this letter."

Now the investigators had three stories of what happened to Lisa Mather with enough inconsistencies in the versions to clearly demonstrate that Matthews was trying to rearrange the facts to mitigate his case.

Edmund Arne Matthews was brought to trial for rape and murder in December 1990. His defense attorney, Rickard Santwier, tried to show that the sex with Lisa Mather was by mutual consent and that no rape had occurred. That would prevent the injury from finding special circumstances of rape committed during a murder, which could make Matthews eligible for California's gas chamber or a sentence of life in prison without the possibility of parole.

Deputy District Attorney Rosalie Morton successfully deflected the defense tactics. On February 14, 1991, the jury found Edmund Matthews guilty of first-degree murder, with special circumstances. After a short penalty phase of the trial, the same jury recommended that Matthews be sentenced to life in prison without the possibility of parole.

Superior Court Judge Ronald S. Coen made the sentence official on May 10, 1991. Edmund Arne Matthews was transported to the California State Prison system to spend the remainder of his life behind bars.

EDITOR'S NOTE:
The names Pierre, Karen Shields, and Sherry Thomas are not the real names of the persons so named in the foregoing story. Fictitious names have been used because there is no reason for public interest in the identities of these persons.

"CURIOUS CASE OF THE KITTY LITTER KILLER"

by Jerry Spangler

SALT LAKE CITY, UT.
APRIL 25, 1987

Detective Sergeant Don Bell—a veteran homicide sleuth for the Salt Lake City Police Department—has handled a lot of missing persons' cases in his day. Most of them have turned out to be teenage runaways, spouses who walk out on their families, people running from a present or a past, and even old folks who have gotten lost or disoriented.

And rarely, very rarely, there have been missing persons who have turned up murdered. April 1987, would be one of those rare occasions.

On April 15, 1987, an employer called Sergeant Bell to report an employee missing. "The last I heard anything was April 6th when a friend of his called and said Earl had asked him to call, that he had some errands to run and would be a little late."

A little late is one thing. But ten days late was something altogether different. Never before had the employee, Homer Earl Elder, missed work without letting his boss know why. Not calling in for 10 days was totally out of character. Elder had

366

been employed at the machine shop for the last four years and had developed a solid reputation for dependability and reliability. An Air Force retiree, he was a hard worker—the kind his employers wished they had more of.

The employers had called Elder's home on repeated occasions, but had received no reply. They had also received several phone calls from a friend of Elder in Virginia who had been unable to reach him. They knew he didn't have a family, and the bottom line, Elder's employers told police, was that they were worried something might have happened to him.

Police were given the missing man's home address and said they would check into the situation. The next day, Sergeant Bell and Detective Jerry Mendez went to Elder's rented two-bedroom house.

"We found everything all locked up," reported Bell. "There was nothing amiss about the home, no doors had been jimmied, the windows were all locked. Inside, everything was in place and nothing appeared to be missing. It was just the way you'd expect it to be if someone had left to go out of town."

One car was in the garage, but a check with the Division of Motor Vehicles revealed Elder owned a newer car which wasn't at the home. Inside the home, police found nothing unusual. The house was remarkably clean and well-cared for. There was no evidence the home had been ransacked by a thief, nor were any valuable items missing. It did appear that a small amount of clothing was missing.

However, two things did catch Sergeant Bell's eye. Someone had been mowing the grass in the backyard, but had left before the job was done. "It was like someone had called him to the phone and there it sat unfinished," Bell said.

Detectives also noticed that Elder's mail had been piling up. A quick glance through incoming letters revealed several uniform letters from a prominent Utah supermarket. "It was the kind of notice you get when your checks bounce," Bell said. "We could see that without opening them." Without a court order, the sleuths could not legally open his mail. But it was an interesting clue, nevertheless.

Having noticed police cars at the Elder residence, the owner of the home came by. Elder was 10 days overdue on his rent and the landlord wanted his money. Did police know where Elder was? Detectives weren't answering questions, they were asking them.

Police questioned the landlord. They asked him when was the last time he had seen Earl. Was he having any financial difficulties? Was he a problem tenant? Did he have a roommate?

The landlord said he had last seen Elder on April 5th, the day before his employer had received the phone call from the unidentified male friend. No, Elder wasn't a problem tenant. In fact, he very much liked Elder who usually paid his rent promptly.

But, the landlord said, Elder had had a friend from Virginia staying with him the last few months. The landlord didn't like the friend staying there. "I had rented the house to Earl, not to this other guy," the landlord told officers.

The landlord had spoken with Earl Elder in early April and Earl had told him the roommate, an Albert Lynn Atkins, would only be staying there temporarily. He was leaving on April 8th to return to Virginia to get his family and move them to Utah. They would be getting their own place to stay. The landlord had noticed Atkins on April 8th, packing Elder's car for the long trip back to Virginia.

Could Elder have gone with Atkins to Virginia? police asked. Possibly, but Earl, as he was known to everyone, had said nothing about going along on the trip.

As police continued questioning the landlord and neighbors who knew the missing man, they learned more about Homer Earl Elder. He was a man who had no real place to go upon his retirement from the Air Force, so he chose to make his home in Salt Lake City. He had rented a small bungalow in the west part of town, landed a job to supplement his Air Force retirement income and had settled into a comfortable bachelor life-style. If he had a family, he never talked about them.

He didn't sound like the kind of man who would simply turn up missing, Sergeant Bell decided. But it wouldn't be the first time detectives had responded on a missing person's case only to find a missing person who didn't want to be found. Especially if he had skipped town, leaving a large number of bad checks behind.

"We asked the landlord to leave the house alone until we could talk with the roommate when he was supposed to return sometime after Easter weekend," said Bell. "And we wanted time to check out the bad checks."

Detectives filed their initial report, and Elder's disappearance was reported in the press the next morning.

Working through Elder's bank and the local supermarkets where the checks had been drawn, detectives retrieved an entire series of checks. All had been written out for $50 cash over the purchase price of miscellaneous food items. The $50 cash-

369

back amount was the maximum the supermarket allowed. "We found he had been writing bad checks all over town, doing the same thing: buying a few food items and getting $50 cash," said Bell.

The bad checks started out at one a day, then increased in frequency until April 6th, and then suddenly stopped. Detectives took the checks to Elder's bank. The bank told authorities the checks did not appear to be forged, that the signatures appeared to be Homer Elder's. "And the bank wanted to talk with him, too. He was way, way overdrawn," Bell said.

The next day, Detective Jerry Mendez received a call from an unidentified man who said he had seen Elder drinking heavily at a local bar on April 6th.

Mendez met with Bell later that day to discuss the case. They had a man with no apparent family ties to the community; a man who wrote bad checks totalling hundreds of dollars in the days preceding his disappearance; a man who had been seen drinking heavily at a local bar; and a man who had disappeared taking only a few clothes. It appeared to be a classsic case of someone stiffing their creditors to start over somewhere else. It had to be. They had seen that scenario all too often.

What's more, detectives discovered this wasn't the first time Homer Elder had disappeared. Going through Elder's Air Force records, Mendez discovered that Elder had a wife and children in Texas. One night, he had simply gathered together a few belongings and disappeared without a word. His family had not heard a word from him since he had abandoned them about four years before.

Detectives were not particularly worried that Elder may have been the victim of foul play. There was no evidence to indicate foul play, but there

370

was a lot of evidence that Elder had written bad checks and simply taken flight. Detectives wanted to talk with one more person before they closed out their involvement in the case. They wanted to talk with the Albert Atkins, most likely the last person to see Elder.

"Then Detective Mendez gets a call from the landlords," explained Bell. "They say, 'We think Earl has run off and we're going to clean the apartment and rent it out.' And by the time Mendez gets down there, they've already moved everything to a storage shed. The inside of the house is bare."

Police were angered that the landlords had started moving things out of the apartment. Perhaps Elder skipped town, but this case was not closed and officers didn't want anyone messing with the scene until they had finished their investigation. Mendez hustled to the scene to talk with the landlords, and when he got there, the owners had something interesting to show him.

When moving the chairs out of the living room, they had discovered a bullet hole in one wall. The hole had been hidden by the back of a recliner chair when officers had made their initial house search. The owners had found the shattered slug lying on top of a magazine in a magazine rack. Mendez chastised the owners, and took the bullet slug back with him to the police lab. There were no traces of blood on it.

Detective Mendez had no longer arrived back at police headquarters when he got another call. The landlord's wife had discovered bloody sheets in the washing machine in the basement of the home. Patrol Officer Bill Poulsen and Patrol Sergeant Sam Hemingway were already at the scene and were requesting detectives.

Mendez, using a hemastick to test for blood traces, tested the sheets in the washing machine. The sheets certainly looked bloody, but the hemastick didn't respond. It wasn't blood, Mendez decided, but rust, perhaps caused by leaving the sheets in the water in the washing machine for a long period of time.

Detective Mendez and Officer Poulsen decided to search the bare house in excruciating detail. While waiting for Mendez to arrive, Poulsen had discovered a couple of rusty, red smears he wanted to test with a hemastick. And while rusty sheets were not indications of foul play, the bullet in the wall was certainly not ordinary.

They started going through the house on their hands and knees. "In the front room area, they found some small pieces of dental material and even part of a gold filling," said Bell. "But they didn't find a speck of blood anywhere, not on the wall, the ceiling or the floors."

Officer Poulsen, who requested to stay at the scene with Mendez because of his fascination with detective work, asked Mendez a million questions. He was fascinated by the hemastick and how it could register even non-visible traces of blood. As Poulsen started nosing around the kitchen area next to the stairwell leading to the basement, he noticed a small red spot between a floor molding and the linoleum flooring. Mendez showed him how to use the hemastick. It flashed a presence of blood.

"This was, after all, a kitchen area, and that there would be blood on a floor in a kitchen was not unusual," said Bell. Then the two officers looked up and noticed a small reddish smear on the door frame. It also tested postive for blood.

Using the hemasticks and flashlights, the officers

combed every inch of the stairwell and basement looking for other blood traces. On a concrete wall next to a crawlspace, Poulsen had earlier spotted what looked like tiny blood droplets. There was not enough of the sample for the hemastick to work.

Mendez and Poulsen started poking around the crawlspace. The ceiling of the crawlspace was no more than four-feet high, forcing officers to stoop as they looked through the storage area. It was littered with garbage: old boxes, paint cans, empty kitty litter bags. Beneath the debris was two or three inches of kitty litter. Beneath that, a concrete floor.

Kitty litter? Detective Mendez had been through the house twice, including a few minutes earlier, in painstaking detail. He could remember nothing indicating that Elder had a cat. There was no cat food in the house, no food dish, no cat, no feces in the kitty litter. So why kitty litter? His curiosity was peaked.

Mendez examined the concrete flooring in some detail. It didn't look as old as the foundation surrounding it. Nor did it look as professionally done. Mendez began chipping away at the concrete floor in the crawlspace. It broke easily.

"Once we got the concrete out, we found more kitty litter," Mendez said. "Another several inches below the kitty litter, I felt a material and recognized it as sleeping bag fabric. And there was something inside it."

Mendez decided to call for assistance before going on. Detective Ken Farnsworth and John responded to help remove the kitty litter—more than 300 pounds of it in all. The sleeping bag was lying horizontal in the hole and, because of the cramped conditions in the crawlspace, it took all three detectives to lift the body, which had been tucked face down in the bag and then tied off with yellow rope.

"We suspected it was Earl Elder because the belt buckle the victim was wearing said 'Earl,'" explained Mendez. "But we couldn't be sure. That was a job for the medical examiner."

So why the kitty litter? Obvious, said Bell. To kill the smell of decaying flesh. "It was a stroke of genius," said Bell. "It would have worked."

Mendez agreed. "The kitty litter did everything it was supposed to. The victim didn't smell like a decomposing body does. It didn't smell bad at all, despite the fact he had been in there two weeks."

The medical examiner's report indicated the victim was a white male in his 40s who had been shot three times, twice in the back and a third time in the back of the head execution-style. The weapon used was a .357 Magnum. No positive identification was made.

Detectives began going over the home again. No gun had been recovered from the home, but sleuths wanted to see if they could determine how the homicide had occurred. Using hemasticks, they went over the entire residence. They found a large section of carpet in the front room (near the bullet hole in the wall) that tested positive for blood, even though there was no visible trace of blood. The carpet smelled of fresh shampoo. Using the location of the blood residue and the location of the bullet hole in the wall, detectives were confident that the victim had been shot—or at least shot at—by someone standing in the doorway of the guest bedroom.

Detectives had been so convinced they were dealing with a simple, straightforward, easy-to-solve missing person's case. Now they were facing a puzzling homicide. Who killed Elder? Was it even Elder or was it the friend who was supposed to go to Virginia? Why? When? Nothing in the missing person's investigation had indicated Elder had any enemies.

Detectives wanted to talk with Albert Lynn Atkins badly, if he was still alive. Perhaps he could shed some light on the case. Atkins, they had learned, had been Elder's best friend for years. Elder was even godfather to one of the Atkins children.

According to Elder's employer, someone claiming to be Atkins had been calling there long distance from Virginia trying to find Earl. Was it really Atkins? If it was, was he genuinely concerned about his missing friend, or was he trying to establish an alibi? Detectives wondered.

Sleuths decided to use a risky tactic rarely used in Salt Lake City police work. They did not report the homicide to the media, and the official reports were kept on their desks for their eyes only. No one besides detectives knew the victim had been found or that a homicide had occurred. Perhaps the killer would make a mistake. Detectives left a card on the front door of the residence asking Atkins to call when he arrived back in Salt Lake City.

"Atkins was not a suspect at this point," explained Mendez. "He was just somebody we thought could help us with the investigation. He would know Earl better than anybody else. We wanted to talk with him as part of the normal course of an investigation."

"I didn't suspect Atkins of anything," said Bell, who supervised the investigation. "I thought it would be pretty weird that if he had killed his best friend that he would come back to town with his

375

wife and kids."

Two days later, Bell received a call from Atkins. "What's going on?" the caller asked. "I tried to use my key on the house, but it wouldn't work. The landlord wouldn't let me in. He told me to call you."

"Earl's missing. Can you come downtown and answer a few questions?" Bell asked.

Bell wasn't certain whose body was in the basement. But when he positively identified Atkins, he was certain it had to be Earl Elder. Bell questioned Atkins about where he had been and when he had left Salt Lake City. Atkins told officers he had been separated from his wife for several months, and that they had decided to start anew in Salt Lake City. He had left Salt Lake on April 8th to drive to Norfolk, Virginia, to pick up his family. His wife quit her job and they sold everything they hadn't been able to fit into "Uncle Earl's" car. They had just arrived that morning. It was good story and it fit the facts known to police.

Nevertheless, detectives wanted to know more about Albert Atkins. Atkins had returned to Utah in February 1987—about two months before Earl disappeared. He had first met Elder in late 1983 when the Atkins family had befriended him. Elder even lived with the Atkins family for a while until he could get on his feet.

"We (Albert Atkins and Earl Elder) discussed it about a month after I was out here, how we would all live together as a family again," Atkins told police. "He was looking forward to my family being here. He loved my wife's cooking and primarily her potato salad. He used to tell her on the phone, 'Get out here quick and make this potato salad.' We discussed how we going to take the boys fishing and things we were going to do together."

It sounded okay, except that Elder had told his landlord that Atkins wouldn't be living with him any longer. Bell wanted to know what Elder had done and said on April 4th and 5th, the weekend before Atkins had left for Virginia. "Do you recall seeing Mr. Elder that Saturday?"

"Yes. We were at home. As a matter of fact, we were cleaning the yard," Atkins responded, no hint of nervousness or concern in his voice. "We spoke with the neighbor, picked up a little bit in the yard and pruned some trees in the back. I was generally cleaning up and he was cutting the grass."

What about Saturday night? questioned Bell.

Earl had mentioned he was going to be bringing a young lady home, "so I just went out and had too much to drink and stayed overnight at a hotel." When Atkins returned to the house Sunday morning, Earl was up with a pot of coffee brewing. "We were just drinking coffee and stuff, ya know just listening to the radio and laying around. Then he got a phone call and went out. I went out about the same time."

Atkins returned home late that evening, but Earl was still up. Earl always stayed up late, often to 1:30 or 2 a.m. Then he was up at 5:30 a.m. for coffee before going to work at 7 a.m. "He always hollered at me to get up before he left. That morning (Monday, April 6th) about six-thirty a.m., he stuck his head in my door and said, 'Hey lazy bones. Are you going to get up?' Earl left the apartment a few minutes later."

"Was the car still there?" asked Bell. Indeed it was, and that was unusual, Atkins said, because Earl always drove himself to work. "Somebody had to have picked him up."

Atkins told detectives how he spent Monday driving to Nevada to gamble. It was a good night:

He won $300. "Me and this other guy on the bus, we hit it big on the craps table. And we got on the bus to go home and we looked at each other and said that was fun. He said, 'I don't want to go yet.' So we both stayed. We stayed overnight and caught the bus back the next day (Tuesday, April 7th)."

Saturday, Sunday and Monday accounted for. What about Tuesday, April 7th?

Atkins told detectives he arrived back in Salt Lake City in the morning, but Earl was not there. He had probably already gone to work, Atkins told police. That afternoon, Atkins went to a local nightclub, picked up a woman and spent the night with her in a motel. "We had dinner and then went back to the room and stayed there all night. The next morning, we had breakfast, we stopped at my place to pick up some cigarettes and then I took her home to her place and dropped her off. I came back to the house, threw my stuff in the trunk of the T-Bird and I hit the road. That was about two p.m."

Somewhere between Salt Lake City and Norfolk, Virginia, Atkins called his wife to let her know when he would be arriving. "Is Earl with you?" his wife had asked him.

"That's the first I knew he was missing. I really wasn't concerned. I figured he was just out with some woman, carousing around. He did that a lot. When she told me he had also been missing work, that was a different story. He never missed work."

On April 9th, Atkins called Elder's employer and talked with a receptionist. He told the woman to file a missing person's report (he didn't know a missing person's report had already been filed). He also called Elder's landlord, who told him to call Detective Mendez. He never called. A week later,

Atkins loaded his family and their belongings into Elder's T-Bird and headed towards Salt Lake City.

It was a good story, repeated with clarity, precise detail and the right amount of emotion. It fit in perfectly with the missing person's case. It didn't fit in so well with a murder case. Bell was growing increasingly suspicious that Atkins wasn't telling the whole truth. An autopsy report put the time of Elder's death between April 4th and April 10th. Where was Atkins when the body was being disposed of? Sergeant Bell decided the time for pleasantries had ended.

"We found a bullet hole in the wall in the living room. You have any knowledge of how the bullet hole got there?"

"I never saw it," Atkins said.

"Does Earl own any guns?"

"I don't believe he does."

"Have you ever seen him with any guns?"

"Just one that I had."

"Where is that gun now?"

"I sold it. In Virginia."

"Do you have any other weapons?"

"Okay, I have a Smith and Wesson three-fifty-seven that belongs to a friend. I took it out of his house one night when he was extremely drunk."

"Do you still have the gun?"

"It's buried."

"Where?"

"In the backseat of my car."

Atkins was being coy—too coy. Could officers have a look at the gun? Atkins still didn't know that officers had found the body. He complied with their request and the interview continued. Detectives went over and over the story, and never once did Atkins slip up or alter his story in any way.

Bell bored in on Atkins about the overdrawn checks. Did Atkins forge those checks? Did he at any time cash Elder's checks? Did he ever use Elder's identification for any purpose? Each time Atkins responded calmly that no he had never forged Earl's checks, yes Earl had written checks out to him, and no he had never used Earl's identification. Detectives pressed him on specific circumstances. He was prepared with detailed answers. He even offered an explanation as to how his own fingerprints came to be found on the checks, even though officers had not solicited that information.

What clothes belonged to Earl? Which furniture? What kind of wallet did Earl have? Did he have credit cards? Was Earl going to move? Who were Earl's friends besides Atkins? Describe the gambling trips in detail. What kind of work are you in? When was your last paycheck? How much did Earl give you? Interrogators probed Atkins' past, his motives for moving to Utah and what kind of marital problems he was having.

Detectives fired hundreds of questions at Atkins in random order and Atkins answered them flawlessly. It was clear he wasn't going to slip up. And just when it appeared Atkins had an airtight story, Sergeant Bell got a phone call from Detective Mendez in the police laboratory. Ballistics on the .357 found in Atkins car and the bullet in Elder's body revealed a perfect match. Now detectives had ammunition to use in their interrogation.

"We got us a problem here, Mr. Atkins," Bell continued. "The problem is I've located Mr. Elder. He's been murdered; he's been shot; he's been killed. There is no pleasant way of doing this. There's been so many questions that are unanswered that I'd say this is one of the strangest

380

cases I have ever worked."

"You're kidding," Atkins said.

"I'm not kidding," said Bell, dead serious. "I know two people lived in that house, neither one of which I could find. When the body was located, I didn't know if it was Mr. Elder or whether it was you. Even after the autopsy I didn't know. When you called this morning, I felt very confident I could rule you out as a victim."

Atkins mumbled "Uh-huh," but said nothing else. Bell continued with his speech. "I am feeling you are responsible for Mr. Elder's death. I have done this for a long time. I have talked to people who have murdered little children, I have talked to people who have murdered their moms and dads, I talked to people who have murdered their wives, their brothers and everyone else. Some are just cold-hearted bastards, there's just no other getting around it. Some of them are sick psychopaths. Some of them should not only be put away for life, they should be put away and killed so they can never get back out.

"Others kill because they are mentally unbalanced," Bell continued. "It's because something happens at one specific instant that they don't have control over it and it just happens. They don't know why they did it."

Then Bell hit him with the bombshell. "The gun taken out of your briefcase positively matches the bullets found in Mr. Elder. That gun was in your possession when Mr. Elder died. Something happened in that house; I don't know what. But there's no question in my mind I'm going to be able to prove homicide. We have too much information. The ballistics information is icing on the cake." Bell was bluffing.

Atkins said nothing at first, then asked Bell for

381

a favor: Could he talk with his wife for a few minutes?

"Before we do that, answer one question. Are you responsible for his death," Bell asked.

"Yes," Atkins replied. "I just felt like I was in a corner and had nowhere to turn and no place to go."

Atkins told detectives how he had forged some checks on Elder's account, driven to Nevada to "hit it big" and then lost it all. He was unable to put the money back into his best friend's account, and he knew Elder would be receiving a bank statement any day. He knew he would be discovered. He knew if it were reported, he would be dropped from the hiring list at a Sale Lake company where he had been accepted for employment.

"I have always had a problem with Nevada. I went up there and lost what money I had," Atkins said. "I thought I would make it back into his account and I didn't. All week long I wracked my brain trying to figure out how to get the money back to Earl. I can't believe what I did. This guy was like a brother, an uncle, a father. This guy was family. I felt I had nothing else to do."

Atkins shot his best friend early Monday morning as he was getting ready for work. Without warning, he fired a shot into Elder's back. "I walked into the living room and shot him. I don't think I could have done it if he was facing me."

Elder dropped to his knees with the first shot. The second one put him on the floor, his torso falling into a chair. A third shot to the back of the head finished him off. "The only thing I hope was he died real quick."

"Then I got scared and I went and got a garbage bag cause I couldn't bear to look at him. This was my best friend in the world. Anyway, I

382

covered him up with the garbage bag."

Atkins then described how he went to several supermarkets cashing checks. "The only thing I could think of was I needed money." And kitty litter. Hundreds of pounds of it. Atkins returned to the house, pulled the body into the basement and used pulleys to lift it into the crawlspace where police found it. He covered the body with kitty litter.

"Did you think about using the kitty litter to absorb the blood or cover up the smell?"

"Never did. It was just fill material, just to fill the hole."

Detectives knew Atkins was telling the truth about one thing: he had killed Homer Earl Elder. But Atkins was filling in the loose ends with a lot of stuff they knew wasn't true. A quick check of certain aspects of Atkins's story confirmed their suspicions. This was not a desperation killing conducted at the last moment. This was a killing planned premeditated to perfection.

The kitty litter was a brilliant stroke of genius. It was no accident. Police later confirmed that Atkins had been purchasing kitty litter several days before the killing. He could have used any of hundreds of different items to cover the body, but he used the one item on the market to cover smells. And it worked.

Atkins said after the killing he drove around, brought a sleeping bag and yellow rope and returned several hours later to dispose of the body. If so, where was the blood?

"A body shot twice in the torso and once in the head would bleed out in a matter of moments," Mendez said. "Yet he says there was very little blood. The reason was he had brought that sleeping bag the day before, he had purchased the rope the day before, he bought the kitty litter the day before, the day of and the day after—just enough each day not to be conspicuous."

Detectives proved their point by going to all of the stores where Atkins had forged checks. Clerks have surprisingly good memories and positively identified Atkins. And the kitty litter. At one store, they identified Atkins as having rented a carpet shampoo cleaner the day of the homicide.

Mendez said evidence is clear that Atkins shot Elder and immediately stuffed his head first into an empty sleeping bag. Tests had shown Elder bled inside the sleeping bag—not on the living room floor as he would have under Atkins' scenario. The clincher, though, was that Atkins said he had put a garbage bag over Elder's head and later stuffed him in the sleeping bag. The medical examiner reported no plastic garbage bag was found in the sleeping bag—as it should have been if Atkins was telling the truth.

Mendez said there was no doubt that Atkins, who prided himself in his knowledge of criminology, planned and carefully executed each step of the crime. He intended all along to get away with murder. And he almost did.

"It could have been the perfect crime," said Mendez. "It would have been the perfect crime if he had had time to finish covering the body with concrete. But he made one mistake: he assumed that Earl had paid the rent. Earl always paid the rent by the fifth of the month. But this month he was late. If he had paid the rent, the owners would never have gone in and started moving out his stuff. They would never have found the bullet hole behind the recliner. They would never have found the sheets in the washer," Mendez said.

According to Mendez's theory, the murder of Homer Earl Elder should have been the perfect crime. But Atkins had not counted on a couple of factors. It took longer than Atkins anticipated to mix and pour concrete. As the hours melted away, so did his window of opportunity to dispose of the body so it would never be found. Atkins had to be in Norfolk by the weekend to pick up his family. That meant leaving no later than Tuesday night.

He had all day Monday and most of the day Tuesday to dispose of the body, but it wasn't enough time to finish the concrete work. He managed to pour several inches of concrete over the body, but he wanted to cover it with 12 to 18 inches — an amount no one would ever break through. He would have to finish it when they got back. After all, no one should be digging around in the basement anyway. The rent was paid until May, or at least Atkins thought it was.

"If Earl had paid his rent, it would have worked to perfection," said Mendez. "And we'd still have a missing person's case on our hands."

Both Mendez and Bell were puzzled at how cold-blooded Atkins was, not just in gunning down his best friend without warning, but in dragging his family to Utah.

"His wife quit her job and they sold everything they had to come to Utah," said Mendez. "Their second day here, we arrest him for murder, we take the car (it was Earl's anyway) and the wife and kids have no money, no way to get back to Virginia."

When his wife learned the tragic news, she responded, "You jerk. You brought us all the way back here to abandon us."

"He was a jerk," said Mendez. "He was a cold-blooded jerk. He even used forged checks after he killed Earl to buy his kids diapers and baskets for Easter."

Atkins got the last laugh, however. Detectives went to prosecutors seeking first-degree, capital murder charges against Atkins. But Atkins gave the inspector a sob story about how he was a combat veteran of the Vietnam war and was under tremendous emotional stress. The prosecutor agreed to let Atkins plead guilty to second-degree murder and even recommended to the judge that Atkins receive a sentence for an even lesser crime of manslaughter (one to 15 years).

"We checked," said Mendez. "He never served in Vietnam."

"NEW MEXICO'S MURDER
MOST FOUL!"

by Gary C. King

The young dark-haired woman, although pudgy
and looking somewhat pregnant, had a pretty face.
Her eyes wide with excitement, she strode out of
her house, raring to go. She had a mission to accomplish and, although it was a dark mission that
no one but she understood, she was nonetheless
full of anticipatory adrenaline as she climbed into
her car and backed onto the street. Today, July 23,
1987, was going to be the day, no doubt about
that. She had waited long enough. She felt aggressive and alive, and she knew she was finally going
to get what she had wanted for such a long, long
time—a baby.

By the time she had driven for a while, thinking
through the details of her mission again and again,
she began to look vacant and spent, her face set in
deep thought as she wheeled her car off Gibson
Boulevard toward the main gate of Kirtland Air
Force Base (AFB).

With temperatures in the 90s and clear, sunny
skies, it was a typically arid day in Albuquerque,
New Mexico. The San Mateo mountains were visible to the west, the Manzano mountains to the
east.

The security policeman on duty, an airman first-class, looked somewhat bored when she pulled up and stopped. Donning sunglasses, the young airman stuck his head out of his small gate-post cubicle and, seeing the small base identification decal on the left front bumper of the woman's car, smiled and saluted his approval for her to pass into the highly secured military installation.

The woman knew exactly where she was going. She drove past the federal townhouses of base housing, past the civil engineering plant and the Veterans Administration hospital, until she reached her destination: a small clinic near the main hospital. Her excitement returned as she pulled into the parking lot, and her vacant look soon turned into one of extreme preoccupation.

After she found a parking space near the clinic's front door, she began her vigil. She watched the people come and go, nervously rubbing her fingernails with her thumb as she scanned the waiting room's interior through a plate-glass window. She disregarded the men, but paid close attention to the women, particularly the pregnant ones going in for a routine prenatal checkup. Not any pregnant woman would do; she had to find one nearing full-term and not accompanied by her husband in order to successfully complete her mission. Finally she found the right one, and her macabre plan was set in motion.

Inside, a pretty young brunette slid off the examining table. When the doctor told her that all was going well, a blush of pleasure rose to her cheeks. Wrapped in a warm bunting of her own feelings of impending motherhood, the young lady expressed her gratitude to the doctor. Even though she'd given birth once before, the miracle of motherhood still seemed to her something wonderful,

388

beyond her.

When the young mother-to-be came out, the woman in the car swiveled her head to keep her in view. Reassured and taking confidence from the gun gripped tightly, she opened the car door and squeezed out of the driver's seat. Getting stiffly to her feet, she stalked the pregnant woman, a deliberate quickness in her every movement.

Her prey, at one point, saw the other woman watching her, coming toward her. Not seeing the gun at first, the woman simply stood there, near her car, watching the other approach. Finally the oncoming woman stopped, stiffening menacingly, and the pregnant woman could see that there was a strange, nervous unease about her. An animal instinct must have told the young mother that all was not going to be well, and when she saw the gun she had to be overcome by horror and a feeling of impending doom.

Motioning with the gun, the woman told her victim to walk ahead of her and to do what she was told. Fearing for her own life and her unborn baby's life, she complied and got into the woman's car. Together they drove away. Panic must have risen in the mother-to-be as they passed the gate guard, especially since they weren't required to stop on the way out. Even though they drove at normal speed, there was simply no way for the pregnant woman to tip off the guard that she was in trouble.

They drove east on Interstate 40 for a short distance, mostly in silence, then south on New Mexico 14, gradually ascending the Manzano Mountains. Several minutes later, the driver stopped the car in a remote mountain area, east of the city. She ordered the pregnant woman out of the car.

A strange, cold excitement filled the kidnapper's whole being as her eyes met the victim's. She took a deep breath, released it, then leaped into movement like a sprung bear trap as she grabbed the other woman by the throat, her fingers closing tightly against the cartilage and bone as they fell to the ground. The pregnant woman gasped and kicked as hard as she could as the other woman's grip tightened. But she couldn't defend herself. Unconsciousness gradually took over, ending the expectant mother's final hair-raising, heart-pounding moments of terror.

Her bloodlust at fever pitch, the kidnapper let out a crazy, full-throated shriek as she searched for something sharp, anything she could use to open up her victim. Finally she decided on a simple key, not large but sharp enough on the edges to do the job.

After exposing the soft flesh of the victim's stomach, the woman scratched feverishly with the key until the skin broke. As she continued to scratch and scrape, a pool of blood bloomed from the victim's abdomen, slowly at first, then poured out into a large puddle as the cut deepened. At last she could see the unborn baby, and she desperately tore more flesh to get at it so she could pull it out of its mother's womb.

Several hours later, back in Albuquerque, a relative of 23-year-old Cindy Lynn Ray's got off duty at Kirtland AFB and returned home only to find that Cindy wasn't home. This was unusual, he thought. It simply wasn't like her to go somewhere without telling someone or leaving a note, particularly since the time of birth was nearing. He knew she'd had an appointment for a routine checkup at the clinic earlier that day, and it was more than a little strange that she hadn't called to let him know

390

how it had gone.

Without hesitation, the relative began calling friends and other relatives to try to determine where she had gone. Much to his dismay, however, no one had seen her. He checked with the clinic and learned that she had kept her appointment and there had been no problems related to the pregnancy. So where could she be? Could she have gone into labor unexpectedly? If so, why hadn't someone called to inform him? Of course if there had been an emergency, there might not have been time for anyone to contact him immediately. but wouldn't someone at least know about it and get in touch with him as soon as possible?

He checked with the hospital, but there was no record of Cindy having been admitted. Under any other circumstances he might have waited a while to see what happened, perhaps for Cindy to call. But with her conditon, he couldn't afford to take chances. He had to act quickly, not only for Cindy's and the baby's sakes, but to quell his own steadily-mounting anxiety. Without wasting a single minute, the worried man notified the police of the suspicious circumstances.

A short time later, a policeman arrived at the relative's home. After attempting to console him, the officer took a detailed statement of the circumstances as the relative knew them. When the officer was satisfied that he had all the necessary particulars, he assured the relative that his department would do all they could and would be in touch as soon as they had something to report.

Meanwhile, at an Albuquerque car dealership, a somewhat distraught young woman entered the showroom just before closing time that same night. She was carrying a baby wrapped in the dress she was wearing. Sales manager Tom Nelson recognized the young woman as having recently visited the dealership with her husband, shopping for a new car. He couldn't immediately remember her name but, seeing her obvious state of distress, he rushed over to her and asked her if she needed his help. He could see from her disheveled state and general nervous condition that she was not there to purchase a car.

After speaking with her for a few minutes, Nelson learned that the woman's name was Darci Kayleen Pierce, 19, and he was informed by her that she'd given birth to the child following a traffic accident. Nelson promptly instructed a salesman to call for an ambulance, after which he notified a relative of Pierce's of the unusual circumstances.

It was a few minutes past 10:00 p.m. when the ambulance arrived. After a brief examination in which vital signs were noted, Pierce and the infant were placed inside. Nelson sent one of the dealership managers with Pierce to the hospital to offer comfort and assistance.

It was about 10:30 p.m. when the ambulance arrived at the University of New Mexico Hospital's emergency entrance. The baby girl weight in at 6 pounds 8 ounces, and doctors determined that she was about two weeks premature. However, she appeared to be in good condition.

Pierce told the emergency room physicians that she had been in an automobile accident and had delivered the baby herself earlier that evening. Results of an additional examination of Pierce and the baby, however, contradicted Pierce's statements. Finding nothing to indicate that Pierce had actually given birth to a child, or to any child for that matter, doctors eventually determined that the baby had been born through Caesarean section. But where was the mother? Suspicious at this point, the medical personnel notified police.

When the police arrived, they were informed by emergency room personnel of the details Pierce provided to them, the inconsistencies revealed by the examination, and of the name of the car dealer who accompanied her to the hospital. A relative of Pierce's told police that the baby wasn't hers. Unfortunately, the relative couldn't tell them *who* the baby belonged to, nor were the police getting much information from Pierce herself at this point. She was taken into custody while investigators tried to ferret out additional information about the bizarre series of events.

Hoping to unravel the mystery as quickly as possible, detectives promptly contacted Tom Nelson, the dealership sales manager. Even though it was late, Nelson was cooperative and provided the sleuths with some significant information. Among the things Nelson recalled was that Darci Pierce and a male relative had been to his dealership a little more than a week before.

"They said they just wrecked one of their cars and the insurance company gave them a settlement," said Nelson. Nelson told lawmen that Pierce said she had only been in the area for a few weeks, but he added that he had since learned she had been there since May.

"The woman appeared to be pregnant, very much so," Nelson said of Pierce's first visit to his dealership. Nelson said the woman had told him a decision on a new car would be made following the birth of her baby.

"The next time I saw her she had a newborn baby, wrapped in the dress she was wearing," Nelson told the detectives. "She told me she had labor pains while driving down the highway, drove off the road, and delivered the baby herself."

He said Pierce had told him she came to his dealership because it was one of the few places in town she could remember how to find. Nelson added that Pierce told him she had bitten the umbilical cord to sever it after delivery.

Nelson told the detectives that he and Pierce talked for a while about babies, and after she became comfortable with him, she asked him to help her. He agreed, and sent her to the hospital with one of the other managers.

"At the time it made me feel pretty good," said Nelson, adding that he called one of Pierce's relatives and informed him that Pierce had given birth to a baby girl. Nelson said the relative "seemed genuinely pleased, but was curious as to why she was at the dealership."

Police Lieutenant Roger Anderson, now assigned to the case, soon saw, after being briefed and studying the reports, that he had his work cut out for him with this one. His analytical mind skeptical of the surface truths he'd been told, Anderson continued to pore over the reports throughout the night. Finally, as dawn came up and painted the eastern sky a delicate rose color while much of the world slept, Anderson considered the various strategies he might use in dealing with Pierce to get her to talk. After deciding on a game plan, he and another investigator approached her with their questions.

After questioning Pierce at length about the circumstances that led up to her arriving at the car dealership, then at the hospital with a newborn baby, its real mother as yet unknown, the detectives finally obtained a significant statement from the woman.

Although specifics of what she told the investigators were not immediately made public, the de-

394

tectives learned enough for them to speculate that another woman had died, probably at the hands of Darci Pierce. After considerable quizzing, Darci agreed to show the investigators where she had obtained the baby and where, most likely, lay the remains of the real mother. Accompanied by a relative and an attorney, Pierce led the law enforcement officials into a remote area of the Manzano Mountains.

Barely 20 minutes later, the officials pulled off the main road at a location designated by Pierce. Most of those present were grim-faced as they climbed out of their cars, and most were prepared for a gruesome discovery. Just what they would find they weren't yet altogether sure of, but most agreed that it would not be pleasant. but it was too fresh and sunny a day to dwell on such disturbing thoughts, particularly before they knew for sure what awaited them.

The officials had walked only a few yards, however, before they saw a sprawled shape lying in the foreground, accentuated by the shadows cast by the morning sun. One of the investigators stopped in mid-stride, cold dread clawing his middle as he recognized the silhouette as a human corpse. As he approached it, his breast rose heavily, and he suddenly felt sick to his stomach. With mute, stupefied faces, the others stared in stunned disbelief at the atrocity that lay before them. It was truly a sight from hell.

The corpse was a young female, the investigators noted. She had sustained a gaping tear near the center of the abdomen. Blood had flowed around and beneath the body and much of it had soaked into the dusty earth. The victim had lost most of her blood virtually all those there believed. There was also dried, frothy saliva around the mouth, and markings in the area of her neck prompted some of those present to suspect that she had been strangled. Lieutenant Anderson, aware of the missing-person report on Cindy Lynn Ray, guessed corectly that this was the body of the expectant mother.

Within minutes after the grisly discovery, Darci Pierce was placed under arrest for suspicion of murder and kidnapping. Several items were confiscated by police at the time of her arrest, including a fake gun and a car key. Meanwhile, Pierce was held in the Bernalillo County Detention Center in Albuquerque.

When the official from the New Mexico Office of the Medical Investigator arrived, he took one look at Cindy Ray's corpse, winced, gulped and momentarily turned away to gain control of his emotions before proceeding. Raising an eyebrow, the normally-phlegmatic doctor positioned himself close to the body, gritting his teeth all the while, and began his preliminary examination.

He noted that the victim's eyes had lost their luster, normal after having been dead and exposed to the elements overnight. Her cheeks were hollow, their luster and resilience also gone, almost completely drained of color. He observed that what had once been a pretty and youthful face was now hideous and leering in its macabre condition. The ghastly sight had pierced the careful psychological armament that had taken years to acquire to deal with such things. But this was just too much. Never could he have prepared himself enough to calmly face this atrocity. To break the overwhelming silence, he immediately began a general conversation to attract anyone who felt like talking, and gradually worked into the specifics of the examination.

By the time the medical examiner had finished, he told the detectives he felt reasonably certain that Cindy Ray died as a result of blood loss and strangulation. He couldn't say for sure at this point if the victim was dead when her abdomen had been ripped open or if she died afterward, but he said additional testing during autopsy might shed more light on the matter. Since much of the placenta, also known as the afterbirth that contains fetal membranes, was present, as was a portion of the umbilical cord, the medical examiner was confident that a Caesarean operation occurred at the location where the victim's body was found. He could not, however, say with certainty that the baby in Darci Pierce's possession when she showed up at the hospital came from Cindy Ray's body. To make that determination, he said, additional tests would have to be conducted.

With the July sun like a fire on the backs of their necks, crime lab technicians and detectives worked at the crime site throughout most of the day. Swabbing their perspiring faces, they collected blood and tissue samples from and near the victim's body, bagged other relevant evidence, and took roll after roll of photographs. When they had finished, they packed up their gear, and Cindy Ray's remains were placed inside a body bag and taken to the county morgue.

Simultaneously, the investigators were faced with the grim task of notifying the victim's relatives of the tragedy. Naturally the young woman's family took her death very hard, but they issued a prepared statement saying they felt no resentment toward the killer.

"It's a tragic thing," said a friend of the family. "That's all you can say about it. Obviously, (they're) relieved that the baby is fine."

397

Meanwhile, the sleuths attempted to establish a link between the victim and the suspect. However, after considerable inquiry, the only link they could find was that each woman had a relative stationed at Kirtland AFB. The two did not appear to know each other.

"Apparently it was a matter of opportunity," said Lieutenant Anderson in a statement to the Associated Press. Although he didn't release specifics of the ongoing investigation, he said his detectives had turned up the fact that Darci Pierce "wanted a baby."

During a press conference, Mary Molina Mescall, police spokeswoman, brought the reporters up to date with what little information she was allowed to release, including the incident with Pierce and the baby at the hospital and the subsequent discovery of Cindy Ray's body.

"It appeared the baby had been taken from Ray's dead body by means of a crude Caesarean operation," said Mescall, who assured anxious reporters that she would call another press conference when more information was available. The county prosecutor was also present but, like other officials, he didn't respond.

Meanwhile, a source close to the investigation said that detectives believed Pierce used a metal key to perform the crude surgery on Cindy Ray. "The official medical report isn't in yet," said the source, "but right now it looks like that's what happened."

During their probe of Darci Pierce's background, investigators soon learned that their suspect was a former resident of Portland, Oregon. A 1985 graduate of LaSalle High School, a private Catholic school in the Portland suburb of Milwaukie, she married shortly after graduation and moved to New Mexico. During interviews in Oregon, investigators learned from one of the suspect's former landladies that Darci was obsessed with motherhood and had once attempted to "take over" a newborn child that belonged to a relative.

Susan Miller, the landlady, described Darci and her husband as "just the loveliest couple," and said they had lived in a duplex apartment in the 9700 block of Southeast Harny Street from May 7, 1985, until January 1987.

"They were excellent tenants, and he was a steady worker," said Miller. "She had an obsession with motherhood, and that's the worst thing I could say about her. They were very nice people." Miller also told the investigators that a female relative lived with the Pierces at the duplex and gave birth to a child. When the baby came, said Miller, Darci tried to "take over the baby."

"(The relative) told me that Darci tried to take over her baby, to take full possession of it," Miller told the detectives. "She even wanted to nurse it. She was obsessed with motherhood. I don't know, maybe that would be a mental problem."

"(Darci) had a miscarriage when she lived here," said Miller, "that's what she told me. She told me the fetus starved to death because her body didn't support nourishment. She told me, 'There will be another time,' when her body had recovered and she would take treatment so she could have other children. Those were her exact words."

"(The relative) said Darci told her she was pregnant when she moved out," continued Miller. "I know she really put on a lot of weight, but it was fat. Even her legs were heavy."

The detectives noted that the auto sales manager in Albuquerque had said that Darci appeared pregnant when she first came to his dealership in May, but they reasoned that she could easily appear to be pregnant at 5 feet 4 inches and 175 pounds. And even though witnesses said that she regularly wore maternity clothes and told people she was pregnant, the sleuths turned up the fact that a medical examination in May showed that she wasn't pregnant.

As the background information on their suspect continued to grow, detectives found a friend of Darci's, the manager of a Beaverton, Oregon hobby shop, who told them he received a letter from her in June in which she said her pregnancy was going well and that everything was fine in her life.

"I've known Darci for over a year, a couple of years," said the hobby shop owner, "and I can't imagine her doing anything like what's been described."

In putting together the profile of their suspect, police learned that Pierce worked as a cashier at a fast-food restaurant in mid-1985 in Portland, but later quit to take a job in the sports department of an east Portland store. Her boss at the store said Darci had worked there for about two years, and confirmed that she had been pregnant but miscarried while employed there.

"She was a good employee, and well-liked by everybody here," said her former boss.

However, one of her former classmates at LaSalle High School described Darci as "just kind of quiet," and a close relative said she "wasn't overly friendly . . . she just kind of stuck to herself."

Another item of interest in Darci's background, the detectives learned, was that she spent a year in South Aftica in a Rotary Club exchange program, according to one of her former teachers at LaSalle.

The teacher recalled that Darci had changed after her trip to South Africa.

Meanwhile, back in New Mexico, Darci Pierce was arraigned in Albuquerque Metropolitan Court on accusations of first-degree murder, kidnapping, and child abuse. Harry Zimmerman, Bernalillo County Assistant District Attorney, told Judge James M. O'Toole that Pierce had a fake gun which allegedly was used to trick the victim. It was also revealed that the child in Darci Pierce's possession when she showed up at the hospital had been confirmed as the victim's, and had since been returned to the victim's relatives.

Dr. Ross Zumwalt, a pathologist from the New Mexico Office of the Medical Investigator, testified that Cindy Ray was alive but unconscious while her baby was being surgically removed from her body. Zumwalt said he had determined that she died of strangulation and loss of blood.

After Pierce entered a plea of not guilty by reason of insanity, Judge O'Toole set bail at $500,000. Unable to raise the bail, Pierce remained incarcerated at the county detention center. Assistant Public Defender John Bogren was appointed as counsel. Following grand jury indictments on the charges a week later, District Attorney Schiff indicated he might seek the death penalty if Pierce was convicted.

Pierce's murder trial began on Monday, March 14, 1988, amid prosecution arguments that Pierce planned her actions and knew what she was doing. Prosecutor Zimmerman said that Pierce chose to steal an unborn baby "to satisfy her obsession to have a child and, perhaps more important, to save her marriage."

Defense Attorney Bogren, however, argued that Pierce was "a loving, caring, compassionate

401

woman," and presented an insanity defense, attempting to appeal to the jurors' sympathy. He argued that Pierce had a double personality, one in which she truly believed she was pregnant and another in which she knew she was not.

The trial took two weeks to complete; on Tuesday, March 30, 1988, the jury was charged with its obligations. District Judge Richard Traub informed the jurors that under New Mexico law, insanity is defined as the result of a mental disease. Three tests must be met, instructed the judge, to classify a person as legally insane: 1) the person did not know what he was doing or understand the consequences of the act; 2) did not know the act was wrong; 3) could not prevent himself from committing the act. If one or more of the three tests for insanity cannot be met, continued the judge, the jury can find the defendant guilty as charged but mentally ill, or innocent. According to state law, said the judge, a defendant can be found mentally ill "if a substantial disorder of thought, mood or behavior impaired his judgment at the time of the commission of the offense." A person found guilty but mentally ill, he concluded, is subject to standard sentences, but the state Corrections Department is required to provide counseling and treatment "as it deems necessary."

Following six hours of gruelling deliberations, the jury found Darci Pierce guilty of first-degree murder, kidnapping, and child abuse. They also found her mentally ill, but not legally insane.

"I just think it's a real sad story," said Defense Attorney Bogren following the verdicts. "It's sad because everybody involved were good people. Two husbands were without wives; mothers were without children. Ironically a baby is born. It's a real sad situation." Bogren said he would appeal the verdict.

On Thursday, April 28, 1988, after hearing testimony from two psychiatrists, Judge Traub sentenced Darci Pierce to life in prison for the killing of Cindy Ray. He also imposed 18 years for kidnapping and 18 months for child abuse, to be served concurrently with the life sentence.

EDITOR'S NOTE:
Tom Nelson and Susan Miller are not the real names of the persons so named in the foregoing story. Fictitious names have been used because there is no reason for public interest in the identities of these persons.

"KILLER LEFT A FEATHER ON HIS VICTIM'S BREAST!"

by Robert Carlsen

UMATILLA COUNTY, ORE.
FEBRUARY 23, 1987

Leah Alice Tahkeal, 20, was a resident of the Umatilla Indian Reservation in Northeastern Oregon. She had always been close to her reservation relatives, so when she hadn't contacted them for several months in the fall of 1986, they became concerned about her welfare.

They knew she lived with a man and another woman at an isolated cabin on his reservation property near the community of Adams. They didn't care for the man, but Leah was an adult capable of making her own decisions, which her relatives respected.

Four days before Christmas 1986, her relatives learned just what a poor decision living with him had been.

After considerable discussion, several men decided they would go to the cabin to check on Leah's welfare. She had a young child who missed her and it wasn't like her not to pay him a visit. Nor was it like her to shun her other relatives.

Even if her living companion could be found,

404

which he couldn't, her relatives didn't trust the guy to give them a straight answer on Leah's well being. The man hadn't been seen in months. They figured he was holed up in the cabin with the women, perhaps forbidding Leah to contact her relatives. He had a reputation for belligerence and violence, and they knew their confrontation with him wouldn't be pleasant. That's why none of them went to the cabin alone. They figured there was safety in numbers. For them, maybe. For Leah and the second woman at the cabin, the numbers hadn't been high enough.

It was Sunday, December 21st, when Leah's relatives arrived at the isolated cabin. Something didn't look right about the place. For one thing, there was too much snow on the roof. The place was poorly insulated and in the winter, with the wood crackling in the pot-bellied stove, all the heat rose to the rafters of the cabin and escaped out the top. Hence, the snow should have been melted. But it wasn't. This indicated there hadn't been a fire in the stove for weeks. That was a bad sign.

"I don't like the looks of this," one of the men said. "Did you notice there weren't any car tracks on the snow when we came? And there's no footprints. This place looks deserted."

However, there was one occupant of the cabin, they soon discovered. She had been ceremoniously placed on the cot, an eagle feather left on her breast to help her spirit into the hereafter.

When the Indians opened the cabin door, the stench was overpowering. It was the smell of rotting meat; the smell of death. For them, the smell of grief. Their beloved Leah lay decaying on the cot. They wailed and cursed the man who'd done this to their beloved Leah.

The Tribal Police were the first notified. Chief

Robert Wilcox notified Pendleton FBI field Agent Mike McPheters. The two had worked closely with one another on other felonies occurring on the Indian reservation, but as they soon would find out, few could compare with the crimes they were about to uncover.

Upon his arrival, Chief Wilcox recognized the Indian custom of placing an eagle feather on a body to help it into another world. Even without looking at any other evidence, the chief could say an Indian did this to the woman, identified by her relatives as Leah Alice Tahkeal.

The body appeared to have laceration and puncture wounds in it, although its state of decay wasn't conducive to close examination by the lawmen at the scene.

FBI Agent McPheters arrived armed with a search warrant issued by a U.S. District Court judge. When Chief Wilcox had been told about the body, he knew it was murder and asked the agent to secure the necessary warrant, thus speeding up the process a bit.

Blood spatters throughout the cabin indicated that some violent acts had occurred there, and the apparent wounds to the body indicated the victim may have been stabbed.

A thorough search of the cabin turned up a large sword which the lawmen speculated could have been used on the victim. More importantly, the lawmen turned up something which led them to a second decomposed body.

What probers found was a spiral notebook in which the killer had jotted down his thoughts prior to and after the murder. One passage read thusly: "I am here to say my last saying. I have killed twice. Whether anyone can believe this, I never meant to. Martina is buried between two pine trees out by the front road, Leah Alice is laying here beside me."

Good Lord, Chief Wilcox thought as the hair on his neck bristled. The guy slept with his murder victim after she was dead! He read on.

"I truly wish I could lay beside her and follow. Although I know in due time I soon will.

"I love Alice, love her so very deeply—and Martina. I have no excuse for these actions except for alcohol and jealousy."

"It looks like we're going to have to do some digging," Chief Wilcox told his Tribal officers and FBI agents. "And look for something in here that will tell us who Martina is."

"No need," said one of the Indians who'd found the body. "Two women lived here. One was Alice. The second was Martina Reed. I don't know her middle name. She was older, Around thirty, I guess. Came from Pendleton."

Chief Wilcox assigned one of his men to find out the background on Martina Reed. Oregon State Police and Pendleton police helped track down this information.

Martina Irene Reed, 30, was a member of the Yurok tribe. She'd come to Oregon from California, police learned. She first arrived in Portland, and about two years prior to her death, moved to Pendleton, and then onto the Umatilla Indian Reservation with the man who eventually would murder her while penning his professions of love for her and Alice.

"If he loved them, he had a hell of a way of showing it," commented one officer while turning the first spade of dirt at the gravesite. "Who did he have to be jealous of way out here? He watched over those women like a vulture, from what I could gather."

The second gravedigger shrugged. "Who knows what makes those guys tick? Walk down any street in the country and you're bound to pass a bomb waiting to go off. They're everywhere. Even out in the middle of nowhere."

"Not a very deep grave," the first gravedigger commented as he dug up the second victim's decayed right arm.

"I'm surprised some animal didn't dig part of it up," his fellow officer said.

"Better tell the chief the information in the notebook was on target. Wonder if there are any more like this out here."

He looked around at the vast acreage. The killer could have buried a thousand bodies and not run out of room, the officer observed.

The body in the grave was decayed beyond recognition, but Chief Wilcox had no reason to doubt it was Martina Reed. To support what he'd already been told about her identity, some papers supporting that statement were found in the cabin.

It was probably for the best that none of her relatives lived on the reservation and were there to see her in that condition, Chief Wilcox thought. They probably wouldn't be able to identify the body, the decomposition was so advanced. And what parent or kid wants to see a relative in that condition?

"Somebody will have to notify her family," the chief said when told she had two children living in California and one in Canada.

"There's no doubt in my mind who we're looking for," Agent McPheters said as he closed the spiral notebook.

"None here," Chief Wilcox agreed. "My only question is where do we start looking? He obviously hadn't been here for months. His last entry

408

in the journal was October 26th. This place hasn't been lived in for a couple of months. The bodies show a couple months worth of decay. Our killer has fled the coop, leaving behind one feather to help his beloved into another world."

The killer was identified as a 36-year-old ex-con named Kendall Arthur, also known as Arthur Kendall and Kenneth Arthur. He wasn't real creative when it came to aliases, Agent McPheters observed. Arthur had lived on the reservation most of his life, except for those periods of time when he was either in jail or briefly off to another city, the investigators learned. He considered the reservation his permanent home, much to the chagrin of others. His reputation was well known on the reservation and beyond.

Kendall Arthur grew up on the Umatilla Reservation. His mother died when he was a youngster and he was reared by relatives. He rented land from one of them and eventually inherited this land. He worked as a farm laborer, and one of his employers, a librarian, hired him to work her land.

"Yeah, he had a temper," she recalled. "But he was one of the best workers I've ever had work for me."

When she learned about the double murder and that Arthur was a suspect, she said, "It's a terrible shock, because he used to come by once in awhile." He'd borrow gasoline occasionally, although he didn't drive because he'd lost his license.

This made the lawmen wonder just how Arthur left the area. Did somebody help him? Of course, the fact that he didn't have a license didn't preclude the possibility that he drove somewhere.

"A stop sign never stopped a car," one officer observed. "It tells the driver to stop the car. It's the driver's decision to obey it. A revoked license never stopped somebody from driving. You either obey the laws, or you don't."

One thing was certain about Arthur's getaway. He had almost a two-month head start on the cops. The last entry in his journal had been October 26th, and the bodies weren't discovered until December 21st. He could have walked on his hands and been a good distance away before the lawmen got wind of the crimes.

The FBI and Tribal Police got a list of Arthur's friends and few relatives. The lawmen started checking with these persons to determine if Arthur had sought their assistance in making his getaway. It didn't surprise the investigators when they came up with negative answers. It appeared Kendall Arthur had made a clean getaway without leaving behind a trace.

If somebody did know of Arthur's whereabouts, it wouldn't have surprised the lawmen that they were keeping their mouths shut out of fear, for Arthur had a bad reputation among the Indians on the reservation.

The Indians didn't care to associate with Arthur, who'd done a stint in jail. It was in jail where Arthur learned to read and write. He also established his reputation as being somebody who others didn't want to mess with. He could take care of himself and on more than one occasion found it necessary to do so, with his adversaries coming out the worse for the wear.

Therefore, when he ended up with two girlfriends at the Thornhollow cabin near Adams, it was no surprise to outsiders that the trio kept to itself. Adams residents figured the young women were terrorized into obedience and meekness. There was no reason to believe that Arthur would be hesitant in being a disciplinarian considering his reputation as a belligerent. But disciplining them with a sword was something nobody had ever suspected he would do.

Dr. William Brady, the state's medical examiner at the time, determined the victims died of what he termed "traumatic asphyxiation," a term that covers a welter of possibilities. Because of the advanced state of decay on the bodies, it was pretty impossible to determine the exact cause of death.

Traumatic asphyxiation is a term which means the victims died from something other than natural causes. The autopsy didn't reveal much the investigators hadn't already determined.

Meanwhile, the search for Kendall Arthur covered a vast area. Pendleton police were busy chasing down possible leads in that city while the Oregon State Police was covering the rural areas. The FBI and Tribal Police plied their trade on the reservation and their work eventually paid off. The lawmen got information from one of their sources that Arthur had made it all the way to Portland, Oregon. He was living somewhere in the northwest section of the city, an area known as Burnside.

The investigation shifted to the west side of the state on December 23rd. FBI agents, armed with photographs of Arthur, started patrolling the Burnside area. December 23rd ticked by without turning up any trace of the suspect.

Theodore M. Gardner, special agent in charge of the FBI's Portland field office, had every available man working the streets in an effort to find Arthur. Arthur was charged in a complaint filed with U.S. Magistrate William Dale in the killings of Leah Alice Tahkeal and Martina Irene Reed. Agent Gardner wanted Arthur off the streets as quickly as possible. The investigation on the Umatilla Indian Reservation was still going on, as investigators started looking for other possible graves on the suspect's property. Although they'd found nothing in Arthur's journal to indicate there were more than two victims, investigators had made contact with persons who claimed that prior to Leah Tahkeal and Martina Reed, Arthur had other girlfriends who apparently weren't seen after shacking up with him for a certain period of time. When his friends had questioned Arthur about their whereabouts, he had told them that the girls had gotten fed up with him and left. Knowing Arthur's disposition, his friends had believed that story the times he'd used it. But after the discovery of the two bodies, they shuddered to think what other secrets the Thornhollow property might hold.

Agent Gardner didn't know if he was looking for a double-homicide suspect or a possible serial killer. Either way, it didn't much matter. He wanted Arthur caught and he wanted it done immediately. He was assuming the worst—that more grisly discoveries were in store at Arthur's Thornhollow property near Adams.

FBI agents were poking their noses in all the known Indian hang-outs in Portland in search of Kendall Arthur. Agents contacted informants and had the streets heavily patrolled. City police and county offices also were on the alert. The suspect's photograph was widely distributed among the lawmen. Every tip on his whereabouts was checked out, all to no avail.

The lawmen had determined that Arthur didn't have a lot of friends or relatives in Portland to whom he could turn for help. He was limited in the number of possible contacts he could make, of this they were certain. They knew he'd eventually have to emerge from his hideout, if for nothing else than to buy groceries. All his known friends had been contacted by agents, and they knew it was a waiting game until the suspect slipped up somewhere.

None of the agents looked forward to spending Christmas spinning their wheels on the streets looking for the suspect. They wanted to get him so they could all breathe easier over the holiday. News about the discovery of the double homicide had hit Portland, and they knew if Arthur was in the area, when he heard about it, he'd be on the move again. And if he slipped through the dragnet, there was no telling where he'd go next.

It was 3:30 in the afternoon of December 24th, when an agent spotted Arthur walking down the street in the Burnside area of Portland. The agent radioed for backup and within minutes FBI agents converged on the scene. Arthur was apparently stunned by all the attention, taken completely by surprise. Obviously, he hadn't been keeping up on the news. The lawmen believe Arthur figured he hadn't been discovered for nearly two months, so he didn't worry about listening for indicators that he'd been found out. The other possibility is that he may not have cared. In his journal found in his cabin, he had hinted about suicide, about not going back to jail, and it all was done in a manner which seemed to indicate he was resigned to the fact that eventually he'd be caught.

"Merry Christmas, Arthur," the suspect was told as agents placed the cuffs on his wrists. "We've got a sleigh waiting to take you downtown."

The apprehension of Kendall Arthur was a gift for all agents in the Portland bureau. Until something else came up, they could enjoy the holiday. Maybe they'd even be able to digest their ham and turkey dinners without another crisis.

If Kendall Arthur's digestion was disturbed, he

413

didn't let anyone in the Multnomah County jail, where he was being housed, know it. He kept mum when advised of his rights and asked if he wanted to make a statement. He didn't. He barely talked to his own attorney.

The first order of business, his attorney determined, was to file a motion to get Arthur's journal declared inadmissible as evidence in court. The journal would leave little doubt in anybody's mind that Arthur murdered the women. Like all good criminal attorneys, Kendall Arthur's lawyer knew that the guilty or innocent verdict is determined long before the matter is even presented to a jury. Good defense attorneys win their cases in pretrial hearings by getting evidence declared inadmissible for one reason or another. That was the defense attorney's intention with the journal. He explained this to his client, who appeared non-committal about the entire matter. Arthur had something up his sleeve, which he wasn't telling anybody, not even his own attorney. He'd simply sit back and wait to see what developed when his case was plopped before a grand jury for indictment.

On Monday, December 29, 1986, Kendall Arthur was arraigned in U.S. District Court in Portland, charged with the murder of his former girlfriend, Leah Tahkeal. He was charged with second-degree murder.

In an affidavit filed with the charge, the prosecutors included a portion of the text from the suspect's notebook. Arthur made an entry in the notebook the morning after the murders:

"I am sober now. It is morning and I see the aftermath of horror. It is so terrible I wish I had never awakened. Alcohol has won. You people will never understand except that I am a twisted person but not until consumed by the booze. I do not

414

know what I am going to do but I hope I die soon. Prison is worse than death."

Although Arthur was originally charged with second-degree murder, that charge was upgraded to first-degree murder and a second first-degree murder charge was added after a federal grand jury indicted him on both counts. Those indictments came on Wednesday, December 31st, two days after his initial arraignment.

While Arthur was being held in Portland, the search for other possible victims continued at his property. But to the relief of investigators, no other bodies were found.

But while Arthur was in custody during January of 1987, he apparently started talking with other prisoners in the Multnomah County Jail. One of those prisoners forwarded some information to a jail guard, and that information sparked new speculation that there still might be more victims.

"We don't know if we have a serial killer here or not," Agent McPheters said. "We have information that there could be another victim or more."

But despite the efforts of the FBI and Tribal Police, no more graves could be found on Arthur's property, and the county jail source dried up. Arthur wasn't talking anymore with him about his former girlfriends.

If Kendall Arthur did leave more than two bodies somewhere in the Thornhollow area on the Umatilla Indian Reservation, it's a secret that will never be told.

On February 23rd, Arthur was scheduled to appear at a pretrial hearing in which his attorney was going to argue that Arthur's notebook shouldn't be admitted as evidence. But at 5 a.m., Kendall Arthur was found hanged inside his jail cell, the cause of death apparently being suicide.

Arthur had tied bedsheets together and tied the sheets to an overhead pipe running through his cell.

The last jail check on Arthur had been made at 3:30 a.m., and it was believed he hanged himself sometime between 4:40 and 5 a.m. when the body was discovered.

Thus ended the case of self-confessed killer Kendall Arthur. His writings left no doubt that he killed Leah Tahkeal and Alice Reed, although it was never proved in court.

Were there more victims? Nobody will ever know for sure unless a shallow grave somewhere near Thornhollow is someday accidentally discovered. Dead men tell no tales, and Arthur left no final note indicating whether any more bodies could be found.

"TERRORIZED HIS VICTIMS WITH A DEAD BODY!"

by Olga Kogan

Ask a woman about her most constant fear and she will likely reply with one word — rape. That's not surprising. The circumstances that can suddenly heighten a woman's latent fear of rape are many and varied: a strange face at a darkened window; the sound of heavy footsteps following a few feet behind; a walk alone through a deserted parking garage. These are enough to send goose bumps up and down the spine of any woman. But there are more frightening reminders of the sex criminals out there — far more frightening, and more deadly, too.

It was not long after ringing in the new year, 1990, that a vicious sex criminal began dropping some of those reminders around the metropolitan area of Chicago. Even in a city where sex crimes are a part of urban life, his bizarre modus operandi made him stick out. In fact, the big-city lawmen could not recall ever having seen or heard of anything quite like him.

It was on the last Sunday of the month when police at Chicago Lawn headquarters got a call from a woman named Dina Cross who told them, through emotional stops-and-starts, that she "needed help because she'd been attacked." A couple of officers

417

were dispatched to the woman's home to take down her story.

The woman was in her late 20s, attractive, and obviously highly upset. The incident that prompted Dina's call to police had occurred the previous night. Not wanting to spend Saturday night alone, Dina had gone to a local lounge-bar on South Archer Avenue. Her intention was not to cruise but just to be with other people and have a good time.

At one point, a bearded man with hair down to his shoulders came up to Dina and started to chat. Unlike many of the men she had met in bars, his manner wasn't aggressive or overbearing. He talked about music and guitar-playing, apparently his favorite activities. Dina felt that maybe he was coming on to her, but she really didn't feel threatened by him, and when she excused herself, he didn't try to pursue her.

At the same bar, Dina met a female acquaintance who told her about a party that was going on that night at a friend's home. She gave Dina the address, and a short time later, Dina left the bar and headed for more action at the private party.

Dina had not been there long before she noticed a familiar face among the crowd of bodies and the lingering clouds of cigarette smoke. The shoulder-length hair and the beard were unmistakable: it was the same guy who'd come up to her at the bar. He gave Dina a little wave of recognition and trundled across the room.

Sitting among the other chatting couples at the party, it was easier for Dina to maintain a conversation with him than it had been at the bar. Besides, by this time, Dina had had a few drinks, it was past midnight, and the guy was telling her interesting stories about his gigs with a local rock band. The hours seemed to change over almost as fast as the discs in

418

the CD player.

It was just about dawn when Dina downed the last drops of her drink and announced it was time to get home. When the man offered her a lift, it was natural that she should accept.

He escorted Dina along the short walk to his parked car, a big, two-door Oldsmobile sedan, rather the worse for wear. The vinyl seat covers were cold from the winter night as the two slid onto the front seat. For some reason, the man didn't start the car engine. Dina wanted him to turn on the car heater as soon as possible to let some warmth in, but he just sat looking at her.

Suddenly, the soft-spoken party guest became unrecognizable. The man's two large hands reached toward Dina, clutching her garments and tugging at them with ferocious energy. Her own hands went up, pushing him away. But even as Dina pushed, she was being pulled closer toward him. Dina screamed and all at once the man stopped jerking.

One of his hands gripped a blanket lying on the backseat and slid it on to the floorboard. The dawn sun was high enough for Dina to get an eyeful of the ghastly object that lay rigid there on the seat—a young woman's corpse!

"Do as I say or you end up like she did," the man told Dina bluntly.

At this point, Dina lost all control of herself. She started waving arms, shouting and kicking with her feet. He began pummeling Dina with his fists. Somehow Dina's hysteria must have given her the strength to fend off the assailant's renewed attack. Dina wrenched open the door and skipped out of the car.

The officers interviewing Dina were a bit incredulous. The woman was asking them to believe that some fellow had driven off to a party with a corpse in the backseat, then invited another woman to his car in order to have sex in the front seat. They had heard of some kinky rapists, but this was a new one on them.

Asked to describe her assailant, the witness said he was on the stocky side, not quite six feet tall, and impressively strong. Dina had gotten a good look at his face during the time they were chatting at the party: dirty blond hair, light-blue eyes, a beard. She also remembered seeing a tattoo of a hawk or an eagle on one arm.

It was an A-one description, particularly the tattoo. The officers felt certain that the witness could identify the man if she saw him again—if they could find him.

The officers headed back to headquarters where they knew their report would raise a few eyebrows among their colleagues. But it turned out that the surprise was on them. A report of a rapist cruising town with a corpse in the backseat was already making the rounds of the station!

The latest report had come in from a female service-station attendant who was working the Clark district. Just after 7:00 a.m. that morning—about an hour after the first incident—a stocky, blond-haired man had come into the station and demanded the contents of the till. At that early hour, that amounted to less than $100. But the man was after more than just cash. He ordered the young attendant outside and into his car.

The woman complied up to that point, fearful for her life. But when he slid the blanket off the backseat and revealed a woman's nude corpse, she told police, "I freaked out.

"He said I'd end up another corpse if I didn't give him sex," the attendant said. "I just started hitting him over and over until finally he let go. Then I just

420

ran and ran."

The man had long hair, a beard—and an eagle tattoo on one arm. Apparently undiscouraged by his failure to rape following the all-night party, he'd immediately gone out looking for still another victim. Meanwhile, the corpse lay under the blanket on the backseat either as some kind of perverse trophy of his previous conquest or as a menace to challenges from future victims.

Even as bulletins were being sent out on the man and his car, police officers were shaking their heads over the weirdness of the case. If the man was as sexually aggressive as it seemed, it would not be long before he began stalking someone else. What frustrated detectives most was that they had an excellent description of the suspect but no name for him. Slyly, he had avoided mentioning even his first name to Dina. When the other party guests were questioned, they all shrugged their shoulders and said they'd figured the stocky blond-haired stranger had been invited by someone else.

Still further sinister reports came in from the overnight patrolmen. An all-night convenience store and a service station in the Archer Avenue area had both been robbed early on Sunday morning. In each case, attendants provided a description of a blue-eyed, bearded man with a stocky build. The fellow was nothing if not brazen.

Lawmen stepped up their canvassing of the area. At the same time, they began a check of their files for a missing woman—the corpse in the backseat of the Oldsmobile. Chicago Lawn Police Office Alex Murphy scanned every missing-person report that had been received at headquarters in the past several days. Armed with a detailed summary of the roving rapist's activities, Murphy had a clear picture of what to look for.

He finally hit on one of the many reports filed on Sunday morning, the morning after the all-night party which almost ended in rape for one of the guests. It concerned the unusual disappearance of Alice Cogler, a petite 29-year-old woman with curly hair and blue eyes. Family members who called police said she failed to come home after work at a popular lounge-bar on South Archer Avenue.

The woman worked as a bartender and knew her way around, her family said. Alice made it a point to let people know where she was going and with whom. If she failed to call home, it meant something had gone wrong.

Chicago Lawn Tactical Unit Lieutenant Dennis Ryan sent detectives to the lounge to investigate. It was a popular place, and Alice Cogler had been a popular employee. The detectives made known the purpose of their visit and soon began getting some interesting responses.

Fellow employees remembered Cogler working on Saturday night. They also recalled that she'd left fairly early — just after nine o'clock. One employee said he saw her talking with a bearded, blond-haired man around that time. He wasn't exactly a regular customer, but for the past month or so he would drop in for a drink from time to time.

Another employee recalled seeing Cogler getting into her car — a 1978 two-door Oldsmobile — along with a bearded man who got in the passenger side. For the first time, lawmen had what looked like a direct link to their suspect. With the eagerness of a blood-hound on a scent, they set about interviewing regular bar patrons, often treasure troves of local gossip.

The description of the stocky blond-haired man drew some shrugs and head-scratching. The name of a motorcycle gang member kept coming up. He had the beard and blond hair and tattoos of the suspect. The only inconsistency was his build: the gang member tipped the scales at over 200 pounds and stood more than six feet. The rapist-killer was stocky, but definitely smaller.

It was when detectives mentioned the suspect's eagle arm tattoo that they hit pay dirt.

"Bob Cloutier has a tattoo like that," remarked one man. "He was here last Saturday night, too."

The name Cloutier rang bells with other bar patrons, too. Detectives were now able to ask more questions.

While lawmen pondered their next move, their worst fears were even then being realized. They got wind of the crime the following Tuesday, when the family of 34-year-old Cynthia Cooney called the police to report her missing. A slim, attractive cashier at a drug store on Archer Avenue, Cynthia was known to have gone to a local bar the previous evening. She drove there in her car, a 1976 Oldsmobile — coincidentally, the same model car the suspect rapist was driving, although from a different year.

The detectives hurriedly reported this new information to the police files department. An all-points bulletin went out for the missing woman's car. Now there were two Oldsmobile sedans on the "hot" list — both of them owned by attractive women apparently kidnapped by the same man.

The police files department came back with some heavy-duty information on Robert "Bob" Cloutier. It wasn't pretty. Less than three months before, a woman who identified herself as Cloutier's girlfriend had filed a complaint against him with police. The two of them had had a quarrel, she explained, and Cloutier decided he could persuade her to see his side of the argument — by whipping her with a chain

423

leash!

When Cloutier was picked up for questioning, lawmen discovered that he'd just been released on parole from one of Illinois' toughest penal institutions: Menard Correctional. He'd been serving a five-year sentence there for armed robbery. The paroled con hadn't lost much time in reinstating himself in the bad graces of the law.

Found guilty of violating parole, Cloutier was given a return ticket to his old cell. But just two months later, a few days before Christmas, prison officials decided to be bighearted and release Cloutier in time so that he could spend the holidays with his family in Chicago.

According to his parole officer, Cloutier had gone the straight and narrow by getting himself a job loading and unloading big-rig trucks for a Windy City firm. The only qualification for that line of work was muscle. Twenty-six-year-old Cloutier was no slouch in that department.

One look at Cloutier's prison mugshot was worth a thousand words. It fit the suspect's description to the last hair on his scruffy beard. Copies were ordered to be distributed among all patrol officers working the metropolitan area, with a special alert put out on the two Oldsmobiles he was thought to be driving.

While headquarters awaited any news from the street patrols, Lieutenant Dennis Ryan, commander of the tactical team, contacted a relative of Cloutier's who lived on South Keeler. Following his latest release from prison, Cloutier had given the relative's address to his parole officer as his place of residence. The relative confessed ignorance of Cloutier's whereabouts: he hadn't been home for a few days. Nonetheless, she had some curious information to offer the lawman. In the last two days, a man had been calling to ask about Bob. The man identified himself as a relative of Alice Cogler's, an employee at a bar that Bob frequented. She was last seen leaving the bar with Bob. Had the two of them gone off together? the caller asked. All of Alice's relatives were worried sick about her.

Lieutenant Ryan knew that there was good cause for alarm. Under his direction, the tactical unit assisted by detectives from the Brighton Park Area violent crime unit under Commander Jon Burge, began an intensive dragnet of Chicago's South Side, focusing especially on Archer Avenue, the killer's main "drag." The searching officers carried a warrant charging Robert Cloutier with two counts of attempted rape. Further charges of murder would likely be leveled following his capture.

News of the rapist's terror rides at night was released to the press, which published Cloutier's mugshot photo as well as photos of the two missing women, Alice Cogler and Cynthia Cooney.

Public safety became an important factor in determining the intensity of the police search. The killer had shown himself capable of bizarre criminal acts. He had a felony record. On top of that, his police file indicated that he was heavily into cocaine among other drugs. The police wanted poster warned, "This man should be considered extremely dangerous."

It was sound advice, as veteran Police Officer Thomas Scott would learn. On February 1st, the Thursday after the weekend of terror, Scott was on routine patrol in Oak Lawn, a south Chicago suburb. As his patrol car approached the corner of Pulaski Road and 99th Street, the officer noticed a stocky man lumbering along the roadside.

Scott's trained memory recalled the bulletin describing a stocky man wanted for attempted rape. This man was stocky, all right, and he was blond-haired; but he was clean-shaven, unlike the suspect. There didn't seem to be enough reason for the officer to interrupt his patrol.

As the police car glided slowly past the man, the officer's eyes met those of the man on foot. The contact lasted only a second — just long enough for the man to realize who was there. He turned his head away immediately and kept on walking, the swagger in his body suddenly turning to stiffness.

The officer drove on a few blocks, then stopped. In 10 years on the force, he'd learned a thing or two about spotting suspicious characters. The fellow on the road had definitely felt ill at ease at the sight of a policeman. Just what was his problem?

Officer Scott dutifully got out of the car and headed back to the direction he'd just come. The stocky figure came presently into view, and as he did so, the officer's hand brushed his open holster, a veteran lawman's instinctive preparation before a potential confrontation.

The stocky man stopped at the sight of the officer. Asked his name and business, the man gave a name and said he was a drifter without work. The officer nodded. Would the man mind rolling up both his sleeves, the officer asked, remembering the eagle tattoo on the suspect's arm that was mentioned in the police bulletin.

The man didn't move. The police officer waited, his eyes fixed on any sudden movements on the man's part, his hand ready to unholster his weapon in a split-second.

But there was no showdown. Robert Cloutier raised his hands in the air and moved to the side of the patrol car. He already knew the routine.

With his gun leveled at the suspect, Officer Scott radioed for backup, then proceeded to pat down the man in a search for concealed weapons. He was

426

clean. His pockets contained no wallet or identification cards of any kind. The sum total of his fortune added up to less than 10 dollars in bills and change. Some car keys on a key ring marked "GM" completed his possessions.

At Oak Lawn Police Headquarters, the arrested man confessed that he was Robert Cloutier. Police in Chicago were notified, and they requested that the suspect be transferred to the Brighton Park Area station for interrogation.

In the interrogation room soon afterward, Chief of Detectives John Townsend and his men confronted the suspect with the evidence. He reacted with little more than a pursing of the lips and a nod of the head. He kidnapped those two women and stole their cars, he admitted.

"Where are the women now?" asked one detective.

"Dead. They're both dead," Cloutier calmly replied.

With an air of resignation bordering on nonchalance, Cloutier conducted the lawmen to a back alley in lower Brighton Park. A brown Oldsmobile sedan was parked there unobtrusively in the shadows.

"Take a look inside the trunk," Cloutier told the detectives.

The lawmen popped open the trunk lid. A woman's naked corpse lay inside. An autopsy would shortly identify her as 29-year-old Alice Cogler.

Cloutier recounted that he'd met her five days earlier at the bar where she worked. She'd kindly offered him a ride home, but when he got into the car with her, something happened. Maybe it was the mixture of cocaine and alcohol that he'd been taking that evening or maybe it was an overwhelming urge to do violence—he didn't know.

Cloutier began fondling her, and when she resisted, he started to beat her with his fists. She was a

427

tiny woman, just under five feet tall, weighing no more than 95 pounds. In just a few seconds, he had his hands around her neck and was choking her. He released his iron grip only when she stopped moving and her body went limp. But then she stirred to life again, which drove him back into a fury.

A spare fan belt was lying on the floorboards. He unlooped it and wrapped it around his victim's throat. This time, he made sure there were no revivals.

Cloutier's reaction to his crime was as cold as the January weather outside. The corpse beside him might just as well have been a box of detergent. Effortlessly, he'd lifted the corpse and placed it on the backseat, covering it with a blanket lying there. It would stay concealed like that until he could take care of his sexual needs, which, with the help of his new set of wheels, he could now proceed to satisfy.

Within an hour of committing murder, Cloutier was sitting on a bar stool, chatting up another woman. When she left the bar to go to a private party, he followed her in his car. A few hours after that, under the pretext of giving her a lift, he had her in the car's front seat, where he tried to repeat the same scene that had occurred there just a short time before—beating and choking her.

When she escaped, his sexual frustration grew still more. He found still another woman to kidnap: a teenage gas station attendant. She, too, managed to get away from him.

By that time, Cloutier had been up all night, but with drugs throbbing in his veins, he still felt wide awake. He wheeled over to the house of a woman whom he knew and had breakfast with her and her small child. Afterward, he drove the stolen car to the alley in Brighton Park, where he abandoned it along with the corpse in the trunk.

One day later, he felt his old urges taking control of him again. That evening he found himself at another Archer Street bar, anxiously looking at the women there. One of them, Cynthia Cooney, offered him a ride home. It was tantamount to an invitation to murder.

Cloutier led the detectives to a spot on the banks of the Des Plaines River not far from an old bridge that led to the suburb of Willow Springs. He had grown up in that area and knew it as only boys who've crisscrossed a region countless times on their bicycles can get to know an area. There were actually two bridges at that spot now—the old span, which was closed after being deemed too dangerous for traffic, and the new span, which was a short ways up the river.

It was to the new bridge that Cloutier said he brought the corpse of his second victim. He had guided the car to about midpoint on the bridge and stopped, mindful of any other vehicles coming on or leaving the span. At that early hour in the morning, there was no one else about.

Taking the partially clothed body from the car, he poised it on the bridge railing and let it fall into the river below. A moment later, the rest of her clothing followed the same route.

Cloutier said he peered down to watch how fast the current would carry away the corpse. To his frustration, he saw that far from transporting it downstream, the water had nudged the corpse to the riverbank, where the body now lay hooked on some driftwood in shallow water. The loose articles of clothing, moreover, had floated downstream to the old bridge, where they remained snagged on the support beams.

Fearful that a passing motorist would see him there and think his presence strange, Cloutier hurriedly got into his car and headed back down to town.

Once Cloutier pointed out to detectives where he last saw the corpse, they had little trouble spotting it, and with the aid of firemen from Willow Springs, the body of Cynthia Cooney was soon retrieved and in the hands of coroner officials. An autopsy later revealed that she had been strangled with a ligature, most likely her own brassiere.

After disposing of his victim in the river, Cloutier drove aimlessly for a while until finally abandoning the car in a restaurant parking lot in the district of Evergreen Park. He then started walking—again without any particular destination—and had reached neighboring Oak Lawn when he was spotted by Officer Scott. The car was still in the restaurant parking lot when police came to retrieve it.

After leading detectives to his victims, Robert Cloutier made a detailed confession of his crimes in the presence of a court reporter. Tired and looking as haggard as a hound-dog left out in the rain, he admitted that he'd gone sleepless ever since the murder of the first woman four days earlier.

On February 1, 1990, the suspect was charged with two counts of first-degree murder along with two counts of aggravated criminal sexual assault for the attempted rape of the two women who managed to escape his clutches.

At his trial in May 1991, for the murder of Alice Cogler, prosecutors accused Cloutier of "keeping her body stretched neatly in the backseat, using it as a weapon to intimidate other would-be victims."

Found guilty as charged, the defendant was given the maximum penalty under Illinois law—death. Robert Cloutier now lives on borrowed time in a death row cell within the Illinois penal system.

APPENDIX

ADDITIONAL COPYRIGHT INFO
TRUE DETECTIVE #13: Bizarre Murders

"He Had Sex with Rosemary's Rosary-Beaded Corpse!" *Master Detective,* February, 1993

"Little Angel was Ravaged by Demented Devil!" *Master Detective,* May, 1992

"Masked Corpse in the Black Bra," *True Detective,* April, 1992

"He Bit Off the Blonde Beauty's Breasts!" *Official Detective,* August, 1992

"Hello Dolly, Goodbye David!" *Official Detective,* April, 1991

"Bizarre Carvings on the Victim's Face," *Inside Detective,* January, 1989

"Freaky Fish Cutter Fileted Females!" *Official Detective,* August, 1992

"Skeleton in the Garter Belt and Nylons," *Official Detective,* January, 1992

"120 Fatal Thrusts with a Tiny, Weird Weapon," *True Detective,* April, 1991

"Finicky Feline Feasted on the Foxy Lady's Flesh!" *True Detective,* August, 1992

"Bizarre Love Bite Murder Case!" *Official Detective,* July, 1990

"Corpse Lover's Unholy Ritual," *Official Detective,* February, 1991

"Trysting Drag Queen and the Cat Man Killer," *Inside Detective,* November, 1989

"Rejected Romeo Fed the Barmaid to the Pigs!" *Inside Detective,* October, 1989

"Killer Stole Her False Teeth for a Souvenir," *Official Detective,* July, 1981

"Strangled Man in the Black Negligee!" *Inside Detective,* October, 1987

"Bizarre Scrawls Beside the Beheaded Bachelor," *Inside Detective,* February, 1989

"Animals Feasted On His Rotting Corpse!" *Front Page Detective,* December, 1992

"The Hairy, Toothless 'Mad Paddler,' " *Official Detective,* July, 1991

"Kinky Clues Surrounded the Slain Gays," *Inside Detective,* February, 1989

"The Caped Count and the Sexy Teen," *Master Detective,* February, 1993

"Curious Case of the Kitty Litter Killer," *Front Page Detective,* January, 1989

"New Mexico's Murder Most Foul!" *Official Detective,* October, 1989

"Killer Left a Feather on his Victim's Breast!" *Inside Detective,* April, 1988

"Terrorized His Victims with a Dead Body!" *Official Detective,* August, 1992

PINNACLE BOOKS HAS
SOMETHING FOR EVERYONE —

MAGICIANS, EXPLORERS, WITCHES AND CATS

THE HANDYMAN (377-3, $3.95/$4.95)
He is a magician who likes hands. He likes their comfortable shape and weight and size. He likes the portability of the hands once they are severed from the rest of the ponderous body. Detective Lanark must discover who The Handyman is before more handless bodies appear.

PASSAGE TO EDEN (538-5, $4.95/$5.95)
Set in a world of prehistoric beauty, here is the epic story of a courageous seafarer whose wanderings lead him to the ends of the old world — and to the discovery of a new world in the rugged, untamed wilderness of northwestern America.

BLACK BODY (505-9, $5.95/$6.95)
An extraordinary chronicle, this is the diary of a witch, a journal of the secrets of her race kept in return for not being burned for her "sin." It is the story of Alba, that rarest of creatures, a white witch: beautiful and able to walk in the human world undetected.

THE WHITE PUMA (532-6, $4.95/NCR)
The white puma has recognized the men who deprived him of his family. Now, like other predators before him, he has become a man-hater. This story is a fitting tribute to this magnificent animal that stands for all living creatures that have become, through man's carelessness, close to disappearing forever from the face of the earth.